TRAVELERS' TALES

PARIS

D0459564

CRITICAL ACCLAIM
FOR *TRAVELERS' TALES*

"Like gourmet chefs sampling the produce in an overstocked French market, the editors of *Travelers' Tales* pick, sift, and prod their way through the weighty shelves of contemporary travel writing, rejecting the second rate and creaming off the very best. They have impeccable taste—a very welcome addition to the genre."
—William Dalrymple, author, *City of Djinns* and *In Xanadu*

"I can't think of a better way to get comfortable with a destination than by delving into *Travelers' Tales*...before reading a guidebook, before seeing a travel agent. The series helps visitors refine their interests and readies them to communicate with the peoples they come in contact with..."
—Paul Glassman, Society of American Travel Writers

"This is the stuff memories can be duplicated from."
—Karen Krebsbach, *Foreign Service Journal*

"...*Travelers' Tales* is a valuable addition to any pre-departure reading list."
—Tony Wheeler, publisher, Lonely Planet Publications

"*Travelers' Tales* delivers something most guidebooks only promise: a real sense of what a country is all about...."
—Steve Silk, *Hartford Courant*

"The *Travelers' Tales* series should become required reading for anyone visiting a foreign country who wants to truly step off the tourist track and experience another culture, another place, first hand."
—Nancy Paradis, *St. Petersburg Times*

"Like having been there, done it, seen it. If there's one thing traditional guidebooks lack, it's the really juicy travel information, the personal stories about back alleys and brief encounters. The *Travelers' Tales* series fills this gap with an approach that's all anecdotes, no directions."
—Jim Gullo, *Diversion*

"...The essays are lyrical, magical, and evocative: some of the images make you want to rinse your mouth out to clear the dust."
—Karen Troianello, *Yakima Herald-Republic*

T R A V E L E R S ' T A L E S

PARIS

Collected and Edited by

JAMES O'REILLY   LARRY HABEGGER

SEAN O'REILLY

TRAVELERS' TALES, INC.
SAN FRANCISCO, CALIFORNIA

Distributed by
O'REILLY AND ASSOCIATES, INC.
101 MORRIS STREET
SEBASTOPOL, CALIFORNIA 95472

Travelers' Tales Paris
Collected and Edited by James O'Reilly, Larry Habegger, and Sean O'Reilly

Credits and copyright notices for the individual articles in this collection are given starting on page 386.

Cover and interior design by Judy Anderson
Cover Stamp by Edie Freedman
Cover photograph: © 1996 Christian Sarramon. An artist by the Seine paints a detail of
    Ile St-Louis.
Illustrations by Nina Stewart
Map by Keith Granger
Page Layout by Cynthia Lamb, using the fonts Bembo and Boulevard

Printing History
March 1997:   First Edition

ISBN: 1-885211-10-4

Take those two words, gold and pleasure, for a lantern, and explore the great cage of Paris.

—HONORÉ DE BALZAC

Table of Contents

ix

Part Five
THE LAST WORD

Preface

TRAVELERS' TALES

We are all outsiders when we travel. Whether we go abroad or roam about our own city or country, we often enter territory so unfamiliar that our frames of reference become inadequate. We need advice not just to avoid offense and danger, but to make our experiences richer, deeper, and more fun.

Traditionally, travel guides have answered the basic questions: what, when, where, how, and how much. A good guidebook is indispensable for all the practical matters that demand attention. More recently, many guidebooks have added bits of experiential insight to their standard fare, but something important is still missing: guidebooks don't really prepare *you*, the individual with feelings and fears, hopes and dreams, goals.

This kind of preparation is best achieved through travelers' tales, for we get our inner landmarks more from anecdote than information. Nothing can replace listening to the experience of others, to the war stories that come out after a few drinks, to the memories that linger and beguile. For millennia it's been this way: at watering holes and wayside inns, the experienced traveler tells those nearby what lies ahead on the ever-mysterious road. Stories stoke the imagination, inspire, frighten, and teach. In stories we see more clearly the urges that bring us to wander, whether it's hunger for change, adventure, self-knowledge, love, curiosity, sorrow, or even something as prosaic as a job assignment or two weeks off.

But travelers' accounts, while profuse, can be hard to track down. Many are simply doomed in a throwaway publishing world. And few of us have the time anyway to read more than one or two books, or the odd pearl found by chance in the Sunday travel section. Wanderers for years, we've often faced this issue. We've always told ourselves when we got home that we would prepare better for the next trip—read more, study more, talk to more people—but life always seems to interfere and we've rarely managed to do so to our satisfaction. That is one reason for this series. We needed a kind of experiential primer that guidebooks don't offer.

Another path that led us to *Travelers' Tales* has been seeing the enormous changes in travel and communications over the last two decades. It is no longer unusual to have ridden a pony across Mongolia, to have celebrated an auspicious birthday on Mt. Kilimanjaro, or honeymooned on the Loire. The one-world monoculture has risen with daunting swiftness, weaving a new cross-cultural rug: no longer is it surprising to encounter former headhunters watching *All-Star Wrestling* on their satellite feed, no longer is it shocking to find the last guy at the end of the earth wearing a Harvard t-shirt and asking if you know Michael Jordan. The global village exists in a rudimentary fashion, but it is real.

In 1980, Paul Fussell wrote in *Abroad: British Literary Traveling Between the Wars* a cranky but wonderful epitaph for travel as it was once known, in which he concluded that "we are all tourists now, and there is no escape." It has been projected by some analysts that by the year 2000, tourism will be the world's largest industry; others say it already is. In either case, this is a horrifying prospect— hordes of us hunting for places that have not been trod on by the rest of us!

Fussell's words have the painful ring of truth, but this is still our world, and it is worth seeing and will be worth seeing next year, or in 50 years, simply because it will always be worth meeting others who continue to see life in different terms than we do despite the best efforts of telecommunication and advertising talents. No amount of creeping homogeneity can quell the endless variation of humanity, and travel in the end is about people, not places. Places only provide different venues, as it were, for life, in which we are all pilgrims who need to talk to each other.

There are also many places around the world where intercultural friction and outright xenophobia is increasing. And the very fact that travel endangers cultures and pristine places more quickly than it used to calls for extraordinary care on the part of today's traveler, a keener sense of personal responsibility. The world is not our private zoo or theme park; we need to be better prepared before we go, so that we might become honored guests and not vilified intruders.

In *Travelers' Tales,* we collect useful and memorable anecdotes to produce the kind of sampler we've always wanted to read before setting out. These stories will show you some of the spectrum of experiences to be had or avoided in each country. The authors come from many walks of life: some are teachers, some are musicians, some are entrepreneurs, all are wanderers with a story to tell. Their stories won't help you be an insider as so many travel books promise—but they will help you to deepen and enrich the experience that you will have as an outsider. Where we've excerpted books, we urge you to go out and read the full work, because no selection can ever do an author justice.

Each *Travelers' Tales* is organized into five simple parts. In the first, we've chosen stories that reflect the ephemeral yet pervasive essence of a country. Part II contains stories about places and activities that others have found worthwhile. In Part III, we've chosen stories by people who have made a special connection between their lives and interests and the people and places they visited. Part IV shows some of the struggles and challenges facing a region and its people, and Part V, "The Last Word," is just that, something of a grace note or harmonic to remind you of the book as a whole.

Our selection of stories in each *Travelers' Tales* is by no means comprehensive, but we are confident it will prime your pump, and make your use of regular guidebooks much more meaningful. *Travelers' Tales* are not meant to replace other guides, but to accompany them. No longer will you have to go to dozens of sources to map the personal side of your journey. You'll be able to reach for *Travelers' Tales,* and truly prepare yourself before you go.

JAMES O'REILLY AND LARRY HABEGGER
Series Editors

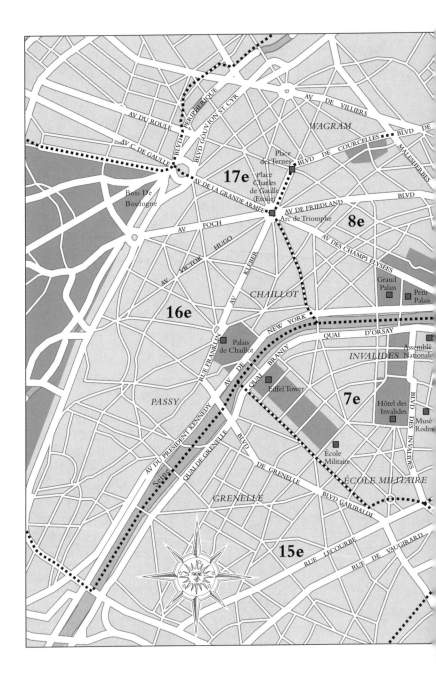

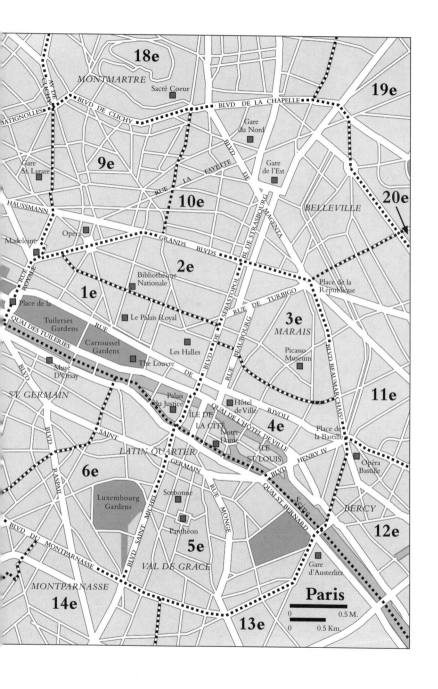

Paris: An Introduction

Imagine leaving this world without ever having seen Paris. For those who have been there, the thought is unthinkable. For those who haven't yet had the chance, the thought is a reminder that their lives will be impoverished until they go, for Paris is the center of the civilized universe, the capital of the Western world, a city of transcendent beauty which belongs to everyone.

It is one of a handful of cities on earth one should endeavor to know over the course of a lifetime, not just in one or two or even a half-dozen visits. Paris—or Parisians—may rebuff you from time to time, but then, that is one of its duties, one of its perverse pleasures. Paris is not lightly seduced, not to be trifled with.

There are those who say darkly that Paris isn't what it used to be; that hordes of visitors have irrevocably changed it for the worse; that in pandering to the needs of tourism the city has become a parody of itself, nothing more than a cultural amusement park. And of course, there is truth to the lament of the cynical, to those weary of slack-jawed foreigners who spout a kind of French which bears more resemblance to the gibberings of the Neolithic than it does the language of Molière and Victor Hugo. But Paris is such a mighty archetype that these things ultimately do not matter.

The images of Paris are familiar to all: barges on the Seine; the Eiffel Tower poking into a summer sunset; the Cathedral of Notre Dame standing stoutly on its island in the middle of the river; the Pei Pyramid glowing before the classical lines of the Louvre; the Basilica of Sacré-Couer stark white above the streets of Montmartre; the Arc de Triomphe dominating the chaotic roundabout of Le Étoile, an architectural key to the Champs Elysées and the grand obelisk at Place de la Concorde, site of the horrors of the

French Revolution; lovers embracing in the Tuileries; the famed headstones of Père-Lachaise cemetery; the ubiquitous cafés and well-dressed Parisians and coiffed dogs; arresting new architecture and the fabulous Métro; the list goes on and on.

There may be no city more uplifting to the human spirit. It is a place to explore the dimensions of yourself or those of someone you love—to walk and talk, to argue about life, to sit and contemplate the events of human history which have played themselves out here on these streets, on the banks of this river.

And yet as heavy with tradition and culture as it is, the City of Light has bestowed on countless millions the gift of the incandescent present, an image, an experience or moment into which all life is condensed, to be reflected upon for years to come. Paris is a place to feel especially alive, and it's here now, waiting for you to come, sample its treasures, and make it yours.

PART ONE

ESSENCE OF PARIS

★ ★ ★

Vive l'Argument

The secrets of Paris are the secrets of love.

IN PARIS, MEN AND WOMEN LOVE WITH THEIR INTELLECT AS MUCH as their emotions. This is in fact a deeply romantic approach to love, one that sees the lover as the most worthy adversary in the world, worthy even of trying to persuade. Of course we are talking about Paris, so the persuasion involves panache, aplomb, and attitude—plenty of attitude.

A young couple enters the Café St-Germain on a November afternoon. His leather jacket is open over a white t-shirt; her heavy gold sweater sets off a mane of black hair. They are beautiful to look at, and clearly in love. They sit, smoke, and drink coffee in a room of spidery mirrored walls and brown marble tables. In fact they sit at the next table and the café is not crowded, so their discussion quickly becomes more interesting than the afternoon newspaper. Love in public is public love, *n'est-ce pas?*

It turns out the young woman is attempting to convince the young man that their relationship should proceed to the ultimate intimacy more or less immediately. Not tomorrow, not tonight, but today, now. The young man sits back in his chair and listens, which means he is resting, marshaling his own arguments for the rebuttal to come. It is a tender scene of young love, in Paris.

There is a famous photo of Simone de Beauvoir and Jean-Paul Sartre, who shared one of the great romances of this century, in Paris or anywhere else. They are sitting at the table in La Coupole where they dined daily for many years. She looks off to the side with a half smile on her lips, he looks down reflectively. What discussions they must have had, I always thought. One day it dawned on me that they didn't go to the same café for 40 years to agree with each other. They went to discuss, to disagree, to *argue*. In fact, their lifelong agreement on where to go for dinner saved invaluable energy for what happened when they got there.

> *Never have I felt so forcefully that our lives have no meaning outside of our love, and that nothing changes that, neither separation, nor passions, nor the war. You said it was a victory for our morality, but it is just as much a victory for our love.*
>
> —Jean-Paul Sartre, in a letter to Simone de Beauvoir

I don't mean they argued as in "had a fight," which you almost never see in Paris, but an *argument* as Aristotle thought of it: a coherent series of logical reasons, advanced to prove a point. What could be more Parisian than that?

The young woman in the café takes the young man's coffee cup from his hand so he cannot hide behind it. It was not religion that invented love, she asserts, leaning forward. It was not your school or your parents, she continues, eyes afire. It is men and women who reinvent love together, and if we two do not make love, love is not made in this world. She crushes out her cigarette and throws her hair back over her shoulder in a flourish of valedictory passion.

You don't have to be Parisian to appreciate this kind of romance, or to participate in it either. An American woman I know spent years trying to convince her Provençal boyfriend that they should leave Paris and live somewhere, anywhere, else. Katie is a professor of economics, a discipline in which so little is actually provable that the ability to persuade is paramount. The discussion about leaving town should have been over in a month. They remained for years. How could this happen? They were in Paris, and in love: the argument illuminated their happiness like a bonfire.

Another Parisian love story, that of Mimi and Rudolfo in Puccini's opera, *La Bohème,* has made millions of people weep. It makes the Parisians I know squirm. They prefer the scenes between the second couple, Musetta and Marcello. I once asked a Frenchwoman to explain this to me. (Of course I started by stating a logical case; I was secretly in love with her, and we were in Paris.) Both Mimi and Musetta leave their artistic lovers to be kept by wealthy men, I argued, so one is no better than the other. Mimi has far lovelier arias, more vulnerability, and one of the most touching deaths in all of theater. Why do you spurn her?

It's not her, the lady said, rolling her eyes. (She was reversing the usual procedure by opening with attitude and then hitting home with logic.) It's the story, she said. Rudolfo and Mimi meet in his room at the beginning, then she dies in his room at the end. But where's the rest? With Musetta and Marcello you get to see them argue a little, so they express their love. The other two, they split up somehow, but we never see it. The real love is all offstage!

Right now, on-stage in the café, the young man reaches for a cigarette. He lights it thoughtfully, blows out a cloud of grey-blue smoke, and considers the intelligent face of his tablemate. I cannot disagree with anything you say, he begins softly. This does not melt the young woman. She is in Paris, and in love. Instead her back stiffens a little.

Even Paris itself, the physical city, is an argument for romance Parisian style. Baron Haussmann's broad boulevards and great monuments argue eloquently that Paris is not like other cities, and its inhabitants not like other city dwellers. Why then should they love like others, with more feeling than reason? Even recent civic "improvements," such as dropping a glass pyramid into the lap of the Louvre—Europe's most romanticized museum—appear intentionally designed to stimulate passionate argument.

The first time I took a woman to Paris, I discovered things about her—and her attitude about our relationship—that were previously unrevealed by years of polite American passion. We were sitting in the cozy corner of a small restaurant in the rue de l'Echaude, savoring winter soup and crisp Sancerre, when she said casually, "This is working out better than I ever thought it would." I believed she was praising either the dinner or my management of our trip, and asked which she meant. "No," she said, "I meant us, the whole thing."

The Louvre was wonderful. I spent three hours sketching one of Michelangelo's slaves. Afterward I hopped on the Métro to try to catch the Rodin museum's last admittance. My luck, it was pouring rain and only the garden was open. Funny how fitting it is to view Rodin's work in the gray Paris mist, soaking cold, the rain tapping softly on black umbrellas.

I missed you as I watched the water fall on the glassy surfaces of fountain pools framing beautiful bodies. His passion touches me the same as the memory of your kiss—like swallowing ice cubes—that sweet, dull ache.

—Gina Granados, "Dear Patrick"

I do not remember any of the courses that followed, nor how we got back to our hotel. I'll never forget the argument that erupted, however, or the heightened passion of the remaining years we shared.

The young man retrieves his coffee cup and gazes into it. When we make this change it will be glorious, he says softly, as if thinking aloud to himself. Our essences will be mixed, our destinies joined in a way that cannot be described, or reversed. He shakes his head slowly at the immensity of it all.

The young woman's body is still wary, but her face is beginning to soften, her eyes to glisten. The young man puts down the coffee cup and takes her hands. He continues speaking to her with such persuasive sincerity that even I am willing to believe anything he says. But what of today? he asks. Once we leave this moment we cannot return to our passionate innocence. When at last we make love, the wanting and waiting will be over, but they will also be gone. Then we cannot go back, he says. Ever.

There is a long moment in which neither of them moves. The sun slides away behind the buildings, and afternoon becomes twilight. An older couple enters the café to warm greetings from other *habitués*; on the sidewalk a man in an elegant overcoat sweeps a woman in furs into his arms; inside, the bartender is talking on the phone with one hand and gesturing dramatically with the other. Yet somehow all is silent, waiting for love to decide the argument.

Finally the young woman extracts her hands from his, sits back, and luxuriously smoothes her hair. It is not clear whether she is savoring victory or accepting defeat. A moment later, the two of them go out together. Do they go to her place and make love, or walk the Seine in silence for hours, arm in arm? Which one of them has prevailed? This is Paris, this is love. The argument continues.

Thom Elkjer is a freelance interviewer and scriptwriter whose work has appeared in print, on stage, and in video. He and his suitcase live in Mill Valley, California.

*

Numerous writers have depicted the famed City of Light as a woman, and I must agree that she is definitely a sensual, voluptuous, sometimes loving, often laughing, playful spirit. She can also be cruel and cold in her sophisticated way, seeming to say, "I am all that is romance and splendor of the past, but if you do not respect my ancient history and try to understand my deeper mystery, then I will show you only one side of myself...the flat dimension of glittering night life, champagne and sequins, the odor of expensive perfume and cigarettes. But I will not unveil my inner beauty that lies within the cracks of every statue, depicting the glory I once knew. You will slumber in a drunken paradise, unable to keep the vigil as the sun rises on wings of fire that kiss the breasts of my monuments to the past. Because my light is invisible to the naked eye, it only touches and blesses those travelers who continue to dream and believe in their own muse with all their heart. For them, I will shine brightly through their tears of pain and infinite joy."

—Carole Brooks, "A Love Affair with the City of Dreams"

JOHN GREGORY DUNNE

Behind the Wheel

Paris satisfies the drives of Private Dunne.

I WAS 22 WHEN I WENT TO PARIS FOR THE FIRST TIME, A MEWLING, puling first-class private in the army of the United States, on a three-day pass from an artillery battalion in divided cold war Germany. I was drawn to the City of Light by Charlie Wales in Scott Fitzgerald's *Babylon Revisited* and by Jake Barnes in Ernest Hemingway's *The Sun Also Rises* and by Henry Miller's *Tropic of Cancer*, drawn by wine and by (let's face it) what opera stage directions call "women of the town." I spoke a little French, *un petit peu*, as I was always quick to say, but I did know the most thrilling word I had ever heard in any language—*apéritif*.

"*Une fine, s'il vous plaît*," I told the barman that first day in Paris (at the Hemingway Bar in the Ritz, where else?) when asked if I would like an *apéritif*. I didn't know what a *fine* was, but if it was good enough for Jake Barnes the night he met Brett Ashley again at the *bal musette* on rue da la Montagne-Ste-Geneviève, it was good enough for me. I had a second *fine à l'eau* (the barman discreetly suggested that cutting the brandy with water might possibly help me make it through the rest of the afternoon) and a third—bad news at lunch, but a gin martini seemed *de trop*, three positively vulgar. Full of brandy, youthful adrenaline, and testos-

8

terone and absent good sense, I decided I must rent a car; I would drive, not so much to see Paris as to take it on in my disorganized (and at this point quite hungover) fashion.

The rental agency to which I was directed by the barman had only one car available, a stick-shift Renault 4CV of uncertain vintage and provenance, more a Tinkertoy with a pushback canvas roof than an automobile.

It was scarcely larger than a carnival bumper car, but no matter; I soon discovered that a bumper car was perfect for what proved to be my first, and what I thought might be my last, destination— the Arc de Triomphe at rush hour. It was like being sucked onto a giant merry-go-round that, as if in a dream, I could not get off. Round and round the Étoile I went, swept by the tide of cars— there a glimpse of the Avenue de Wagram, and a moment later Wagram again, then a third time, a fourth, and always over my left shoulder the Arc, my lodestar.

By the fifth time around, however, I began getting into it, feeling the rush, waving now, shouting, cursing, exuberantly singing "La Marseillaise," cutting cars off, flipping other drivers the bird, and then suddenly, as if I had been ejected by a slingshot, I was off that demented carousel and onto the relatively safe haven of the Champs-Elysées. I could, however, only feel disappointment; the ride around the Étoile had been so exhilarating that I turned right around and went back again. It was as if I had finished basic training—now it was time for advanced Étoile maneuvers, except this time I would choose where to get off. And so, supremely confident, moving easily with the flow, darting through openings, I exited onto all the great avenues branching out from the Arc— Champs-Elysées, Marceau, Iéna, Kléber, Victor-Hugo, Foch, Grande-Armée, Carnot, MacMahon, Wagram, Hoche, Friedland. I will not say that I underwent an epiphany that afternoon, but in some inchoate way I realized that the only way I wanted to experience Paris was in an automobile.

Ever since that first trip I have always rented a car immediately upon my return, more than twenty times now, and on my first day in the city, sane and sentient wife in tow and protesting vigorously,

I make for the Étoile at rush hour: it is the way I let Paris welcome me back. Here a confession is in order that will perhaps explain my need for wheels. I have an aversion to sightseeing and little affinity for museums, monuments, cathedrals, shrines, grottoes, tombs, castles, and palaces. No organized bus tours for me, no group forays to Notre Dame or the Orangerie or the Palais du Luxembourg, no checklist of sites and sights to be ticked off: if this is the 7th *arrondissement*, it must be the Eiffel Tower, the École Militaire, the Invalides with Napoleon's tomb. Guidebooks leave me numb, except for the odd nonessential fact that I might later put in a book of my own. My heart leaps, for example, to learn that the Florentines, while laying siege to Siena in the 13th century, catapulted excrement and dead donkeys over the city's walls in hopes of starting a plague. Or that the Germans, during the Nazi occupation of France, added their own savage wrinkle to the guillotine: unlike the French, they made each condemned prisoner face upward, and taped his eyes open so that the unfortunate victim's last terrifying sight was the blade heading toward his neck.

I have an image fixed for ever in my mind of young, blond, admirably coifed, and chicly clothed young mothers in the driver's seats of Renault 5s (the other part of this encapsulation of the essence of Frenchness), a Stuyvesant or a Virginia Slim or a Blue Blush by Helena Rubinstein held firmly in their lips (otherwise they would be biting them), a scarf by Hermés caressing their lovely necks, their Louis Vuitton bags by their sides, and two well-dressed small children strapped into the back seat—bearing down on the Étoile like tank commanders, shaking their hands with irritation (hand held palm upward, fingers splayed, and shaken up and down) at some offending other driver. Mais, qu'est-ce que tu fous?— What the hell are you doing?— they mutter under their breath as the battle ensues. Ta gueule, salaud—Up yours, you bastard (very rough translation)—they say.

—Richard Bernstein, Fragile Glory: A Portrait of France and the French

What a car provides is the opportunity for unexpected adventure, a freedom to explore, to be overtaken by what might not interest others. A wrong turn, a one-way street running in the opposite direction from where I'm headed—getting lost is in fact the larger purpose. Exposure to the mundane puts me in touch with the rhythm of a place. I saw the locks of the Canal St-Martin and the slums of Belleville and Ménilmontant on market day before I saw the sublime stained-glass windows of Sainte-Chapelle. I did not visit the Louvre until my sixth trip to Paris, and then only because a cloudburst had rendered my windshield wipers inoperable and the Quai des Tuileries impassable. I pulled under a tree, sure that in such a storm I would not get a traffic ticket, and ducked inside with my wife to escape the rain. We walked upstairs, smack into the *Mona Lisa*. How much better to be favored by the Gioconda smile that way, the first time, rather than as a sightseeing duty.

In a car, on a given day, I can visit any number of destinations and never see a tourist gazing at a green *Michelin* guide. Sometimes I invent whimsical expeditions. One afternoon it was to find the apartments of American writers who had once lived in Paris (the addresses provided in an estimable volume, Brian Morton's *Americans in Paris*). I zipped from the building on rue de Tilsitt, near the Étoile, which Scott and Zelda Fitzgerald had occupied for a time in 1925, when they were in the chips, to the house on the Ile St-Louis where James Jones held court, to the sawmill on rue Notre-Dame-des-Champs in the 6th *arrondissement*, above which Hemingway, almost broke, had lived in 1924, and then to the two apartments across the street from each other on rue de Varenne where Edith Wharton passed her Paris years. Close by the Invalides, rue de Varenne is the same street to which Wharton's memorable creation (and perhaps fictional alter ego) Countess Olenska exiled herself from Newland Archer in *The Age of Innocence*.

On another, more *louche* foray I set out to locate some of the old *maisons de tolérance*, or brothels, that Brassaï had photographed in *The Secret Paris of the Thirties*. At the Chabanais, not far from the Place de L'Opéra, the Prince of Wales—later King Edward VII, a regular—had a Hindu room set up in homage to his mother, Queen Victoria, empress of India. In a nearby *maison* on rue des

Martyrs, an elderly president of the French senate had years before expired in the arms of his Venus, a minor scandal at the time. On Boulevard Edgar-Quinet, near the Montparnasse cemetery, I found the site of the Sphinx, one of the few brothels where customers could bring their wives and children. It was a Wednesday, and the street alongside what had once been the most famous whorehouse in Paris was closed for market day. At covered stalls with a staggering variety of fish, meat, fruit, vegetables, and cheeses, I watched as the farmers and the bourgeois matrons of the *quartier* haggled endlessly. I bought some chestnuts and then wandered through the cemetery examining the dates on the crypts and monuments; it was a history of France since the Revolution.

On this eccentric one-day tour I had managed to see a huge part of the city and its quotidian life, past and present, which would not have been possible had I not been driving. Each day has its structuring destinations. Sunday is park day—Parc des Buttes Chaumont in the 19th *arrondissement*, Montsouris in the 14th, Monceau in the 8th. It is to Monceau that my wife and I drive every Sunday morning to read the English papers and to watch the beautiful neighborhood children at play, many the sons and daughters of the diplomatic corps from the nearby embassies. Monceau is the most cosmopolitan of these parks, almost a child's fairy kingdom, alive with the squeals of preschoolers. In a sandbox full of forts and castles and battlements, Linda, a tiny black girl, shouts at Abdul, equally tiny in his pink Lacoste polo shirt. The merry-go-round doesn't have just horses but also a fire engine, a tank, a stagecoach, two motorcycles, a Paris-Lyons bus, and a rocket ship.

Then across the Seine to Parc Montsouris at the southern edge of the city. Like Monceau, Montsouris is a mix of nationalities—in this case students from the foreign dormitories at Cité Universitaire across the street. The students lend the park its raffish air of young love and unlimited possibilities. Adjacent to Montsouris is rue Georges-Braque, where the painter had his studio, and overlooking the park are the spacious *ateliers* of contemporary artists. Some of the nearby streets are cobblestoned and lined with ivy-covered cottages, giving the area a strange, almost Bavarian Mother Hubbard quality that makes it unlike any other place I have seen in Paris.

I suppose my favorite park, though, is Buttes Chaumont in the northwestern part of the city. I discovered it quite by accident driving back to Paris from the World War I battlefield at Château-Thierry. There was a *déviation* in the road. I of course got lost, then suddenly came upon this park in what seemed to be a working-class district. On an adjoining street, old men were playing *boules*. Buttes Chaumont is one of the highest spots in Paris with a view of almost the entire city. Its hills are impossibly steep—vertical and vertiginous. Walking there is a workout. The park has a lake and a suspension bridge which at one time was called Pont des Suicides because, like the Golden Gate in San Francisco, it seemed to invite jumpers. It was the contention of Louis Aragon, former literary godfather of the French Communist Party, that before the city erected metal grilles along its sides, the bridge claimed victims even from passersby who had no intention of killing themselves but were suddenly tempted by the abyss.

Cemeteries always attract. My wife and I first drove to Père Lachaise in the 20th *arrondissement* with our daughter, who wanted to see the putative grave of rock-and-roll legend Jim Morrison. She was then fourteen, convinced that Morrison was alive and living in the Philippines. If he's in the Philippines, we asked, then who's buried in his plot at Père Lachaise? Logic did not prevail; she obviously viewed our reasoning as heresy. I wondered how we would find the grave, but I needn't have worried. Whitewashed on various crypts was the single word "Jim" and, under the name, an arrow pointing visitors through the cemetery toward Morrison's monument. Lounging around the grave, draped over the adjoining stones, were denizens of what must have been the last hippie enclaves from around the world; the smell of their marijuana gave an immediate contact high. The monument, topped by a bust of the singer with a head of curls that would have done credit to Louis XIV, was covered with graffiti "Antonio, Stefano, Giulio, Paolo, Fabio—12/8/82. Music Is Your Only Friend Until the

End." We left our daughter to commune with the living dead and went to pay our respects to Oscar Wilde.

Having driven in Paris for more than 30 years, I know the city even better than Manhattan, where I live and where I rarely ever drive except to get out of town on weekends. New York's outer boroughs are *terra incognita* to me, as Pantin and St-Denis are not. Parking in Paris is easy: you can pull up anyplace, sometimes even on the sidewalks. At night I always leave my car on the street, without worrying as I do in New York that I will find it in the morning absent tires and radio. Years ago, hopelessly lost in the cobweb of streets high in Montmartre, I came upon a launderette near the basilica of Sacré-Coeur. I still take my washing up there, lugging it out to my rental car, past the concierge's desk and the steely eyes of assistant managers in morning dress, who I know are wondering why I bother to stay at the Ritz or the Plaza Athénée if I choose not to pay $75 to get some socks and underwear done by the hotel laundry.

There are closer self-service places, but speed is not the point. How I get there depends on my mood. I might go by way of the Jardin des Plantes. Or the Bois de Vincennes. Or the Place des Vosges in the Marais. Or the apartment house where Gertrude Stein and Alice B. Toklas resided on the rue de Fleurus. Or the hotel on Boulevard des Batignolles where Josephine Baker lived with a lover, a parrot, two rabbits, a snake, and a pig. It is perhaps not your way to see Paris, but in 30 years, there is very little that I have missed.

John Gregory Dunne is the author of ten books including Playground, True Confessions, Dutch Shea, Jr., Harp, *and* The Red White and Blue. *His screen credits, written with his wife, Joan Didion, include* A Star is Born, True Confessions *(based on his novel), and* Play It as It Lays *(based on Didion's novel). He and his wife live in New York.*

★

I'd been in Paris five days. I'd walked around in my sensible shoes—that is, a pair of sneakers that made my feet feel as if they were in clouds. Five days in Paris, watching gorgeous French women with thin legs and highly fashionable shoes stride seductively around the city.

On Day 6, I looked at my own highly fashionable shoes, which were sitting untouched in the hotel closet. "Wear us," they called.

"Why not?" I thought. I'd worn said shoes for ten-hour workdays. Marched to and from parking lots, up and down stairs, into offices, even for a couple of spins around a mall. Never a problem. Never a rub. Never a blister. I strapped them on.

My husband looked at my feet. "You wearing those?" he asked, tremulously.

"Sure. They're comfortable," I assured him.

Two hours later, there I was in Père Lachaise cemetery, wandering among the illustrious dead, my feet weeping silently. Two gravediggers stood waist-high in a newly dug hole. I considered lying down.

—Jill Schensul, "The Splendor and the Pain: Touring Paris in Heels,"
The Bergen Record

JOSEPH DIEDRICH

⋆ ⋆ ⋆

The Gift

For everything there is a season.

THAT MARCH WAS A BAD TIME TO BE IN PARIS. A HARD, UNPLEAS-
ant wind whipped the branches of the bare trees and drove gusts
of cold rain through the streets. Heavy traffic splashed through
pools of standing water. Huddled pedestrians ducked into doorways. The taxis had all gone to wherever taxis go when it rains.

I had come to Paris to meet my wife to try to revive a marriage
already broken by a year of separation, and it wasn't working. Our
favorite little hotel was damp and underheated. Our favorite little
restaurant had lost its Michelin star and deserved to lose it. My
wife and I had changed as well. Too much had been said and done
in the past year. We just couldn't put it together again. Humpty
Dumpty.

To avoid another evening of strained conversation at a table for
two we arranged to have dinner with some old friends who lived
in the 6th *arrondissement*, an Englishman and his delightful
American wife. I had heard that she was having some trouble with
leukemia but I hadn't known how bad it was. At dinner we realized two things: that Peggy was dying and that she was someone
whom we both would miss very much. We all tried to keep the
evening light and happy, and we almost succeeded.

My wife and I didn't talk very much on the way back to our hotel. When we got there, we tried to make love in the clammy bed and failed hopelessly. When I finally shut my eyes she was still crying. The next day we went out to Orly and I put her on her plane for London. We promised that we would try again, knowing that we never would, and we never did.

I waited until her plane had left and then I went back into Paris, feeling a black sense of failure, of things not done, of paths not taken. That which I did, I should not have done. That which I should have done, I did not do. I thought of our twelve-year-old in her boarding school in England, of how much she wanted her family back, and of how I had failed her yet again. I didn't know where to go or what to do, and I didn't care. I just gave myself over to my misery and let it lead me where it would.

I remember ordering lunch in a bistro somewhere and leaving it on the table. I remember going to see the Impressionists again and finding the usually vibrant paintings as bleak and as grey as the day outside—and as the man who viewed them. Then I went back to the empty room in the sad little hotel and laid on the bed and tried to weep. I couldn't do that either.

I didn't want to see any of the people I knew in Paris that evening so I ate alone in a *brasserie* near St-Germain. A notice pinned to the wall advertised someone singing Argentine folk songs that evening at a café somewhere, so I wrote down the address and went to hear him. I lived in South America for a while and I know and like Argentine folk music, much of which has a rough, bittersweet feeling that I thought might fit that particular evening.

The café was in a dingy street on the wrong side of the Boul Mich and stank of brown tobacco. A handful of men in working clothes were drinking silently at the bar. When I asked about the Argentine folk concert the bartender shrugged, pointed to a closed door, and said that it was supposed to be in the back room there. He also supposed that it would start whenever the singer showed up. I ordered a drink and sat down at a table to wait. No one else came into the place.

Then a shabby old man carrying a wet guitar case came in from the street. He went to the bar, drank a cognac in one gulp and said something to the bartender who pointed at me. The old man shook his head sadly and walked over to the closed door.

"We will get started," he said. "Please come in." None of the other men at the bar moved.

"Am I the only one?" I asked the bartender as I paid for my drink.

"The other one is already in there."

A woman in a dark dress was sitting alone in the inner room, which had chairs for perhaps 80 people. Except for a small bulb hanging from a cord over the little stage the place was in gloom. The old man fiddled with his guitar case for a moment, then he said: "My friends, it seems there are only the three of us. Why don't you bring chairs down here and we will sit around this table while I sing. We will make a little party." He paused and cleared his throat. "Perhaps someone could find a bottle of cognac for us?"

I went out for a bottle and a pitcher of water. Then the woman and I moved our chairs down to the little table on the stage where the old man sat. He poured the drinks and raised his glass in salute.

"To Argentina," he said and emptied his glass.

He began with a lovely old song from Cajamarca. His voice was worn and lived in, and fitted the song well. While he sang I had a chance to study the woman next to me. In the dim light she looked to be in her late twenties, slender, and expensively dressed. She sat with a hand held against her cheek, hiding much of her face. What I could see looked lovely. She spoke Spanish like an Argentinean in a soft and cultivated voice.

After a while the old man began to sing some of Jorge Cafrune's songs. Cafrune was a middle-aged, black-bearded, whiskey-voiced drunk who used to sing songs that he wrote himself for drinks and tips in some of the roughest cantinas in the country towns of northern Argentina. Then someone discovered him and brought him on tour to Paris where he became rich and famous overnight. Then he went back to Argentina and fell off a horse while drunk and was killed by a passing car. He left behind some of the most haunting music in South America.

I knew the song the old man was singing, so I joined in. (Sometimes I fool with my guitar and sing folk songs late at night when no one is listening, or even when they are, and sometimes when I have had too much wine or cognac.) Then the woman, who had scarcely spoken until then, began to sing along in a soft throaty voice. She sang very well.

Her name was Susanna. She told about meeting Cafrune at a party in Buenos Aires and that he was nice until he got drunk, which he did as quickly as possible.

"He was a rough man," she said in her soft voice. "But the songs he wrote—the words, the music—they are pure poetry."

After that Susanna and the old man sang together—she seemed to know all of the old songs—and I joined in when I could. It turned out to be a good party, the three of us, the guitar and the bottle of brandy in the grubby back room.

It was still early when the old man got too drunk to sing any more. The rain had stopped and Susanna and I walked back to the Boul Mich and up the Avenue St-Germain.

"Let's go somewhere else," I said. "This evening is too nice to stop now."

"You have seen my face?" It was more of a statement than a question.

"Yes."

"I am not pretty any more."

"Yes you are."

"It is nice of you to say so, but I know better. The left side, the side towards you, that is how I used to look. The right side, well, I was in a car that crashed and afterwards a fire...." She looked down for a moment, obviously remembering. "It was much worse at first," she went on. "My right cheek was gone and half of my mouth. I couldn't speak intelligibly. I had to be fed with a tube. Since then I have been to the plastic surgeon many times. I have come to Paris to see another one."

"And what does he say?"

"He says that I will need two or three more reconstructive surgeries. After that he can begin with the skin grafts. Maybe four more years. I will never look like I used to look, but at least I won't frighten children any more."

"That's nonsense, Susanna. You are lovely. Everyone past 25 has scars. Your's just happen to be where they can be seen."

She smiled. "All right, have it your way. We don't know each other well enough to bicker. Now let's go in the Rotonde and have café royal. I will buy because I sing better than you do."

Sitting at the table, Susanna looked at me carefully. "Your scars are inside, are they not?"

"Yes."

"And fairly new?"

"Yes."

"*Pues entonces.* Now we will talk no more about scars."

"I'll drink to that," I said. And we did.

To speak of love is to make love.

—Honoré de Balzac

We left the Rotonde and went out into the cool night and the quiet street. Susanna's hotel was nearby and I offered to walk with her to the door. We turned off the St-Germain at the Café de Flore and went down the empty street. I don't know why I chose that particular street. There were several ways we could have walked to her hotel.

"Excuse me," Susanna said. She had stopped and was staring at a building across the street. "Number seventeen. That is the house where my husband had a room when he was a student, and had run away from the killings in Argentina. How did we happen to come here?"

I had wondered if she was married and had begun to hope, very much, that she was not. "Where is he—your husband?" I ventured.

"He was in the car. He died in the crash." She took a deep breath. "Our daughter too. Only she died in the hospital three days later. I was driving and it was my fault and yet I did not die. At least not entirely." She put her hands to her face and began to weep silently. I put my arms around her, rather awkwardly.

"I'm sorry," she said, not moving. "I had almost forgotten about it for a while this evening, which makes it worse somehow. Will you please stay out with me until I can stop behaving like this? I can't face an empty hotel room just yet." She began to shiver. "I'm so cold. Can we go inside somewhere?"

Most of the cafés and the bars were closed for the night, but on the corner ahead the lights were on in a Russian restaurant and the door stood open. We went in. The place was empty except for about a dozen people seated around a long table at the back of the room. A man came out from behind the bar carrying a concertina.

"I am sorry," he said, coming over to us, "but we are closed. This is a private party." Then he looked at Susanna's tear-streaked, ravaged face and said, "But I do not think that we are so closed, pretty lady, that you and your friend cannot sit at this little table here while I bring you some hot borscht and some cold vodka."

rench science fiction writer René Barjavel wrote of the transforming power of Paris in his novel The Ice People *(published in France as* La Nuit des Temps*):*

"Paris is the loveliest garden in the world for a woman: she can become a flower herself, a flower among other flowers—that's the miracle of Paris, and that's where I'm taking you!"

"I don't understand."

"You don't have to understand, you have to see. Paris will heal you. Paris will cure you of the past!"

—JO'R, LH, and SO'R

We sat at the table in the dimly lit restaurant and ate the borscht and drank the vodka, and after a while Susanna's tears stopped. The people at the long table were singing Russian songs accompanied by the owner on his concertina. The party must have been going on for quite a while, for they were all quite drunk.

We were just getting ready to leave when the door from the street opened and a young man came in alone. He was dressed in black trousers and an open-necked white shirt with a black overcoat slung over his shoulders. He had dark hair, dark eyes, high cheekbones, and was deathly pale. He was also very, very drunk.

Susanna stared at him as he walked by our table. "My god," she whispered. "He's beautiful." And he was.

The people at the party in the back called out to him and he walked carefully over to the long table, drank a proffered glass of vodka neat, draped his overcoat over the back of a chair, and sat. A hush fell over the party. Then he began to sing.

I don't know what it was that he sang. I had never heard such music before and I have never heard it since. Whatever it was— gypsy, Tatar, Cossack—it was the most beautiful music Susanna and I had ever heard. A cynic would say that it just fit the mood of the night, but I don't think so. The young man had a superb voice. He sat with his eyes closed and his head back and sang songs which told of longing and heartache and loss and loneliness and love and redemption. You didn't need to understand the words. He sang for nearly half an hour. Then he slumped back in his chair, motionless, his eyes still closed.

No one at the party spoke after that. The people stood up, quietly put on their coats, and began to leave. Susanna and I left too.

"I think those songs were meant for me, somehow," she said as we walked through the quiet streets. "I was being egotistical with my sorrow, thinking no one else had ever suffered so. And they have, haven't they?"

"Yes."

"And yet you can go on and find redemption and peace and beauty—and even love if you are lucky."

"Maybe we are lucky," I said, knowing that we were.

Then we turned together, there, in the middle of the empty street, and kissed. We kissed for a long time, feeling the loss and the loneliness and the hopelessness beginning to go.

Then we walked back to Susanna's hotel together.

That was 20 years ago. We have been together ever since.

Joseph Diedrich is a retired Pan Am pilot who spends his time traveling, sailing, trekking, and "messing about." He and his wife live in Mallorca, Spain. This story was the first-place winner in a Paris writing contest sponsored by Travelers' Tales.

✦

Le Pont Mirabeau

Under the Pont Mirabeau flows the Seine
And our loves
Must I remember again
Joy always follows pain

Night comes hour's refrain
Days depart I still remain

Hand in Hand, toe to toe
While underneath
Our arms' bridge flows
Eternal gaze of the weary billow

Night comes hour's refrain
Days depart I still remain

Love runs away like a stream
Love runs away
How slow life seems
And how violent our dreams

Night comes hour's refrain
Days depart I still remain

Days depart, weeks in their train
Await time past
And loves in vain
Under the Pont Mirabeau flows the Seine

Night comes hour's refrain
Days depart I still remain

—Guillaume Apollinaire, "Le Pont Mirabeau,"
translated by Thérèse Lung

HERBERT GOLD

On the Left Bank

*What is the meaning of life? There's still time
to figure it out in the world's most famous
living museum.*

As was said of all Paris, the Left Bank is the Capital of Hope and the Paradise of Misery, where one can live in continual expectation, relishing failure and the pleasures of melancholy if one chooses. During my student days there, Jonathan Cape, an English publisher, used to take the boat-train over from London on weekends and lead me on walks through the Paris of *his* youth—here he rejected James Joyce ("Bloody crossword puzzle"); there he knew a lady with plump arms and eyes of a heartbreaking sadness, right there, on the rue de Tournon. Maybe, if I listened, he would publish my first novel in England; he didn't, but this stately, white-haired relic became one of my favorite ambulatory monuments.

The Left Bank, or *Rive Gauche,* comprises half of the great city of Paris, so of course it includes working-class and middle-class districts, the monstrous Manhattanized skyscraper of Maine-Montparnasse, offices and businesses and quietly expensive neighborhoods where people live quietly expensive lives. Its monuments, such as the Eiffel Tower, its museums, such as the great Rodin Museum in its classic hotel, and its historic refuges, such as the Roman baths from 200 A.D. in the Cluny complex, have little to do with what we think of when we think Rive Gauche. The spirit of the place is more truly expressed by the little passage near St-Germain-des-Prés where Dr. Guillotine perfected his "philanthropic decapitating machine." The enduring legend of the Left Bank comes out of the 5th, 6th, 7th and 14th *arrondissements*: the Latin Quarter, the Sorbonne, the warren of medieval streets near the Place St-André des Art (including the narrowest street in Paris, the Street of the Fishing Cat—*rue du Chat-qui-Pêche*), the spirits of Sartre and Genet and Camus at St-Germain-des-Prés, and the ghosts of the painters and writers of Montparnasse, where Gertrude Stein made so many remarks and Hemingway paid attention.

This legendary lifestyle adjusts and survives in its own way. Take, for example, the *cinémathèque* phenomenon—the countless little rooms where movie-crazed Parisians can assuage their indiscriminate passion for Jerry Lewis and Eric von Stroheim, Akira Kurosawa and Laurel and Hardy, Charlie Chaplin ("Charlot") and Ingmar Bergman and *le film noir américain*, which generally means cheapie gangster movies of the '40s and '50s. It sometimes seems as if Left Bankers make their livings selling each other movie tickets and ancestral antiques, like Jimmy Durante surviving on a desert island by peddling newspapers.

Despite the accelerated rusting of time, the Left Bank retains its consistency. In the crowds, a visitor still walks with Abelard in the Sorbonne; he meets the obsessed outcasts of Balzac, the cavorting bohemians of Henri Murger, the anxious Existentialists of Sartre and Simone de Beauvoir, and the ghosts jostle each other. An ear to history picks up the steps of the Roman legions marching south past the baths and amphitheaters at Cluny, past the rue de la Huchette, where the tourists come to hear guitarists, past the ancient Romanesque church of St-Julien le Pauvre, where I saw a priest sweeping with a crooked straw broom that looked as if it had been bought in a crooked-straw-broom sale 300 years ago. And at many corners stand the urns, still filled with fresh flowers, for those who died to liberate Paris from the Nazis. Students, bureaucrats and widows live in buildings where Verlaine, Oscar Wilde, gener-

als, composers, heroes, saints, and revolutionists once sojourned. As
did Benjamin Franklin; as did I, age 24.

A person who sits at a Left Bank café—which I have been
doing for a generation now, studying literature, studying the newspapers, studying the pretty young women, studying my fellow
studiers—will notice several brands of professional café sitters.
There are those who carry a lot of mouth, filtering reality through
laughter, companionship, and discussion. And there are many who
carry a load of silence: who sit brooding and watching, smoking,
munching, or sipping, waiting for the meaning of life to reveal itself, or merely for the day to end and the time to go back into un-
observed privacy. The proper pursuit of a Left Bank café sitter is
to practice an agile, caffeine or alcohol-released singing of the Left
Bank arias of flirtation and commitment, while watching with
irony over all the surrounding aspects of self. After all, there is time
enough in this thousand-year operetta to be both solemn and
giddy. There are other people. It may not matter. And even if I
won't live forever, which is always a possibility, Paris surely will.

The Left Bank still bravely attempts to shoulder the burden of
classic bohemia, but as it grows massive and expensive, other places
come along to do the job: London, New York, San Francisco, a
piece of every college town. There used to be (perhaps still is) a
Left Bank bar or gallery or café in my other hometown,
Cleveland, and elsewhere, too. Rive Gauche is a magic international phrase, evoking the universe of wine, garlic, fun and endless
youth. (Maybe it was only a frame shop in Cleveland.)

Allen Ginsberg once took me to a vegetarian restaurant on the
rue Cardinal Lemoine called Auberge Inn—a triple pun, since
auberge means inn and *aubergine* is eggplant (well, it's funnier if it
sneaks up on you without translation). There Allen sang a
Buddhist country-western rock song about love and death, clack-
ing his musical tools, and a young man tried to pay for our tea, saying, "I want to pay! I must pay! I've never paid a check before!"

I looked at the unhealthy vegetarians, dreaming in their Levis,
strumming away and singing their versions of Judy Collins and

Bob Dylan songs, and remembered Baudelaire's relevant Left Bank question: *When shall we get on toward happiness?*

Each new generation makes what progress it can. France itself, and even Paris, tends to be settled, materialistic, and family-oriented. The excess rootless hope and dreaming are shipped across the Seine to the Left Bank to be marinated in the cafés, parks, *brasseries*, garret rooms, discotheques, student clubs, *cinémathèque,* tryout night spots, and, in more organized fashion, in the various schools and institutes—medical, dental, liberal arts, language, art, music, and drama—that have traditionally supported much of the youthy bustle of these few square miles on the bank of the slow river that are devoted to the Elders and Youngers of Hope and Misery.

"Take those two words, gold and pleasure, for a lantern, and explore the great cage of Paris," Balzac commanded. One of his print shops on one of the narrow lanes off the rue de Seine is memorialized with a plaque, but my favorite of Balzac's streets is the rue Mouffetard, which runs upward into the Place de la Contrescarpe, where until a few years ago one of the last *vespasiennes* of Paris could be found, offering relief to the kidneys

A t the origins of William Burroughs's career as drug addict, collector of boys, Bohemian wanderer, and loyal accountant of his dreads, there seemed to be a midwestern American moroseness, a passion to relieve boredom, find something to do, manage to fill the hours of his time on earth. It was appropriate that he was a son of the manufacturer of Burroughs calculating machines. Thanks to the good equipment he had inherited, and hard work, he tinkered with the controls until he opened the locks into his nightmares. He won a partial victory. It wasn't easy. The morose mask became permanent, even in his peaceful and rewarded last years.

During a filmed interview, Allen Ginsberg said that everyone needs love, everyone wants love, a speaking from the heart, that's what we're all after—love— "Isn't that what you want, Bill?"

Staring coolly into the camera, Burroughs muttered through his teeth: "Not really."

—Herbert Gold, *Bohemia: Where Art, Angst, Love and Strong Coffee Meet*

of men while affording everyone a view of their feet and their polite, abstracted, thoughtfully concentrating faces. Now the rue
Mouffetard—pawn-shops, Left Bank proletariat, the boarding-
house in *Père Goriot* where Vautrin and Rastignac lived—has become La Yuppieville, with trendy restaurants and antique shops and
even, Lord forgive us, a t-shirt store or two. Several generations
ago, another novelist, Huysmans, made an odd remark: "Paris is a
sinister Chicago." It must mean *something*—probably that
Huysmans never visited Chicago, but being French he wasn't
stopped by lack of knowledge. The artistic vitality of Paris is running a bit thin these days, but there is still enough to spread a sheen
and gloss over the damp, gray, lovely city and conceal its mourn-
fulness with good cheer.

The Left Bank tries to save the past, both the ancient traditions
and the two centuries of bohemia. It tries to non conform and yet
enrich itself. The result is the preservation of the charming tangle
of medieval streets near the Seine and the dizzy street life of the
rue de la Huchette and St-Germain-des-Prés and the cafés near
the Sorbonne and Montparnasse. The result is also the plastic, glass,
steel, and aluminum international skyscraper inflicted on the
Maine-Montparnasse neighborhood, where once the streets were
sweetly sordid. The City of Light is also the City of Neon Light.

Sobriety hides in the religious corners—the square of St.
Sulpice, for example, the stately gray medieval church of St-
Germain-des-Prés and all the lovely chapels and agreeable, foot-
wearying sanctified enclaves—because, after all, this is still right-
thinking France, even if it is also the Left Bank. Sobriety is stowed
and spills out of vital junctions that reflect the ancient linkage of
piety and marketplace. In front of the Hôtel Madison, where I used
to stay—along with Alexander Calder, the mobile maker and Elie
Wiesel, the writer—there is a statue of Denis Diderot, encyclope-
dist, philosopher, atheist, joy giving novelist, occasional jailbird. His
finger is uplifted in warning. If one follows his pointing, it becomes clear that he is shaking his finger at the great church across
the Boulevard St-Germain.

Sometimes the young and the discontented of Paris pick up cobblestones to demand virtue, or use the majestic sycamore trees to build barricades. After the "events" of 1968, many of the cobblestone streets were tarred over, many of the trees removed. This is a good French way to deal with unrest. There is equal justice for all in Paris, Anatole France noticed. Neither the rich nor the poor are allowed to sleep under the bridges.

The Left Bank is the original opera set—*La Bohème's* Mimi and Rodolfo warbling and dancing and embracing through a cutesy decor of chimney pots and narrow winding streets and four cafés at every corner. Well, that paroxysm of fantasy has subsided. Housing pressure takes precedence; both artists and real people live where they can. Where there used to be four cafés at every corner, there are now perhaps only two—the others replaced by a video-rental emporium, a mini-micro supermarket, even an amazing junk-food trough.

But there are still those two cafés at each corner (and a few on the block in between) with their terraces, serving the *flâneur,* the street wanderer who wants to share in the contemporary medley of musical comedy and rock 'n' roll. The splendid cafés of an earlier time, the Flore, the Deux Magots, the Coupole, the Brasserie Lipp, are still the splendid cafés of today. Hemingway, Sartre and Gertrude Stein have gone to the Great Café in the Sky, but I met a Moroccan film director's girlfriend at the Deux Magots. Surrealism, Dadaism, Existentialism, even Communism, have been replaced by Structuralism and Deconstructionism and a heavy fragrance of consumerism. Often the artists are merely playing themselves, merchandising the style, so one must search and poke to find the brooding old Left Bank.

The daughters of the lovely, vicious green-skinned girls of pre-beatnik Paris, the girls of the postwar *zazou* persuasion—such as Juliette Greco when she sang of dead leaves, *Les Feuilles Mortes*—now look out for their health, take vitamins and have learned to stride along more like Americans and less like foot-bound Chinese maidens. There are Zen, Encounter, yogurt, and tennis and mountain-climbing shops. Well, let's not exaggerate. You can find a few runners along the Seine, watching out for the loose bricks, the winos and the fishermen, but they are likely to be Americans or laborers in the giant UNESCO complex, infected by contemporary ways of relieving world-historical anxiety. Today's Left Bank beauties have better teeth, cleaner hair, longer legs than they used to. This is not really a regression, unless one is hopelessly sentimental about the old garret, hot-plate, no-heating days of Paris bohemia, when changing residences meant throwing one's books out the window in the night while the landlord, to whom one owed rent, was busy sleeping off her day's wine.

Wine is more expensive now.

The concierge doesn't always dress in the black of grief and gloom.

My old concierge now has a daughter who is a ballet dancer, a *rat d'opéra*.

Cheap living and feudal luxury still exist side by side. The Faubourg St-Germain, traditional resort of the rich and aristocratic, also rents rooms to students and artists; great restaurants look only a bit more discreet than the neighborhood *brasseries*. Although the medieval walls of Paris are down, replaced by speedways, there is still a sense of concentration within limits, of a continuing dense urban unit. On the same brief turn up one of the streets off St-Germain-des-Prés—the rue des Ciseaux, say—rank smells and delicious whiffs struggle for control of the stroller's nose. The Left Bank is a place of lazy enjoyment and of irritability; coffee, wine, garlic, bread, fruit, spices. The open-air market at rue de Buci lacks only Gene Kelly to tap-dance his way past the cheeses and apples. If it's April, this must be Paris.

In the old days, I would buy my lunch at an open-air market and eat it on a bench along the Seine, or in the garden of the little Ukrainian church at the corner of the rue des Sts-Pères and the Boulevard St-Germain. Now I often do the same thing, joining other picnickers in the Place de Fürstemberg, outside the Delacroix Museum, and then sitting over an espresso or a *citron pressé* at the Deux Magots or the Flore, the Bonaparte or the Old

Navy, watching the ghosts of both the past and the future. No matter how loafingly the body coils or uncoils on wire or wicker chairs, Rive Gauche Present invites contemplation of Left Bank Past.

Symbolic of both the change and the sameness is the adventure of the St-Germain-des-Prés wino called *P'tit Louis*, or Little Louie. He was selected as a photographic model by Timberland Shoes, which had decided that the one thing a Left Bank hobo needs is a sturdy, long-lasting pair of American boots. After auditioning more than 50 "personalities of the sidewalk," the advertising agency chose P'tit Louis because of his authentic hat, nose, overcoat, and grizzled style.

The day I read about this in the morning *Figaro*, I happened to meet Little Louie on the steps of the philosophical and geographical institute located between the Café aux Deux Magots and the Café Bonaparte, where he was being asked about his views of the world by a French television team with the usual tense and worn international media faces. He was earnestly discoursing on the life of a *clochard* (a word that means one who sleeps under bridges and clocks) while occasionally taking a deep puff on his cigar or an even deeper drag on his bottle of Gros Rouge—for inspirational purposes only, of course. He was wearing The Shoes. He was not wearing socks. Today he was, as everyone is supposed to be for fifteen minutes of a lifetime, a Star.

Later that day I had lunch at *chez* Lipp, the *brasserie* of politicians, *littéraires*, filmmakers, the famous, and those who want to look at the famous, and I failed to recognize Leslie Caron at the next table. I too have grown older. Nearby, poodles were yipping in the laps of their lovely mistresses, who were feeding them morsels of sausage. (Poodles don't develop cellulite.) My friend at lunch, a journalist who has lived most of his life in Paris, a man who ranks high in the Café-sitting Olympics, stipulated that the Left Bank isn't what it used to be, and nothing is, but it is still "agreeable." The pickpockets and the arrogant waiters are more fun than elsewhere, the people are still humble and modest (and proud of it, in that French way), and the rusty treasure of a place is still a treasure, even polished up for display in a living museum of impacted time. If a person can be entertained anywhere, or bemused by the nearness of history, he can be bemused and entertained here.

"Let's search the Left Bank," I proposed to a friend. "Let's try to find a bad meal."

We succeeded. It was in an Algerian restaurant on the rue Xavier Privas, because we wanted couscous, that North African specialty of grains and vegetables and spices and various meats. But we cheated: it was a restaurant aimed like a missile at tourists, with a barker outside; and even here the food was merely mediocre, perhaps even *interesting*, which of course is not a word of highest commendation for food. One can eat poorly only with the greatest difficulty in the myriad small restaurants of the Rive Gauche.

Paris is still Paris, portions of the Left Bank are still something of the bohemian nation, but of course elements of *Bon Chic, Bon Genre*—the French version of gentrification, yuppification—have turned many of the former attic rooms into pretty studios. When I was a poor student and would-bee buzzing around St-Germain-des-Prés, Montparnasse and the Latin Quarter, I knew a little hotel in the rue de l'Odéon where other would-bees stayed for 50 or 60 cents a night. The "facility" was between each two floors. There was no shower or bath, so part of our social life consisted of meeting at public bath houses, carrying our towels. ("We always knew Paris would be like this!")

Now I was paying several hundred times as much to stay in the same hotel, but an elevator had taken the space once given to the water closets, there was a neat little bathroom in each room, and strategic antique beams had been exposed. All over the Left Bank, the little boardinghouses that recalled Balzac and Wilde and the Existentialists and waves of foreigners washing up on the shores of bohemia have become pretty and clean and healthy: "Nostalgia," as Simone Signoret wrote, "is not what it used to be." Yet the shadows of the lovers and philosophers and wine drinkers remain in corporeal new lovers, thinkers, flirters, café sitters. There are still plane trees and cobblestones and little squares like the Place de

Fürstemberg, where I heard a flamenco group howling magnificently of jealousy and loss. There are still international beatniks and hippies in the Place de la Contrescarpe; even a few French ones. The Rive Gauche is still a country of the mind, a nation of smoke in the head, the republic of imagination, the place of strict welcome to the amusing from everywhere, a purgatory of hanging loose.

"Money can't buy happiness," admitted my friend Claude Roy, a writer who lives on the rue Dauphine, but a person can use it well and happily here to buy his fruit, cheese and wine at the rue de Buci street market, books at Le Divan or La Hune, paintings in the dozens of galleries, all within a few minutes' stroll of his apartment. In a shop on the rue de Tournon that sells toy soldiers of ancient breed—Napoleon, Lafayette, Joan of Arc—I saw a newer toy soldier, of painted lead, in a black hat and cape. It was one of the heroic battlers in the wars of the Left Bank circa 1930, a tall, thin, Irish toy soldier—James Joyce. The pen can be both as mighty and as leaden as the sword.

Come with me down this street and meet the ghosts of our earliest years. Run, schoolboy, run, with your sachel bouncing between your shoulderblades— shout, shout for no reason, for the pleasure of being alive, glance quickly into the antique shop, where the grey cat sleeps amid the yataghans, parasols, and fans, run on past the shop where the embroideress is ruining her eyesight stitching initials onto snow-white sheets, run past the bearded chiropodist as he surveys the long pavement from his window, run as far as the bronze lion guarding the entrance to the Villa Fodor. But you're so quick, I've lost sight of you. Have you slipped into the church where the candle flames flicker in front of the grotto of Lourdes? Are you hurtling down the rue Raynouard, where the cab horses needed to be reined in? I'll not go chasing after you, little ghost from 1908. Too much has changed for the worse in our city to let me smile at you as cheerfully as I should like.

—Julian Green, *Paris*, translated by J. A. Underwood

Without going out of its way to welcome the stranger, the Rive Gauche has evolved an immense traditional hospitality. Hardly anyone rejects her embrace—although, as anyone who has been the victim of Parisian impatience can attest, sometimes the embrace is pretty cool. It requires an ability to fight back, which was lacking in the tourist I saw desperately shouting. "Diet pop! All I want is a diet pop! Why can't I get a diet pop!" on the terrace of La Palette, on the rue de Seine, near various art schools. This is one of my favorite cafés, but the burly waiter, who must have attended Berlitz Anti-Charm School, kept asking, "*Champagne? Cognac? Faites un bel effort, monsieur!*" ("Make a beautiful effort, sir!"), as if he didn't understand. Of course the waiter understood the tourist's wish. Of course he likes to play his games. Of course the art students and Rive Gauche locals—including an African prince in his robes, Swedish explorers, tousled philosophers, and me—were sadistically entertained by this unwinnable battle.

S hakespeare and Company is an irreplaceable institution: it is an English-language outpost if you need that, but more fundamentally it is a place to renew yourself, a place that embodies a belief in books and in people, a place with a liberal, literate heart and soul—and in that sense a place that symbolizes part of the special spirit of the city. That spirit extends to the chalkboard notices scrawled outside the door, too, source of some of Paris' prime wisdom and deals, where I found the following: "Paris bookseller looking for outdoor girl to build cabin in north woods. If she will cook him trout for breakfast every morning, he will tell her dog stories every night."

—Donald W. George,
"The Liberation of Paris,"
San Francisco Examiner

One of the special pleasures of the Left Bank is browsing the different bookstores specializing in English and American books. First among equals is the famous Shakespeare and Company of George Whitman, who used to hint that he was descended from Walt Whitman. His shop on the rue de la Bûcherie, a few steps from the Seine, has been a hangout for poets and college kids since it was called Le Mistral many years ago, before George adopted the name of Sylvia Beach's bookstore-publishing company, which first printed James Joyce. He keeps open late at night and has frequent mass Sunday teas for visiting geniuses. He is, as e. e. cummings once said about someone else, a delectable mountain, albeit a skinny and irascible one.

The Rive Gauche is a swamp filled with birds and giants, a continent of fantasy, a very lazy but agitated ancient kingdom in the midst of the 20th century, a *flâneur* among the world's earnest, a place to miss nothing but also to do nothing, a silence surrounded by noise, a sausage, a beer, a giggle, a dream of the past for those who have a shrug for the future, a baguette, a bottle of red, a bevy of students, a guitar jangle, a festive street orchestra that—I actually saw this—could not pass the hat because they had left it at home. In other words, the Left Bank is a delirious confusion and fantasy.

Like the rest of Paris, the Left Bank really used to be what we still think it is. It is heading toward being a Rive Gauche Museum. That's the truth and should be accepted. But the flower and bird markets still exist; so do the café sitters and their crises of exhilaration (call it inspiration, call it *joie de vivre*), and, in that magic light of the Ile de France, so does their gracious melancholy (call it pensive, call it acceptance of the mysteries of being).

One night on the rue de la Huchette, I came upon a group of buskers singing a stirring version of "Let It Be," that anthem of the late Sixties. They sounded exactly like the Beatles, except that they were singing in Korean. My French friends, a novelist and a psychiatrist who live upstairs from this year-round music festival, said they sometimes couldn't decide whether to drop coins or bags of water on the entertainers. A few years ago this pedestrian quarter, surfeited with Danish Joan Baezes and Israeli Bob Dylans, was blanketed with revolutionary posters proclaiming *a bas les gratteurs de guitares*! (Down With the Guitar-Scrapers!)

My personal law for survival and thriving on the Rive Gauche is to enjoy the monuments, parks, museums, churches and great public buildings, but pay attention first of all to the people. They are the distilled essence of France, essence of Paris—beautiful, ugly, surly, funny, greedy, generous, friendly, rude, seething with energetic complication. The best, useless and most fruitful occupation is to find a café terrace, buy a newspaper or a guidebook or anybook to prop against your cup or glass, and join the interlocking dramas of the street and the little stage on which you sit—the scholars, the mumblers, the lovers, the brooders, the debaters, those looking deeply into their liquids or into each other's eyes. Now you're there. This was the place.

Against all odds, even against the march of history, it still is.

Herbert Gold is the author of many books, including Lovers and Cohorts, Fathers, Family, Best Nightmare on Earth: A Life in Haiti, *and* Bohemia: Where Art, Angst, Love and Strong Coffee Meet. *He lives in San Francisco.*

★

Night after night I pored over my *Philosophical Dictionary* and my other books. What seemed obscure or unintelligible I attributed to my ignorance and stupidity, and I persisted. I recall how I suffered over certain passages of Sartre's *Being and Nothingness*, unable to make head or tail of them. My confidence was further shaken by the fact that other sections were clear and easy to comprehend, as were the same ideas expressed in his plays, essays, pamphlets. Recently I returned to that book, and reading it again in the light of experience realized that I was not entirely to blame, that certain sentences and paragraphs are indeed cloudy to the point of meaninglessness (perhaps written under the influence of drugs). I then understood why Heidegger, whose philosophy had been a powerful influence on Sartre's development, had described the book as "muck"—not that *he* was a model of clarity!

—Shusha Guppy, *A Girl in Paris*

LYNN SCHNURNBERGER

The Mystical Scarf-Tying Gene

Don't let the canons of fashion get you down.

"NO, I CANNOT SELL MADAME A STRAPLESS BRA," THE PERFECTLY coiffed French saleswoman said haughtily, looking at me somewhat lower than in the eye. "Your breasts are too large." (Actually, what she really said was, "*Votre poitrine est trop grosse.*")

At the time, I was living in a small town in the French countryside and was married to a Frenchman, and until that day I had never shopped in Paris. Now I stood in an elegant lingerie shop on the rue de Rivoli, opposite the Louvre museum and the Tuileries Gardens. The windows of the shop were filled with delicate Dior camisoles and saucy Saint Laurent panties. I was embarrassed. Did she mean that they didn't have bras in my size (which I had not yet disclosed)? Or that she had them, but wouldn't sell one to me?

The *vendeuse* rolled her eyes in exasperation. "*Non, non,* Madame does not understand. It's simply that you have, well, American breasts…. It just would not be right," she sniffed. Ah, the perils of shopping in Paris.

Now, I'm no shopping slouch. In fact, as a TV reporter in New York, I'm known as a shopping expert. I studied shopping at the hem of a master—my mother, a redheaded fashion plate who used her first Depression-era paycheck as a down payment on monogrammed silk underwear.

During my formative years, it was my mother who tooled around town in a two-toned turquoise-and-white Ford Fairlaine convertible and matching leather jacket. It was she who taught me to elbow my way through Filene's Basement and emerge unbruised with an under $20 Norma Kamali pantsuit. And it was she who showed me how to walk into Henri Bendel (when Buster, the doorman, still tipped his hat and scrutinized all those who dared enter) with a certain *élan* and drop $400 on a sweater that "we understood."

But shopping in Paris, where dressing is an art form, requires a whole different set of instincts. Whether one is stalking the *atelier* of some trendy new designer, perusing the Courreges boutique, or combing the racks at Tati (a K Mart with style), one finds oneself shoulder-to-shoulder with some of the most chic women in the world. They may live in a city with cobblestone streets, but they're wearing spike heels or four-inch-high platforms. From the art student with multi-looped earrings bracketing her Mohawk haircut to the "Madame Figaro" turned out in exquisitely accessorized pastel suits, these women are together. *Put* together.

I wanted to put myself together, too, but the obstacles seemed daunting. There was the intimidating process of buying things in a foreign language, the unfamiliar terrain and clothing sizes, the thought of stepping into a community changing room with an impeccably turned out Frenchwoman who probably looked more chic in her underwear than I did in the I-can't-afford-it-anyway $750 designer dress I was trying on. (I'm convinced that all Frenchwomen are born completely crease-free, with a unique and mystical scarf-tying gene.)

Slowly, though, I began to overcome the intimidation and the fear. I learned about the Paris that is all *haute couture* and little gold chairs, and the trendy Les Halles boutiques where gamine salesgirls sport purple lipstick and black, boxy dresses. I learned the latest slang: for instance, it used to be chic to say that some new idea or style was "brancher-wired," plugged in. Now, the hip French simply exclaim "Decker!" (pronounced deck-AIR)—trendy shorthand for Black & Decker, contemporary provider of all things plugged in.

I also learned about browsing. The French expression for this, *faire les vitrines*, sounded to me suspiciously like "make the latrines." Anyway, as it turns out, this is mostly an American pastime. Just try entering the house of Chanel to "look around." Even in the local Benetton shop, a salesgirl will immediately appear behind you. *"Voulez-vous quelque chose, Madame?"* the voice inquires, its tone an implied question about your lineage, your taste, your credit line.

"Non, je regarde."

You walk over to a stack of blouses. She walks over to the stack of blouses. You finger the gray chiffon. She eyes you suspiciously.

"Would you like to try on the gray chiffon?"

"No, thank you. I'm still just looking."

You move to the right. She moves to the right. You to the left, she to the left. Suddenly you feel like the prey of Inspector Clouseau.

Perhaps French salespeople are more attentive (just try to round up a salesperson in Bloomingdale's when you need help). Or maybe they're more persistent (personally, I'd rather be left alone). Perhaps the French consumer is less frivolous (and actually goes to a store to buy something). Or less curious. I'm not sure. All I know is that it's a difference that took some

From Aristotle to Cuvier, from Pliny to Blainville, natural science has made great strides. Each scientist has brought his aggregate of observations and studies to this field. Intrepid explorers have traveled the world over and have made important discoveries, but for the most part they have brought back only small black, yellow, or multicolored furs. It was helpful to learn that bears eat honey and have a weakness for cream tarts.

I admit that those are very great discoveries. But no one has yet thought about discussing the Clerk, *the most interesting animal of our era. No one has specialized narrowly enough, or meditated, observed, and traveled sufficiently to be in a position to speak with reasonable authority on the* Clerk.

—Gustave Flaubert, *Early Writings*, translated by Robert Griffin getting used to. Standing in front of a mirror at home and practicing a scowl, a firm *je regarde*, and an arch of the eyebrow helped immeasurably.

And when you actually find something you wish to buy (that you'll be *allowed* to buy—witness my encounter with the lady in the lingerie shop), there's the embarrassment of not understanding what it costs. Do you want to stand there counting on your fingers (in front of the impeccably dressed, crease-free, perfectly scarf-tied salesperson) or juggling your pocket calculator? It lacks a certain *je ne sais quoi*, if you know what I mean. A friend remembers saying "I'll take it!" and then quickly handing over every franc in her pocketbook in exchange for a thin, flat box containing one thin, flat (albeit elegant) Hermès scarf. How many Eiffel Tower bracelets, pink mesh stockings, berets, or bottles of Chanel No. 5 could she have gotten if only she'd correctly calculated the exchange rate?

People have asked me if I've noticed that at least the French are nicer to the Americans these days. "Is it because of the favorable exchange rate?" they want to know. "Not exactly," I answer sagely. "The Japanese have had the most money to spend lately, so the French now treat the Japanese even worse than they did the Americans."

Living in France, I soon found that just like Frenchwomen I gradually bought fewer pieces of clothing, but more carefully selected ones. I found that I relished the opportunity to try on new personalities: after all, I could play out my fantasy of strutting into a bistro wearing patterned black stockings and a graffiti-covered micromini, absolutely confident that no one I know would recognize me. I even prevailed upon my French tutor to devote one of our lessons to teaching me how to tie a scarf *à la française*. And eventually I came to think of shopping in Paris as a great adventure—almost as if the FBI had relocated me to a new life, with a new name, language, identity, and size. But it took time, and it wasn't easy.

As for bras, I never did understand the imperious declaration of the lingerie saleswoman: were my breasts really too large, or was

her remark just an example of Gallic snobbery? After that encounter, I called New York and had my bras sent from Ezra Cohen
on the Lower East Side. I wore them under my latest Claude
Montana and Agnes B sundresses. And if that's not a cross-cultural
experience, then I don't know what is.

Lynn Schnurnberger is the author of Let There Be Clothes: 40,000
Years of Fashion. *She is happily remarried and living (and shopping) with
her husband and daughter in New York.*

★

After dinner we felt like seeing such Parisian specialties as we might see
without distressing exertion, and so we sauntered through the brilliant
streets and looked at the dainty trifles in variety stores and jewelry shops.
Occasionally, merely for the pleasure of being cruel, we put unoffending
Frenchmen on the rack with questions framed in the incomprehensible
jargon of their native language, and while they writhed, we impaled
them, we peppered them, we scarified them, with their own vile verbs
and participles.

—Mark Twain (1869)

JACK E. BRONSTON

Le Paris Profond

The author's favorite companion is Vie et Histoire.

TRAVELERS NOD KNOWLEDGEABLY WHEN PARIS IS DESCRIBED AS beautiful, but even knowledgeable travelers would be hard-pressed if they were asked what it is that makes Paris beautiful. The closest they come is to talk about the way in which the lines and color of its buildings and open spaces have a harmonious flow and unity or to describe the way in which the natural light of Paris under an open sky flatters its surface and emphasizes those harmonies. But to find how Paris achieves that effect is a further challenge comparable to reading a score at a concert—as we begin to understand the components of those harmonies, they become more precious and more meaningful.

I've had an unusual opportunity to get beneath the surface of Paris and to understand how it has achieved its mysterious effect. Thanks to my wife's profession and my own curiosity, I have a routine which I have followed for several years which has enabled me to uncover some of the beauty secrets of the city.

My wife is a professional photographer which is reason enough for me as her personal "photo assistant" to look at the city of Paris more closely. Thus, the development of our routine—Sandra's work begins in the morning and lasts through the day and early evening. My services as porter, traffic-diverter, and location spotter are appreciated, but mostly after dusk when tripod and complex equipment—and my company—become more essential. Otherwise, from morning to mid-afternoon, my assistance is dispensable. I am therefore free to wander the *arrondissement du mois* with the intelligent and diligent companion to whom I dedicate these pages.

There are twenty *arrondissements* in Paris and each is the subject of a twenty-volume encyclopedia called *Vie et Histoire*—one for each. They are handsome, beautifully illustrated volumes dealing, as they each proclaim, with "*Histoire, Anecdotes, Célébrités, Curiosités, Promenades, Monuments, Musées, Jardins.*"

For good measure, they contain *Dictionnaires des rues* and, being French, *Vie pratique*. They are written (in French) with that precise scholarship and ironic sense of French history which reflects the serious but affectionate view which the French take of their history, their milieu and what they consider to be their somewhat eccentric but profound national character.

For each visit, I pick one of the *arrondissement* volumes. Even in the more obscure sections I have picked, I have never been disappointed. The avenue-by-avenue, sometimes building-by-building *promenades* which the demanding scholars have laid out in these volumes are long and physically tiring. But visiting the Place St-Georges in the IXe, la rue Mouffe in the Ve, the Bibliotheque d'Arsenal in the IVe or the Church of St. Vincent de Paul in the Xe—to take four happy surprises—are all the revival one needs. And there is always the sidewalk café restorative where no one cares how little you order or how long you stay.

The volumes usually begin with "*Découvertes archéologiques*" (a Parisian obsession tending to prove the continuity of the French persona); they then move to the medieval bishops and religious orders who built the churches, convents, and monasteries which fixed the original sectors, lanes, and lines of Paris (obliterated now, as the text mourns, by some depredation of the modern city). The authors gamely try to make the *arrondissement*'s Middle Ages as distinctive and fascinating as possible. Then we accelerate to those bloody outbreaks of the Parisian spirit—the feudal rivalries and broken heads of the holy orders in the VIe, Le Tumulte de Saint-Medard in 1557 as the Reformation advanced, St. Bartholomew as it declined, the Revolution, the Commune, the effects of wars and sieges on the city. All of this turbulent history is described in these volumes with scholarly neutrality. The events themselves come alive on the carefully planned *promenades* as one walks by and into the ancient buildings of Paris, explores its streets and alleys, or reads the historical markers which might be hidden from the casual passer-by.

As all of this architecture, carefully planned open space, statuary and buildings with their decorative alcoves gradually seep in to the now-weary walker, he begins to sense the underlying harmony of the city. Even the more prosaic, more modern buildings—anything after Napoleon III is modern—are built with a feeling for their place in the whole. It is not accidental. The French live and regulate their public lives by establishing what they consider to be exclusively French standards—the various Academies in their dictatorial prescriptions over the centuries have long been a source of amusement, especially in their often blind and stubborn adherence to tradition. But that tradition tends to achieve a harmony of thought and esthetic—and architecture—which the French, at any rate, consider a necessary form of discipline against their occasionally anarchic tendencies. The flow of the city expresses that discipline and that harmony.

But on to the *promenades*, each of which begins with the call, "*A pied....*" They are carefully planned, but need a word of warning. The abiding Parisian concern about usable space and Gallic precision dictates that there is no skipping of street numbers for buildings—32 is followed by 34 which is followed by 36 *ad ultimatum* with many a *bis* and 1/2 thrown in for good measure. Of course there are *pairs* and *impairs* sides of the street which seem consistent within an avenue, but not always uniformly north and south or east and west.

And don't expect the *pairs* to bear any relationship in number to the *impairs*—number 35 is seldom opposite 34 on the other side of the street, a disheartening fact at the end of a long tour *à pied* when the traveller standing at 56 is directed to an architectural curiosity at 59 which turns out to be several hundred yards away. The street names themselves can be quite confusing: there is "rue Condorcet" and "Cité Condorcet," "rue Chaptal," and "Cité Chaptal," to say nothing of large numbers of "Impasses" and "passages" which divert the earnest seeker into blind or confusing alleys.

To take you through a *promenade* as described in an *arrondissement* volume, I would choose the 9th which offers beauty, variety, and richness of tradition. It lies behind the Opera, which it encompasses (illustrated in the volume by a beautiful cross-section of the building), and includes the Gare St-Lazare, the incomparable churches of the Trinité and Notre-Dame de Lorettes, stretching to the Place Pigalle and the Boulevard Montmartre. I "covered" it in

arisians affectionately call it the Rallye Transparisien, *but we call it the Paris scavenger hunt. What you're looking for are one or all of 135 bronze discs (about five inches in diameter, with raised letters reading "Arago," and two small inlaid letters, N and S, indicating north and south) imbedded in streets, sidewalks, courtyards, and gardens. Playing connect the dots, these discs form a line called the Paris Meridian that runs from the southern to the northern edges of the city. Extending this imaginary line beyond the city limits around the world splits the earth into two equal halves: a meridian. Parisians with lots of time on their hands proudly boast having located all 135 discs. Others, less in the know, scratch their heads in wonder every time they stumble across one.*

—*Paris Notes*

four days and, as I open the volume again, I feel that I barely touched its luminous quality.

The *promenades* are themselves mercifully subdivided for practical exploration. In the case of the IXe, there are six such walks. One of them is called "la rue Blanche to the Place St-Georges" which I would like here to revisit because I think that this sub-*promenade* helps disclose the secret of the city's beauty most dramatically.

We begin at the Church of Ste-Trinité where la rue Blanche originates. The Church was built during the Second Empire on a spectacular intersection which is now being beautified into an even lovelier garden square. Ste-Trinité reflects what one might call the French dilemma or, more generously, the French charm— it is so carried away by its own aesthetic that it may have forgotten its original religious function. It combines the qualities of a grand Salon, a stately Chambre and a concert hall within the space and context of a church which is itself half-Gothic and half-Renaissance. I hesitate to call the event serendipitous, but I attended a funeral there on my *promenade* which gave the church the opportunity to manifest one of its few continuing functions in modern French society.

The rue Blanche leads into the quarter traditionally favored by French artists in all fields—mostly, the successful ones who were able to build houses for themselves which are at once unique, occasionally eccentric and yet, through some unseen discipline, harmonious. Music, drama and painting are all represented in schools of drama and music, places of birth and death (including the mysterious death of Victor Hugo), personal museums and former theatres. One of my favorites is the Musée Gustave Moreau (where I am the centerpiece of one of my wife's exhibition photographs) which houses 850 of his paintings and, they say, 7,000 of his drawings. And there is another jewel of a private museum waiting nearby where the descendants of the Brothers Scheffer have preserved their *ateliers* set in a pretty, hidden courtyard in two delightful buildings, one of

> *Gautier said that the Paris of his youth had become unrecognisable. When I walk down from Passy towards the Seine, I sometimes wonder where I am and whether I have not been dreaming. My sole consolation in disaster lies in the depths of the as yet intact avenue Henri-Martin when, in early summer, the impenetrable vault of the horse-chestnut trees protects a residue of coolness, and I spy, in this verdant tunnel lit by shafts of sunlight, a lone horseman, oblivious of his time, fleeing at full gallop in the direction of Yesterday.*
>
> —Julian Green, *Paris*, translated by J. A. Underwood

which is described by the scholars as "*une petite merveille de bon goût
et du plus absolu dernier cri!*"

Around the corner is the former Grand Guignol, the precursor of palatial movie houses and gory cinema around the world
(*précurseur de l'hémoglobine cinématographique*). Although it reopened
as a legitimate theatre in 1962 after 66 years of terrifying movies,
it is closed today. Rue Pigalle is, as the guide says, a kind of axis
for smaller side-streets with the homes of proud names in French
culture: Vuillard, Bonnard, Maurice Denis, Degas, Delaroche, and
toward the rue de Martyrs and rue Taitbout, Chopin at number 5
and George Sand at number 9 (*naturellement*), with Alexandre
Dumas and Delacroix on the nearby rue de Lorette. Interspersed
with these stylish locales are theatres, art schools, and small parks.
However, if one ventures to the end of rue Pigalle, 20th-century
pornography and its clientele dominate the boulevard between
Place Pigalle and Place de Clichy with a concentration that is
formidable.

But a clue to the secret of Paris lies at the end of this sub-*promenade*. Following the text, one makes a turn and suddenly looks up
to one of the prettiest sites in Paris—Place St-Georges with its
central statue of the designer Gavarni.

Place St-Georges was once a fountain in a square provided by
the ladies of the quarter with water for the horses of this artistic
neighborhood. Then came the Métro near the turn of the century
with a stop at St-Georges, destroying the fountain. But instead of
dooming the square, the incursion (now discreetly hidden) became
a challenge which was answered by a typically Parisian response.
The lovely statue-monument of Gavarni took the place of the
fountain and became the center of a tranquil, tree-lined square surrounded by classic architecture. This includes the superb former
residence of Adolphe Thiers, a museum or two, and the home of
"la Paiva," a grand performing *artiste*.

When I think of the harmony of Paris as the critical element of
its beauty, I think of Place St-Georges. The large ochre residence
of Thiers, with its triangular Greek cornice, ceiling balustrade, and
deep classic windows, is on one side of the square opposite the

half-gothic, half-renaissance residence of la Paiva. The charming bust of Gavarni studying his plans in the center of the square unifies the whole; the buildings and statue echo each other's light stone sculpture and quietly ornate decor.

Perhaps the square was carefully planned that way or perhaps it was simply that instinctive sense of the harmony of space and structure which pervades the city and guided the reconstruction of the square. I recall it as I saw it one day in bright sunshine at the end of my walk with my thumb marking my place in the *Vie et Histoire* volume. The Place St-Georges, its trees and the buildings around it were open to the sky, the sounds of the city were muted, Mr. Gavarni studied his designs atop his decorated column—and I thought to myself, "Paris is beautiful."

Jack E. Bronston's international travel began during World War II when he was a Russian and Japanese interpreter for the Marines in North China. He graduated from Harvard Law School in 1948 and served twenty years in the New York State Senate. He and his wife, Sandra Baker, a photographer, live in New York where he continues to practice law.

★

We made a good decision, not to have a car in Paris. No more fretting over repairs, parking, premiums, is there enough gas? For excursions outside Paris we take the train, or find a reasonable weekend car rental. In Paris the Métro works remarkably well. Maps are clear and easy to follow, with their ribbons of color to mark the different lines, and the trains are frequent and graffiti-free. There is no sense of menace; young musicians play their saxes and guitars, an occasional orator presents his opinion of French politics, beggars implore politely, "*Excusez-moi, madame*, but I'm hungry...." I always reward the puppeteers, who sling a velvet curtain across the car and present a lively little show with their ten decorated fingers.

Buses are even better. Sitting in a warm comfortable seat, gazing out of clean, clear windows at the passing sights, I roam the city armed with the yellow *Le Guide Paris-Bus*. It is quiet, other than a pleasant voice announcing the stops, although recently we had an international colloquy going. An Italian couple asked the French woman in front of me how to get to Étoile, and before we were finished, we all had our maps out, chatting animatedly, even the German man across the aisle piped in with his suggestion. You would have thought we were solving a problem of the world; we did, in fact, put together a nice little tour for our new Italian friends.

I walk in Paris, sometimes hours a day, and I observe, discover, reacquaint. Having mothballed my American walking shoes in capitulation to Parisian fashion, some days the soles are weary, which has led me to yet another Parisian delight: our neighborhood *podologue*, who will pare nails, shave calluses, and always finish with a foot massage. I still don't miss my car.

—Ann Davis Colton, "Letter from Paris," *Paris Notes*

Internal Affairs

A woman explores the Kingdom of Euphemism.

"MADAME!" THE RECEPTIONIST BECKONS. GINGERLY, MY ALARMING symptom and I sit where she motions, here in the foyer of a Paris gynecologist's office. The chairs are Louis something and gold frou-frou gilds the walls in that fancy French style so swell in a château but frankly not the sort of comfort I need now that the doctor refuses to see me. Not until I fill out the fat clipboard of forms on my lap, that is, and bypass the problem that has me stalled and gnawing my pencil at Question 2: "What brings you to the doctor today?" Through the smoked glass door to the examination room I see the shadow of him hiding in back; he is perched on a stool, twiddling his instruments, waiting. His concern hangs on him like his white coat two sizes too big—just about the size mine should be for I have recently discovered a secret so hush-hush here in France that any American worth her women's rights would marvel at the good fortune: here, there is no "down there."

That's right. For millions of Frenchwomen, when it comes to the subject of their bodies, here, there are no ovaries to speak of, no fallopian tubes to point out, no uterus to note, nor vagina. Nor are there breasts or PMS. If that sounds bad, what's worse is the alarming symptom I woke up with today is located in a place on my body which in France is not on the map, territory as yet un-charted, for no words exist to describe it.

My French friend, Eve-Marie, first shared the shocking fact of her country's lack of even a single serviceable cervix the June day we strolled the Champs Elysées, shopping.

"I must visit the pharmacist to buy Tampax for my little business affair," she said suddenly. "And pick-up some Midol, too, for my difficulty of the stomach." Although Eve-Marie spoke French, the English translation that spontaneously sprung into my head whenever she said this or that clearly popped up "business affair;" there was no mistaking it, "stomach."

"You mean, menstrual cramps, *non*?" I asked. My friend stared at me with an expression as vacant as those of the stone statues in the Louvre.

"*Comment?*" she said, listlessly, and I translated, "Hunh?"

Once at the drugstore, Eve-Marie was more forthright. "I would like something, *s'il vous plaît*, for my abdomen itch," she commanded and the pharmacist without so much as a mouth twitch of confusion slapped onto the counter a box of Monistat 7. "*Voilà.*"

Eve-Marie! I thought, flabbergasted. *Abdomen itch?* Why, the way she, a grown woman, verbally tip-toed around her bodily topics seemed a show of immaturity no better than if she'd confessed to her gynecologist some trouble with her "tee-tee," or suggested to her husband that he be more attentive to her "fou-fou" in bed. Embarrassing.

I confronted her later over coffee. "Eve-Marie," I said, being firm, "surely the pharmacists of France, professionals whose life work is to dispense products for every possible intimate situation, surely *they* won't be shocked at the mention of, say, a yeast infection?"

"You mean abdomen itch," my friend corrected.

"I mean, when it comes to problems like your menstrual cramps..."

"*Excusez-moi*, but it's difficulty of the stomach," my friend clarified.

"…you could just explain in plain French the exact spot in your pelvic region where…"

"If it's my lingering belly thing we're talking about then don't be absurd," said Eve-Marie, by now in a bit of a snit. "The pharmacist knows enough to hand over the K-Y jelly."

Our chat left me shattered. Long ago liberated enough to call a woman's givens by their proper names, I, like many Americans, can publicly mouth without stutter the word "menstruation." I can say it, yes, "breasts," and not collapse into a heap of preteenish snickers. Yet here in France, where women's rights ostensibly are so far advanced that RU-486 has been in use for *years* and sunbathing topless is *de rigueur*, Eve-Marie can't bring herself to actually say "premenstrual syndrome."

"Of course, you are referring to that which arrives each month like a hair in the soup," she said when I mentioned it. Of course.

So I zap the television one day desperate to comprehend Eve-Marie's coyness and there they are: commercials for "throat supporters," which in fact are *brassières*; ads for a product that provides relief from the pain and bloating of your "business affair" (Pamprin); soap opera girlfriends deep in tortured conversation over the grief of a sister's "accident" (miscarriage), in tears over a mother's fatal "heart trouble" (breast cancer). I flip through Larousse's French-English dictionary frantic for an answer and there they aren't: "clitoris," "labia," "G-spot," "vagina." These and other words for women's sexual reproductive accouterments simply can't be found. Stripped. They have been stripped from the French vocabulary as smoothly as unwanted body hair after a hot wax job.

The French have taste in all they do,
Which we are quite without;
For Nature, that to them gave goût
To us gave only gout.
—Erskine (1850)

It occurs to me that the language itself might be the douche that cleanses French of all natural, healthy expressions for the nature of womanhood. After all, as one of the world's most beautiful "romance languages," it gives itself the kiss of *politesse* by prac-

ticing excellent linguistic hygiene with many things coarse in life.
It pretties-up the crude, it adds glamour to the average. In France,
for example, criminals are not arrested, rather, they are "invited" to
jail. A "nice to meet you" upon meeting someone new in French
becomes "Enchanted!" Even a backyard tool shed behind a house
in Provence is known as a "château."

Obviously, in this neck of the woods a woman's parts are perfumed by expressions that leave the feminine sex to parade
through life as does Catherine Denueve through those French *films
noirs*—as an illusion of beauty. Mystery. A symbol creature of ef-
fortless perfection. Problem is, these parts are often drenched in
euphemisms so strong their very existence seems to cease and, as
the pain my alarming symptom makes plain, I have a problem that
must be described and "belly itch" isn't it.

"*Madame!*" the receptionist beckons again, anxious to retrieve
her clipboard of forms. This time she slits her eyes at me for causing a scheduling logjam and keeping the doctor stool-sitting
longer than he likes. "*Alors, fini?*"

Question 2 looms. Suddenly, I am seized with the peculiar per-
versity of a traveler an ocean from home, alone, and frankly ap-
palled to her very pituitary by the pitiful recognition given to
Frenchwomen's otherwise self-respecting sex characteristics. If
Eve-Marie and her millions of French sisters can't, I decide, I *will*
give voice to the oppressed, to the neglected. Yes, the revolution
for a freely recognized PMS starts right here, right now, with me.

What *am* I doing in the doctor's office today? I write furiously,
in capital letters to express the militancy of my ideals: "I have had
a bad MENSTRUAL pain in my left OVARY or maybe my FALLOPIAN
TUBE, or else my UTERUS, I don't know. But one thing's for sure:
the pain isn't anything that possibly can be mistaken for a soup
hair."

There. I hand the receptionist my clipboard. "*Well,*" she sniffs.
"*Bravo.*" She briskly disappears only to reappear trailing the doctor.
Worry weights his head which hangs as heavy as a water balloon.

"Madame, I don't understand," he says, oozing woe. "What *can*
we do for you today?"

Suddenly, my body cries out in pain and panic. Cramp! Suddenly, my fantasy cause doesn't seem so hot a priority. I mean, what if I, self-styled figurehead for all disenfranchised vaginas, am picked-off prematurely by a fatal faction of pelvic inflammatory disease? What if my plans for a family are assassinated here in France by an emergency hysterectomy performed right here, right now? Oh, God. My courage spontaneously aborts and I blurt in one breath: "It was right after my last little business affair when I suffered an abdomen itch followed by bad stomach difficulty. I'm scared it might be sexually transmitted heart trouble I got from my boyfriend."

"Why didn't you just say so!" rejoices the doctor, relieved. "We'll conduct an exam *tout de suite* and have you fixed up in no time. Right this way, Madame, *merci.*"

And you know, he did. It was only a minor belly thing, after all, caused by my too-tight push-up throat supporter.

Colette O'Connor is a traveler whose world of late has been Paris. She is a freelance writer whose work has appeared in the Los Angeles Times, Washington Post, Contra Costa Times, Women's Sports & Fitness, *and other major dailies and magazines.*

★

As a foreigner, being pregnant in Paris and preparing for your *accouchement* (giving of birth) can be both exciting and a bit scary. On one hand, you should be very pleased that, attitudinally, Parisians are very open and accepting about such natural phenomena as pregnancy and giving birth. The *accouchement* is not seen as a medical or surgical intervention; nonetheless, most Parisian women give birth in hospital *Maternité* wards or private clinics, and a large percentage opt for the epidermie (*péridurale*) procedure of painless but sensitized birthing. The *péridurale* procedure was devised by a Parisian doctor at La Pitié Hospital, the largest teaching hospital in France, located between the Gare d'Austerlitz and the Porte d'Italie. Hospital aesthetics in Paris may not meet the visual expectations of visitors used to more clinically antiseptic environs. Less attention is given to the public relations and image of hospitals in France than in the U.S. There are few frills in Paris hospitals, and it is primarily for reasons of comfort and not medical ones that many women have their babies in clinics. Also, in clinics the post-partum stay can be up to ten days, whereas hospitals keep new mothers for four or five days, which in itself is substantially longer than in the U.S. or U.K.

Many women and their men attend midwife (*sage-femme*) birthing classes, which are also reimbursed in part by the *Sécurité Sociale*. Almost all babies are delivered by *sages-femmes*, except in the case of complications or Caesarians. One absolutely wonderful place for birthing classes with highly trained and culturally sensitive midwives is the Centre de préparation à la naissance, 55, rue de la Roquette in the 11th.

—David Applefield, *Paris Inside-Out: The Insider's Guide for Visitors, Residents, Professionals & Students on Living in Paris*

St-Germain-des-Prés

This is a place where thought was turned into smoke.

THE LEGEND OF ST-GERMAIN-DES-PRÉS AS THE INTELLECTUAL centre of Paris had reached Persia by the end of the 40s and gradually spread among the young progressives. Through articles, photographs, and films we learnt the topography of the area: a maze of cobblestoned streets clustered around the square, dominated by the abbey and its graceful 11th-century tower—the oldest in the city. We knew of the cafés Flore and Deux Magots, where Sartre, Simone de Beauvoir, Albert Camus, and many other authors had written the books we read in translation. We had heard about Le Tabou, where Juliette Gréco had first sung the songs of Jacques Prévert and Raymond Queneaux, and launched the fashion for a pale complexion and disillusion. All you had to do was hop on an aeroplane and disembark in Paris, and there they would all be, waiting for you!

In reality by the mid-50s the writers, singers, and actors had mostly disappeared, having moved from their dingy hotels to apartments acquired with their earnings, while the developers and financiers had moved in. But many of the old *habitués* still lived in the district, and sometimes went to the cafés and restaurants they had made famous. It was not unusual to see a short, tubby man, with balding head and strabismic eyes behind thick glasses rush down the boulevard towards his home in the square—and recognize Sartre; or to see Simone Signoret and Yves Montand having a drink with friends at the Flore. But if the stars appeared occasionally, those in supporting roles—writers and poets of various nationalities living in Paris, actors and film-stars, chanteurs and impresarios—were regular visitors, and you could count on seeing them if you went to the cafés at certain times of the day, or at night after the shows.

All this was enough to attract intellectual tourism, and put prices up beyond the reach of students, who increasingly favoured the less expensive establishments further down the Boulevard St-Michel. By the 60s many of the small food shops had become boutiques, the run-down hotels where impecunious writers and artists had lived were refurbished into three-star hotels, and the apartments had been bought up and restored—yet another twist in the fortunes of a district which had fluctuated from commercial prosperity in the Middle Ages to dilapidation at the beginning of this century, when its derelict buildings had become the abode of students from the Beaux Arts and other university annexes. Yet despite it all, the area retained something of its village atmosphere, as it still does, with crowded street-markets, food-stands and flower-sellers suffusing the air with varied fragrances, antiques and exotica shops, while the presence of important cultural institutions such as the Institute and the Academy, and of major publishing houses ensures its continued intellectual prestige.

But St-Germain was a mental space far more than just a geographical district, for it symbolized the triumph of France's spirit after collapse on the battlefield. Germany had aimed its guns against culture, and lost; France had used culture as its weapon and won, wiping out the shame of military defeat. Jean-Paul Sartre (whose name more than any other was associated with the district) was one of a group of extraordinary French men and women in the forefront of European thought, who shaped their epoch: Simone de Beauvoir, Raymond Aron, Claude Lévi-Strauss, Simone Weil, Albert Camus....

Out of their writings here, in St-Germain, was born the philosophy of Existentialism, a philosophy popularized above all by Sartre's fiction. Each generation of students has its particular vocabulary, based on the prevalent ideas of its time. Ours was compounds of Existentialism, Marxism, Psychoanalysis.... At that time in Paris the majority of young people who called themselves "Existentialists" had no more read Sartre and Camus than most Communists had read Marx, but the ideas were in the air, and the post-war climate propitious for their spread.

I like Sartre's face. Some say it is ugly. It cannot be ugly: his intelligence irradiates his features. Hidden ugliness is the most repulsive; Sartre's face has the candor of an erupting volcano. When he enters the Dôme or La Coupole, he is like a suppressed bull.... Some faces are stingy, denying one even the flicker of eyelids. They appear starched. I love his lower lip like a white Negro's, his squint, his wandering eye, his shipwrecked eye, a slipstream of light when he enters our troubled waters.

—Violette Leduc, *La Folie en tête,* 1970

I was given Sartre's lecture "Existentialism is a Humanism" and later ploughed through numerous volumes of Sartre, as well as Camus. Philosophical choices depend on temperament and circumstance, and at the time Existentialism, as I understood it, suited mine: it was an expression of exile. It proposed that man is alone, "abandoned" in the universe; and free, and that the price of his freedom is perpetual anxiety; that there is no predetermined destiny, since we choose what we wish to be and thereby make our own destinies; that life has no meaning save what we give it; and that art and literature can redeem existence, which is fundamentally absurd. Most people, it says, refuse their freedom and take refuge in fantasy and self-deception, which leads them to "bad-faith" and "inauthenticity." But freedom is exercised within a "situation" which can change by "action" (notably political action), and this makes commitment unavoidable.

Existentialism was a hard philosophy to live by, as it put the responsibility of life squarely on man's own shoulders, offering him no alibis and no comfort. Amazingly, Sartre himself found it too hard to bear: he tried to reconcile Existentialism with Marxism—an attempted "squaring of the circle" which led him to compromise and to personal "inauthenticity." He and Simone de Beauvoir aligned themselves with the Communist Party and became staunch fellow-travellers. They established a kind of intellectual terrorism by declaring "all anti-communists are swine," broke with their friends—Camus, Aron, Koestler, even the suave Merleau-Ponty—and surrounded themselves with younger cronies, many their ex-students. By 1957, after the Hungarian uprising and the Khrushchev Report, most Communist intellectuals had left the Party or been expelled, but Sartre continued to "believe." Later, when asked why he had concealed the existence of concentration camps in Russia, about which he had known for a long time, he replied: "One should not drive Billancourt [i.e. the Renault car workers] to despair"—a quote that has become famous since as a supreme example of "treason of the clerks." Towards the end of his life, when he was ill and almost blind, and history—to which he had sacrificed truth—had moved on and left him behind, he declared: "I'm not a Marxist."

Sartre was not alone in this political trajectory; countless other Left-wing intellectuals and fellow-travellers followed it. Disillusioned with Russia, they kept finding promised lands, in China, Cuba.... "Something in them aspires to slavery" is how Camus described their attitude.

By contrast Camus remained honourable and true to himself till the end of his life. He and Sartre had quarrelled after the publication of Camus' *The Rebel* in the early 50s—a dispute chronicled in numerous volumes since. Suffice it to say that Camus contrasted man's continuing metaphysical and political revolt with the banality of "revolution:" the one a refusal of injustice and an affirmation of human dignity,

> *A Sunday morning full of wind and sunlight. Over the large pool the wind splatters the waters of the fountain; the tiny sailboats on the windswept water and the swallows around the huge trees. Two youths discussing: "You who believe in human dignity."*
>
> —Albert Camus, *Notebooks 1942-1951*

the other a suspension of human values for the sake of a "*programme*," a hypothetical better future. "I rebel, therefore we are" against "the end justifies the means," which sanctions violence, deceit and terrorism.

More than a decade before it became a commonplace, he understood the nature of totalitarianism and denounced it—the irrational totalitarianism of Fascism as well as the rational totalitarianism of Communism. Not wishing to align himself with either the Left or the Right, he became increasingly isolated, a lone voice crying in the wilderness. Stoically, he stood his ground, won the Nobel Prize in 1958, and died in a car crash in January 1960. And then, what posthumous triumph over his persecutors! All his predications came true and by the time that Eastern Europe collapsed in 1989-90 not a single intellectual of note was left in the French Communist Party.

Camus embodied a temperament both rebellious and mystical, but always on the side of life and joy. Unable to endorse a philosophy which says that moral principles have to be sacrificed until they can be resurrected in a "better future," I found myself more and more drawn to his position.

Although married with two children, Camus was known to have extramarital love-affairs. His two marriages and major relationships have been chronicled in his biographies as well as in contemporary *romans à clef*—notably in Simone de Beauvoir's *The Mandarins*, published in 1954. At that time Camus's main "companion" was an ex-pupil of Tania's, a celebrated actress, whom I had met and admired greatly. But so many beautiful women came into his orbit: young aspiring actresses, would-be writers, society-hostesses. Clearly, he had no trouble making new conquests, and in this he was no different from countless other writers and artists; St-Germain was always rife with gossip about love-affairs among intellectuals.

"There are absolute loves and contingent loves," Sartre had told Simone de Beauvoir, assuring her that theirs was of the first variety while his and her other affairs were of the second. The formula had become famous and provided a model for their followers. The American writer Nelson Elgren, with whom de Beauvoir had a long affair, commented: "How can love be contingent? Contingent upon what?" I agreed with him: this was surely promiscuity dressed up in philosophical garb? And it was not for me: I was truly innocent, and I did not see any reason to change my behaviour—it would be inauthentic!

One of Camus's conquests was Antonella, a student at Tania's who was among the first to befriend me. She was of Italian origin and very attractive—tall, slim, with a dark complexion and grey-green eyes which seemed to be always moist with tears. She had studied Italian at the university, then married a fellow student and produced a son, while writing short-stories and fairy-tales, a couple of which had been published. One day she had written a fan-letter to Camus, which had led to their meeting and later to an affair. For Camus it was evidently a short, inconsequential encounter, like grabbing a chocolate bar on your way home to dinner, but for Antonella it was serious. She had fallen hopelessly in love with him. She had left her husband and taken her little son to live with a schoolteacher girlfriend, hoping that Camus would make a commitment to her.

Instead, gently and politely he had made it clear to her that he had no intention of doing any such thing, telling her that he was incapable of love in her sense, and that he would always be her friend, as he was with many other women. But no more. Antonella was heart-broken. She was now 25, and had built a whole emotional edifice on very little, certainly no pledge. She lived for the rare occasions when she saw him—taking up acting was one of the ways in which she sought to remain in his life.

I n Paris, one never sees the look of defeat, no ancient sense of being crushed or, rather, of life's crushingness. In Paris, in France generally, everyone is all right, No Thank You! They're in control. They've got it covered or, at the least, they can and are taking care of themselves. Their lives, whether intellectual, executive, punk kid with a motorcycle, waiter, all are made to seem intact. You're supposed to think that no one has called for help in France since Olivier sounded his horn at Rouncevalles.

—Stuart Miller,
Understanding Europeans

She confided in me, and wept profusely, and I was sad not to be able to do anything about it. Despite being so influenced by his thought, I resented Camus for being the cause of her suffering. Then Tania, my drama teacher, cast me as Olga, the revolutionary heroine of his play *The Just*, and later when he came to see *The House of Bernarda Alba* I was introduced. He was courteous and charming, paid me the usual compliments, adding some specific remarks that made me believe them. He hoped to set up his own company, he said, and suggested I audition for him. To be part of a group of actors under his direction was to acquire a family security in doing worthwhile work while earning a modest living—it was a dream! But because of my feelings about what he had done to Antonella I never took up his offer to audition, and eventually left Paris a few days before he died. It was one of those "missed appointments" with which life is pock-marked, part of that mass of regrets that we accumulate.

Not that we did not meet again—once. One day I bumped into him on the Boulevard St-Germain, coming out of a café near his publishers' offices, and we stopped for a chat. He said he had an appointment, but would see me the next evening at six o'clock in the same place.

I believed that we would talk about the theatre, his plans, ideas and books, but when I told Pierre he laughed: "How can you survive with such naïveté? Is it not possible that he might like you as an actress and an adventure?" and he gave me a lecture about Camus's philosophy and how it tallied with his way of life—*joie de vivre,* multiplicity of experience, Mediterranean equilibrium and clarity—all as remedies against the angst and feeling of the absurd. So I did not go to my appointment, and never saw Camus again, but instead wrote and told him honestly that I was afraid of him, and had been warned against him. He sent me a gentle, kind letter, and we exchanged a couple more. I threw away most of my letters, diaries and notes when I left Paris, but his are among the few I have kept.

I was told that when he died, apart from his widow and the actress who was his acknowledged companion, many other unknown "widows" appeared in Paris, all claiming to have been great loves of his. Antonella was one of them.

Shusha Guppy is a journalist, singer, and author of Looking Back, *a collection of ten in-depth interviews with women writers, and the memoirs* The Blindfold Horse *and* A Girl in Paris, *from which this story was taken.*

∗

As Marie-Sylvie took the microphone at the Café des Phares in Paris one recent Sunday, an angry murmur ran around the room. There was one chair left and several people wanted it.

How would the protagonists decide who should sit? Would existentialism help? Or utilitarianism? Or religion perhaps? Not exactly.

"Get lost," said a middle-aged man with curly gray hair. "I was here first and I'm keeping this place for my girlfriend. Find somewhere else."

His intervention may have lacked courtesy but at least it settled the issue beyond doubt—a rare achievement for a follower of the popular philosophy movement that started here in the Café des Phares on the Place de la Bastille and is spreading across France.

Its founder, Marc Sautet, recently opened France's first philosophy practice, where patients can shed their metaphysical angst rather as they might try to shed more mundane forms of angst at the psychiatrist's.

What is the purpose of human existence? What is existence? Does existence exist? For a fee, Sautet will discuss all this and more in a one-to-one conversation in his office at the end of a dark corridor in the Marais district.

—Adam Sage, "French Revolutionaries Chew the Fat in Cafés,"
The London Observer

EDMUND WHITE

The Concierge

A fond look at a Parisian tradition.

THE CONCIERGE IS A DISAPPEARING INSTITUTION, THOUGH THE memory of this domestic Cerberus and spy remains potent for most Parisians. If someone becomes really detailed, spiteful, and petty in his gossip, he's likely to be upbraided with the rhetorical question "What are you, a concierge?" For the French protect their privacy with a sacred fury and prefer the permissiveness of sophisticated silence to the pleasure of spicy gossip (or "crusty," as they say—*croustillant*).

We have a concierge, Madame Denise, who is sweet, funny, and, above all, discreet. She lives in her little *loge* at the rear of the courtyard. Her windows are bedecked with impeccably white lace curtains in which swans and swains are picked out in eyelets.

Everyone in the neighborhood likes her. The Indian restaurant a block away gives her curries too strong for her stomach—but not for Fred's [the author's dog]. The nearby funeral parlor gives her slightly faded flower arrangements; on some days our narrow, rainy courtyard is carpeted with anthuriums or gladioli or mountains of chrysanthemums denuded of their satin sashes spelling out the name of the deceased. At Christmas time she receives a prematurely browning and shedding pine tree, which she decorates with a string of lights she runs on a cord out from under her door into the part of the courtyard sheltered from the rain.

Madame Denise takes in packages for us but also shipments for the bookstore on the street level, cleverly named Mona Lisait ("Mona was reading," not a bad name for a store selling art books); the boys who work there in return trundle out the garbage can for her every night. But Madame Denise's greatest admirer is the *coiffeuse* in the shop next to Mona Lisait, a stunning young *beur* (a French-born Arab) who tries out all the latest hairstyles on Madame Denise. One day our concierge will look like a Roman matron, the next like a Neapolitan tart, then a week later she'll become a Tonkinese princess or a cabaret singer of the 1940s, startlingly resembling the imposing, throaty, lesbian chanteuse Suzy Solidor. Of course constant variety is the very source of the *parisienne's* power to bewitch us, but it's somewhat disconcerting to see your motherly (and normally brunette) concierge coiffed with a bright red punk's coxcomb at eight in the morning (or—to be more honest—at ten).

Madame Denise lives with her son, who looks so solid, so ageless that at first I mistook him for her husband. In fact he looks a bit like the cowardly criminal in a Jean Gabin gangster film, with his pencil-thin mustache, sleeveless yoke-necked t-shirt and surprisingly silent way of walking (or rolling by), as if on casters. To be sure, he's not at all a gangster; on the contrary, he has a medal for 25 years of faithful service sweeping up at the town hall, the gleaming white Hôtel de Ville just two blocks away, and his mother showed it to me proudly. We've never seen him with another human being except his mother. "I've tried to persuade him to marry," she says with the cooing regret and feigned annoyance of the Triumphant Mom, "but he's a quiet boy, a real loner, and he's comfortable here."

One of his *relations*, or "contacts," at the Hôtel de Ville is a strange little burn victim with a molting wig and a crablike gait, an old *monsieur* who works as a bookkeeper for the mayor; he comes once a year to the *loge* to sort out Madame Denise's taxes, and she in turn prepares for him skate and capers in black butter.

Loge is the word not only for a concierge's apartment but also for an actor's dressing room, and Madame Denise, in her modest, smiling way, has a flair for the theatrical. An excitable French photographer, sent over by British *Vogue*, wanted to set up a shot in which Madame Denise would open her door slightly and with a smile hand me my morning mail while Fred looked on approvingly. We had to repeat this little scene twenty times but each time Madame Denise was just as natural, unaffected, gay—a born star. One day she showed me a glossy German photographic study of the concierges of Paris in which she figures prominently as the genuine French article (most of the few remaining concierges are Portuguese, which means their entryways smell of salted cod, their national dish, instead of *raie au beurre noir*).

Even better, Madame Denise is from the Nord-Pas-de-Calais region, considered the best breeding ground for conscientious, hardworking concierges. She was born in Lille and brought up there, in a boisterous, sentimental, accordion-playing café, and she "descended on" Paris 28 years ago with her husband, who promptly died. Luckily she found her position as a concierge and has held on to it tenaciously ever since. She has never traveled and doesn't seem to approve of it; she shakes her head tragically whenever we take off for Italy or Nice or London or the States. "Never a moment of repose," she laments. Of course she does her own traveling, through stamp-collecting, and she has my permission to cut out with a big pair of scissors the canceled stamps on my mail from Greece, Austria, Thailand, and other exotic places (she loves the *Porgy and Bess* commemorative stamps from the States).

In the afternoon she begins to socialize. She'll stand at the bar of Les Piétons just next door with the whores, all of whom she knows by name. If she's not at Piétons, she's at the other corner bar, the Royal St-Martin. Sometimes, when we catch her coming back from the bar, she tells us of the famous movie star who used to live in our apartment, and of her many loves. We exchange stories about some of the gallant adventures of our handsome landlord and new "crusty" details about his cheapness; like all French he fancies himself a *bricoleur*, a weekend Mr. Fix-it, and would rather attempt five times in a row to repair our leaking hot-water heater than call in a proper plumber.

She knows we're gay and says nothing, but does not resort to the polite fiction used by the restaurateur on the corner of referring to Hubert as my "son" (*votre fiston*), a particularly difficult lie to sustain given my American accent. She also knows Hubert is ill, and when he's in a bad way she'll offer to shop or cook for us; she asked only once what was wrong with him, and I, in my best French way, became evasive, giving her her cue to retreat into her usual discretion.

She has seen everything in her work and has a name for most of her observations. One day she was washing up some human *merde* left in the entryway, by one of the local bums no doubt. Bright-eyed and uncomprehending, I said, "What's that you're cleaning up, Madame Denise?"

"*Une sentinelle, Monsieur*" (a sentry).

"What's a *sentinelle*, Madame Denise? I don't know that word."

She turned on me a weary, faintly superior and terminally sophisticated face: "Just think about it another little moment, Monsieur White."

Edmund White has taught literature and creative writing at several universities including Yale and Johns Hopkins. He is the author of several books including Forgetting Elena, Nocturnes for the King of Naples, States of Desire: Travels in Gay America, *and the award-winning* Genet: A Biography. *This story was excerpted from his book,* Our Paris: Sketches from Memory, *which was illustrated by Hubert Sorin who died of AIDS in 1994. He lives in Paris.*

✳

More and more landlords are deciding to eliminate the concierge. The escalating cost of construction provides an excellent argument for the termination of an ongoing contract. Selling the ground floor apartment to finance renovation makes perfect sense—on paper. Won't a maintenance crew be more efficient in keeping the building clean? Why not install a row of mailboxes, instead of having letters hand-delivered? And a *digicode*? Is it really necessary to pay a concierge to keep watch when modernization has transformed the apartment building into a fortress with locks and security systems?

The concierge appears to be an anachronism as we approach the 21st century. Well, perhaps. But, she remains that extra dimension that makes urban life more pleasant. It is the concierge who gives each building its soul. Once she is eliminated, the human factor will be lost forever.

—Alexandra Grabbe, *French Graffiti*

KATYA MACKLOVICH

Paris in Pink

Living well is indeed the best revenge.

IT WASN'T SUPPOSED TO BE THIS WAY. ME SITTING ALONE AT LES Deux Magots trying to make glass after glass of *vin ordinaire* fill the expanse of a hot September afternoon. I was supposed to be in Paris with Tim, the man I had been living with for the last two years, the man who had hinted for months that he was going to ask me to marry him somewhere in this city of romance. We had planned this trip together for nearly a year. We had made lists of all the places we would see. For months I had practiced accepting his proposal while dreaming of the moment I would be transported forever out of the dungeon of single supplements and spinsterhood.

Instead, one night three weeks before we were to leave for Paris, Tim told me that he didn't love me anymore, wanted me to move out as soon as possible, and I could have the tickets to Paris, he had other plans. His other plans were SooZan, the former wife of his best friend: a woman as pretentious and phony as the spelling of her name. She called. Tim ran to her. I got booted.

I have very little memory of the next three weeks. I truly don't know how I managed to pack, to get on the airplane or even how I got to the Hôtel du Quai Voltaire, the small, antique-filled hotel we had chosen because it had sounded so romantic: all its rooms had French windows opening onto the Seine, with the Louvre as backdrop. All I remember is my friend Debbie telling me that if I wanted to regain my confidence with men, I needed to parade myself down the boulevards of Paris, *tout de suite*, and let the men follow after me like poodles in heat.

"If you stay home and wallow in self-pity, you'll find that by the time you're ready to get back out there, you'll have become ITM," she warned me. ITM was Debbie-talk for "Invisible to Men," a state of perennial spinsterhood and a purgatory of the worst kind. So I went to Paris alone, a sad, frowzy, 35-year-old. I dragged myself down the Champs Elysées, the rue de Rivoli, and the other boulevards. I scanned the city from the rooftop café at La Samaritaine, paraded myself through the corridors of the Louvre, the Musée d'Orsay and L'Orangerie, and took bus tours to the Eiffel Tower, Napoleon's tomb and Sacré-Coeur. Not a sniff. Not even a leer, or a wink. Nothing. I had indeed become ITM, a truly unpleasant state in a city that was certainly God's prototype for Noah's Ark.

For five nights I lay awake weeping. I left the windows wide open to let in the breeze off the river. But the open windows also let in the light and noise of the *bateaux mouches*, the boats that plowed up and down the river until well past midnight, playing music, displaying silhouettes of lovers embracing along their rails, and periodically shining spotlights onto couples kissing, and more, along the river's walks. I was being smacked hard with reminders of what I had lost. I had never been to Paris before and now the city would be so associated with these lonely memories that I didn't think I could bear to ever come back.

I had been sitting at this prime sidewalk table for hours, determined to get drunk. Instead all that I was developing was a ripping great migraine from the lethal combination of strangling heat, the rivers of *vin rouge* I had been consuming, and the incessant chords of an accordion player on the corner, who swayed rhythmically while producing noises like frogs being passed through a sieve, in three-quarter time. Meanwhile, my waiter was trying to mentally levitate me away from this famous café and across the boulevard

St-Germain to some other establishment at which he collected no tips. I started crying. My face got red and wet, my nose ran.

"Madame, Madame," my waiter said, shaking his head sympathetically at me. "Thees man you cry for ees not worth it." And then he handed me a napkin to blow my nose in. I nodded, thanked him, paid my bill and went back to my hotel room. How did he know? How embarrassing!

I decided to leave Paris, to take a train somewhere else for a few days. I found the number my British friend Michael had given me for his old school chum who lived in the Hague and worked for NATO. The Netherlands, perfect. Perhaps he was someone with whom I could have a drink or share a meal. I dialed the number and a voice, rich and burnished by years in an English public school confirmed that he was indeed, Neville Darnay. I told him that I was a friend of Michael's, currently in Paris but thinking of traveling up to the Hague. Could we get together for a drink, perhaps? In a voice as smooth and creamy as caramel, he told me that he was going to be in Paris the next day for a meeting. If it finished early enough, perhaps we could have that drink in Paris? He took my hotel number and promised to call either way. No trip to the Hague for me.

The next morning I felt better for some reason. Perhaps getting drunk really did help. Perhaps it was the prospect of sitting and talking in English with a native speaker, even if it was only for a few hours. I decided that I would pamper myself, treat myself to some new clothes from Le Bon Marche. I bought three clinging summer dresses, all in different shades of pink. "*Je déteste rouge*," I had protested to the saleswoman. "Oh but pink, eet ees Madame's color, and eet shows off Madame's figure so well," I had been assured. I was talked into a pair of pale pink sandals as well.

I wore one of the dresses out of the store. It was cooler and lighter than any clothes I had brought with me. As I walked back towards the hotel, a man on the street smiled at me. "*Ça va?*" he said. I smiled back. Then an old man doffed his cap at me and smiled a toothless grin. I smiled. "What was going on here? Was it the dress? Was that all it took, a skimpy, thin, pink dress?" I wondered. But it did seem as simple as that. Suddenly, men of all ages were nodding, and smiling and acknowledging my presence as I swished past. I decided to go completely mad, and spent the afternoon having the gray in my hair replaced by the reddish highlights I had had as a child, a shorter haircut, a manicure, a pedicure, a massage. By late afternoon I was poorer, but pink and perfumed.

At the hotel, Neville had left a message to meet him in the bar at the George V Hotel at five o'clock. I decided to take my time and walk slowly across the river, through the Jardin de Tuileries, and along the Champs Elysées. This time I saw men's eyes follow me, undress me. I walked slower, exaggerated the swing of my hips. An old man with brown teeth offered to buy me dinner. I declined politely. By the time I got to the hotel bar, I was feeling as sexy as I had ever felt, and then I saw what had to be him: a handsome man in a pale blue shirt, pale linen suit and large brown briefcase. He looked crisp and English. He had shaggy, graying hair and a moustache. I froze for a moment. He was almost too good-looking! "Neville?" I inquired. "Katya?" he replied. I smiled, and he stood up, held out his hand and escorted me to a chair.

We ordered some wine and talked. First about Michael, then about nearly everything else: our work, the theater, movies, books, politics. I saw nothing in that room but him. After more than two hours I asked him when he had to leave. He asked me if I was hungry. I nodded.

He made a telephone call and then we took a cab to the restaurant, Campagne et Provence, along the Quai de la Tournelle. The food had the full-bodied flavor of the south of France. His voice had the rich romantic tones of the actor, Ronald Colman. We drank champagne. I smiled a lot. I was light-headed and falling in love. I have no recollection of the decor, or the other diners. I only saw him across from me.

Dessert was a *tarte tatin* served with a dollop of lavender ice cream, fragrant with the scent of the pale purple flowers. He scooped some ice cream onto a spoon and beckoned me to lean forward and open my mouth. He fed me. He fed me some more, and then he leaned across the table and kissed me hard, his tongue sharing the taste of apples and flowers with me. I felt the tiny hairs on the back of my neck rise. My heart beat so wildly I was certain he could see it through the thin fabric of my dress.

"Let's go," he whispered. I was powerless to refuse. I didn't want to refuse.

We walked along the river. The sky above the twin towers of Notre Dame was lapis blue streaked with deep pink. A full moon was rising. He took my hand, then he slipped his arm around my waist and pulled me to him. I had the chills, I was shaking. We stopped. He pulled me closer and we kissed, at first slowly, just lips, then our mouths began devouring each other. His hands teased the small of my back, while my hands found their way under his shirt. My temperature rose wildly and I felt my nipples harden, my crotch pulse. A *bateau mouche* slipped past us on the river, and suddenly we were bathed in bright pink light. From the boat came whistles and applause. "Oh my God!" I shouted. "We're making love in public." "Hmmm," he said while nibbling the cradle of my neck. And then the boat moved on, the light was gone, and he held me against him. His heart was beating as fast as mine. I was melting into him.

We climbed back up to the street. At the foot of the boulevard St-Michel, a young man was playing a tarantella on the accordion. People were strolling about. It was a warm, calm night. Neville let go of me and I momentarily thought I would crumple. He dropped some coins into the man's hat, whispered something; the man nodded. With a flourish, the man started playing "La Vie en Rose," a song made famous by Edith Piaf, a song I had always thought downright sappy.

"Do you know this song?" he asked me. I nodded. It was the story of a woman telling how, when her lover held her close in his arms, all of the troubles of life disappeared from view, and for that moment life was beautiful, pink and rosy: *la vie en rose*. "I asked him to play it for you," he said. Then he kissed me gently. I trembled. I listened to the music as Neville pressed me to him. He stood behind me and encircled me with his arms. I had been wrong. It was a lovely song. The accordion was a lovely instrument. Everything was lovely. Then the song ended and I was back in reality.

Sin is whatever obscures the soul.

—*La Symphonie Pastorale*

"Don't you have to leave?" I asked.

"I don't have to be back until Monday," he answered.

"But, aren't you married?"

He nodded. "She's decided to stay in the Algarve another few weeks."

I didn't need to know anything else.

We went back to my room and made love by the pale pink light of the moon. Then we ran the bath and slept in each other's arms in the cooling water. We spent the next three days together: eating, making love, sitting in cafés staring into each other's eyes, holding hands. We wandered about the bookstores of the Left Bank, and bought each other tiny gifts from the *bouquinistes* along the river. At night, I would put on a new pink dress and we would dine elegantly, drink fine wine and champagne. Then, Neville would take me in his arms as we sat some place with a view: the steps of Sacré-Coeur, the top of the Eiffel Tower, the tip of the Ile St-Louis. We synchronized our breathing. We found secret places to make love while Paris winked her glowing pink lights knowingly in our direction. And then we'd go back to the hotel and make love again. It was the best three days of my life.

Early Monday morning I rode in the taxi with Neville to the Gare du Nord. We stood on the platform entangled in each other until the train started to leave. He ran on board, and then poked his head out a window and blew me a kiss. I stood on the platform watching his train disappear. His scent lingered about me, and I could still feel his last kiss. I was too happy to cry.

I have been back to Paris many, many times since. I always wear pink. And I always stop and secretly smile whenever I hear the accordion.

Katya Macklovich was stolen by gypsies when she was a little girl. Although she was ultimately recovered by her grandfather, that brief experience gave her a taste for adventure and travel that shall last the length of her life. She is an artist and poet living in San Francisco, at least for now.

✳

Among the enduring icons of Paris is Edith Piaf, the tiny singer who burned herself out more than 30 years ago but who remains for Parisians, and for the French generally, the embodiment of some cherished values: a gritty romanticism, a profligate willingness to give everything for love and art, and a love of Paris that embraces equally its squalor and splendor. "My heart," she sang, "is at the corner of a street / And often rolls into the gutter."

And it was almost in the gutter of the 20th *arrondissement*, legend incorrectly claimed, that Edith Gassion was born in 1915 when her father failed to get a doctor in time and Edith's mother gave birth on a policeman's cape on the steps of 72 rue de Belleville. Fifteen years later, and long since abandoned by her mother, Edith left her father to begin a career as a street singer in the district's Belleville-Ménilmontant neighborhood.

Later she would describe the years 1930 to 1935 as an "endless walk." This was the depths of the Depression, and Edith and her companion Simone Berteaut were just two of a hungry, shifting crowd of singers, jugglers, beggars, and mimes who worked the city's streets, courtyards, and squares hoping to hear the ring of coins on the cobblestones. When a passing cabaret owner heard Piaf in 1935, he was astonished by a voice that seemed to fill every inch of her body and by an almost alarming intensity of delivery. He dubbed her "*Môme Piaf*"—the Little Sparrow— and took her off the streets and put her on the road to stardom.

And yet in important ways Piaf remained to the end a person of the streets, closely identified with the working-class neighborhood of Belleville-Ménilmontant. Speaking of her impoverished beginnings there, of that endless walk that would begin again each morning with the thin and dirty teenager gargling coffee to loosen her vocal cords, she said, "I wouldn't be Piaf if I hadn't gone through all that."

—Frederick Turner, "The Echoes of Piaf in Paris," *The New York Times*

HELEN DUDAR

✦ ✦ ✦

The Hungry Museum

*Cézanne said, "The Louvre is the book
from which we learn to read."*

THE WIDOW LADY FROM TROY, NEW YORK, WAS OFFENDED, INDEED
seriously shocked. For some months of 1830-31, Emma Willard
was in residence in Paris. She had, of course, toured the Louvre
Museum—or perhaps only as much of it as a virtuous person
could endure. As her journal would report, the place was an offense against decency, its walls crowded with works more suitable
to dens of iniquity than to a public collection of art. Now, Emma
Willard was an early feminist, a pioneer educator of women; don't
even ask how she could have known anything about the decor of
iniquitous dens. It is likely that she was shaken by images of naked
creatures celebrating a few of life's pleasures. Even more offensive
was the cavalier way in which sacred and profane works were allowed to mingle. In Mrs. Willard's eyes, the morality of all Paris was
imperiled.

Sixteen decades later, the relentlessly modernized Louvre is not
so much a shock as a bombardment of surprises. One recent season, a devotee of vintage monster films could take in King Kong
and Godzilla in a single sitting or spend an entire day listening to
expert discussions of the iconoclastic American architect Frank
Gehry, perhaps hoping for a gorilla to appear. In the fairly new, im-

mense underground-entrance space below I. M. Pei's celebrated glass pyramid, dedicated shoppers roamed through boutiques crammed with expensive knickknackery and shawls priced at $300. There were not only cafés for light bites but a gourmet restaurant where, at last, a finicky diner could encounter what national standards currently consider a "correct meal;" there were concerts and art lectures and a post office handy for mailing souvenir cards; there were stacks of videocassettes on Louvre masterworks turned out with Hollywoodian finesse by a new department of cultural affairs.

And borrowing a leaf from enterprising American museums, the Louvre was now available for private parties. On Tuesdays, when the museum is closed, the same subterranean entrance area known as the Cour Napoleon, which displays no art that might be endangered by revelers, may be rented for dinners for a maximum of 1,000 persons. The price: $50,000 to $100,000.

If there is any trauma in the renewal of this storied institution, it is to be suffered in its acreage—miles of hard flooring to be traversed by a serious visitor bent on exploring riches beyond the *Mona Lisa* and the *Winged Victory*. Ten years into what has, without exaggeration, been called the Grand Louvre project—at a cost that has so far scaled the $1 billion mark—the place is bigger than ever and still growing.

In November of 1993 the museum at last became the sole occupant of the rambling old palace it calls home. It occupied and opened the Richelieu Wing, the long arm of the building on the north side of the grounds. A

After spending countless hours in the Louvre and other august institutions, I've come to the conclusion that they are in desperate need of a Sleep Program, whereby one could, for a fee, sleep on a cot before a great work of art. Sleep fundraisers, done selectively, would not only augment the coffers of perennially fund-hungry institutions, but provide culture lovers with a unique way to worship, to study, and to dream. (Of course, tests would first need to be conducted on the effects of morning breath and gas on the most delicate works of art.)

—James O'Reilly,
"Sleeping with Giants"

shabby warren of offices that housed the French Ministry of
Finance for more than a century had been gutted and transformed
into an elegant sprawl of spaces for art—more than 100 rooms.
With the 39 others opened last year in another wing, the museum
has doubled its exhibition space.

And there is still more. Inaugurated simultaneously with the
Richelieu was an immense underground facility wearing the imposing title of the Carrousel du Louvre. For years now, at the western end of the museum grounds, workmen have been burrowing
under the gardens known as the Carrousel. The place was a mess,
a perpetual chaos of noise and dirt and disorder, embellished with
hopeful signs promising an up-to-date array of amenities. The
completed space has its own access to a Métro station and several
museum necessities—a laboratory, an amphitheater—but its main
purpose was to alleviate burdensome traffic problems.

Until this year, the busy thoroughfare along the Seine River on
the south side of the Louvre has been cluttered with parked and
double-parked tour buses, the vehicles that shepherd fully one-
third of the daily visitors to the museum. Now, at last, underground
parking space has been provided for 80 buses and 600 cars. And
significantly, there is also space for 60 new shops. Because neither
the city nor the state would come up with sufficient funds to pay
for a parking installation, rent money from the boutiques, when
they are fully leased, will eventually cover the high cost of building underground.

There is no progress without pain. In the quiet of cramped cu-
ratorial offices—17th-century rooms equipped with up-to-date
computers—staff people sit worrying about the kind of unwelcome visitors this new shoppers' paradise is apt to attract. Not far
from the Louvre is a similar underground mall, the Forum des
Halles, which replaced the legendary wholesale food markets of
Paris. It seems to house a floating population of *voyous*, young and
vaguely menacing layabouts from the suburbs who spend hours
just hanging around.

In its long, checkered history, the Louvre has survived worse, including the demanding tastes of twenty monarchs, most of whom

lived elsewhere; the dictates of at least fifteen architects who built, tore down and rebuilt segments of the palace for eight centuries; a few revolutions; several names, one of which was Palace of the People; serious fires; the untidy housekeeping of artists allowed to work there; and the greed of the Nazi invaders. In World War II, the Louvre's cherished contents were packed up and trucked to hiding places in *châteaux* scattered throughout the countryside.

The inauguration of two new major installations was timed to coincide with a significant anniversary—the bicentennial of the birth of the Louvre as a public institution. It formally opened November 18, 1793, at the end of the French Revolution, as the Central Museum of the Arts, with a collection of 538 works, most of them acquired by generations of French royalty. These were augmented by art that had lately been confiscated from cathedrals and the great homes of members of the nobility who had either fled or been parted from their heads. For a long time, the premises were primarily devoted to a small army of copyists—spiritual ancestors of the needy artists who today can still be found turning out clumsy replicas of great paintings. In the early years they were the only people allowed in daily; the general public could visit every ten days. Not long after the opening, the name was changed to the Napoleon Museum; the collection had been brilliantly enlarged by a conqueror who knew a thing or two about looting.

Neither the name nor Napoleon's booty would survive Waterloo. In an effort to savor all the stolen art before it was retrieved by the prior owners, in the summer of 1815 an English miniaturist named Andrew Robertson scooped up his spare cash and rushed to Paris. As he recounted in his journal, Robertson haunted the museum, hoping to see everything before the Italians, Prussians, Austrians, Spanish, and Dutch, in turn, arrived and packed up their national treasures. To the French, their claims were a cultural insult. As one outraged Parisian insisted to the visiting artist, "France was the garden and cradle of the arts—the only place where these things ought to be...." Actually, the repatriation efforts were not entirely completed. The Italians accepted a boring Charles Lebrun and left behind a first-rate Veronese; they took

back inlaid marble tables and did not bother with so-called primitive works, which tastemakers of the period rejected as "bar-
barous." Over time, bequests, purchases, and astute explorations
would fill empty spaces and crowd basement storage rooms. The
Vénus de Milo, found by French archaeologists digging around the
Mediterranean basin, arrived in 1821. For much of the 19th century, the French burrowed through ancient sites in the Middle
East, shipping home masterworks of great pre-Islamic civilizations.
The result is perhaps the largest and most diverse assemblage of art
in the world.

Housing the works and showing them in improved surroundings proved to be a major priority for the President, François
Mitterrand; the Grand Louvre project was the subject of his first
press conference on taking office in 1981. It is invariably perceived
as part of Mitterrand's "edifice complex"—he launched a good
number of building projects. On the other hand, the professionals
who occupy the Louvre had been wringing their hands over space
problems for half a century. As the museum's director, Michel
Laclotte, puts it, "It was a dream for generations, from the 1930s
on, to have the Richelieu"—the wing occupied until now by the
Ministry of Finance.

It would take some time to persuade the ministry to relocate to
new headquarters on the edge of Paris. For one two-year period,
while the bureaucrats managed to delay their departure, construction work could be pursued only during the night hours, at great
expense and inconvenience.

As urgently needed as the Richelieu Wing was a central reception area. There were a half-dozen ways into the Louvre but no
suitable gathering place for the large classes of chattering children
and the big tour groups shepherded into the museum all day long;
there was no auditorium for film, lecture and music programs; and
there were hardly any of the merchandising facilities that today's
museums thrive on. To find a workable solution and to oversee the
platoon of architects who would eventually take on assignments
for parts of the huge project, Mitterrand chose I. M. Pei, one of
America's most distinguished architects, whose best-known design

was probably the masterly East Building of the National Gallery of Art in Washington, D.C.

Great space for new facilities was to be found only underground. For a time it looked as if nothing at all would rise on the surface of the court, but Pei felt that a marker of some kind was needed, a structure that could also bring daylight into the installation. He thought of domes, he toyed with cubes; he chose a pyramid, a 71-foot-high structure made with panes of clear glass that would reflect the ornate facades surrounding it and the ever-changing sky above. To say that the reaction was hostile scarcely describes the explosion of abuse that greeted his design. "Fit only for Disneyland!" and "The Luna Park of the Louvre!" the critics cried.

To this day, some Parisians insist the opposition was not wholly esthetic. Some of the anger was focused on the fact that Mitterrand had chosen his chief architect without competition (Pei does not participate in competitions). There was, as well, the automatic resistance of conservatives to a Socialist president's building ambitions. As one Parisian woman involved in the arts recalled, the opposition view was: "How dare Mitterrand touch the Louvre? How dare a Socialist do this?"

> *I*n Paris a building is never just a building. New public architecture gets served up as a gourmand's feast of allegory and national politics. I. M. Pei's pyramid at the Louvre is not just a new entrance to an old museum but a central eye for all of Paris, regenerating all that is old, redefining the entire city around its single glass point like a magic crystal in Superman's Fortress of Solitude.
>
> —Alastair Gordon,
> *Architecture View*

In Pei's New York office, the published insults are preserved in a foot-thick file. A man of resolute high spirits, Pei now says with a laugh, "I was hurt but not mortally so." He had the firm support not only of the Mitterrand government but, eventually, of the entire Louvre staff. Still, in the early days, during frequent business trips to Paris, he could sense the public hostility even in casual encounters. Some of the animosity abated after a full-scale prototype, without glass, went up on the site in 1985, conveying a sense of what the courtyard would look like with this large, spare addition. And after the 1989 opening, public opinion was swiftly transformed. "People stopped me on the street and thanked me," Pei recalls. He would repeat himself brilliantly in the design for the Carrousel du Louvre. Daylight pours into that underground space through another big pyramid, this one inverted so that its point becomes a beacon in a great space.

Pyramid bashing has now faded, to be replaced by agitation over the Tuileries. The Grand Louvre project includes restoration of those splendid formal gardens that stretch from the museum grounds as far as the Place de la Concorde. One citizens' group organized a protest, enlisting American support and contributions, with flyers that instructed the public on "How to Stop the Massacre." The victim of the massacre, in their eyes, was a piece of history—Le Notre's incomparable 17th-century gardens—and the means was their growing commercialization. In recent years, garden space has been rented out for three-week street fairs, a giant bookseller's exhibition and what seemed to be the last straw—a skating rink.

As one architect involved in the project sums it up, the conflict is a battle between two groups: the functionaries who oversee the Tuileries and who, to support the gardens, will rent a plot to any entrepreneur able to pay congenial sums of francs for the privilege; and on the other side, the strict preservationists who don't want to see anyone even walking on the grass. The resolution will likely be a compromise. The street fairs, popular events for children, have already been reduced from two a year to one.

Whatever pride Parisians take in the Louvre is hardly translated into a notable local presence in its galleries. Since the pyramid reception hall opened, the number of visitors has gone from three million a year to more than five million. The majority are foreign, and about one-seventh of all visitors are North American; the proportion from the city and suburbs is said to have risen from a sparse 31 percent to 36 percent. Even so, people in the businesses and professions of the arts insist that although they are often at the Louvre, their friends never go. Among knowledgeable residents there is an amiably cynical rule that residents of this culture-ridden city turn up at the pyramid in large numbers, lunch in the gourmet restaurant, take in a lecture or film, pause to inspect the glorious bookshop and go home without ever having stopped to inspect a work of art.

Apparently many do not even wander beyond the great entrance hall for the short walk to one of the newest—and oldest—works on display. Even before digging began, French archaeologists told Pei and the builders that they would find vestiges of the first royal dwelling on the grounds. What the excavation actually uncovered were substantial sections of walls, towers and wells of the austere 12th-century fortified castle that was the first Louvre—an impressive and strangely touching remnant of the city's early history.

Recent innovations trouble some Louvre professionals. Without prompting, a curator suddenly offers an explanation for an unexpected detail on the Louvre's one-page map. Published in six languages and color-coded to help tourists find their way through confusing spaces, it provides the precise location of six masterworks that many first-time visitors feel it is crucial to see—among them, the *Mona Lisa*, the *Vénus de Milo* and the *Winged Victory*. No museum is happy to encourage tourists to proceed through the building at a gallop primarily or exclusively in order to stand before a half-dozen celebrated pieces. But something had to be done for the peace of mind

In the 12th century, Paris was France's largest city, but the royal court was in neighboring Senlis. In 1180, this was to change when a young boy of fifteen became King Philippe-Auguste of France. From the very first years of his reign, Philippe took it upon himself to transform Paris into the finest city in the western world. He had the streets paved, laid the groundwork for the creation of the University of Paris, and, upon leaving for the Crusades, gave the order to build a fortress to protect his beloved Paris from invaders.

A castle called the Louvre was built on the most vulnerable site in Paris. It was a massive square structure with a central tower topped with a pointed roof. It housed royal prisoners, the crown jewels, and the kingdom's charters.

—France Today

of those staff members who preside over the information desk: they were bored beyond endurance by the number of tourists wanting directions to those works.

In fact, the museum administration appears to be singularly attentive to the comforts of its 1,300 employees. Michel Laclotte, a small, brisk, unpretentious man, is the first scholar ever to head the museum, and one would expect his interests to focus chiefly on the art inventory and its proper display. Nevertheless, since his arrival the Louvre has found room for an employee health club complete with weight machines, a lending library and a part-time social worker available to help staff members with financial or domestic problems.

Of the six stellar pieces listed on the map, Leonardo da Vinci's *Mona Lisa* is not only a point of pride but a source of torment. Posing the question as "one of the crucial issues" confronting the museum, his words edged in irony, Pierre Rosenberg, the Louvre's curator of paintings, asks, "What are we to do with the terrible *Mona Lisa*?" With her faint cryptic smile and her sly eyes, this 16th-century portrait is an object of great beauty and greater fame, rendered even more famous by theft. In 1911 it was stolen and kept hidden for two years by an Italian workman who thought it belonged back home where its model had lived.

In high tourist season, when the noise level and the crowds in the pyramid reception hall resemble the Miami airport on Christmas travel days, the groups of guided tourists rooted before the painting create day-long bottlenecks. Their presence makes it a chore to move through the Grand Gallery and nearly impossible to approach the art on neighboring walls. In fact, one of

I n order to make culture a game, my wife and I buy postcards and catalogs of pieces of art and encourage our daughters to find as many as they can in a given museum. And so I will always remember the Mona Lisa this way: armed with a catalog, my three-year old Mary disappeared, munchkin-like, into a herd of grownups swarming the fabled painting. Soon I heard a shriek from the front of the crowd, "Daddy! I found her!"

—James O'Reilly,
On and Off the Autoroute

the few depressing sights in the Louvre is to observe visitors gazing raptly at the portrait and scarcely casting a glance at two splendid Leonardo paintings that hang nearby, the *Virgin of the Rocks* and the *Virgin and Child with Saint Anne.*

Rosenberg has finally concluded that the only solution is to give the Mona Lisa a room of its own. "It is a little bit sad," he notes. After all, what a museum of this size has to offer is context—a number of major works by a master, in the company of the paintings of some of his important teachers and followers. In this case, however, the obligation to educate has been vanquished by human traffic problems.

By Rosenberg's estimate, the range and depth of the Louvre's painting collection is matched only by the National Gallery in London. The public had a chance to experience the depth at the end of 1992 when the Louvre opened 39 refurbished rooms in the Cour Carrée, the oldest part of the museum, showing only 18th- and 19th-century works of French art. One-fifth of the exhibition had been in storage for years.

Reviews were mixed. Some critics thought the installations were entirely wonderful, "a sumptuous gift." A serious French arts magazine complained about the murky colors of the painted walls—too dark—and suggested that under the natural lighting some still lifes looked as if they were in an "advanced state of decomposition." Interspersed among pieces by such important painters as David and Ingres were fairly underwhelming efforts by such secondary figures as Flandrin and Chasseriau. In all, the galleries show 700 paintings, about a hundred pastels, drawings and miniatures, and a captivating three-walled woodland scene executed by Corot for the bathroom of a patron's home. Taking in the entire survey of two centuries of art in a single visit is something like consuming three gourmet meals in one day.

But the Louvre was not meant for visual snacking. The new Richelieu installation is a feast: 860 paintings of the Northern European school, including the Dutch, Flemish, and German treasures in the collection; 3,000 large and small antiquities from the Middle Eastern excavations; 33 rooms of French sculpture; a string

of rooms for a prime collection of objects of decorative art—
among them, at last, the space to hang 80 large, rare Renaissance
tapestries.

Interestingly, it was a sudden inspiration for the Richelieu in
the planning stage that Pei believes won him the unwavering
support he needed from key figures at the museum. In the hard
winter days of 1982, bruised by the fierce attacks on his designs,
Pei went off to Arcachon, a summer resort in southwestern
France, to talk things over with the Louvre staff and with Emile
Biasini, the agile civil servant whom Mitterrand had chosen to co-
ordinate the project for the government. The Richelieu had one
small and two large courtyards where Ministry of Finance functionaries habitually parked their cars. Pei proposed installing glass
roofs over them so that the museum could use those gloriously
decorated spaces to display large works of sculpture, including
some eroded outdoor pieces removed from the adjoining
Tuileries. The smaller space would be set aside for some of the rare
pieces from the Middle East.

It was, he says now, one of those obvious lightning-bolt solu-
tions that, with luck, arrive in an architect's moments of desperation. If the Louvre leadership had been vacillating about his ideas,
it became at that moment a solid constituency for Pei's leadership.

Theoretically, the construction rigs and the workmen should be
gone soon. But nobody believes it. Pierre Rosenberg is given to
saying that, like the great castles and manor houses of Europe that
are eternally engaged in addition and renovation, the Louvre will
forever be a work in progress. Michel Laclotte is wryly certain that
when the last picture has been hung and the last piece of carved
ivory placed in its glass case, the curators of all seven departments
will probably be heard complaining that they must have space,
more space.

Helen Dudar is a freelance writer and former staff member of the New
York Post. *Her work has appeared in the* Wall Street Journal, The New
York Times, Smithsonian, *and other major U.S. publications. She lives in
New York with her husband, author Peter Goldman.*

✳

Suddenly Rosy, my ten year old, gasps, stiffens like a pointer, and darts down the wide corridor, brown hair and jacket flying behind her. Dodging the multitudes in her wake, I take off in pursuit, leaving Grandma with the guidebook: I have no idea what has spooked Rosy, but, since a very dapper French gentleman inexplicably stooped at a street corner earlier this morning to untie my shoelace, I am prepared for just about anything. I catch up as she skids to a stop in her little sneakers before the broad staircase, eyes and mouth agape, gazing upward, her face rapt with astonishment.

Towering above us, three or four times larger than life, and blazing ivory and gold in a pool of afternoon sunlight, is the marble statue of Nike, the *Winged Victory of Samothrace*. The familiar headless figure is arrested in a movement so animated with vitality it is as though she has flashed through the ages and materialized on the pedestal before us to herald the fulfillment of some ancient prophesy. My daughter, who is bored with art and hates museums, has stopped breathing in spite of her exertion, and silently slips her hand into mine. Rosy has found a symbol to mirror her innermost fantasies, a goddess so invincibly unfettered, so inspired with freedom and urgency and power that we can all only pause to pay homage as my mother quietly arrives at my side.

—Lois MacLean, "Rosy in Paris"

* * *

Excusez-moi, Je Suis Sick as a Dog

When laid low in Paris, help is close at hand.

IF YOUR WORST TRAVELLING NIGHTMARE IS WAKING UP IN A strange hotel room knowing you are really sick, let me reassure you. If it should happen in Paris you have it made.

The French are really into handy telephone numbers. Allô Vert, for example, is not a number for a football squad but a help line if your green plant has gone yellow. There's a number to call if you need a Grandmother in a hurry. For example, if you are a working woman and your child is suddenly ill, who will hasten to the house while you sort something out? Dial-a-Granny, that's who. And so it goes, with the solution for just about every imaginable problem just a telephone call away.

And that includes the problem of the individual, local or visitor, who becomes *malade*. In that case, SOS Médecin is at your service. A while ago, holidaying in Paris with a friend, I experienced this for myself.

The procedure is extremely simple. Every hotel desk has this handy number...it is also listed in the "What's on in Paris" type magazines which appear weekly. Depending on the state of your health and/or your French, you or the kindly hotel desk clerk simply dial this number and before you can say "*Mon Dieu*," help will be on the way.

I finally decided to ask for help about 5:00 p.m. on Friday afternoon. My friend, who had awakened that morning feeling pretty miserable, was suddenly running a spectacularly high fever. Not that I could explain how high...as my thermometer was in a different scale from theirs. But I showed it to the lady in reception, pointing maniacally at the little red line way above which the mercury most obviously was—in any language. She nodded calmly but seriously (the French take ill health very seriously) and dialed the SOS number.

"They come *immédiatement*, Madame," she assured me. I had hardly retraced my steps up to the room when the phone rang with a sad message from Madame. "SOS is *désolé*, Madame, but it is the hour of the rush and they will be retarded in arriving. Patient yourself for twenty minutes I am afraid."

As I had not expected help to be beamed in, twenty minutes did not seem too long to wait. But in fifteen minutes they were there, a pair of very serious looking young men, who immediately upon entering our two-star hotel room, gave it the air of a surgical suite.

Most efficiently they re-checked the temperature, prodded and poked. Looked down throat, in ears, up nose. Listened to chest. They murmured questions in Franglais and accepted answers such as "ouch" or "stop that," seeming to find them meaningful.

The prodding over, they pulled the two rickety breakfast chairs up to the rickety table for the dignified conference. Some slight differences of opinion were thrashed out between them most eloquently. ("*Ah, mais oui!*" "*Alors!*") I felt I was listening to a rather advanced tape on Teach Yourself French. Then they

The French have one of the world's highest rates of pharmaceutical consumption.

—JO'R, LH, and SO'R

began filling out prescriptions. Rather a lot of them.

It remained only to hand over the franc notes. (Madame had

told me the price previously—250 francs. At that time it compared very favourably with the cost of a housecall back home in Dublin, but like fevers, the prices of things tend to mount steadily in France.)

With considerable reassuring shaking of my hand and studiously unworried shoulder shrugging they indicated that my friend seemed to be suffering from a virus, but to be on the safe side had written prescriptions covering a wide variety of look-alike ailments.

I was guided to the window where they pointed out the pharmacy across the street. In common with all open-for-business French pharmacies, it could be identified by its lit Green Cross shop sign. I could also see the doctors' white car with the solemn black letters—SOS Médecin—across its side.

The two had hardly left the room when Madame was on the phone to me again. In passing, the Médecins had mentioned to her that the shop across the street would soon be closing and to save me having to walk a short distance away to the area's on-duty pharmacy, I should be advised to go as quickly as possible to have the prescriptions filled.

The visit to the pharmacy passed without words—prescription handed over, pre-packed medicines handed back. The story ended happily. The patient was sufficiently recovered the next morning to totter out and see some sights.

But for me, "SOS Médecin at work" was a more Parisian sight than the Bluebell girls could ever be!

Maryalicia Post is a freelance journalist who lives in Dublin. She travels widely but Paris is her favorite destination—in sickness or in health.

★

My little cousins call them "toilets of death." Legend has it that a woman, desperate to use a Parisian pay toilet but lacking correct change, had dashed in after a previous patron but before the toilet had begun its automatic cleaning cycle. Inside, she was trapped and killed by the fumes. When I told my friends about this, they were understandably concerned, nature's call aside.

Finally, a volunteer stepped forth bravely into the green plastic shell, leaving the rest of us huddled outside. We must have brightened many a Frenchman's night: seven American tourists clumped nervously outside a public toilet, praying for their friend's survival. She emerged unscathed, though later admitting to a fierce adrenaline rush, and the rest of us took our turns in relative peace.

—Arwen O'Reilly, "Paris Vignettes"

JAN MORRIS

Within the Périphérique

Paris exerts an unusual gravity.

PROUD WELSH PATRIOT THOUGH I AM, AND THEREFORE FRANCO-
phile almost by historical definition (for did not the French come
to our help in our last great rising against the English?), I generally
get no nearer to the heart of Paris than the Périphérique. I shy
away from the city centre like a horse frightened by a ghost, and
the spectres that scare me are my own insular prejudices.

To name a few at random, I do not much like the songs of
Edith Piaf, the boulevards of Baron Haussmann, the furniture of
Louis XIV, the sound of Gertrude Stein, the vainglory of
Napoleon or the conceit of Charles de Gaulle. I distrust, at one
level, people who turn ideas into movements; at another, ideas
themselves if too pressingly articulated. In a paranoia common but
not often acknowledged among Britons of my World War II generation, deep in my semi-conscious I probably resent the fact that,
while London was blitzed in victory, Paris remained inviolate in
defeat.

Yet I am haunted, as so many of us are, by the suspicion that
Paris knows something other cities don't, that it has an advantage
over them somehow, and is handling our brutal century more in-
telligently. So when invited to spend a long weekend in the place,

I determined to restrain all bigotries, whether of taste or of bias, and look at Paris once more altogether from scratch—exploring my own intuitions about the place as I wandered footloose, Friday night to Tuesday morning, through what they used to call (but not lately, I notice, the idiom being too slushy perhaps for modern Paris) the City of Light.

I arrived after dark, and when I walked the next morning out of my hotel near the Bastille, almost the first thing I saw, through a bright-lit first-floor window, was a middle-aged scrawny man flexing his upper torso rhythmically before a mirror to a muffled beat of not very heavy rock. He clenched his modest muscles, he moved his head this way and that like a woman trying on a wedding hat. I could not resist stopping to stare, and doubtless sensing my gaze on the back of his neck, he turned and gave me, still twitching, a mordant, joyless smile. I thought of using him as an image in this essay, but when it actually came to the point I could think of nothing he was imaginal of.

Whenever I reached a high viewpoint I was at once excited and disturbed by the spectacle of La Défense, Paris's newest quarter, baleful beyond my Périphérique. Its skyscrapers seemed to me to stand there resentfully, brooding over their exclusion from the city centre. They have an allegorical look, especially seen through the imperial frame of the Arc de Triomphe, as though they represent a future being kept calculatingly at bay or in reserve.

Certainly with calculation, either way, for carefully selected envoys of Modernism have of course been allowed to enter the gates, and actually there is something about the ambience, or perhaps merely the design of Paris, that makes futurism seem easily at home. Place de la Concorde, especially after dark with its lights and streaming cars, seems to me very like a space launchpad, preparing to send its obelisk into orbit. The cruelly disciplined Seine, for my tastes the most overrated riverscape in the world, provides the perfect channel for those glass-roofed restaurant boats which glide beneath the bridges at night, headlights blazing.

Seen from the top of the Montparnasse Tower Paris looks an utterly modern city, laid out by computer beneath the vapour trails of its jets, while if you need a human figure to represent the coming age, you could hardly choose better than the solitary police-woman who, bathed in unearthly floodlight, patrols Place de l'Hôtel de Ville at midnight with her pistol at her hip.

thousand years from now, perhaps, a man will stand as I am standing behind a windowpane and look as I am looking at this landscape of houses behind trees and this sky scattering spring rain. I try to imagine having crossed that great space of time and being that man. What is he thinking about? Is he happy? Does he sometimes wonder what he is doing on this earth and why at one period rather than another? What does he believe? What can he see? This same curiosity that he arouses in me, others had about us before they passed away in the days when Lutetia was first emerging from the mud. Maybe on this very spot where I am standing a Barbarian mused about the men that were to come. And here am I, dreaming of that Paris of the future, raised up on the space that is now ours, where shuttered concrete, glass, steel, and possibly other materials as yet unknown will be the ingredients of a limitless beauty.

—Julian Green, *Paris* translated by J. A. Underwood

The Centre Pompidou, which seemed a few years ago so reckless an imposition, already appears perfectly at home, its pipes and girders almost as organic as the sinuosities of Art Nouveau, its forecourt ever more reminiscent of the great square at Marrakesh. Like many an exaggerated emblem of Parisian assertion—the Arc de Triomphe, the Panthéon, the Eiffel Tower, the Opera, the Champs-Elysées itself—it has been reduced by sheer osmosis to a proper metaphysical size. As to I. M. Pei's Louvre Pyramid, I foresee that it will soon be cherished as an integral and indeed redemptive part of the monstrous palace around it. Already it provides, with its Napoleonic connotations, one of the city's most truly characteristic *coups d'œil*. Spouted around by its rumbling fountains, glassy as the sky above, seen through the gateway to the east it looks to me as though it has been dropped there ready-made from some meticulously navigated spacecraft.

In the Musée d'Orsay eight very, very small children sit on the floor around one of Gauguin's Tahiti paintings. They are addressed with an exquisite lack of condescension by their teacher, who explains in detail the composition of the picture, the flow of its colours, the relationship between its characters, human and animal. What fortunate infants, I think as I eavesdrop, to be born in such a city, to live among such beauties, to be treated with such courtesy! They listen with intense intelligence, their eyes shifting from teacher to painting and back again; but when they take up their drawing boards to copy the masterpiece, starting with an oblong frame to set the proportions, hastily I move on in case they one and all prove to be without talent.

I am agitated by the timelessly emblematic quality of Paris. It is not like other capitals, living for the moment and the cash. It is as though the whole place consciously stands for something or other, so that almost nothing is simply itself. Just as in Mao's China every single action, public or personal, had to fall into a political category, so in Paris I sometimes feel that every street, every event, every gesture is dedicated to some aspect of Parisness.

Elsewhere civic generalizations are generally out of date, overtaken by shifting styles and standards. Here they remain almost disconcertingly valid. The plan of the *arrondissements* still provides a sociological and aesthetic index to the city, and here as almost nowhere else the idea of a city quarter is not obsolete. There really are whores around Pigalle, there really are tramps beside the river, there really are Breton cafés around the Gare de Montparnasse, you really can buy a live common-or-garden hen on the Quai de la Mégisserie. Publishers visibly frequent St-Germain-des-Prés, and hardly had I read in my guidebook that the Café Floré, where I had stopped for a cup of chocolate, had lately become a homosexual rendezvous than I was greeted by an eminent gay novelist of my acquaintance.

Clichés come true, too. Parisian chic exists, Parisian live-and-let-live lives on—where but in this capital would the layabouts be left in peace on the warm floors of Beaubourg? Black people walk about Paris with such elegance, such panache of cape and flaunt of fur, that they might be living models of negritude. The Lebanese, the Vietnamese and the North Africans, however intrusive they may seem to the more racist of the *indigènes*, to an eye from across La Manche truly do appear to have been gracefully assimilated.

Just over the hill from Place du Tertre, I found myself wandering through a district which appeared so entirely and authentically petit bourgeois that girls still played hopscotch in its streets and neighbours actually talked to each other—I saw it!—out of their windows; and on the Sunday morning I walked from the Arénes de Lutece, where elderly gents were playing *boules* in the pale sunshine, to Place de la Contrescarpe, where the butcher and the baker faced each other in almost rural intimacy, where pigeons and drop-outs lazed bucolically around the square, and where I could hear from far down rue Mouffetard the strains of an ebullient brass band.

How is it done? By a natural conservatism, perhaps a cautious view of change, and possibly not least of all by a serious acceptance of surprise as a constructive element of municipal style. The surprise indeed often seems as deliberate as everything else. The Métro is purposefully impregnated with variety, to dispel the sense of menace that other subways have; and when one morning I saw a small fire on the track down there, extinguished not with extinguishers (none of which could be made to work) but by a man jumping off the platform and stamping it out, I really thought it might have been specifically arranged for our distraction.

I helped a blind woman over a street-crossing near the Gare de Lyon. She looked particularly irritable, cross, and demanding, but though born and bred in the 12th Arrondissement, turned out to be diffidently gentle. It was a lesson to me not to misjudge the hard-mouthed, sharp-eyed, fast-shoving, middle-aged Parisian housewife, who may well be sweeter than she allows. I took the blind lady first to the post office, then to the pharmacy, and when I left her she said: "Now I give you back your liberty."

Sometimes it seems to me that Paris is marking time. Emerging from a recent past without, not to put too fine a point upon it, all that much honour, it is girding itself for a future to which it already seems much better attuned than most of its peers. Perhaps the Centre Pompidou digital clock, ticking away the seconds towards the end of the century, is counting down for the city itself; perhaps the escalators, elevators, and walkways, which already move faster here than they do elsewhere in the world, are being imperceptibly speeded up, year by year, to accustom Parisians to the pace of the millennium. The ideas, it appears, are on hold— one hears of no successors to Existentialism or Structuralism—and French films, books and plays also seem to be holding their fire.

But then they are in the wrong language. That's the underlying reason, I dare say, why Paris gives me this watching, waiting, plotting impression. The most obvious anomaly of the city today, the most obvious cause for civic neurosis, is the fact that the French language has lost its cachet. Except among captive cultures like the Gabonese, I would guess that Spanish, German, Russian, even Chinese, and Japanese, are all more in demand in the language classes of the world. Not to mention, of course, English. The Parisian complex about the English language must hit every stranger in the eye. Walking down the short arcade which connects the Centre Pompidou with the new Quartier de l'Horloge, I noted the following shop signs: Paris Basket, Tie Break, New York New York, Scoop, Blue Way, Award's Academy, Yellow, Bubble-gum, and Lady—all in 100 metres of Parisian shopping! The graffiti of Paris, if they are not of the mindless Manhattan sort which disfigure the Métro trains, frequently indulge themselves in Anglicisms such as Fuck Off Skinheads, Kill The Cops, or Crack Snack; as for Richard Branson's Virgin Megastore on the Champs-Elysées, it is like a people's temple, before whose alien gods all young Paris dances.

Nevertheless I still get the sensation that Paris may be stealing a march on us all. Cities do not think or conspire, of course, and one should not think of them anthropomorphically, but sometimes one senses that a profound historical instinct animates the spirit of a place, and I sense it about Paris now. I feel that it aspires to be, not the political capital, but the most resplendent and influential metropolis of the terrific new Europe. Figuratively, those skyscrapers are held at a distance only while the future they represent is assessed and prepared for. The Centre Pompidou, the Pei Pyramid, the Montparnasse Tower have been allowed in as one might permit double agents into the halls of chancery, and the plan that won the competition for the new Seine bridge is, I note, the most insidiously Modernist of the entries. Technically, Paris seems to me more ready than any other European capital for the opportunities of a 21st-century federal continent; only the language, only the magnificent language, preys on its mind, inhibits its manners, and breaks out in Franglais.

Wandering into Notre-Dame on a Sunday night, I found a choir and orchestra celestially performing Bach's Christmas Oratorio. *The cathedral was full, a reverent multitude of young people sitting on the floor, if they could not get a seat in the nave, or simply milling about like me. It was magical. All Paris seemed to be there, singing its heart out or half-lost in the marvel of it all. When I discovered that the choir and orchestra came from Germany, and realized that half the listeners were as foreign as I was, it only seemed more magical still.*

So I left Paris as I came, in an ambiguous frame of mind. More clearly than ever I realized it to be one member of the supreme metropolitan trinity, with New York and London, one of the three cities where anything can happen, anything can be found, anything can be done, everyone comes. "Drop a plumb-line into Paris," Balzac said, "and you would never find bottom." It is an impertinence even to try to gauge the condition or the intention of such a prodigy.

Yet at the end no one ever left Paris willingly. The city became a state of mind which you carried with you for the rest of your life: you interiorized your displacement, your deracination. Real exile begins when you no longer pine for "home," when it has been lost forever, buried in the recesses of the psyche, and the only home you have is Memory.

—Shusha Guppy, *A Girl in Paris*

Yet whether it be out of historicism or out of the collective unconscious of my own people, the city still leaves me uneasy. Just as I think I have exorcized my prejudices, new ones materialize. I feel that Paris, though patently more clever than most of its peers, is not necessarily more wise. I feel that given the chance, more readily than most capitals it would impose its will upon the rest of us. It seems to me somehow too harmonious for our times, without its natural element of chaos. I miss the unpremeditated clash of styles and patterns, and of all the street musicians who entertained me during my visit, the ones that beguiled me most were an un-kempt English rock group—somehow they seemed more spontaneously outrageous than the rest.

For it is a humourless city at heart, I cannot help feeling; grand, of course, beautiful, brilliant, inexhaustible, indestructible, in many ways incomparable, but short on natural fun or fantasy. Perhaps that's why, when I drive by on the Périphérique, superstition keeps me out.

Jan Morris has been wandering the world and writing about her experiences for more than 40 years. She is the author of numerous books and her essays about travel are among the classics of the genre. She lives in Wales.

★

The Parisians have been very good at creating visual delights. They have managed it partly by cunningly enhancing what was there already—the river especially—but partly by the most brilliant and inventive creation. One of their fertile techniques has been to use or if necessary invent forms that are not merely striking in themselves but have a double role: for example, things that can be seen *through*—the Arc de Triomphe or the Carrousel or the Porte Saint-Denis or the transparent Pei Pyramid—or seen *around*—the Vendôme column, the Concorde obelisk—or seen *between*—the long lines of clipped trees in the Palais Royal, the Jardin des Plantes and the Luxembourg Gardens—or seen *underneath*—the pretty bridges, the great arch of the Eiffel Tower or the new Défense arch. I have seen no other city where such devices have been so widely and so skillfully deployed. It is this combination of imagination and ruthlessness that gives Paris its unique character.

—David Gentleman, *David Gentleman's Paris*

PART TWO

SOME THINGS TO DO

The Empire of Death

Do you know what's in store for you?

Un monstre sans raison aussi bien que sans yeux est la Divinité que l'on adore dans ces lieux on l'appelle la mort et son cruel empire s'étend également sur tout ce qui respire.

(A monster without reason and without eyes is the God one worships in those places where one recognizes death and his cruel empire extends equally over all who breathe.)

OSSUARY, FROM THE LATIN FOR BONES, MEANS A CONTAINER OR vault for the remains of the dead. A friend who'd lived in Paris had placed the Municipal Ossuary, the Paris Catacombs, on our must-see list. I wasn't entirely convinced. As much as I loved the busy, funereal jumble of Père-Lachaise Cemetery, the Paris Catacombs would be an encounter with death of a more embodied nature. I'd never seen a defleshed human skull before, never confronted the harsh reality of our interior structures. Death had come and gone from Père-Lachaise; in the catacombs, death lingered. Despite my curiosity, I was in no hurry to look the grave in the eye—such eyes as it had.

However, Paris during the Gulf War was bitter cold and increasingly menacing. While my husband and I had heard from

103

friends about the anti-American protests in Barcelona, the propriety of the *International Herald Tribune* had shielded us from the war's reality. Several days into our trip, we stepped out of the medieval splendor of the Musée de Cluny to find police cars and paddy wagons lining Boulevard Saint Michel. The sidewalks stretched away, ominously vacant. Turning a corner to escape, I stopped short in front of the dripping muzzle of a water cannon. The police had tested it in anticipation of the protest march.

Mason and I decided to avoid the Left Bank for a while. Our solution was to go underground.

> *Heureux celui qui a toujours devant les yeux l'heure de sa mort et qui se dispose tous les jours à mourir.*
>
> (Happy are they who have always before their eyes the hour of death and who prepare all their days to die.)

For centuries, Christian philosophy taught that the soul was fundamental and the body mere dross, to be discarded. Simultaneously, the Church preached of the bodily resurrection. When the trumpet sounded on the final day, the dead would rise out of their graves to be judged. Bodiless spirits could not rise. Therefore, bodies could not be cremated or otherwise destroyed. They had to be buried, preferably in hallowed ground. Of course, such an interment required a donation to the church. Aristocrats and wealthy merchants might purchase coveted space inside the sanctuaries, but everyone else squeezed into the churchyards. The clergy were not eager to part with a guaranteed source of income by condoning burial in just any old place.

Unfortunately, the dead piled up faster than churches could be built.

The Cimetière des Innocents (near Les Halles) served as Paris's chief graveyard since the Middle Ages. For over 500 years, corpses were laid cheek by jowl in 30-foot pits, then blanketed thinly with earth. Cadavers were stacked layer upon layer, until they filled the graves. An estimated 2,000 bodies were interred there each year. Five hundred times 2,000...my mind boggled.

The Cemetery of the Holy Innocents, glutted with corpses, inspired a theme in medieval art that found its highest expression in the woodcuts of Hans Holbein the Younger. The first known *Danse Macabre* was painted as a mural on the surrounding walls in 1424. The *Danse Macabre*, or Dance of Death, depicted the equality of all humanity before Death. Rank, wealth, and privilege offered no protection. Death, personified as a gaunt, anonymous corpse, always led his chosen victim away. In one of the earliest Parisian illustrated books, woodcuts thought to have been based on the Holy Innocents' murals show Death emasculated and naked, his abdomen yawning open upon shadows.

> *Insensé que vous êtes, vous promettez-vous de vivre longtemps, vous qui ne pouvez compter sur un seul jour.*
>
> (Fool that you are, you promise yourself to live a long time, you who are unable to count on a single day.)

*L*et the dead join the dance! Begin dancing when midnight sounds and the entire nave rocks with the strains of its mournful harmony. Black clouds fill the sky, owls fly above the ruins, the universe becomes filled with ghosts and demons, and funereal voices, moans, and sighs are heard. Then the tombs open a crack, skeletons with earth still clinging to their bones cast off their shrouds. They stand up, walk, and dance. Let the dead begin dancing! Leave your tombs, now that the hour has struck. Listen to the droning ring of the bells as they murmur, "Don't stop!" Dance, now that you're dead, now that life and misfortune have left your flesh! Have at it! There will be no tomorrow to your celebrations, for they will be as eternal as death, so dance! Rejoice in your oblivion. You'll have no more cares or labors, since you no longer exist. No more misery for you in your nonbeing. Ah, my dead ones, dance!

—Gustave Flaubert, *Early Writings,* translated by Robert Griffin

The origins of the word *catacomb* are uncertain. Linguists suggest it comes from the Greek *kata kumbas*, which means near the low place. It's unclear why this Greek phrase became attached to a district in Rome where, in the 2nd century A.D., Christians buried their dead. Now the word is applied to any underground burial place.

The catacombs of Paris began as a network of quarries beneath the city. They provided stone to rebuild Paris according to Baron Haussmann's plan. After they'd been mined, the tunnels stood empty and unused.

Concurrent with the reconstruction of Paris in the 1780s, a movement gained momentum to clean out the old churchyards. The Revolution had loosened the grip of the Catholic Church in France. With Reason as the new philosophy, people questioned the Church's system of mass graves.

Accounts of the period speak of pestilential hellholes, jammed with liquefying cadavers. One report claimed that the notorious Cimetière des Innocents broke through an adjoining wall to spill corpses into an apartment building. Fearing epidemics, the city fathers voted to excavate the Parisian graveyards.

Beginning at dusk, charnel pits around Paris were emptied out by bonfire light. It was impossible even to consider individualizing the remains. The bones, loaded respectfully onto carts, were followed to the underground quarry by priests chanting the funeral service.

In 1786, once the ossuary was full, the Archbishop of Paris consecrated the residues of approximately five million people. Among the now-anonymous dead were Lavoisier, the father of modern chemistry; Madame de Pompadour, Louis XV's girlfriend; alchemist, spy, and reputed immortal Saint Germain; the philosopher of the Enlightenment, Montessqieu; Mirabeau, who advocated constitutional monarchy and whose corpse was ejected from the Panthéon; Danton, who participated in storming the Bastille and was guillotined during the Reign of Terror; Robespierre, who engineered the Reign of Terror and became its prey; and numberless victims of the guillotine.

In 1874, the Municipal Ossuary opened to viewers, including Bismarck and Napoleon III.

Venez, gens du monde, venez dans ces demeures silencieuses, et votre

*âme alors tranquille sera frappée de la voix qui s'élève de leur in-
térieur: "C'est ici le plus grand des maîtres, le Tombeau."*

(Come, people of the world, come into the silent resting
places and your tranquil soul will be struck by the voice that
rises inside them: "This here is the greatest of masters, the
tomb.")

"Come, people of the world!" I imagined a barker calling. "Step
right up. Here is the Greatest of Masters!" Who wouldn't be
tempted to pay the admission and take a look? The more I considered the exploration before me, the more my curiosity increased. What could possibly be down there?

A spiral staircase of stone wound down and down and down
until it reached a path paved with dressed stone and edged with
pebbles. The stone was a buttery yellow, warmed by bare light
bulbs on the arcing ceiling. I couldn't touch the sides of the tunnel when I stretched out my hands, but I didn't reach up to measure the short distance overhead. A sign said we were twenty meters below the streets of Paris, deeper than the Métro. Thank
goodness Paris isn't prone to earthquakes.

My guidebook recommended keeping close to a tour group, as
the tunnels stretch for miles. It related a cautionary tale about a
Parisian who went downstairs to check his wine cellar and took a
wrong turn. Seven years later, he was discovered, mummified.

Permanent Parisians, a guide to the dead in Paris, said there were
no catacomb tours and you were on your own. It suggested you
take a flashlight. I wondered if a ball of string was in order, too.

As we discussed the discrepancy, my husband turned a corner to
find a large tour group blocking the tunnel ahead of us. The guide
talked interminably in French about the composition of the rock,
the excavation of the tunnels, the quarriers themselves. While the
quarry is historically significant, in terms of the architecture of
modern Paris, that wasn't nearly so interesting as death.

A child of eight, bored by the lecture, started crawling up the
side of the cavern where the group clustered. The soft rock crum-
bled and shifted under his feet. My sleeping claustrophobia in-

stantly burned white hot. If he caused a cave-in, I thought, I'd drag my broken body through the rubble and…The boy's father persuaded him to stop fooling around, averting multiple catastrophes.

Some Germans pushed forward through the crowd. The guide blathered on without stopping them, so Mason and I followed.

We found a pair of niches carved with miniature cityscapes. *Permanent Parisians* said that the stonemason who sculpted them had been a prisoner in the city they represented. After he finished the carving, he tried to cut steps down from the street so the public could view his masterpiece. The stairway excavation caused a cave-in. The story, surely romanticized, said that he died with his chisel in hand.

Next we came upon steps down to a well of perfectly clear water. Though the stone stairs looked sturdy enough, an iron gate blocked them off. A plaque said that the quarrymen used to drink the water. They called the well Samaritaine, after the woman Jesus met at the well. I wondered if this well had any connection to the department store. We could only look down into the shimmering water from what seemed like a balcony.

Eventually we reached a doorway, the first since we'd come underground. Wooden obelisks, painted white and black, flanked yawning darkness. Above the lintel, a sign warned, "*Arrêtez. C'est ici l'empire de la mort.*" Stop. Beyond this is Death's Kingdom.

The warning had frightened away the Nazis, who never discovered the French Resistance, hiding in the catacombs after August 1944. Right beneath the Parisian streets, the Resistance had concealed a radio capable of reaching London. They worked in the tunnels until the liberators came. How terrifying could the Kingdom of Death be?

We paused outside the doorway, while I gathered my courage. Taking my husband's hand, I stepped through the portal, into the empire of Death.

Pensez le matin que vous n'irez peut-être pas jusqu'au au soir et au soir que vous n'irez peut-être pas jusqu'au au matin.

(Think in the morning that perhaps you won't last until

evening, and in the evening that you won't last until
morning.)

Inside, the brown knobs of fibulas and femurs stacked higher
than our heads. Skulls formed contrasting lines among the leg
bones, a decorative motif. The round domed craniums were naked
and sad. Empty eye sockets gazed patiently at us.

Bone upon bone upon bone. The sheer number of these
anonymous *memento mori* was staggering. I had trouble grasping
the concept of 5 million skulls, 10 million shin bones, 60 million
ribs.... If a human body has 206 bones, there must be over a bil-
lion bones stacked in the catacomb tunnels, assuming, that is, that
the gravediggers found everything. I imagined some *bourgeoise* matron trying to gather herself together after the Trump of Doom
sounded. The hipbone's connected to the backbone.... Which one
of these backbones is mine?

Now that I thought of it, I wondered where the remainders of
the skeletons lay. I expected to stroll past towers of hipbones and
stacks of shoulder blades. Instead, we saw nothing but skulls and
long bones. Everything else must have been tucked away. I stopped
in the midst of a passage so narrow my elbows could have touched
bones on either side. The caverns must have been enormous before these mortal remains filled them.

Mason and I photographed everything that struck a chord in us:
the walls and pillars and columns of bones, the piles that had collapsed and spilled their sad relics onto the stone floor, the arrangements of skulls and crossbones. I worried that the gloom might be
too much for my little camera, even with the flash. Shadows lurked
beyond the occasional round fluorescent light fixtures.

Beautiful inscriptions graced plaques set amongst the remains.
Here and there a yellow spotlight cast a narrow beam, but overall I
was glad I'd brought that flashlight. Other visitors burned their fingers while lighting matches to read the inspirational words. One
plaque spoke of shadows among shadows, another about the empty
eyes of skulls and the full eyes of God. All men fall, several said. If you
have seen a man breathe his last, you know what is in store for you.

Why, I wondered, is Death female in French?

Où est-elle, la Mort? Toujours futur ou passé. A peine est-elle présente, que déjà elle n'est plus.

(Where is Death? Always in the future or the past. As soon as it is present, it is already gone.)

After 200 years and at least two burials, some of the bones were beginning to decompose. White down grew on one wall of shinbones. Elsewhere, two skulls had turned quite green. Some craniums sported round holes. I imagined someone grasping a skull, only to have it crunch beneath his fingertips like eggshell.

I discovered that I'm funny about human bones. I find something especially creepy about the geometry of a skull, inside which someone once lived and loved and dreamed. A skull, more than any other relic, seems too personal to be examined by a stranger. All those skulls, all those empty eyes, unnerved me the most.

Throughout the catacombs, everything was well within reach. Although a sign had cautioned us not to touch, nothing prevented us. We could have easily taken a souvenir. As an intellectual exercise, we speculated on how one might sneak human remains through customs.

In reality, I had no desire to touch the bones or to allow them to touch me. Little matter that they could not possibly be

I felt uncomfortable among all these human remains and tried not to think at all, but simply to follow the crowd as it moved on. My companion had not much to say; nor had I. Suddenly a burst of laughter broke from a small group of youngsters who were holding their burning candles beneath some of the skulls as if to try whether they would burn. I was at once jolted into remembering my nationality. I have been living away from China for many years and have acquired many Western habits, but my early up-bringing in ancestor worship had not entirely left me. Worshipping one's ancestors is not a bad practice; there is nothing silly in according one's forbears due respect. To hold a lighted candle under skulls is a bad joke. Who knew whether those very skulls did not belong to the youngsters' own long-deceased ancestors?

—Chiang Yee,
The Silent Traveller in Paris

contagious after so many years postmortem. I did not want to feel the brittle evidence of death beneath my fingers. If looking into the void meant the void looked back, I expected that touching Death meant that Death returned the gesture. You see where fondling Yorick's skull got Hamlet. I kept my hands jammed resolutely into my pockets.

> *Si vous avez vu quelquefois mourir un homme, considérez toujours que le même sort vous attend.*

> (If you have ever seen a man die, consider always that the same fate awaits you.)

One of the guidebooks had warned us to take sweaters but, compared to the January winds outside, the tunnels were comfortably warm. It might have been cozy, if it hadn't been so damp.

Tiny nubbins, future stalactites, hung from the ceiling. Water dripped incessantly, puddling on the floor. I didn't want any of that water falling into my face. The sound, when the two of us stood alone amidst the dead, was like slowly falling tears. The atmosphere definitely affected me.

The catacombs provided a perfect cathedral in which to meditate on the folly of human aspirations, to think about the war in the Persian Gulf. Death was so universal, so inescapable, why seek to hasten it? There were so many things I had yet to do before I could surrender to Death. Did those American boys in the foreign sand feel the same? Did the Iraqi boys? Wars should always be considered among *memento mori* like these. Perhaps life would seem more precious to the politicians who wage them.

We rounded a bend in the tunnels in time to see a man in another group stumble. His friends snatched him back before he could topple into the stacked bones. What a nightmare that would be: falling into the arms of Death, hearing them snap beneath you. Once you stopped falling, the other bones would tumble down over your face. I shivered with empathy at his near escape.

Mason was glad when we encountered the family with the small boy again. Imagine, he said to me, the dreams you would have if your parents had brought you here as a child. Instead I imagined the dreams I would have that night. This might be a good night to drink red wine before bed.

The ossuary seemed to go on and on. I wondered if we'd gotten lost, since we separated from the tour, but locked gates clearly delimited the direction we could go. When at last we climbed the tall steps of the spiral staircase to the exit, we found ourselves on an unfamiliar street. The pedometer said we had gone only a mile underground.

White powder edged our shoes, dried residue of the moisture on the path. The chilly January wind felt fresh on my face and in my lungs. I thanked goodness to find myself alive and in Paris.

I linked arms with Mason. If we weren't going to last until evening, I said, we'd better locate a *pâtisserie*. I had a burning desire for an apple tart.

On Loren Rhoads's first visit to the Catacombs she was overwhelmed by the emotional confrontation with "Death." She is not sure she could have survived it if her husband had not been there to hold her hand.

★

A brisk fifteen-minute walk away the word *museum* takes on new meaning at the Museum of the Sewers. Entered through what looks like a big manhole on the sidewalk at the southern end of the Pont de l'Alma, it is both museum and sewers, that is, a section of the sewers—*les égouts* in French—that has been adapted to give tourists an idea of what the entire 1,320-mile network looks—and smells—like. (Actually, it doesn't smell too bad—a sort of musty damp smell most of the time.) It has a little museum, with paintings, drawings, and photographs accompanied by texts—in French, English, German, and Spanish—explaining how the sewers were built and work.

For centuries the city's sewage ended up in the Seine, which also provided some of its drinking water. Not a good idea, concluded Napoleon, who ordered construction of the first underground sewage canals to take the waste away from the river. By 1850 there were already 100 miles of canals, but the real turning point came in the second half of the 19th century, when Baron Haussmann tore down central Paris to make way for the broad avenues and fine buildings to be seen today. He assigned an engineer, Eugene Belgrand, the job of building a proper sewer network beneath the newly transformed city. His legacy is one of the most extensive urban sewer systems in the world. Much of what exists today was his work....

The underground network, though, serves other purposes. In *Les Misérables*, the Victor Hugo novel that became a hit musical, Jean Valjean saves his wounded enemy, Marius, by carrying him to safety through the sewers. During World War II, when Paris was occupied by Nazi Germany, the French Resistance would hide and plot there. Today the city's water supply, telephone and electricity lines, and pipes carrying compressed air to hospitals run through the network of underground canals. Even the turn-of-the-century system of delivering express letters through pneumatic tubes survives. It now connects only Government ministries and Parliament, but it explains the occasional rattling sound that can be heard at the Museum of the Sewers.

—Alan Riding, "The Sights Beneath the Sidewalks,"
The New York Times

MICHELE ANNA JORDAN

Paris Rapture

Testing one's mettle in the City of Light.

I ARRIVED AT THE GARE DE LYON ON THE NIGHT TRAIN FROM Milan at 7:22 a.m. Having treated myself to a first-class sleeper (the best travel money I have ever spent), I was in pretty good shape: well-rested, not wrinkled, and most importantly, not carsick. A porter helped me get my luggage to a locker and by 9:30, I had a hotel room nearby and was ready for my single day in the City of Light when it began to rain. After a long hot bath, it still was pouring but I was not to be daunted. I opened my red umbrella and hit the street, determined for adventure. I was one of the only people in sight but I hurried on, ignoring the water seeping into my red shoes and splashing against my legs.

I walked to the nearby Bastille in search of an interesting restaurant. I was longing for oysters, but more than that I wanted authenticity, a place without tourists where the waiter would not condescendingly address me in English as I struggled to speak my best French. Alas, I had left behind my *Food Lover's Guide to Paris* and would have to rely solely on my good instincts, which were a little frayed after nearly three weeks on the road.

I walked for what seemed like hours, and after lingering in a lavish outdoor market a stone's throw from the Seine, intuition

114

served me well. I settled into a comfortable table in a small wine bar that had simply looked right. Soon, I was sipping champagne and nibbling walnuts while I slowly considered each menu item. If I had but one meal in Paris, I told myself, it would be grand. Three hours later the singularly most indulgent, decadent solo activity I have pursued concluded with a strong cup of *café crème*. Every minute had been divine.

I followed my flute of champagne with the richest, densest slab of *foie gras* I have ever tasted, served with sweet butter and a basket of crispy toast and accompanied voluptuously by a 1988 Roumaud Sauternes, a truly rapturous combination. I ate slowly, relishing each bite and reading from a favorite book, Greil Marcus's *In the Fascist Bathroom* (known in its American edition as *Ranters and Crowd Pleasers*). Throughout my travels this tome on punk music is the one book that held up to all of my culinary indulgences. Everything else paled in comparison to what I was eating and drinking but

H ow could such a simple blend of sugar, butter, eggs, flour, and a touch of lemon unleash the flood of memories that filled those volumes of prose we know as Remembrance of Things Past? *For Proust, the memories began one wintry day when his mother sent out for "one of those squat, plump little cakes called* petites madeleines *which look as though they have been moulded in the fluted valve of a scallop shell." With his* madeleines *Proust drank an infusion of* tilleul, *a tea prepared from the dried blossoms of the linden tree.*

Proust continued: "I raised to my lips a spoonful of the tea in which I had soaked a morsel of the cake. No sooner had the warm liquid mixed with the crumbs touched my palate than a shudder ran through me and I stopped, intent upon the extraordinary thing that had happened to me. An exquisite pleasure had invaded my senses."

—Patricia Wells, *The Food Lover's Guide to France*

Marcus's tight, intense essays formed the perfect literary counterpart to my gastronomic adventures, perhaps because he, too, eats with relish and enthusiasm. It helped that I knew that the final piece, a bizarre story called "I Am a Cliché," had been at least partially inspired by a solo meal he'd had in Paris a few years earlier.

My *foie gras* was followed by an enormous portion of *steak tartare*, the most ethereal version I've encountered, if indeed you can apply the term ethereal to a mound of chopped raw beef and in my lexicon you can. An accompanying side dish of *pommes à l'huile* and tiny leaves of *mâche* in a delicate vinaigrette added both virtue and contrast, while a glass of 1990 Pierredon—a very pleasant Bordeaux—fit like the proverbial glove.

Nearly all French eateries, even the lowliest cafés and bars, offer a cheese course and here there was an interesting selection rarely if ever seen in America. A thick slice of Cantal, a tangy hard cheese from Auvergne garnished with white raisins soaked in Sauternes and a final glass of Bordeaux (St. Estephe Beau Site) alongside, brought the extravaganza to a delightful close.

I ate and read with languorous pleasure, recalling musical moments that resonated with Marcus's. Seconds after I came across a reference to "Bette Davis Eyes" by Kim Carnes, the song began to play on the wine bar's radio. The rain stopped, a bit of sun broke through the grey day and I wished the moment could last forever, so complete did life seem there in that tiny dark café.

Following whatever you want to call what I had just done—my indulgence, my feast, my folly—I walked for several hours, not with any particular purpose but simply to absorb through my pores as much of Paris as I could. A well-known destination—the Louvre, say, or the glittering activity of the Champs-Elysées— seemed pointless with such limited time, particularly since my meal had lasted until late in the afternoon. I also knew that I had a hidden agenda—secretly, I was hoping that if I walked enough I might be hungry again before day's end.

After relaxing briefly in my hotel room, I set out again, this time crossing the Seine and thinking I might walk to Notre Dame. But adventures unfolded quickly and among other things, I found myself assisting an old woman across the street. She had been leaning against the traffic signal in the center of the road, unable to go on. An hour later, I had gotten her to the train station and comfortably situated in a wheelchair, with a porter to escort her onto the train to Lourdes and its healing waters, where she would seek relief from the various afflictions of age. She was from Florida and had made many trips to Europe by herself. As I walked back to the street, I wondered how she made it on her own, if someone like me came to her rescue in other places.

It was now close to 11:00 p.m., and everything was drawing to a close, my day in Paris, my extended European adventures, my energy, and my appetite. I walked purposefully towards my hotel, the sensible thing to do. But across from the Gare de Lyon, seafood restaurants still bustled with the night's lingering customers. Oysters of every sort and size beckoned from mounds of ice. What the hell, I said, and walked in.

Ten minutes later, I was seated at a window table before a towering platter of ice and oysters, a half bottle of a crisp, flinty Sancerre chilling next to me. I ate the oysters ever so slowly and after the first two, closed my book and looked out onto the Parisian streets. The contrast to my earlier meal was significant. Then everything had been so dark and rich, so nearly sexual in its voluptuousness, that each bite filled me with guilty pleasure. Now, it was all lean and bright and spare and I felt myself growing lighter as I lingered over each oyster. I am sure I glowed with contentment.

The streets were crowded and as I watched the couples in love, the old men, the women walking small dogs, a woman caught my eye. She and a friend stopped and surveyed the scene: me in front of my icy tray of oyster shells, with rosy cheeks and a glass of wine in hand. They gave me an enthusiastic nod, a smile, a thumbs-up salute, and as they walked away I felt as if my whole day had just been blessed.

Michele Anna Jordan is the author of nine books, including Polenta, The Good Cook's *series* (Oil & Vinegar; Mustard; Tomatoes; *and* Days: A Food Lover's Journal), *and* California Home Cooking. *She writes for numerous publications including* au Juice *and* San Francisco Focus Magazine *and is host of "Mouthful with Michele Anna Jordan" on Sonoma County's NPR affiliate. Jordan makers her home in both San Francisco and Sebastopol, California.*

✳

Paris can be many things for lovers, but for me, it will always be the place where my kid sister fell head-over-heels—for chocolate.

Emily was sweet 17 and I, her guide, was a worldly 24 when we arrived that summer in Paris. The first morning in our little hotel near the Luxembourg Gardens, we woke to a rap-rap-rapping and a voice singsonging "*Bonjour.*" Emily opened the door and brought in the breakfast tray that I had ordered the night before: a baguette with fruity jam, strong milky café au lait for me, and for Emily, the drink that would change her life. When she lifted the white china bowl to her lips and took her first sip of that steamy, creamy *chocolat chaud*, she knew that she had found true love.

Emily had tasted hot chocolate before, of course. Even at her tender age, she was well on her way to becoming a confirmed chocoholic. But somehow, in Paris, the chocolate was richer, unexpectedly different, like the gangly boy next door you've known all your life, who suddenly catches your eye and he's become a strikingly handsome man.

Every night, my sister curled up in her bed and talked about her new *amour*, its smells, its look, its feel in her mouth, shivering with anticipation about her next encounter. She bounded out of bed when she heard the morning tap on our door, scooping her bowl off the tray with both hands. She held it up to her nose to let the warm, moist sweetness circle her face. "Ah," she sighed. "Chocolate...."

I've been back to Paris several times now. I've walked with my husband along the Seine. We've sipped red wine by night and savored buttery croissants as the morning sun peeked across our bed. Emily is grown-up now, too, a sophisticated New Yorker with a husband of her own. But I know she still remembers that tender early love. And as the matchmaker who paired her with that special first *amour*, I will always remember Paris as the City of Chocolate.

—Carolyn B. Heller, "The City of Chocolate"

Illumined in Sainte-Chapelle

*Louis IX left Notre Dame to the ordinary folk and heard Mass
himself across the square, in his exquisite private chapel.*

AFTER VISITING NOTRE DAME, I HEADED ACROSS THE STREET,
nose in a map, driven by a faint memory of a passing mention of
a small church "with the best stained glass outside of Chartres."

Sainte-Chapelle. That must be it, I thought. But where was it?
On the map it looked like it was actually in the courtyard of the
police headquarters building, the Palais de Justice. And indeed it
was. As we approached, it seemed we had to go through metal de-
tectors to get anywhere near.

With my wife and daughters in tow, I walked to the back of a
courtyard, rounded the bend and entered a small, low-ceilinged
Romanesque chapel. It was quite pretty, but it hardly justified the
high praise I'd heard.

Then I noticed that people armed with guidebooks were passing by with hardly a glance at the frescoes and stained glass I was
trying to admire. Instead, they were streaming right to a doorway
in the back wall of the chapel. There must be more through there,
I said to myself.

We squeezed through the narrow doorway and up a circular
stone staircase…into Glory.

With the perfect proportions of a Gothic cathedral, but only the

119

size of a vest pocket, Sainte-Chapelle seems somehow to bring into vibrant coexistence the magnificence of those cathedrals and the intimacy of a space meant for more ordinary living.

And the stained glass! Narrow ribs of soaring stone separate band after band of illumination—what seems like more glass than all of Notre Dame in a space one-tenth the size. Colors so exquisite that they seem more real than those we ordinarily know. Shafts of brilliance from every side, as if we'd found our way to the heart of a jewel, to the heart of a dragon's hoard of jewels.

I lay on the floor for a few precious moments, soaking it all in without having to divert even the attention it requires to stand, until the embarrassment of my daughters and the disapproval of the guard reeled me back, a fish torn from what ought to be my natural element, afloat in those seas of light.

Tim O'Reilly is the author of Frank Herbert, *a biography of the late science fiction writer, and the author and editor of many a technical tome. His company, O'Reilly and Associates, publishes computer books and software, the* Whole Internet Catalog *and other Internet and World Wide Web publications.*

★

Sainte-Chapelle: magical, a labour of love. As I wait for you in the chapel I marvel at how time has left this magical space untouched. The late light streams bright colors through warm air—casting wine reds and luminous yellows on mosaics of royal blue and gold, musical patterns placed with loving, whimsical hands. As we join hands in the nave I'm amazed by the depth of light in your eyes, your face lyrical and surrounded by stained glass of incredible height and detail. Paris: Could we stay here forever? I love you.

—Gina Granados, "Dear Patrick"

HERBERT GOLD

On Ile St-Louis

A Cleveland native discovers a village universe.

AN ISLAND PRIME, AN ISLAND AT THE SECRET HEART OF PARIS, floating in time and space across a footbridge on the shady side of the Cathedral of Notre Dame de Paris, the Ile St-Louis may also be the most ambiguous orphan island there is—city and not a city, village and metropolis, provincial and centrally urban, serene and hyped by hundreds of years of noisy lovers of solitude.

Unique it is, possessed of itself, even self-congratulatory, yet available to all who choose to stroll from the population sink of contemporary Paris to a place that has no Métro stop or depressed highway. One could live there forever and do it in a short span of time, and I did.

Just after World War II, I came to study philosophy amid the existentialists of St-Germain-des-Prés. The first winter was bitter cold, with food rationing and no heat, and we philosophers—that is, admirers of Juliette Greco with her long nose, hoarse voice, black jeans and sweaters—had to find cafés to do our deep think-ing in.

In existential pursuit of the largest café au lait and most tooth-rotting but warming chocolate, I bought a bicycle to widen my field of operations, showing a certain Cleveland shrewdness by paying $8 for the rustiest, most battered bicycle I could find so that I could leave it unlocked.

Behind Notre-Dame, across the narrow footbridge of the Pont St-Louis, on the tranquil Ile St-Louis, which did little business and did it negligently, I leaned my bike against a café that served large coffees, rich chocolate and few customers. I remember it as Aux Alsaciennes, because it served Alsatian sausage, corned beef and cabbage, *choucroute garnie* at lunchtime; but for many years, now that the place had been discovered, it has been called the Brasserie de St-Louis-en-l'Ile.

Somehow, here I couldn't think about Bergson and Diderot and the hyphen between them, a little-known idea-smith named Maine de Biran, my thesis. Maybe it was the action of pumping a rusty bicycle; maybe it was the red-faced waiters, the black-dressed postwar girls with bruised eyes; but on the Ile St-Louis I graciously allowed the history of philosophy to continue on its way without me.

My bike had no carrier for books; instead, I could stick a notebook under the seat. While warming myself at Aux Alsaciennes, I began to write a novel.

Nearly two years later, when the stationery store lady wrapped the package for mailing to Viking Press, she figured out what it was and gave it a sharp slap, crying out, "*Merde!*" I was startled because I thought I knew what that word meant and took it as a judgment of my coffee-and-*choucroute*-fueled eighteen-month creative frenzy, but she explained that it meant good luck!

(The book, *Birth of a Hero*, about a Resistance hero who happened to be stuck all his life in Cleveland, was published. I went home to Cleveland to buy the three-cent stamp with my picture on it but they were still using George Washington. I like that first novel now mostly because it instructed me that I had the right to do it.)

At some point in the creative process, I left a GI overcoat—the vestmental equivalent of my bicycle—on a rack at the *brasserie*. The waiters kept asking when I would take it again, but spring came, the birds sang on the Ile St-Louis and other birds allowed me to buy them hot chocolate; I was too overwrought.

Later, I decided to see how long the coat would live on the coat rack. As the years went by, I committed more novels, visited Paris as a tourist, and came to the Ile St-Louis to check on my coat. It was still there. "Soon," I promised the waiters.

One May in the early '60s, I noticed that the narrow, swaying footbridge across which I used to wheel my rustmobile had been replaced by a wider, stabler cement product, although it was still blocked to automobiles. And my coat was gone from the café, which had changed its name to the Brasserie de St-Louis-en-l'Ile. And that *tout Paris* had discovered the happy place that in my secret mustard-loving heart will always be Aux Alsaciennes.

Anciently, the Ile St-Louis was two islands, Ile Notre-Dame and *Ile-aux-Vaches* (Cow Island). You can buy old maps that show the walls of medieval Paris and this tiny pasture in the Seine, from which cows and milk were brought by dinghy into the city. In the 17th century the places were joined, and in a burst of elegant speculation, bankruptcies and re-speculation, a dense web of *hôtels* (fine mansions) were spun.

The Hôtel Lambert and the Hôtel de Lauzun are two noble examples, but the entire island,

I often write at the Café Beaubourg, which strikes the English, who love crowded, smoky pubs, as disagreeably austere and new, but which I find airy and calm although there's always something to see. It was built at the end of the 1980s, right across from the Centre Georges Pompidou and the giant digital clock that counts down the seconds that remain until the end of the century. At the corner is the always busy fountain designed by Niki de Saint-Phalle and her husband, Jean Tinguely, with a pair of red lips, water squirting from the tits of one of Niki's famous fat ladies, or nans, a top hat that spins, a treble clef in black metal, and so on, all bobbling and twirling—and soaking passersby on windy days. Fred [the author's dog] likes to walk by here because I encourage him to defecate on the grill above the underground center for experimental music, directed by Pierre Boulez, who once refused to give me an interview.

—Edmund White, *Our Paris: Sketches from Memory*

its narrow pre-Detroit and even pre-Citroën streets, its encircling
quays for strolling and breeze-taking by the Seine, has a comfort-
ingly unified classical pattern.

The decoration and architecture date from a single period of
French elegance and are protected by fanatic preservationists,
among whom was former president Georges Pompidou, who
helped stuff other districts of Paris with freeways and skyscrapers.
(Pompidou lived on the Ile St-Louis.)

There is an ice cream shop, Berthillon, with perhaps the best
and certainly the most chic sherbets in France. Usually the lines
stretch out onto the street—people waiting for their *glace café, sor-
bet, crème*—as others in other places wait in line to pay taxes or to
see if their portrait is on the three-cent stamp.

There is but one church on the island, St-Louis-en-l'Ile—
lovely, tranquil, softly flowing, with devout deacons scrubbing the
stone with straw brooms from a stock that seems to have been purchased by some 17th-century financial genius of a priest who
feared inflation in the straw-broom market.

Contemporary Paris discovered it could find quadruple use for
the Ile St-Louis: as an elegant residential quarter of the 4th
arrondissement; as a strolling museum neighborhood, a sort of
Tricolorland with no parking meters, no movie house or cemetery
(if people die, they have to be taken to the Continent); as a quiet
corner for small restaurants, antiquaries, bars, book shops, hotels,
Mme. Blanvillain's 160-year-old olive shop (she was not the
founder), and a pheasant-plucker named Turpin in case you need
your pheasant plucked; and the fourth use is optional.

On my most recent visit, the spirit of the place was expressed
by the aforementioned Berthillon, the studio for ice cream mas-
terpieces with the 17th century aspect. It was early July. A cheer-
ful sign said: "Open Wednesday, 14 September." Where else would
an ice cream shop close for the hot months?

I was relieved by this assurance of little change in the weekend-
maddened, vacation-crazed spirit of the French *commerçant.* No
matter how greedy he might seem to mere mortals, plucking

money from the air and sewing it into his mattress, the flight to seaside or country cottage remains sacred.

Throwing duffel on bed, not even glancing at the exchange rate, I seized a notebook in jet-lagged claws and made a quick tour of the few streets and circumnavigating quays of the island, trying to find what had changed, what had remained the same, and what might persuade my body that it was time to sleep. The fact that I had cleverly scheduled my visit to come near the July 14 celebration, when France dances and drinks and makes new friends in the street till dawn—all because their ancestors tore down the Bastille—did not induce thoughts of prudent shut-eye.

(In my student days, when an American friend studying in Belgium bicycled into Paris for the first time, he happened to arrive on Bastille Day and found colorful lights strung from everywhere, accordions, embraces, a fierce festival glitter in every eye. He fell upon my little room crying, "Oh, I always knew Paris would be like this!")

A street sweeper with the timid face of a peasant come to the metropolis was scrubbing down the stones in front of the St-Louis-en-l'Ile. No change here.

Libella, the Polish bookstore on the rue St-Louis-en-l'Ile, reminded me that Paris has always been everyone's other home. The wall above Libella bears a stone plaque telling us that in 1799 the engineer Philippe Lebon discovered, in this building, the principle of lighting and heating with gas—the word "principle" and past experience suggest that the French did not actually get around to doing it for a while.

The island is crowded with such notices—tributes to poets, advisers to kings, soldier heroes, men of God, and even a film critic immortalized on a plaque affixed to the place where he analyzed Jerry Lewis as *auteur.*

There is also a plaque on the wall of the Ferdinand Halphep Foundation in the rue des Deux-Ponts:

> To the Memory
> Of the 112 Inhabitants

Of This Building
including 40 Children
Deported and Killed
In the Concentration Camps in 1942.

No island is entire of itself, exempt from history. Across the street, in the ice cream shops, bistros, the Bateau Bar—50 brands of beer from all nations—gratification proceeds on its necessary course.

One in two French people have never set foot in a café.
—*Paris Notes*

It was time to sit at a café table for the island equivalent of my typical San Francisco after-racquetball vitamin and health hi-pro yogurt shake; in this case, a coffee with "yak"—cognac.

Two helmeted Vespa people came skidding to a stop in front of me. Like space warriors, they were encased in huge plastic headgear. Evidently they knew each other, because they fell to kissing, their helmets thudding together. I peeked at their faces when they came apart. They were both about 60 years old and hadn't seen each other in hours.

A fisherman nearby, when I asked what he caught with all his equipment, assured me that trout hover near the fresh underground springs at the head of the island.

"And what else?"

"A moment of meditation. A view of Notre-Dame. There are gargoyles, sir. At this season, there are roses."

During the morning, a fisherman was catching roses; that night in front of the footbridge leading to Aux Alsaciennes, the Communist Party sponsored a rock celebration of Bastille Day. A girl in a "Wichita University Long Island" t-shirt danced to a French knockoff of "Lady Jane" and other Rolling Stones' hits. Instead of a male partner, she held a contribution box for *Humanité*, the party newspaper.

The little park at the end of the island where the Pont de Sully links the left and right banks of Paris—leading to the workers' quarter of Bastille in one direction, the Quartier Latin in the other—has a grand stone monument to "Barye 1795-1875" at its entrance. The sculptor seems to be telling a busy story, including naked lads, heroes, a foot on a screaming animal, a sword, a staff, a few less boyish youths. Who the heck was Barye 1795-1875?

He may be there to provide a little relaxation from all the really famous people who lived and live on the Ile St-Louis. (He turns out to have been a watercolorist.)

The Square Barye, surrounded by the Seine on three sides, is quiet, peaceful, scholarly, artistic, with occasional summer concerts; kids sleeping on their backpacks, workmen with bottles of *rouge*; Swedish *au pair* girls watching the babies and sunning themselves with that passionate solar intensity only Swedish girls achieve— happy sunbathers when it's hot and moonbathing when it's not; haggard widows in black, wincing with their memories; birds chirping and barbered bushes and peeling-bark trees and neat cinder paths: all honor to Barye 1795-1875!

Three small hotels on the island located on the rue St-Louis-en-l'Ile, a few steps from each other, have been converted from 17th-century houses: the Lutece, the Deux-Iles and the St-Louis.

When I telephoned the Lutece from San Francisco for a reservation, the place was booked, but the good madame leaned out the window and yelled next door to the Deux-Iles to ask if they had a place. Also booked. So was the St-Louis. But on my arrival, I managed to persuade the daughter of the proprietor of the St-Louis to find me a corner room.

On the short walk home—saying "home" comes quickly in this island universe—I noticed that Hippolyte Taine and Georges Sandoul did their work in the same building. Marc Chagall and Charles Baudelaire, Voltaire and Mme. Pompidou, dukes and barons, and *chanteurs de charme*, plus a stray prince or princess, and inventor or hero—who didn't have a connection with the Ile St-Louis?

The Ile St-Louis is like France itself—an ideal of grace and proportion—but it differs from the rest of France in that it lives up to itself. Under constant repair and renovation, it remains intact. It is a small place derived from long experience. It has strength enough, and isolation enough, to endure with a certain smugness the troubles of the city and the world at whose center it rests.

The self-love is mitigated partly by success at guarding itself and partly by the ironic shrugs of its inhabitants, who, despite whatever aristocratic names of glamorous professions, live among broken-veined *clochards* (hobos) with unbagged bottles, tourists with unbagged guidebooks, Bohemians with bagged eyes.

The actual troubles of the world do not miss the Ile St-Louis—one doesn't string hammocks between the plane trees here—but the air seems to contain fewer mites and less nefarious Paris ozone.

The lack of buses, the narrow streets, the breeze down the Seine help. And as to perhaps the most dangerous variety of Paris smog, the Ile St-Louis seems to have discovered the unanswerable French reply to babble, noise, advice, and theory—*silence*.

One can, of course, easily get off this island, either by walking on the water of the Seine or, in a less saintly way, by taking a stroll of about two minutes across the slim bridges to the Left Bank, the Right Bank or the bustling and official neighbor, the Ile de la Cité.

Island fever is not a great danger, despite the insular pleasures of neatness, shape, control. Some people even say they never go to "Paris." (In 1924, there was an attempt to secede from Paris and France, and Ile St-Louis passports were issued.) Monsieur Filleui, the fishmonger, used to advertise:"Deliveries on the Island and on the Continent."

The Ile St-Louis, an elsewhere village universe, happens also to be an island by the merest accident of being surrounded by water. Its bridges reach inward to shadow worlds of history and dream; and outward toward the furor of contemporary Paris.

Shaded and sunny, surrounded by the waters of the Seine like a moat, it remains a kind of castle keep that is powerful enough in its own identity to hold Paris at bridge's length, a breath away. Amazingly, it has occurred to no one powerful enough to do anything about it that this place, too, could be high-rised, filthied, thoroughfared, developed. There is no Métro station. The breezes down the Seine keep busy, sweeping and caressing.

Despite the claims of metropolis on all sides, the Ile St-Louis still expresses the shadow presence of the Ile Notre-Dame and the Ile-aux-Vaches. The ancestor islands make a claim to be remembered because they have been forgotten, and both the aristocratic and the chic who live here, and the *gratteurs de guitare*, who occasionally come to serenade the ghosts of counts and courtesans, know that they tread in a palimpsest of footsteps, including ancient Gauls, Romans and now, chirping and clicking beneath the willows, the occasional polyester-clad, camera-breasted tourist.

A more characteristic sight is that of the professional anguish of a French intellectual walking his dog. The rich tend to live like Bohemians here. (Only the poor, as Anatole France said, are forbidden to beg.)

The Ile St-Louis is one of the places where a postwar generation of Americans in Paris loosened its military discipline—if we happened to have any—studied peace and art and history and depravity (called it freedom, called it fulfilling ourselves), lived in awe before our fantasy of France (still do just a little).

We bought old bicycles and new notebooks. We pretended to be students, artists, philosophers, and lovers, and, out of our pretensions, sometimes learned to be a little of these things.

Remarks are not literature, Gertrude Stein said, and islands are not the world. But some remarks can tell us what literature is about, some islands can tell us what a sweeter, more defined world might be. In Spinoza's view, freedom consists of knowing what the limits are. I came to Paris as a philosophy student but left it as a novelist. On the Ile St-Louis, I am still home free, watching the Seine flow and eddy and flow again.

Herbert Gold also contributed "On the Left Bank" in Part I.

✳

I walked outside, planning to stroll around in search of a last image to match that picture in my mind of a wonderful old man offering me the first waters of the Seine cupped in his hands. The moon mugged me. I mean, this was a moon, so huge and round it looked like an orange. I watched until it was no longer startling, just an unbelievably lovely source of light that splashed gold over the estuary. Its human face seemed animated, but this was no man. I swear to God, Sequana [goddess of the Seine] was talking to me.

—Mort Rosenblum, *Secret Life of the Seine*

★ ★ ★

Les Girls

Ladies and gentlemen…

HER NAKED BODY IS PERFECT: THIS IS WHY YOU ARE HERE. IN semi-darkness she lies just out of reach on a circular platform tilted toward you, a girl with long red hair and a hard, impudent body. She wears only a brief patch at her crotch; leather thongs at her breasts and hips exaggerate her nakedness. Smoke billows and climbs a pyramid of light behind her. She watches you defiantly as her dais revolves slowly; she seems bound to it by centrifugal force. A filigree of laser light sizzles across her body. Somewhere a hoarse black voice sings a blues, but you are beyond the reach of words.

She tosses herself against the dais, pouts, snarls, her hair tawny against her white flesh. She rears up onto her knees, arches her back like a pacing panther whose fur has come up. You can feel the confident muscles in her long legs. Her hair streams through her fingers and turns to smoke as she writhes onto her back again.

Suddenly a greater voltage of lightning shakes her. She reaches down, pulls off the patch at her crotch. Bolts of electricity cross her body as the dais revolves faster. She spreads her legs wide as the dais turns her from you, closes them as it brings her back, now spreads again as she is whirled away, arching, taunting, open.…

The most invigorating music hall in France, the Crazy Horse Saloon of Paris, isn't really a music hall at all. Cabaret-size, it calls itself erotic theater and boasts "the most beautiful *femmes fatales* in the world." Since opening in 1951, the Crazy Horse has become an institution in Paris nightlife and its lighting effects have been copied worldwide. Its origins lie partly in striptease, partly in a French talent for sensuality, but it has little to do with the Folies Bergère/Moulin Rouge tradition. Located on the swank Avenue George V, across from Yves Saint-Laurent and next to Balenciaga,

Alain Bernardin died in 1994.
—JO'R, LH, and SO'R

its high style is very much its own, continuously under the guidance of its founder and owner, Alain Bernardin.

How to describe such a spectacle? For two hours, one's senses are blasted by variations on a single theme: eighteen naked young women with perfect bodies as individual as their faces, close to you yet not close enough, in tableaux that range from the near trashy to the near sublime. The tone is never leering, more a kind of holy lasciviousness. A show consists of group numbers and a dozen solos or duets, interspersed with a couple of comic acts to re-whet the appetite. Bernardin christens his dancers with names like Zaza Vesuvio, Vanity Obelisk, Tipsy Tipperary, Pearly Offshore, Lulu Paladin and Tiny Semaphore. Bathed in enigmatic light, all-powerful in their physical glory, they become, as Bernardin puts it, "the most inaccessible puzzles of nude women in the world."

Past the street-level lobby guarded by doormen dressed like Royal Canadian Mounted Police, downstairs into the small, 420-seat theater, in sumptuous red with an Art Deco aspect. The stage is downright tiny, flanked by nude golden statues and hidden behind a silver curtain. Signs everywhere proclaim "THERE IS ONLY ONE REAL CRAZY HORSE." The crowd is mixed, about three men to every woman. This show is necessary to any young man's education: a few very happy teenage boys accompany their parents. I stand at the bar along with mostly veterans and locals, as it affords the same view for half price. On my right is a Swiss engineer who attends the show with clockwork regularity, on my left one of the most beautiful brunettes in Paris, accompanied by a gentleman older and seemingly richer than either her or me.

A siren goes off, louder and louder. Then trumpets, martial drums and the voice of a British sergeant barking commands. The glittering curtain pulls open, and there they are, the famous line of proud-breasted girls in boots, white gloves, great black beefeater hats and nothing else save tiny black triangular *cache-sexes*. (Velcro is crucial to the Crazy Horse.) Lifting their knees high to military music, these soldiers march, salute, and about-face; the audience applauds this inspiring sight. White horsehair tassels dangle suggestively between the girls' legs, front and back.

In "*Rouge et Noir*," two incandescent girls, one in a black wig, one in a red one, wearing gloves and throat ribbons, take turns provocatively balancing across a leather armchair fitted with stirrups. "Bananas" is a group number in silver porcupine wigs: a funky golliwog's cakewalk, a nude rain dance, a toy waddle, done with high energy.

Now "Jailbirds," to urgent string music powered by bongos. Vertical black bars front the shadowy stage. A sultry redhead struggles, drapes her legs around the cage and arabesques at the audience. A brunette lies on a black altar and grinds her rump against the bars. A blonde girl caresses her. Each girl broods to her own tormented rhythms, trying to escape. The cape is whacked furiously as the naked bodies hurl themselves faster and faster, pinioned, scissoring around the bars, straining as the music ends.

The finale is a swaggering strut to horns: eighteen girls in blonde, black and blue wigs—wearing only black gloves, G-strings, garters, and stockings—swing and slide their buttocks down illuminated firemen's poles. By now their incendiary attitudes seem normal. Is there gentle sarcasm in the lyrics?

> *You're not too short*
> *You're not too tall*
> *You're not too round*
> *You turn me on.*

The Swiss engineer, so help me, sings along.

Alain Bernardin is a tall man with doubting eyes, thinning hair and the long face of a bloodhound. In his seventies, fit, calm, he looks a good twenty years younger, with the tanned health one associates with aging movie stars. He has three children by a former wife, but in 1985 he married Lova Moor, a blonde dancer and longtime star at the Crazy.

We meet in the modern, red subterranean offices of the theater. Bernardin is dressed casually, in a black shirt with streaks of color like the lighting effects in his show. Since the beginning, it has been all his—his design, his property, his "mistress"—and it has made him very wealthy. His staff calls him Le Boss. He chooses the girls, and he trains them; he estimates he has baptized 250 by now.

"I am looking for a cannon," says Bernardin, "an aggressive girl, who doesn't have fear in her eyes. A sparkling, brilliant, bewitching sorceress. One in fifty. I can recognize her in a second. First, she must have marvelous breasts. Then she must have trained already as a dancer. And she must be a 'good girl.' I don't find them, they find me. We have girls from all over Europe, from South Africa, Australia, New Zealand, even Hungary and Romania. We almost never have American dancers. Many, many English. English girls are all out to leave Mama. Many Russians, Czechs, and Poles. Polish girls are crazy, but they have strong temperament and personality. They're great onstage. Offstage, they're gold diggers. Our youngest dancer is eighteen, the oldest is twenty-eight. I want to provoke the public by putting them in the path of these cannons. If you give them their cleaning woman, they won't come. They want a dream money can't buy, inaccessible because of me—Pygmalion. And I try not to fall in love with my Galateas."

For his corps of twenty-four dancers, Bernardin takes about five new girls a year; more than a hundred audition. They average about five years in the show. Afterward, he says, a few become singers or dancers on TV. Others marry. Stripping, he points out, encourages ideas of domesticity.

"When I was eighteen, I worked at the Ritz hotel in London.

Then I was in the army. After the war, I opened a small, success-ful restaurant. In those days, the girls at, say, the Moulin Rouge, were not moving, not dancing, not teasing. They stood there with silly things like the Eiffel Tower on their heads. I had a shock of an idea: to bring burlesque to Paris, not in an American style but in a French style. Not a seventy-year-old doing a striptease but girls of eighteen, *sportives.* Originally, I wanted a wild-West saloon, with a country-and-western orchestra and lassos. In 1950, I sold my restaurant and rented this place. I had one girl at first, but at least she moved. After a year I understood I had to have five girls. Success was immediate. I designed the costumes, the dances. Even now I design everything.

"In 1958, by accident, I invented a lighting for the nude. In those days we projected each girl's name on the curtain. One night the curtain opened too soon, so the slide got projected on the girl. This way nudity can be artistic; the light clothes the body."

Bernardin is proud he can pay his dancers "twice as much" as the other Paris *spectacles.* The girls earn between $30,000 and $45,000 a year; the Crazy Horse maintains savings accounts for them. Renovations have brought the place up-to-the-minute. The lights and the three tape decks are controlled by computer. Backstage, most dancers have their own tiny *loges*, festooned with pictures, letters, personal effects. There are showers, a spaceship-style lounge with TV monitors, also an extensive room for daily rehearsals run by either of the choreographers, Molly Molloy and Sofia Balma.

"Salvador Dali must've come twenty times. He used to say, 'The Crazy Horse girls are all virgins.' One evening, he arrived and Andy Warhol was here. Dali said, 'Tonight the omens are not good.' He turned on his cane and left. Elvis came one night, brought by a mutual friend. He said, 'I'll come only if you give me a girl for the night.' So the friend had to loan Elvis his fiancée.

"Rostropovich came and spoke Russian with several dancers. Balanchine visited all the time. Bob Fosse kissed the carpet. Woody Allen used the Crazy Horse in *What's New, Pussycat?* Gypsy Rose Lee told me, 'We weren't like this. We weren't beautiful, we weren't young; we were actresses. It took us ten minutes to remove a glove.'"

A sloe-eyed brunette trips in, shoots Bernardin an intense look, then disappears into the *coulisses*. "A new girl," he says. "French. About half are French. French girls aren't as serious as the others. In England, nightclub work is considered a profession. In France, show business isn't taken seriously, not even theater. French talent never goes in the direction of cabarets. And it's a very difficult form to master. Everyone thinks it's easy because it looks easy. They don't realize how long it takes to perfect."

> *To achieve harmony in bad taste is the height of elegance.*
>
> —Jean Genet, *The Thief's Journal* (*Le Journal du Voleur*) [1949]

Bernardin has a reputation for protecting the girls with military strictness. It's forbidden for the dancers to meet anyone within two blocks of the theater; security is extensive. "There's a bad reputation, because outside France, the cabarets are bordellos," he says. "Frenchmen ask me how many girls are at the bar. I tell them, 'If I wanted to run a bordello, that's a profession too, but I run a theater.' Everyone knows there's no question of meeting the girls.

"In 1962 we did a Nazi parody. The music was a German military march; Bertha Von Paraboum wore a feather boa and a G-string in the shape of a swastika. The French were shocked, the Americans were shocked, the Germans were shocked. We even got letters of protest from old Nazis. The publicity was enormous. Now everyone's done everything; you can't scandalize anymore. Anyway, a porno show is boring, precisely because it leaves nothing to the imagination. I want a show of superb quality. I tell the girls to be like a painting by Modigliani. When I see them out there, I imagine making love to them. Everyone does, that's the idea. How wonderful, no?"

Night. We are no longer in Paris, but rather an apartment in East Berlin as it used to be. German voices drift up from the street through a blue window with venetian blinds. A brief flood of pale light as the door opens, revealing a balance beam in the center of the apartment.

A blonde with a ponytail enters, her face an impassive mask. She wears a white silk blouse, a black leather miniskirt. She tunes a radio to a blaring trumpet, hot and slow, then begins a limbering exercise against the balance beam. The radio bursts with static.

Suddenly we overhear the crackling walkie-talkie voices of two CIA agents on stakeout, filming her. Now we realize she's a spy. One agent says, "No wonder politicians run their mouths when they're in the sack with her." She tears off her skirt, runs her long legs caressingly along the balance beam to German music from the Thirties. Off comes the silk blouse. She's in only a black G-string and shoes. A measured swagger against the bar. In her eyes we see only a concentration on her body's movements. Does she know she's being watched? Is she deliberately tormenting them? They have turned into cheap voyeurs, their words banal against her beauty.

And now the G-string too comes off. Her hair comes undone as she throws herself violently along the exercise bar, whipping her body back and forth. Her big gulping eyes send astonished looks out as if startled by her own fiery intensity. A smile of pride in what her body can do; the music winds down, languorously she collapses, hangs from the bar, a gentle amusement playing across her face.

She knows.

To see a performance makes one wonder, naturally and perversely, what these girls look like with their clothes *on*. Albert Camus spoke for many of us when he said, "It hurts me to confess it, but I would gladly trade ten conversations with Einstein for one first encounter with a pretty chorus girl." Luckier than Camus, I meet with three star *danseuses*. All are well-spoken, smart, confident, and proud of the show; they are lovely without the public prettiness of models, with dancers' long bodies and healthy energy.

Akky, 24, Dutch, is the glowing blonde from the spy number. In jeans and a halter top, her midriff bare, she seems conscious of her physical presence, and I would guess she is the best-traveled. She's been at the Crazy for two years. Both the other girls are British. Friday, 22, with black hair pulled up from a no-nonsense practical face, wears a short skirt and high boots. She has been dancing here for about eight months now and has a winning brashness. Paula, 21, is a freckled redhead with a penetrating gaze, her long legs in jeans. Having been here only two months, she strikes me as the shyest.

FRIDAY: Half of us have good ballet training, the rest have some jazz training. When I was young, I wanted to be the good classical ballerina. Then I got interested in cabaret and show dancing.

AKKY: Everywhere I auditioned for ballet companies—Holland, Germany, and France—I was too tall. So I started doing cabaret work.

PAULA: I saw an ad for auditions in a trade weekly. I sent in a photo, and Bernardin flew me over with five other girls. After seeing the show, I thought, Can I dance nude?

FRIDAY: The audition's always the same. You improvise to "Menergy," the gayest song ever. It's bizarre and nerve-racking.

AKKY: It's the only place I know where they have you improvise. You're alone onstage, naked, and he's out there. It's not long. If you have the right style, they see immediately. We're classier than any other nude show; some dressed girls dancing can be much more vulgar than we are. We don't have to pull faces to be sexy; we have to be careful not to add too much. I don't think about the fact I'm taking off my clothes. Onstage we feel protected by the lighting.

PAULA: You can see only about the first couple of rows.

FRIDAY: You feel completely dressed. You're in full body makeup, and you've got lights, music, props. You become that number; you are that story. You're not a girl onstage taking off her clothes.

I wonder how they answer when people ask what they do.

AKKY: It depends who's asking. There are a lot of frustrated people out there. Some guys, I see they've heard about the Crazy Horse on TV, but they really have no idea. You can't explain it. My parents have come to see it and they think it's fantastic.

PAULA: I was in a restaurant the other day, talking to this American girl who was in Paris on holiday. She'd gone to the Lido, one of the big music halls. She said to me, "I was shocked! Those girls are topless!" When I told her what I did, her face fell.

FRIDAY: I'm proud to work at the Crazy. I say, "I'm not a topless dancer, I'm a nude dancer." Dancing here makes you appreciate what you have and make the most of it while you've got it. I've always been very shy of my body. I was always the person who wore baggy clothes, I felt self-conscious at dance class. I really hated myself when I came to the Crazy. Subconsciously, working in the nude, you put a check on your weight or your body.

AKKY: I see these young American women dressed like little girls, in prim and proper clothes, with little-girl shoes, very fake. I promise you, these women have wilder fantasies than I've got.

On asking their full names, I realize they've given me their stage identities: Akky Masterpiece, Paula Flashback, Friday Trampoline.

"*La Leçon d'Erotisme* with Friday Trampoline."

On a black stage, an enormous sofa in the shape of two red, ideal feminine lips. Friday in black negligee, black patent-leather shoes, black stockings, black garter belt, one black glove, with a black crucifix around her neck (a characteristic Bernardin touch). Her raven hair magnificently foaming, one pouting breast exposed, at first she sits ladylike on the two red lips. Then, as a husky-voiced French *chanteuse* whispers about the art of seduction, Friday insinuates herself across the lips, making sly love to them.

Slowly she pulls off her negligee. Very slowly she turns so we can admire the superb back view. She waits, her body stretched out, a hand on her hip. Off comes the garter. She wriggles lasciviously, lets her body wink at us, knowing everybody is watching her tiniest gesture as the *chanteuse* explains the "erotic lesson." Slowly she rubs the length of her body in all kinds of gyrations, straddling those fortunate lips. Purring against them, she falls asleep.

Near me, an Englishman says, "I want to be a student again."

Another view, less admiring, from a former soloist. Having started at age nineteen, she recently left after two years. Driven, smart, confident, she now runs her own successful small business.

"To dance at the Crazy changes you. Bernardin's strategy is to make girls feel like stars, even though they're only dancers. When you're given the ecstasy of being a star at twenty, this makes problems. You don't become confident. You lead a double life. You are strong onstage; offstage you're weak. You depend on the show to feel beautiful. The dancers end up wearing enormous amounts of makeup in the daytime without realizing it, because they can't bear not being looked at.

"The soloists are hated by the others. They're not paid more, but they're less likely to be fired by Bernardin, who can fire you at any time. Five minutes late and you're fined 50 francs. Everyone is scared of him because he can send them packing. I never felt badly treated myself, but he knows these are weak girls. I suppose he feels loved with all these women around.

"You become a night creature. After dancing and a cold shower you don't feel sleepy, even though it's two or three in the morning. It's hard to be in a relationship with a man who lives by day, so you end up going out with other people who live by night. Men are very aggressive because they know you're a Crazy Horse girl. I lost two years of my life this way, even though I did become adult very quickly. The dancers stay there a long time because they're afraid of leaving the life of the night and frightened of the normal life of the day. The dancers who stay on feel old, and they're very hard on the young girls who arrive. And the waiting around kills you.

"After the Crazy Horse factory, what's left? Only huge egos. They dream of becoming actresses or singers, but it never happens. They're not dancers; three hours' practice every day and any girl can do that. They end up as luxury courtesans, or married to some dismal older man. At first I liked being in a *spectacle*, and I was paid enough to live in Paris on my own, but I had problems for a long time after."

Her naked body is perfect, lying like a sacrifice on that tilted platform as smoke billows. Can this be the shy Paula I interviewed? Suddenly she pulls off the patch at her crotch; the audience holds its breath as her dais revolves faster and lightning engulfs her. As the platform turns her away, she spreads her legs wide, teasing. A thousand eyes are fastened on the tufts of her pubic hair, emphatic in the weak, smoky light, on her strong legs as she brings them together, opens them wide again, but never at the moment when the dais turns her to us. She tosses her head once; darkness closes in too quickly on her. The image of her lies burned on the darkness for an instant, then she is gone, gone, gone.

Anthony Weller is a writer and poet whose novel The Garden of the Peacocks *was published by Marlowe and Company.*

✳

No city has been more feminized than Paris, more effectively moulded to the contours of the female myth. It is the only one to have seen a particular culture of prostitution, even an architecture of the courtesan, an architecture whose apotheosis is the Hotel Paiva. The Paris of the Second Empire was a satrapy of the courtesan, not only as the West's first society to be dominated by the cult of woman, but also as the first in which the self-made by the cult of woman, the prostitute-capitalist, was a formidable controller of blocks of shares in South American railways and nickel mines in Noumea. For the first time the sex-fantasy puppet persisting aimlessly through history is able to turn the tables on the society that breeds and tames her. The first empress of the City of Women is a whore, Thèrése Lachmann, La Marquisa de Paiva and later countess Henckel von Donnesmarck, the daughter of a weaver in the foreign ghetto in Moscow, anthrophage and female vampire, consumer of aristocrats and agent of social cancer: the richest prostitute in human history and the builder and owner of the most expensive house—in relative terms—ever constructed in the City. The most terrifying incarnation of the will to power and money of the nineteenth century is a sex goddess actively laying the foundations of the worship machine of Hollywood. For the Parisian prostitute is the foundation of all female screen idols of the twentieth century. Marie Duplessis, the Dame aux Camélias, emerges a century later, both figuratively and literally, as Greta Garbo.

—Lawrence Osborne, *Paris Dreambook: An Unconventional Guide to the Splendor and Squalor of the City*

DAVID ROBERTS

*⃰ *

Bonjour, Chaos

Not far from Paris, there's a great place to monkey around.

I AM NO LOVER OF FORESTS, THE BIRCH MAZES OF THE Adirondacks, the hideous brush-choked ravines of the Cascades, the gauntlet of squat taiga enfilading the Alaska Highway—such woods have always seemed to me landscapes of gloom, brewed up by Darwin's mutative riot at its most careless. Even the open lodgepole and ponderosa stands of my boyhood Colorado served only as glades of passage, gateways to the bursting promise that timberline laid bare.

But Fontainebleau is a forest I can love. Thirty miles southeast of Paris, bisected by the roaring Autoroute du Soleil, Bleau—as the climbers call it—should not be confused with wilderness. From about 1130 to 1840, the forest was the hunting ground for the rulers of France. The palace of Fontainebleau, exceeded in magnificence only by Versailles, served for centuries as the swankiest hunting lodge in the world; thus the 62,000 acres of surrounding woods are crisscrossed with hand-cobbled carriage roads that meet in puzzling *carrefours* in the middle of nowhere.

Despite its name—an antique contraction of *fontaine de belle eau*—the forest is all but waterless, a desert out of which pines, oaks, beeches, and wild cherry trees somehow connive to spring. Aeons flooded the plain with limestone; millennial rains wore this softer stuff away, leaving woods strewn with grotesque sandstone monuments up to 50 feet high. The homely taxonomy of English calls such an assemblage a "boulder pile"; in French, it forms a *chaos*.

During the last hundred years, many of the best mountaineers in the world, from Pierre Allan to Guido Magnone to Catherine Destivelle, found in Bleau a nursery for their youth and a Sorbonne for their maturity. Today Parisian office workers routinely shut off their word processors at 5:30 and careen down the *autoroute* for an evening's sport at Bleau. No major city in the world has a more genial rock garden so close at hand.

On my last visit to Fontainebleau I discovered the ideal way to apprehend the place. Shunning the thronged cafés that edge toward the palace, I alighted in the one-street town of Barbizon, at the Hôtellerie du Bas-Bréau [formerly the Hôtel Siron]. The very same inn had, in the 19th century, sheltered the salon of a lively gang of painters who trooped daily into the forest, armed with canvas and easel.

Most people understand the Bleau's sandstone is unique and doesn't need any manipulation. You'll find big slopes, tiny edges, soft pockets— any kind of hold you could imagine, with a very pleasant feel. When you climb at Fontainebleau you rarely rip up your fingertips, but after three or four days your skin is as pink and soft as a baby's, so worn that you cannot touch anything.

—Baptiste Briand, "The Magic Forest," *Climbing*

No group of artists has fallen into a moldier neglect than the Barbizon School: Corot, Millet, Théodore Rousseau, and their lesser-known cronies. Often they are damned with the faint praise of serving as "precursors to the Impressionists." To my mind, however, the savage woodland epiphanies of Corot are far more powerful than Seurat's picnics. Sleeping at the Bas-Bréu, visiting the small museums housed in the ateliers of Millet and Rousseau, venturing into the forest, I began to see Fontainebleau through the painters' eyes, to recover the revolutionary fervor with which their landscapes teem.

These were the first Europeans who dared to paint for nature's sake, rather than as a backdrop for mythology or history. Trees, rocks, light, and shade—these made as noble a subject as the martyrdoms of saints, declared Rousseau. The Barbizon paintings seize upon the disorder of nature: ancient oaks are tortured by the twisting agonies of arboreal thirst; even a restful clearing brims with fathomless mysteries. So dark are their canvasses that the artists' detractors accused them of painting with prune juice.

Yet what a raucous, hedonistic band the Barbizon School was! Coyly, the painters posted a sign in the salon declaring, "Under pain of fine, visitors are forbidden to excite the artists." Yet by moonlight, they marched with their admirers into the forest to the tread of trumpets, built campfires in caves, drank flagons of wine, and made love all night. Their number included Lazare Bruandet, gentle as a lamb while he painted but a great brawler when drunk, who accosted strangers at the Siron and once threw his wife out the window; Stamati Bulgari, the eccentric military hero who held a parasol while he painted; and Rousseau, the nervous insomniac, whose passion for the forest amounted to a private religion. When King Louis Philippe ordered 15 million pines, not native to Fontainebleau, to be planted there in regimental rows, Rousseau organized expeditions into the woods to tear the trees up by the roots.

Steeped in these 19th-century glimmerings, I set out into the woods each day on my own excursions. In my pack I stuffed a loaf of hearty bread, cheese, and a bottle of wine. For many a lazy hour I followed the blue dots of the old Denecourt trails, named after Claude-François Denecourt, who had been a soldier under Napoleon before he settled near Fontainebleau in 1832 and set out to handcraft *sentiers* that eschewed the rectangular logic of the king's roads in favor of winding tours.

Denecourt's paths seek out every *chaos* in the forest: they deliberately scuttle through natural tunnels, or corkscrew around a handsome boulder, or linger on a ledge with a view of acres and acres of sand. Coming upon caves in which outlaws and hermits and society's castoffs once lived, I recaptured the medieval fear of the forest as a dangerous, alien place.

Every day I chose a bouldering circuit, Bleau's specialty. Each circuit contains a numbered sequence of boulder problems, as many as 70 or 80, that weave in and out of a particular *chaos*. The rocks are neatly painted with tiny arrows, numbers, and parenthesized dots indicating a jump. Color-coordinated by difficulty, the circuits range from the yellow *peu difficile* to the fiendish black *extrêmement difficile*. In the United States, eco-vigilantes would have squelched such desecration of the scenery before it got started; at Fontainebleau, the circuits integrate the human and the natural, as do the formal gardens of the palace.

I had lost for good, I thought, the urge to boulder: at stateside crags, the scene reeks for me of chalk-dust and ego and painful calisthenics. But Bleau reawakened a sense of play. On a warm, windy day, with no one else in sight, I puttered through the 71 problems on the blue (*difficile*) circuit at Manoury: I tackled the Mustard Pot and the Camembert Traverse, was stumped by the Drunkard's Arête and the Subway Handle, but managed Toto's Slide.

Then I lounged on a sandstone table and opened a bottle of wine. Rousseau's gnarled oaks swayed in the breeze, and Corot's umbrageous glooms flickered on the periphery. As the Beaujolais worked its charm, I lapsed into wistfulness, ruing the eternal injustice of having been born too late.

David Roberts is a freelance writer living in Cambridge, Massachusetts. He is the author of eight books, most recently Once They Moved Like the Wind: Cochise, Geronimo, and the Apache Wars. *He writes regularly for* National Geographic, Smithsonian, Men's Journal, Outside, *and other magazines.*

✦

For centuries the Fontainebleau forest had a very bad reputation. It was synonymous with darkness and fear, inhabited by demons, dwarves, and witches. Eventually, kings came to hunt in the forest, but people still avoided it, except the brigands, who would hide behind trees to ambush the unwary, cut their throats, and steal their money. At the beginning of the 19th century, entrepreneurs took interest in the rocks of the Fontainebleau woods, finding useful materials to pave muddy roads. The soft sandstone was easily cut, and many quarries were created. The woods lost their dark reputation. Writers, poets, and painters started to praise the Fontainebleau's forest. Footpaths were created and more and more people walked the woods, sometimes sleeping under the oddly shaped rocks. At the start of this century the first serious scramblers approached the rocks, and Fontainebleau climbing was born.

—Baptiste Briand, "The Magic Forest," *Climbing*

Monsieur Fix-It

A search for the holy grail ends in hardware heaven.

WE HAD ONLY ONE DAY LEFT IN PARIS. MY FRIEND FATIMA wanted to go to the Louvre, and since I had other things to do, we agreed to meet later in the day at a favorite café. We were both breathless with stories when we reconvened.

"You won't believe all that I say," she was saying excitedly as I tried in vain to recite all the accounts of my own ingenious discoveries.

"But the crowds," I complained.

"Yes, the crowds were fearful," Fatima concurred, each of us expounding on lines and elbows. Finally we stopped trying to talk at the same time and laughed at the absurdity: we had had the same afternoon—hers at the world's greatest museum; mine at its greatest hardware store.

I had browsed for hours, outlasted the peak-hour rush of shoppers and acquired bags full of trophies at the BHV, a sprawling department store on the rue de Rivoli across from the Hôtel de Ville, Paris' city hall. At the BHV (the letters stand for the seldom-used name, Bazar de l'Hôtel de Ville) my passion for gadgets and gizmos found ultimate gratification in the basement hardware department. BHV's management insists that there is more hardware for sale in its *sous-sol* (basement) than under any other roof on the planet. Certainly this hardware junkie wouldn't dispute the claim.

On more than one trip to Rome or Frankfurt—and once going to Addis Ababa—I have booked myself through Paris to shop for hardware (and to eat, of course). I've held off on home repairs until I could get back to the rue de Rivoli and buy just the right faucet or latch among the possibilities that fill a full city block. Some think it's quite mad (or at least pretentious) to go to Europe for hardware, passing perfectly good malls on the way to the airport. And to Paris, yet!—blasphemy to every junior high school English teacher who ever canted that edifying ditty "Oh, London is a man's town, there's power in the air; and Paris is a woman's town, with flowers in her hair." My Paris has flowers, too—and nuts and bolts and gadgets too inscrutable ever to see the fluorescence of an American shopping mall.

I discovered the BHV years ago when a Parisian friend suggested I might find there a little window ventilator like those I had seen in French kitchens. The one I wanted required no electricity—its silent spin was powered by variations in barometric pressure. I knew what made it go, but I didn't know what it was called, and I'd never seen one for sale.

The BHV saleswoman listened intently as I undertook to clarify my grail. Was it a fan, perhaps? No, not exactly. A gyrating showerhead? A motor of some kind? Electric? Battery-powered? Windup? Solar? No, not that either (although I was getting the idea that this place had potential). As her eyes followed my finger drawing ever-more-rapid circles in the air, she ignited with comprehension. *"Ah, oui! Un aérateur!"*

She led me to a whole wall of *aérateurs*. They came in plastic or metal, in decorator colors and in sizes that ranged from the diameter of a coffee cup to that of a soccer ball. I bought four clear-plastic ones, and they spin to this day.

The BHV has just about anything that can reasonably be classified as hardware and countless items that stretch the point—for instance, in the automotive section, just opposite snow chains and some 200 shades of touch-up paint, you'll find the complete library of Michelin guides and maps. The BHV never stocks just one of anything. On my most recent visit I noted more than a dozen styles of gardening gloves; 25 or so versions of the distinctive Parisian mailbox, with racks underneath for newspapers and magazines; perhaps 50 different flashlights, both functional and designer models.

Hinges, locks, knobs and handles fill long aisles, floor to ceiling, with styles that number in the thousands and range from medieval black iron to Louis XIV to *Starship Enterprise*. In the BHV's basement you'll find country weather vanes from any French province you wish to restage back home, shoe trees in the wood of your choice, or a bicycle lock that exactly balances your imperatives for security and esthetics. If you can't find a portable cement mixer anywhere else, you can pick one up in Paris.

The BHV eschews the usual French word for hardware, *quincaillerie*, preferring *bricolage*—loosely, do-it-yourself. At last count the store stocked more than 350,000 items in its *départment de bricolage*. That figure is even more remarkable when you consider that many home-decorating items (unusual carved moldings, ceiling medallions, paints, and a compelling selection of wallpapers and coverings) aren't included. They're on the fourth floor, with the largest cache of designer toilet seats ever uncovered.

Store statistics confirm what has long seemed evident: on all but one of eight floors—the ground level, where cosmetics and perfumes are sold—male shoppers outnumber the ladies at the BHV. Men predominate even in a third-floor kitchenware department that is about twice the size of Bloomingdales'. (The selection of steak knives is bewildering.)

The fact that the BHV is a power bazaar might have something to do with its imperial origins. The store was incorporated in 1854 as Bazar Napoléon by a former street merchant, Xavier Ruel, who had been rewarded for saving the life of Empress Eugénie, wife of Napoléon III. Ruel chose rue de Rivoli for his Second Empire building (still in use) because he correctly reckoned that it would become Paris' busiest thoroughfare.

More visitors probably stroll past the BHV each day than by both the main locations of the Galeries Lafayette and Printemps department stores. But more might not recognize the black-domed building as a department store. The BHV—Napoleon's name was not dropped until 1884, almost ten years into the Third Republic—gives short shrift to "visual merchandising" (a.k.a. window dressing). In fact, some days the iron gates over display windows remain shut, and several window spaces have been rented to street vendors selling schlock. Before venturing inside to search for my *aérateur* I thought the place was a warehouse.

Every Parisian I've asked says he (or she) shops there, but I've seen the BHV mentioned in few guides to the city. Apparently the management hasn't noticed the slight. There's a Tourist Welcome Center on the ground floor to help you find things, and bilingual agents at the sixth-floor customer-service department can arrange shipping when you toss baggage allowance to the wind and buy too much. Announcements in English are made over the public-address system, and most salesclerks speak enough of the language to tell you to stand right there, they'll be back with someone fluent.

D own the street from Le Printemps is the glass-domed Galeries Lafayette, another megalith of consumption on the Parisian grand magasin scene.

In the toy department, I was sure that I had found the perfect gifts for my step-nieces: Barbies dressed like "Apache dancers," in tight, front-slitted black skirts, red and white striped shirts, and black berets. They were packaged in screaming pink telephone booth-like boxes with French sayings, such as "Bonjour, ça va?" and "Je t'aime," scattered about the surface like confetti. And best of all, these dolls spoke French! "Elle parle!" the box shouted in large blue letters.

I took one of the dolls out of its box and pushed the button on its back. In a voice that trilled like Edith Piaf singing, the doll said, "Je t'aime. Je t'aime." I hit the button again. This time, in a dense, nasal patois, the doll seemed to say, "Voulez-vous rester avec moi?" Nah, I must have misunderstood it. I put the doll back in the box before I heard too much and took it and its twin to the cashier.

—Claudia J. Martin,
"Service by Committee"

Once I eavesdropped as two BHV cashiers read to each other from mimeographed sheets, practicing the English equivalents of *la plume de ma tante est sur la table*. When one of the grandmotherly cashiers spotted me, I feared I had embarrassed her. But she hoisted her shoulders, smiled proudly and glued together the words: "Hello. Do you speak English, too?" I often tell the story when Anglophones proffer that old (and essentially untrue) cliché that Parisians could if they would, but they won't.

The best way to approach hardware shopping at the BHV is to allow plenty of time; try to get the lay of the land while you're still on the stairs leading down to the basement (be prepared for aisles that extend to the vanishing point—I still get lost), then start prospecting. Help is always around if you need it, but finding things yourself is more rewarding—and you're almost guaranteed to stumble upon items you need but didn't know existed. My prize find is a set of long steel keys with handles on one end and threaded points on the other. It took me a while to puzzle out their purpose, but a dollar's investment means I'll never again have to use a hammer and nail to make starter holes for wood screws. Less constructive but more envied is the *Fermé le mardi* (Closed Tuesday) sign I bought for my kitchen.

Join the huddles around live demonstrations of the newest widgets, and for hands-on entertainment drop by the plumbing section where dozens of novel faucets and showerheads are connected to the Paris water system, ready for testing. When you find something you want to buy, ask a salesperson to write up your order and take the sales slip to a cashier, who will stamp it *paid* (the BHV takes all charge cards). Then go searching for the salesperson again, to claim your purchase. It's a time-consuming routine, but its charm grows on you. For a break from nuts and bolts, head upstairs to the sixth-floor *salon de thé*. Now, really—name one shopping-mall hardware outlet with a decent *salon de thé*.

The late Coleman Lollar once boasted that one-third of the hardware in his house hailed from the BHV.

＊

Whoever goes in search of anything, must come to this, either to say that he has found it, or that it is not to be found, or that he is yet upon the quest.

—Montaigne

The Source

Visit a distant and little-known part of Paris.

PAUL LAMARCHE, KEEPER OF THE SEINE, SCAMPERED OVER THE last traces of a vast Gallo-Roman temple to show me the river's source. He was into his 90s, quick, sturdy, with an elfin twinkle in his eye. Those old guys in Armenia last long on yogurt, but Lamarche thrives on the magical waters of the Seine.

"Look at this," Lamarche said, bending over a tiny stream trickling down a groove in the rock. He dislodged a stone and seized a waterbug, like a minuscule shrimp. "Any kind of pollution kills these things," he explained. "You won't find any cleaner water." He cupped his hands in the furry green moss and thrust his face into the cool liquid. I did the same. Water never tasted better.

The old man fell silent to let me ponder the past. Instead, my mind flashed ahead to the immediate future. I could imagine splashing water into guests' whisky aboard *La Vieille* [the author's boat and river home] and mentioning casually that I had scooped it from the Seine. A sadist's dream.

We were on the Langres Plateau in the Côte d'Or, up to our ankles in red poppies and talking over the bussing hum of cicadas. Wild roses and columbines fringed the rocks, and rich, fragrant grass hid little yellow buds. Lamarche first saw this enchanted

154

source when he was six. "We hiked down from Chanceaux to say *bonjour* to the goddess," he said, nodding toward a Rubenesque statue in a fake grotto built by the city of Paris to honor Sequana.

The plaque says she was put there by Napoleon III, but Paul knows the statue was replaced in 1928. Once water spouted from her left arm, as though she were personally filling the river, but in dry years the pressure was not strong enough. Now water burbles ignobly from somewhere near her feet. In any case, her cave is not the actual source.

"The river really starts here," Lamarche said, pointing to a rusty grate by a few chunks of marble column, all that remains of the biggest temple in ancient Gaul. "And there and there." Water oozed from two other breaks in the rock at the base of a low cliff, in a clump of trees. "Then it goes underground and loops around to the grotto."

He was enjoying himself, poking holes in the first few fibs the Seine's curators sought to perpetrate on the public. The river was his life, and Sequana his beloved ancestor. After checking out the world in the military, Lamarche came home to Saint-Germain-Source-Seine, the village nearby. In 1953, he settled into the old caretaker's farmhouse just below the grotto and opened the Café Sequana. His wife, Monique, made omelettes and strong coffee. At the source, Lamarche planted two willows, under which picnickers can dangle their toes in cool water, and shaped the small park. With money left over, he built the first bridge over the Seine, a funny little miniature of the vaulted spans farther down.

These days, mostly, he and Monique tend their fields. The grotto is left open to the public and needs only a casual eye. But when anyone stops to ask, the old man seizes a fat iron key and shows off the real thing.

Lamarche took me to the gate and worked at the rusted padlock. For several minutes, he jiggled the key and muttered darkly. Finally, he worked it loose. My friend Jeannette, meantime, simply walked past the locked gate; the fence had long since collapsed. Inside, Lamarche showed us a heavy slice of column that looters had tried to roll into a pickup. He had run them off. "They've taken everything," he said, shaking his head at nonspecific sacrilege over the last two millennia.

The park belongs to Paris. After all these years, the source of the Seine, deep in the belly of Burgundy, is still a colony of the French capital. Napoleon III claimed it last century when such symbolism was pregnant with political import. Now, only a curiosity, the symbol still fits. When the river gets bigger, it is pushed around with Paris in mind. Downstream from Paris, it runs thick with urban waste.

Although Lamarche plants the flowers, trims the trees, and cleans up after slobs, what he likes best is talking to visitors. He wants people to get Sequana's story straight. Which is not so easy to do. The *Dictionnaire Etymologique des Noms de Rivières et de Montagnes en France* offers eleven lines on the name *Seine.* This, via a string of variants used over the centuries, evolved into *Seine. Squan*, apparently, was a Gallic word meaning twisting, or tranquil, or both. The Romans added a few vowels. Later, French settled on a single syllable.

An eighteen-inch-high statue of the goddess has survived in a museum at Dijon. She is in flowing Greco-Roman robes, standing in a boat with a bow shaped like the head of swan; in the swan's mouth is a small round object, a pomegranate or a tennis ball. For myth spinners, it is a promising start.

Archeologists, in fact, have put together a detailed account of the daily goings-on at the temple to Sequana. Reading it, I half-suspected that some clumsy printer had substituted pages from a modern guide to Lourdes. The Gauls' first temple was made of wood and clay earth, but Romans later hauled in enough slabs of marble and hewn stone for a vast religious complex. The waters trickled among high columns and past inner recesses reserved for holy business. Downstream, they widened into a pool where the masses took the cure.

Gauls, Romans, and foreign tourists covered great distances, hobbling on foot or in fancy carriages. Priests received offerings in temple alcoves. Pilgrims sealed vows by pitching coins or jewelry into the water. Artisans fashioned replicas of limbs in need of curing, and they charged an arm and a leg. In bronze, wood, or soft rock, they depicted familiar-looking maladies—tumors, poxes, and deformities—which the Seine was enlisted to heal. Souvenir stands sold kitschy statuettes; had transport been better, they might have come from Taiwan.

The temple thrived as a sacred health spa and also as a vacation getaway from a bustling Gallo-Roman settlement downstream started by a tribe of Gauls, fishermen, and water traders known as the Parisii. *Par*, in Celtic, means boat. By then, the Parisii's capital on an island in the Seine, now the Ile de la Cité, was rolling in resource. The settlement, as well as the region near Sequana's temple and the river that linked them, were at the crux of a new world taking shape.

About six centuries before Christ, and the Romans, the Greeks had found a more direct route to Britain than sailing by Gibraltar and up rough open seas. They needed English tin and copper to make bronze, buying it with Mediterranean wine. Greek traders followed the Rhône to the Saône until they ran out of river. Crews humped their cargo overland to the headwaters of the Seine. From there, it was only water to the Thames. The Greeks enriched not only the *entrepôt* region of Vix, not far from the source, but also Gallic villages clustered along the river.

Germans, meantime, carted their heavy metals from Spain, in exchange for honey, amber, and furs. That required crossing the Seine. Wagoners settled on the Parisii's village, where flat rocks on either bank flanked an island made of silt. For much of the year, horses could ford the river; it was twice as wide then as it is now and a whole lot shallower. When the water was high, Gauls ferried the wagons across, for a price.

The island was perfectly placed. Forests hemmed in the river basin, and bandits cruised the few rutted roads. Anyone

Paris was born on what is now Ile de la Cité, a small island in the Seine. On its coat of arms, the city's symbol is a boat shaped like an island.

—JO'R, LH, and SO'R

with a choice preferred the Seine—peaceful, dependable, and free of muggers. And road convoys had to get over the river. Seven thousand strong, behind a stockade, the Parisii ran a bustling market and a mint that stamped gold coins. Politics were shaped by the watermen, the *nautes*, who ruled the wavelets until A.D. 52.

But after Rome conquered the British isles, Caesar realized he had to fuel his legionnaires there with home-grown olive oil. Like all other roads, he decided, the Seine would lead to Rome. His armies seized everything along the old Greek route. On their island redoubt, the Gauls fought back.

Caesar reported humbly: "Labienus exhorted his soldiers to remember their past bravery, their happiest combats, and to conduct themselves as if Caesar, who so often had led them to victory, were there in person." Romans routed the right flank, but the Parisii's general, Camulogenus, held the center. "All were encircled and massacred," Caesar wrote, adding that horsemen cut down those who fled. We have no Gallic version, but the battle was likely the origin of Parisian driving habits.

Having burned their town rather than leave it to Caesar, the Gauls started fresh on the island. On the river's left bank, a gleaming Roman city offered the usual colonial amenities: temples, baths, a theater, aqueducts, and stone streets, along with a port. Stone pillars and wooden planks made up the first Petit Pont. Gauls ran their own port on the island. The whole place was called Lutetia, a name that lingers today on a fancy hotel façade and a hundred other places.

The Romans built a temple to Jupiter atop a shrine to a Gallic god; Notre-Dame, on the same spot, now blots out both deities. By then, the Gauls had joined the invaders they could not beat. The *nautes* offered a statue to honor the Roman god and continued their lucrative river traffic.

Late in the 3rd century, France was rearranged by the muscular Teutonic tourism that got to be a habit. Franks swept southwest from the Rhine estuary. They eventually settled most of the country, hence the name France. But Burgundians from the central Rhine, tall Wagnerian blondes with a power problem, made straight for the Seine. In A.D. 276, they trashed Lutetia, burning the Roman sector. Failing to dislodge the Gauls from their island, they moved up-stream and razed Sequana's temple.

A Seine biographer, Anthony Glyn, reckons the Germanic invaders smashed the temple because they did not like female deities. In fact, centuries later, a monk named Seigne (pronounced "Seine") was sainted and recruited as patron of the river, which explains those impressive church towers at Saint-Seine-L'Abbaye, a few miles toward Dijon on the other side of the hill from the source. But he didn't take; Sequana has eclipsed Saint Seigne, whatever his role.

The Roman Empire was crumbling fast. In Lutetia, Gallo-Romans had shaped a new culture. Freed of Mediterranean keepers, they took the old name, Paris. And they looked mostly downstream, toward England and northern Europe, where trade was brisk. Wine from Burgundy and Champagne floated down the Seine. But not much came from beyond, overland from the Saône. Gradually, Sequana's shrine lost its pre-Michelin stars and slipped into the mists.

I started my river journey on foot. This line might have carried some power in a Richard Burton diary, with chilling detail of treacherous porters and mosquitos the size of turkey buzzards, but walking down the Seine is not what you'd call hardship. In fact, I didn't go very far before I hopped back into an open car and followed the farmer's roads and narrow strips of blacktop to the first proper bridge across the river. A very short bridge.

My original idea had been a single journey, from first trickle to final rollers, in some form of conveyance. Paul Theroux suggested a kayak, the way he'd do it. Another old pro urged something more French, like a rubber Zodiac. Had I talked to Mark Spitz, I probably would have considered the butterfly stroke. But the Seine, often submissive, needs a minimum of conquering. To live her secret life, you've got to take it slowly, in various ways at different times. My exploring would take me among old books, into rusting engine compartments, and, as far as I could go, into the thoughts of river people. More than a journey, this was a quest. I was after the soul of the Seine. Scrapping all plans, I simply set out.

The countryside is picturebook France, rolling, rich and rock walled. In its early stages, the Seine winds among fields and occasionally disappears in a brushy tangle. At any point, during the first few miles, you can hop across without getting your feet wet. Soon it widens into a respectable stream, snaking in even loops across fruited meadows. This is the deepest, greenest, richest heartland of Old Europe.

The Seine is formalized at Billy-lès-Chanceaux, its name on the enameled plate bolted to the stone bridge. It flows past a line of tile-roofed and shuttered buildings, the town hall and bourgeois homes, set on the cobbled quai as if the place were a busy port. Jeannette and I settled down to watch life. An ancient tractor clattered across the bridge. Some kids did a Flying Wallenda act over the water. A mother herded her toddlers homeward, a duck with ducklings. We laid out a lunch on the grass. It was less elaborate than Manet's, but we got the feeling. This was one lovely river.

Then we meandered downstream, stopping to sniff at kitchen windows and craning our necks over tumble-down stone walls to see gardens gone wild. Whenever we found a bridge, we crossed it and watched clear water swirling slowly around the pilings. If a side road climbed a wooded rise, we followed it.

France is particularly well endowed for this sort of sweet exploration. The Institut Géographique National (IGN) puts out a series of blue-bordered maps on a scale of one to twenty-five thousand. Two inches are devoted to each mile on the ground, enough room for street grids of hamlets and the shapes of château outbuildings. Each caprice of a stream bed is traced in and out of green-shaded splotches. A practiced eye can almost pick out the places with cozy little cafés run by accomplished grandmothers, causing the practiced palate to moisten noticeably.

Thanks to the IGN, I could follow highways too insignificant for any color at all, doubling back to thwart dead ends and recrossing the Seine yet again whenever I liked the cut of a barn. There is a certain pleasant sameness in the river's early stages. As in much of France beyond the cities, most people are linked to farms or are shopkeepers who earn their living one baguette at a time. In terms of nature, however, all around is heavy on *luxe, calme et volupté*.

Hard times had begun to bite when I first tracked the river in 1992, and things were getting worse. The European Community, an imperfect union, bettered few lives. Farm subsidies plummeted, prices sagged, and agro-industry suffered. Other sectors stagnated, drying the national resource pool. Elsewhere, rural families were migrating to cities. The Seine's waters hardly shielded people nearby from the world beyond. But, I suspected, only desperation could dislodge many of them from their natural paradise.

Conflicting sensations came back, time and again, as I explored the river. Try as you might to avoid it, the Seine at its gentlest pushes you toward grandiose metaphor. It is a silver thread woven into a rich Old World tapestry, an inlay of precious metal...and so on. Then you turn another corner and find some architectural atrocity at the edge of a village gone modern. People are kind beyond belief, or porcine putzes. In microcosm, the Seine is France.

At Bar-sur-Seine, well before the boats start, Antoine Richard fished for supper. His secret spot was just below the picturesque wreckage of a wooden wheel that had churned up electricity not long after Thomas Edison invented light bulbs. A few days earlier, he had pulled out 23 trout. A fireman in his twenties, Richard spends his down time along the river.

The occasional French monarch dreamed of bringing boats up this high. Under orders from Napoleon, engineers once tried to dredge a channel near Bar and line it with rock walls. But the river bed is too porous in its early stages, and the emperor's canal would not hold water. As a result, the Seine's gently sloping grass banks are just about the way nature wants them.

"Such tranquillity, beauty," Richard reflected, pausing to let the scene speak for itself. Bright flowers climb mossy village walls. Up the graveled road was a regulation church with a pointy steeple. The cafés and shops had not changed for generations and likely never will. Ah, the poetry of *la France éternelle*. And then the other side. I asked about pollution.

"It's not too bad here," Richard said. "You can still catch *l'ombre*, as far down as Fourchière." That was not so far down. "Then it disappears." *Ombre*, a delicate white fish like a trout, can't handle dirty water. Farther down, fishermen have to settle for carp, chub, roach, bream, eels, and other hardy species. A few hours' drive from the source, the Seine looked fresh and alive. But Paul Lamarche's tiny bugs wouldn't stand a chance.

At Fourchière, a gas-station owner in greasy overalls said that, in fact, the odd *ombre* still lurked in the river. He eyed me carefully and added, "*Ici c'est une societé privée.*" This was confusing. *Societé* can mean "association" but also "company." Had some business cornered fishing rights? The man explained, "*C'est réservé aux gens du pays.*" Another two-way meaning: *pays* usually means "country," and he might have been saying that only French people could fish there. He wasn't. The other meaning is "around here." He meant that the Seine, in that area, belonged only to Fourchière's people. But the bakery sold me bread.

Châtillon-sur-Seine is the first real town on the river. As in Paris, the water splits into two branches around an island of buildings in fitted rock that go back a half dozen centuries. But in Châtillon the channels are a coin's toss wide, and you can see bottom. At midnight, time tun-

In the Middle Ages people believed that bodies drowned in the Seine could be located by setting afloat in the river a votive candle on a wooden disc and noting where it stopped or went out. It was doubly important to find drowned bodies before the authorities did, because a huge fee of 101 écus, the equivalent of a year's pay for a manual laborer, is said to have been charged for the delivery of a loved one from the morgue at the Châtelet. One version of a story told about a bridge and its fires has it that a poor old widow whose son had drowned had set a candle afloat in hopes of finding his body. The candle floated close to a straw-laden barge, setting it on fire. The barge touched the wooden scaffolding of a pillar of the bridge itself. In three days the raging fire destroyed the bridge and the houses on it.

—Alison and Sonia Landes,
Pariswalks

nels you backward. Cobblestone streets, laid out for horses and slop buckets, echo footsteps. Rusty hinges hold up shutters in wood petrified with age. People have snapped off their lights, leaving only a flickering glow of street lanterns that might be oil torches. A fortified hilltop church stands above the river. From some angles, it is a brooding hulk. From others, it is a graceful sweep of towers and ramparts.

The river hairpins and eddies into a mystical pool under a rock outcropping. In fact, this is the Douix, perhaps the world's shortest river, and the first tributary of the Seine. The Douix gushes up from the cliff at rates approaching a thousand gallons a second. It boils over a natural fall of ragged rock. From source to mouth, it is 100 yards long. In the darkness, it churns and rushes, blowing off mists. When the upper Seine was a highway, this had to be a Druid rest area.

A number of years back, say about 50 million or so, when the Seine's bed was on the floor of a shallow inland sea, France was as warm as the Caribbean. Off and on during those Paleocene times, waves covered a broad sweep of Western Europe, leaving islands of rich vegetation and small tropical beasts. Each dose of salt water lasted two to four million years. In between, the land dried and life forms nestled in the sediment to fossilize for the later amusement of geologists. Remains of two thousand mollusks have been found in the Paris basin, many of them dead ringers for the shells that get tossed out each night after a *fruits de mer* feast in Les Halles.

As time marched on, old sands and clays hardened into new formations. The limestone deposits that characterize Paris began in a subepoch called, naturally, Lutecian. Successive layers of gypsum, clay, and sand already had taken shape by the Pleistocene epoch, a million years ago, when giant ice cubes elsewhere on the planet scraped slowly past and redecorated the scenery. Toward the end of the Quaternary period, the banks of the Seine were somewhat as we find them. Rich alluvial soil goes down yards deep on a sandy, porous base. In the heart of Paris, where wagons could cross once wheels appeared, hard calcified rock forms a solid foundation for a city.

A visitor today can sit on the bank under leafy trees and taste the fruits of this geological C.V. The chalky hillsides and plains produce grapes to kill for. And, above Châtillon, the northbound Seine flows into Champagne, where a monk named Dom Pérignon figured out a splendid use for them.

In these sorts of settings, one is well advised to husband the adjectives and go easy on superlatives. That said, there may be no place better than Vix, anywhere, to uncork a bottle and contemplate peace on earth. Two millennia after thriving as a crossroads of world trade, Vix has dropped from the map. Its ancient treasures—some gold and jewelry, but especially a stunning cast-bronze five-foot-six-inch-high Grecian urn from the tomb of a princess—are five miles away in Châtillon. The highway misses it by a mile. No one mentioned it to me; flashing by in the car, I saw a sign and hung a right.

Unvisited, Vix remains in a mossy-tile, pre-neon state, its falling-down walls half hidden in bursts of bright flowers. The Seine makes a gentle bend into the village and flows under three arches of a stone bridge. It is wide and clear as glass, with whorls of weeds under its rippled surface. In the falling light of dusk, fishermen in waders tie flies to their lines and snake them over the water.

For a while, I fussed with my cameras. By placing my car near the bridge, I could get high enough to picture the chipped "La Seine" sign, with a spray of red flowers in the foreground and the rich green far bank as a backdrop. After half a roll, I gave up. The power was not visual but spiritual, and every sense went into the picture: perfumes, ripplings and rustlings, balmy air you could feel.

A few couples, some young, some ancient, watched the bushy-haired man with Paris plates crawl over his car and twist into odd positions. Most quickly lost interest. They had come to see the river at sundown, a specialty of Vix that is now into its third millennium and shows no sign of losing its glory.

Approaching a man with a fly rod, I fished for quotes. Yes, outsiders were welcome to try their luck in the Seine, he said, and I was happy to hear it. Like picture-taking, words fell short. What could he tell me that I could not feel by sitting there quietly? Here in Vix, it all fell together: the cycles of geology, the waves of history, the link to modern times. Light was dwindling fast, and people were expecting me a long way down the road. I sat, and sat, and sat.

Mort Rosenblum is the former editor-in-chief of the International Herald Tribune *and the author of* Mission to Civilize, Back Home, *and* Who Stole the News. *This story was excerpted from his book* The Secret Life of the Seine.

✶

> *L'aurore grelottante en robe rose et verte*
> *S'avançait lentement sur la Seine déserte*
>
> The glittering dawn, in robe of red and green,
> Moving slowly, on the Seine was seen.
>
> —Baudelaire

DONALD W. GEORGE

In Notre Dame

The author is moved by the Unseen.

NOTRE DAME FROM THE OUTSIDE IS MAGNIFICENT, MONUMENTAL, solidly of the Earth and yet soaringly not. But for all its monumental permanence, its context is clearly the present: visitors pose, focus, click; portable stalls sell sandwiches and postcards; tourist groups shuffle by in ragtag formation.

Walk through those massive, humbling doors, though, and suddenly you breathe the air of antiquity. Let your mind and eyes adjust to the inner light, and you begin to realize that there is much more to Paris than the life of its streets, and a small sense of its magnificent and moving past comes back to you.

When I entered Notre Dame on my most recent trip, I was overwhelmed by the solid, soaring arches and columns I had forgotten, by the depth and texture of the stained-glass windows with their luminous blues and reds and greens. I thought of how many people had worked to build this magnificence, and of how many people since then had stood, perhaps on the very same stones as I, and marveled at it. I thought of all the faith and hope and sacrifice it manifests. I walked through the fervent space, awed by the art and the hush that seemed to resonate with the whispers of centuries, and just when I was beginning to feel too small and insignificant and was getting ready to leave, I saw a simple sign over a tiny stone basin of water, on a column near the doors.

The sign said, "In the name of the Father and the Son and the Holy Spirit" in seven languages, with pictures that showed a hand dipping into the water, then touching a forehead.

I touched my hand to the cool, still water, then brought it to my head, and as I did so, chills ran through my body and tears streamed into my eyes.

Somehow that simple act had forged a palpable contact with ages past, had put everything into startling focus: the ceaseless flow of pilgrims to this special place, the ceaseless procession of hands to water and fingers to forehead, all sharing this basin, this gesture.

I felt a new sense of the history that flows with us and around us and beyond us all—of the plodding, tireless path of humankind and of the sluggish, often violent spread of Christianity through Europe and the rest of the world—and a new sense of the flow of my own history, too: my Protestant upbringing, a pastor whose notions of Christian love have had a deep and abiding influence on my life, the old and still inconceivable idea of God.

For a few moments I lost all sense of place and time—then a door opened and a tourist group entered, looking up and around in wonder, and I walked into the world of sunlight and spire again.

I stopped, blinked at the sandwich stalls and postcard vendors, then turned back toward that stony symmetry and thought: sometimes you feel so small and insignificant in the crush of history that you lose all sense of purpose and self. Then something will happen to make you realize that every act and every encounter has its own precious meaning and lesson, and that history is simply the sum of all these.

Sometimes it comes together, as it did for me that moment in Notre Dame; sometimes the world is reduced to a simple sign, a stone basin, the touch of water to head—and the vast pageant of the past and the living parade of the present take on a new, and renewing, symmetry and sense.

For eight years Donald W. George was the award-winning travel editor of the San Francisco Examiner. *His career as a peripatetic scribbler started in Paris, where he lived and worked and fell in love (several times) the summer between his junior and senior years at Princeton. He is the editor of the forthcoming* Travelers' Tales Japan.

★

A bench at the entrance to the Métro, Champs-Elysée:

As I sit in Paris in the rain I try to imagine each passerby in 16th- or 15th-century dress. The images are quite vivid, as I've soaked up enough Tintorettos, Titians, and Lottos to last till the next millennium.

Ever bright in my mind are the twisted, tortured torsos of slaves, the brilliant detail of saintly robe, the cool, smooth feel of carved stone limbs, and the myriad of churches and museums. Such passion, such epiphany, such intensive labor and detail in every craftsman-trade, from glass and mosaic to stone work, wood carving, and masonry.

Paris now feels like a weathered and paved-over metropolis of modernity and bustling tourists. Looking deeper and deeper though I can see vividly Paris as it once was: a glorious daunting fountain of song.

Paris's soul is still here, as solid as the faded marble façades and cobblestone walkways. I'm awed that we've regressed so far. What men 600 years ago erected, carved, created without use of modern amenities puts us to shame. In each detail, archway, window I see a masterpiece taking a man's entire lifetime to create. Perhaps that's why the city has such soul—from every artisan and slave buried, celebrated within it.

No wonder modern man is lost, living in a wasteland of convenience—only 200 souls per building, only 2 days of ethereal spontaneity per painting. Sainte-Chapelle must be at least 50,000 souls—200 mosaic artists, 10 architects over 200 years, 100 masons, 2,000 slaves—the *Assumption* at least 2 years. And imagine, making paint for each pigment, etching each chip of stone. No wonder they did it right—such effort, such time required—every stroke counts.

—Gina Granados, "Dear Patrick"

FRANÇOIS MASPERO

★ ★ ★

A Reminiscence at the Air Museum

The history of aviation lifts off in the Paris suburb
of Le Bourget.

THE AIR MUSEUM IS OPEN, AND IS AS EMPTY AS THE FLANDERS
road was 200 years ago. The young man in uniform behind the
ticket counter is bored: he thought it would be fun to do his national service in the air force, but it's not. Was he posted there by
chance? Not exactly. Family connections. His father knows the
general who runs the Air Museum. But if he had known, he would
have tried to get invalided out.

The concourse of the former airport is entirely devoted to the
early days of aviation up to the end of the First World War. First
there are the new life-size reconstruction's of old—even legendary—contraptions such as Leonardo da Vinci's; and even, in
some cases, genuine creations built from plans which were never
executed. A perfectly painted hot-air balloon (to a scale of 1:16)
rises and falls in time to blasts of hot air. You can admire Francesco
Lana's airship (1670), a wooden skiff suspended from four copper
spheres, propelled by a sail and oars; and nearer our own time,
Cayley's heliplane (1843), a huge spring equipped with propellers
and rotors; or Charles Renault's ten-wing glider. Then come the
first machines that actually dragged themselves off the ground:
Count Massia's glider, which, with blinding logic, equipped man

169

with what he lacked—two wings and a tail; those by Lilienthal and the Wright brothers; and, of course, Clément Ader's plane. The accompanying notes tell us that Clément Ader—who would have thought it?—was a victim of the Dreyfus Affair: "The Dreyfus Affair erupted in 1894, complicated by sluggish finances, a situation whose fatal consequences Ader failed to recognize." Ader, as we know, got airborne for a few metres of runway at Satory camp, though he failed to convince the assembled military. But it wasn't the bad weather, or the weight of his steam machine, or of course the dull-witted army brass which caused him to crash: if he fell to earth, Dreyfus was to blame.

The Air Museum is a marvel. You could spend hours there dreaming. There is the same sheer quiet you get at high altitude. Hanging from the ceiling, the Morane, Spad, Caudron, Bréguet, Fokker and De Havilland are as dazzling as the day they were born. And there's a *nacelle* of the first Zeppelin: it's all cramped, it's the one with the engine. François would so like to see inside the *nacelle* of a 1930s Zeppelin, the one which flew its passengers from Hamburg to New York, and where, as legend has it, piano recitals were given on board.

Parked in adjacent halls are more recent planes. François would have liked to see again the fabulous airships of his childhood, from the time when air transport was a byword for unimaginable luxury. One was the Latécoère 631, "the biggest hydroplane in the world." He remembers religiously exploring the cabin of one of them (or was it simply a life-size model?) at the 1937 Paris Exhibition: he was only five years old at the time, and it was one of his most magnificent memories of that brief but fabulous pre-war period; what has stuck in his mind—and who knows if it is somehow linked to reality?—is that it had several bridges, an interior staircase and cabins with bunk beds, like a boat. And maybe there was a lounge, and a bar? And a piano? When, as a grown-up, he had to catch a plane for the first time—it must have been a Languedoc or a DC4—everything seemed very cramped, as if progress had come to a halt with the war and could from then on offer human beings only small and utilitarian things. Later still, he rediscovered that feeling of vastness and interior luxury on board a six-engine, twelve-prop Aeroflot Tupolev: this aircraft was flying a route for which it had probably not been intended, and to ease the length of the journey (a nonstop, seventeen-hour flight), half the seats had been taken out: there was room to play dominoes (double-dozen dominoes!) on real tables, and chat in small groups. From the corny chandeliers hanging from the high ceiling, and the curtains, down to the mysterious staircase adorned with a copper balustrade descending goodness knows where, everything seemed straight out of a Jules Verne story, a *Nautilus* where no one had spring-cleaned for years, or like the Czar's saloon carriage as it appears in old issues of *Illustration*. But you could tell it was a Soviet plane: there was no toilet paper. The Latécoère, though, came to a sorry end. During the war, the individual parts were hidden by patriotic engineers. After the Liberation, it was seen as a desirable symbol of rediscovered French greatness. In the eyes of the world it was supposed to be the Concorde of its time. In 1948 its inaugural flight made the front page of all the newspapers. The next chapter was cruel indeed: somewhere over the Caribbean it started to fall apart. A propeller came off, sliced through the fuselage and severed a journalist's arm—oh, the shame of it! The Latécoère 631 was heard of no more.

He would also have liked to see the 1950s clippers again, the last planes you could still say looked like "large birds," such as the Superconstellation, with its slim, curved cockpit and three fins; that was in the days when the air hostesses used to offer you sweets because sucking them was supposed to unblock your ears. Or a good old DC3, like ones you still find on airfields in Africa and Latin America, whose nuts were tightened after the stops; through the portholes you could see the wings beating in thin air.

Mostly there are the planes he saw in the 1940s, gleaming and raking their machine-gun fire, and sometimes nose-diving with long trails of smoke. Spitfires and Lightnings, bearers of death and yet messengers of freedom. It could have been the exhilarating

sight of so many planes skimming through the clouds, despite all
the bombs and exploding ground-to-air shells which for two years
rained down on his head, or maybe the fairy-tale memory of the
Latécoère, but at the age of thirteen François felt a strong aero-
nautical calling. Every Thursday he would drag his cousins along
to "The Small Wings of the French Air Club" to construct
wooden model gliders (ah, the CB32, with its triangular fuselage!),
which they never managed to assemble completely because all the
parts were missing and the glue was duff. This vocation went into
tailspin in the third form after he had founded and presided over
the *Avionnet Club*, whose aim was to promote paper arrows and
planes in all their forms, but which met with no sympathy from
the school's senior authorities, the teachers and headmaster, and
thus became the first of his ventures to be scuppered by the disapproval of serious people. But today one of his cousins is a colonel
in the air force, and François remains convinced (even if no one
else is) that he was behind this fine career.

Might this explain why the first jet planes, in a different hall, are
more sinister, more directly threatening and cruel? Great metal
bodies devoid of a sense of speed and space-conquering freedom,
leaving just the faintest reflection of cold-blooded murder on their
grey riveted forms. Like a gloomy pets cemetery, calling to mind
the birds of prey at the Botanical Gardens. The place has the atmosphere of a port's backstreets where retired test pilots go to
dream nostalgic dreams, bald gentlemen trying to explain to their
grandsons how they climbed in there to storm the skies, trying to
tell them that in those cockpits they experienced moments of brief
and intense happiness which, as they sadly realize once more, are
impossible to convey.

Outside in the sun on the old runway, a Concorde and a
Caravelle display rotten entrails inside their fuselages, their sides
flaking off with a vengeance. A state of total decay. It seems there
should be other big planes here, but apparently they are being repaired for the air show next door, preparations for which are well
under way. Under a wing of the Concorde, a gentleman complains

that no one's interested in aviation any more. There's been an exhibition, he says, at the Grand Palais, which got only 300 visitors per day, and next door some painter or other, "Degas, I think it was," was pulling in 9000: it's not right.

No, it's not right.

A worried-looking individual appears from between two hangars and questions them in an improbable language. After several attempts, it transpires that he knows a few words of German and is looking for the way out. François suggests that the best way to get out might well be where he came in, but all of a sudden the man seems freed from worry and anxiety, utters "*unmöglich*" a few times and hurries off towards the barriers behind which the air show is being prepared. They conclude that he's a spy. Bulgarian, decides François.

Should one talk about Le Bourget's finest hours? On one side of the airport car park is a statue of a woman taking to the skies, a monument to Nungesser and Coli, and Lindbergh: "In honour of all those who tried and he who succeeded."

François Maspero, formerly one of France's leading radical publishers, is the author of two novels, Le Sourire du Chat *(translated as* Cat's Grin*) and* Le Figuier. *He has also written the text accompanying the latest collection of Anaïk Frantz's photographs,* Paris, Bout du Monde.

✳

Another off-season treat was a visit to one of the *Marché aux puces* (Market of Fleas). The largest Paris flea market, open on Saturdays, Sundays, and Mondays, is on the edge of the city in a grimy, no-frills town called Saint-Ouen. On a Saturday morning, it attracts lovers of the second-hand, the rare, and the unusual. In October or November there are few tourists to clutter the stalls and few pickpockets, and normally taciturn dealers have more time to talk.

This Market of Fleas is the best-known market of its kind in the world, with more than three thousand separate stalls in various buildings, under tarpaulins, and along rambling alley-ways covered with tin roofs. There is china, porcelain, furniture, postcards, posters, lamps, rugs, silverware, toys, and *objets d'art*. There is, in short, little that cannot be unearthed here.

The market was founded in 1885, when the city fathers banished the junkmen and ragpickers of Paris to this neighborhood near Porte de Clignancourt, just beyond the Paris city limits. The "market of fleas" was no doubt an apt description of conditions at that time and for years after. It became a weekend market that took advantage of the large numbers of Parisians passing through Saint-Ouen to flee the city for a day in the country. Most of the dealers here are specialists and the chances of unearthing a Matisse are virtually nil. But there are savings of fifteen percent to twenty percent off city prices.

—Everett Potter, "Paris in Winter," *Relax*

TARAS GRESCOE

* * *

Real Life House of Horrors

What resides in Paris's least-known museum?
Come and see.

THERE ARE PARTS OF PARIS THAT NEVER MAKE IT INTO THE guidebooks, and the Fragonard Museum is one of them. Its home, the little bedroom community of Maisons-Alfort, at the confluence of the Seine and the Marne just south of the Bois de Vincennes, is only twenty minutes upstream from the Louvre by even the slowest *péniche*, but a skein of TGV tracks, elevated Métro lines, and Périphérique off-ramps has lately transformed this nondescript suburb into a commuter belt no man's land.

Since the 18th century, in fact, Maisons-Alfort has been noted for only two things. The first is its proximity to a grim enclave in Charenton, the mental hospital whose walls are visible across the water. The second is the presence of one of the world's oldest veterinary schools. The sprawling École Vétérinaire d'Alfort, with its spike-topped stone walls and slit-windowed turrets, looks as intimidating and inescapable as the most Zolaesque lunatic asylum. On this overcast afternoon, however, the knowledge that it also houses a museum filled with the grotesque work of an anatomist—one declared mad by his contemporaries—makes it downright terrifying.

Honoré Fragonard, the first director of the school, spent his life

175

in the *terrain vague* between science and art, using bodies rather than clay for raw material, and Paris's least-known museum is filled with some of the most disturbing sculptures ever created. The school still treats animals large and small; however, if the young woman carrying her poodle across a courtyard knew what was hidden away in the museum's collections, she might turn and run.

The few rusty signs that point to the museum's entrance aren't likely to excite much suspicion. The name Fragonard has long since been associated with the refined pursuits of the upper echelons of French culture: the paintings of Honoré's cousin Jean Honoré Fragonard hang in the Louvre, and there are two Fragonard Museums of Perfume in the city. But Fragonard the anatomist had other interests.

Born in the Provençal town of Grasse, he trained to be a surgeon and was named director of the world's first veterinary school in Lyons. In 1776, at the age of 33, Fragonard came to what was then the newly-opened École Royale Vétérinaire. (Today the full name is École Nationale Vétérinaire d'Alfort.)

The sickly-sweet smell of formaldehyde is the first thing to greet a visitor at the entrance to the three-room museum. The second is the hand-lettered sign on a desk in front of the skeleton of a rhinoceros: "Unfortunately, we have too few visitors. If you enjoy the museum, why not send us your friends—if not your enemies."

After buying my ticket from a man who immediately returns to the dissection room below, I'm alone for the afternoon. Apart from the cracking of the herringbone parquet underfoot, and the occasional sounds of horse's hooves striking gravel in the courtyard below, a sepulchral silence reigns over the rows of tall exhibition cases.

As I roam from cabinet to

> *reud said of the French, "They are a people of psychic epidemics, of massive historic convulsions...." He observed the French up close during several long trips to the country; the first took place from October 1885 to February 1886. During this time he fell in love with the city, but was not impressed with Parisians, whom he found deceitful, unkind, and "possessed with thousands of demons."*
>
> —*Paris Notes*

cabinet in the first of three linked rooms, it's hard to say whether the items in the collection, most of which date from the 19th and early 20th centuries, were chosen because they were instructive, bizarre, or simply beautiful. There's a jewel box of iridescent, perfect pearls—formed in the kidneys of cows. A piglet displayed in the cross-section has undergone "diaphanisation"—its organs have been treated with a chemical that makes them transparent—so that it resembles some kind of ghostly deep-sea fish. The pale blue fetus of a horse, injected with mercury to highlight the vessels in its outer membranes, floats in a jar, surrounded by a tracery of quicksilver. Ostensibly, all the works are meant to illustrate some principle of anatomy; at some point, however, their anonymous creators must have yielded to a stronger impulse.

The cabinets devoted to teratology, the study of monstrosities, are a journey through Greek and Roman mythology. There is the head of a Cyclops—a colt with a malformed facial bone that caused it to develop one huge eye. A siren floats in a cracked jar of liquid—in reality a baby, born in Maisons-Alfort, whose joined legs make it look like a mermaid. There are monsters whose birth would have augured the outbreak of a dozen Athenian Plagues: Siamese twin lambs, locked chest-to-chest in a permanent waltz; chicken skulls the size of basketballs; a ten-legged sheep, floating in a tank of formaldehyde. It makes a show by the British artist Damien Hirst look like a trip to the petting zoo.

As shocking as they are, these mutations do nothing to prepare the visitor for the contents of the museum's third room. Beyond a central chamber packed with the

To know Paris is to know a great deal.
—Henry Miller

skeletons of ostriches, camels, and lions caught in midroar, the work of Fragonard, the oldest part of the collection, appears.

The silhouette of a horse in full gallop, mounted by a stiff-backed rider, attracts the visitor to the display case of this final room. As one draws closer, however, it becomes clear that something is wrong. This horse has no skin. Although it's caught in midstride, it looks as if it's been flayed alive. Every cord of its flexed muscles is visible; bulging blue veins stretch over its jaws, tendons and ligaments strain to raise the out-thrust neck. The upright rider, arms bent as if to grip reins and a whip, is not exactly a skeleton, but neither is it human, rather an accumulation of brown ligaments, red arteries, yellow tendons. The shining orbs of his eyes stare fixedly into the distance, over rows of gritted teeth. It's Dürer's *Horsemen of the Apocalypse* by way of Madame Tussaud (she was a contemporary of Fragonard's), except that this is no waxworks—these are real bodies that have been carefully stripped of their skin and elaborately posed.

There are over a dozen other flayed figures, or *écorchés*, on display in the room. The bust of a man, skin peeled away from the skull, is mounted on a pedestal. An antelope whose flesh seems to have exploded away from its bones looks at the spectator in dumb shock; a llama, its tongue lolling, rears back in surprise. Of the 3,000 preparations of cadavers and body parts Honoré Fragonard created in his lifetime, about 50 were *écorchés* like the ones in this museum. Dissecting cadavers at the rate of two a week, Fragonard started to develop the techniques that would allow him to preserve and pose his *écorchés*. Although he never revealed his special recipe, he probably followed a technique used by other anatomists, preserving body parts by soaking them in *eau-de-vie* or another alcohol, mixed with pepper and herbs. While they were still supple, Fragonard injected the veins, bronchial tubes, and arteries with colored wax or tallow mixed with turpentine. They were then stretched on a frame in the desired position and left to dry.

While Fragonard was still perfecting his technique, the head of the school, an ambitious aristocrat, was quietly spreading the word that he had a madman on his staff. In the salons of Paris, rumor had it that the figure on the horse was Fragonard's fiancée—who had succumbed to grief after her parents forbade their marriage. (A close inspection of the *Horseman* reveals the rumor was unfounded.) In 1771, at the age of 39, Fragonard was dismissed from the school. If he was insane—and all indications are that he remained perfectly lucid until his death at the age of 66—his brand of folly was particularly in vogue with the European upper classes.

Aristocrats kept him employed creating preparations for their private cabinets of *curiosités* right up to the beginning of the French Revolution. (He died in 1799.)

As the initial horror of Fragonard's creations wears off, questions arise. If this is supposed to be an anatomy lesson, why the elaborate theatricality of the poses? If, on the other hand, this is meant to be art, what kind of sculptor, using what standard of beauty, would devote his life to creating such prodigious monstrosities? Unfortunately, the only possible response to these questions lies in the silence of this neglected museum, in the works themselves. Taciturn in his lifetime, Fragonard spent his days and nights curved over cadavers, and never published a single volume to explain his techniques and motivations. When asked what he was up to in his secluded study, the anatomist's only response was an enigmatic smile and an entreaty, one that is just as valid today: *Venez et voyez.* Come and see.

Taras Grescoe is a freelance writer who lives in Montreal. He's a regular contributor to several publications including Canadian Geographic, The New York Times, Ecotraveler, The Times of London, Islands Magazine, Saveur, *Hong Kong's* Discovery Magazine, *and* Paris Boulevard. *Some readers have detected a slightly morbid streak in his choice of subject matter—bizarre museums, catastrophic floods, chefs who cook with insects—but Grescoe claims that these are the only things that can get him worked up enough to leave the house these days.*

✳

Everything in this city has a quality that defies analysis but enables you to say without any hesitation: "That is Paris"—even if it is only a milk can dangling from a door knob, or one of those coarse brooms sweeping up the leaves at the pavement's edge in October with a sound like the sea, or an array of tired-looking volumes in a bookseller's box on the embankment between the pont Neuf and the pont Royal. Why this should be so I do not know, but Paris sets its seal on everything that belongs to it. The tourists are too distracted or in too much of a hurry to notice it, but the heart of the true Parisian will beat faster, if he is away from Paris, at the memory of a few pots of flowers on a windowsill, or a popular refrain whistled by a butcher's boy as he cycles by. Show him a photograph of a baker's shop with a child eating a croissant, or a photograph of a table or a chair on a pavement with a waiter standing beside them in his white apron, a towel under his arm, and he will think: "That is neither Toulouse nor Lyon nor Marseille, though the casual observer might be deceived. That is Paris. Good or bad, what Paris produces is Paris, be it a letter, a bit of bread, a pair of socks, or a poem. What we give the world, we have borrowed from no one; it is ours. It may be taken from us, stolen from us, but imitated?—never."

                                   —Julian Green, *Paris*, translated by J. A. Underwood

The Fairy Palace

Twenty-nine miles southeast of Paris lies the
other Versailles, Vaux-le-Vicomte.

THERE MAY BE MORE BEAUTIFUL PLACES THAN VAUX-LE-VICOMTE, but I haven't seen them. It is today, as the king's mistress exclaimed when she saw it for the first time over three hundred years ago, a "veritable fairy palace." It is a palace that was built with an extravagance that astounded a very extravagant king.

While both Vaux-le-Vicomte and Versailles were built to impress—and they do—and both palaces were designed by the same team of artists, Vaux is to Versailles as an artist's sketch is to a ponderous finished oil painting. Vaux is human in scale, "of superb and elegant proportions," while Versailles is intentionally overwhelming. In addition to possessing that sense of grandeur and splendor associated with the Age of Louis XIV, Vaux is filled with life and with a sensuous vitality I have found nowhere else.

Seen from the gardens, this domed Baroque palace, which seems to float upon the square reflecting pool, is a gem. And walking inside the château is, for me, like walking inside a many-faceted jewel. Its rooms are elaborately ornamented in a form of decoration first hinted at in Fontainebleau: a breathtaking combination of stucco, gilding, and painting. The subjects are mythological in an idealized, rational, classical landscape. In the Room of the

Muses, where Molière's plays were performed for Nicolas
Fouquet, and Voltaire's performed a generation later, eight muses
luxuriously recline in pairs at the corners of the ceiling. Clio, the
Muse of History, with Prudence and Fidelity at her side, occupies
the center, holding a key: meaning that the past is the key to the
future. Thalia, the Muse of Comedy, draped in blue velvet, holds a
smiling mask in her hand, and a garland of red flowers flows from
her hair; above her, an eagle holds a banner with Fouquet's motto
("*Quo non ascendum*"—"How high shall I not climb?") in his beak.
Euterpe, the Muse of Music, is playing the flute. Terpsichore, the
Muse of Dance, is holding a lute; Calliope, the Muse of Oratory,
a book; Urania, the Muse of Astronomy, a compass and a globe.
The goddess of night, dressed in a film of black, is drawn through
the clouds by two black horses. The carvings, unable to contain
their joy at being at Vaux, seem to burst out of the Baroque frames
created to hold them.

Notably unfinished is the domed grand salon, far more Roman
and Imperial than the rest of the château. On its ceiling, now an
empty sky, Le Brun was to have painted symbolic pictures of
Fouquet's accomplishments.

The gardens at Vaux and those at Versailles were both designed
by Le Nôtre, and both were based on the principles of geometry,
perspective, illusion, and control of nature by man. As is the case
with all Le Nôtre's gardens, they were designed so as not to interfere with the view of the palace, but to enhance it and to harmo-
nize with it. The major differences between the gardens at Vaux
and at Versailles are the scale and the thematic treatments. The
scale is much grander at Versailles. At Vaux, the park, with its statues of mythological Greek gods, succeeds in creating what the ancient Greeks once envisioned: the Elysian Fields, the pagan paradise that only those favored by the gods could enter. At Versailles,
on the other hand, the central theme compares Louis XIV to
Apollo, the Sun God, around whom the universe is in orbit.

Visiting Vaux the first time, after having just seen Le Nôtre's
gardens at Dampierre and Sceaux, I understood the theme and
variations of his designs. Nearest the château on either side of the

central *allée* are two long parterres with intricate swirling designs, which are laid out on the landscape like two elegantly woven oriental carpets. The central *allée* leads from the center of the château terrace into the distance, to a huge statue of the Farnese Hercules, the Greek hero who could not be defeated. Along the way are green parterres crossed by gravel paths and by canals—first two small canals and then the Grand Canal. Each difference in gradation creates illusion and surprise. Carefully pruned shrubs look more carved than real. Rather than colorful flowers, there are graceful plumes of water spouting from a multitude of elaborate fountains. The gardens must be seen when the fountains are in operation, and they are best seen when you look back at the château from the Hercules statue, which stands in the center of a long, sweeping vista bordered by forests on both sides. (It takes about a half hour to walk from the château to the statue.) When Louis XIV walked from the palace to the canal, he passed through crystal walls of water, spouting from a hundred jets, such as those seen today at Sceaux. A 17th-century visitor to Vaux commented, "The air was filled with the sounds of a thousand fountains falling into marvelously fashioned basins, as if it were the throne of Neptune." From the Farnese Hercules you can see the cascades, invisible from the château, where Madame de Sévigné liked to bathe beneath the watchful eyes of the Greek river gods, who recline in hidden grottoes. As I stood here, with the pagan gods in careful attendance, it did appear, as my little book on gardens suggested, that I was in an earthly paradise, and I wished with all my heart to be swimming where Madame de Sévigné swam.

The story of Vaux-le-Vicomte is inseparable from the story of the great party its creator, Nicolas Fouquet, gave there—the party he gave for Louis XIV which so angered the king that he imprisoned the host for the rest of his life.

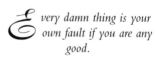

very damn thing is your own fault if you are any good.

—Ernest Hemingway

Fouquet was one of the most unscrupulous, and perhaps the most ambitious, of all Louis XIV's unscrupulous and ambitious ministers. Born in 1615, the descendant of a long line of wealthy judges, he was sent to study with the Jesuits, but his father, soon realizing that his second son was ill-suited for the priesthood, purchased for him, when Nicolas was only sixteen, the position of *avocat* at the Parliament of Paris. From that time on, thanks to the nimbleness of his mind and his boundless energy, his rise was unmarred by setbacks of any kind. At eighteen he was *conseiller* to the Parliament of Metz; at twenty-one, *maître des requêtes*. At thirty-five he purchased the post of *procureur général*, the chief prosecuting officer of the Parliament of Paris. At thirty-six he married Marie-Madeleine Jeannin de Castille, whose immense dowry was added to his growing fortune. Serving as an official in the royal army, he became the cardinal's protégé; when Mazarin was sent into exile during the Fronde, Fouquet protected the cardinal's interests and property until he returned to power in 1653. Mazarin rewarded Fouquet with the post of superintendent of finances, recommending him to the young king by saying, "If they could get women and building out of his head, great things might be done with him."

The great things Fouquet did, however, were at least as much in his own behalf as in the king's. As superintendent of finances, he paid the government's bills partly by borrowing on his own credit, but in the process hopelessly intermingled the public purse with his own; he successfully kept the royal armies outfitted and provisioned and the royal coffers filled, but more successfully, and fraudulently, filled his own. His position as *procureur général* (attorney general) shielded him from investigation, as did Mazarin's favor. Fouquet, noted Louis's mistress Athénaïs de Montespan, was,

> envied by a thousand, provoked indeed a certain amount of
> spite; yet all such vain efforts...to slander him troubled him
> but little. My lord the Cardinal was his support, and so long
> as the main column stood firm, M. Fouquet, lavish of gifts
> to his protector, had really nothing to fear.

But eventually even Mazarin became alarmed at the extent to which Fouquet was diverting the nation's taxes. About to launch an inquiry into Fouquet's activities, however, the aging cardinal realized that the investigation would reveal the immense gifts his protégé had made to *him*—and he let Fouquet off with a warning.

But Fouquet was much more than a financier. He was also a remarkable patron of the arts, a man of superb taste, possessing an uncanny ability to recognize and inspire great talent—in both young and old—in all the arts. He seems to have thought of himself as a 17th-century Maecenas, the ancient Roman patron of the arts who, like himself, was both an adviser to a great ruler (Maecenas to the emperor Augustus) and the most renowned literary patron of his day (among Maecenas's protégés were Horace and Virgil). Comparing the Age of Louis XIV to the Age of Augustus was not uncommon—and there are indeed similarities. It wasn't merely that Voltaire, writing less than a generation later, compared the Grand Siècle to the Augustan Age, or that, as a 20th-century historian of Louis's reign wrote, "Not since Augustus had any monarchy been so adorned with great writers, painters, sculptors, and architects." The people who lived during France's Golden Age saw themselves as the embodiment of all that was to be admired in the ancient world. Louis XIV certainly saw himself as a modern Augustus, and so did artists of his age. In the statue of Louis by Girardon at Vaux, the king is dressed as a Roman emperor, as he is in the painting by Mignard, and the statue in the Venus Drawing Room and the carved medallion in the War Room at Versailles. Louis considered the wall of the Roman Theater of Orange, the one containing the statue of Augustus, "the finest wall in my kingdom." When he tore down the medieval walls surrounding Paris, he built at the entrance to the city a series of triumphal arches, such as Augustus had built at the entrances to Roman cities.

Fouquet gathered around his table, for which the food was prepared by the renowned chef Vatel, France's most celebrated artists and authors, such as Jean de La Fontaine, Paul Scarron, Mademoiselle de Scudéry, Madame de Sévigné. And he was attracted not merely by fame but by talent. The reputation of playwright Pierre Corneille, who did not adhere to the Aristotelian unities of time, place, and action that the Academy considered indispensable in the Golden Age, was so low in 1659 that, unable to bear the prospect of more vicious attacks by French literary critics, he had not written a play in eight years, and, impoverished and depressed, was determined never to write again. Fouquet, however, recognized Corneille's greatness and gave him both a pension and praise—as well as an idea for a new play. He kept encouraging Corneille until he began writing again. Watching Fouquet provide artists with pensions, private rooms in his château, meals prepared by a great chef, and scintillating conversation, an admirer wrote that he had the "true fiber of humanity: he could touch its spring in others and they would answer to him." The artists themselves adored him. For example, from 1654 on, he gave the absentminded La Fontaine a thousand livres a year, the condition being that every three months he was to present Fouquet with a new poem. Books were dedicated to Fouquet, and he appeared as a character in Mademoiselle de Scudéry's novel *Clélie,* in which he is described as a "man who makes nothing but what is great, and whose mind by its vast range cannot conceive little designs."

All of Nicolas Fouquet's love for the arts was poured into Vaux-le-Vicomte.

At the time he bought the property, it held only a tiny fortress and three little villages. The first thing he did was raze them. The second was to plant a forest where they had stood. In the 17th century a forest signified more than trees to a man intent on rising above his station. Like the feudal tower, which was a symbol of feudal authority, the forest was a symbol of a feudal lord's rights, a place where he could hunt and cut down trees for firewood, while the peasantry was forbidden to do so. And Fouquet—whose motto was "How high shall I not climb?"—was very intent upon rising above his station. Then he instructed Le Nôtre to design a park so that it seemed to be carved out of the forest.

To build Vaux he brought together a team of relatively unknown young men whose work had caught his keen eye: the architect Louis Le Vau; the painter Charles Le Brun; and Gilles Guérin and Thibault Poissant for sculpture. Le Brun had a talent for organizing groups of artists. He suggested to Fouquet that

André Le Nôtre, with whom he had developed a friendship while an apprentice in the workshop of Simon Vouet, join the team to design the gardens, and Fouquet agreed. Fouquet gave Le Brun the opportunity to deploy his full artistic talents in the decoration of his château, and Le Brun never again painted as sensuously and movingly as he did at Vaux. His work at Versailles is generally agreed to lack the vitality it has here. The allegorical paintings at Vaux are by his own brush; he provided the designs for the garden sculptures and for the decorative sculptures in the château; and he drew the cartoons for tapestries, which were manufactured at Maincy, where a factory was created to supply Fouquet's needs. Eighteen thousand men worked on building Vaux and its gardens.

Fouquet commissioned and oversaw every detail of construction. You know this, for example, when you look at Le Nôtre's planned landscape designs, now hanging on a wall in the château, and then see Fouquet's alterations in the actual gardens. He filled Vaux's library with 38,544 manuscripts, many of them very rare. Ancient Greek marble statues, 17th-century busts of Socrates and Seneca, tables of porphyry, rare mosaics, a copy of the Talmud, several old copies of the Bible, and other treasures filled its rooms.

When the château was completed, he invited the king and his entire court—all the hundreds of courtiers—to a great *fête* in the king's honor, to take place at Vaux on August 17, 1661. Louis accepted the invitation, but he had already become suspicious of the methods by which his superintendent of finances had obtained the funds to build Vaux. He was beginning to wonder how high Fouquet's ultimate ambitions might reach, and, in fact, had begun subtly to undermine the sources of his power.

Louis's suspicions had been awakened a few months before, when, on March 9, 1661, the dying Mazarin had warned the 22-year-old king about Fouquet's financial manipulations and had recommended another young minister, Colbert, as a safeguard against them.

Colbert found six million livres Mazarin had squirreled away in various places in the Château of Vincennes (that was in addition to the fortune, estimated to be as high as forty million livres, he left his nieces) and shrewdly turned the money over to Louis. From that moment, Louis trusted him implicitly; he would write in his memoirs, "To keep an eye on Fouquet, I associated with him Colbert...in whom I had all possible confidence, for I knew his intelligence and application and honesty." Louis appointed Colbert as Fouquet's "assistant," which meant that every afternoon Fouquet went over accounts with Louis, and every evening Colbert would show Louis how Fouquet had falsified those accounts.

Colbert began to intrigue against Fouquet—and Fouquet, supremely overconfident, didn't bother to defend himself at first. In the meantime, he had purchased his own island—Belle-Ile-en-Mer, off the coast of Brittany—and begun repairing the existing ramparts to create a fortress there. And under the pretext of nurturing an infant sardine industry, he was in effect creating his own fleet by purchasing armed vessels from Holland, which he added to his whaling fleet.

Nothing is so dangerous as weakness, of whatever kind it may be. To command others, one must rise above them; and after having heard all sides, one must decide on what must be done with an open mind, always keeping in view to order or execute nothing unworthy of oneself, of the character one bears, or of the grandeur of the State....

—Louis XIV

But Louis XIV, although certain Fouquet was guilty of embezzlement, did not yet feel in a position to arrest his financial minister. He was too powerful and too popular. His popularity extended from the Parliament of Paris, where his position as *procureur général* protected him from investigation, to the coterie of artists he subsidized, and most important, to Louis's own mother, Anne of Austria, whom Fouquet had often supplied with funds and who was very fond of him.

But Anne's fondness was about to be destroyed—by her old friend the Duchess of Chevreuse. When, on June 27, 1661, the queen mother visited the duchess at Dampierre, Colbert was there; his daughter was about to marry the duchess's son, bringing with her a large dowry, and Colbert and the duchess had become allies. They told Anne how Fouquet was extending his power, buying the support of members of the Parliament and promoting his friends and relatives by means of public money. By the time the queen mother completed her visit to Dampierre, her mind was so poisoned she was ready to accept Fouquet's arrest.

When he learned from spies of Colbert's success in turning the queen mother against him, Fouquet tried to persuade Louis's mistress, Louise de La Vallière, to intercede with the king on his behalf, using a technique that had proved successful with other women. As the keen-eyed Athénaïs de Montespan, whom Louise had brought to court to amuse the king with her charming banter, reported:

> M. Fouquet has one great defect: he took it into his head that every woman is devoid of willpower and of resistance if only one dazzles her eyes with gold. Another prejudice of his was to believe, as an article of faith, that, if possessed of gold and jewels, the most ordinary of men can inspire affection.

> Making this two-fold error his starting point as a principle that was incontestable, he was wont to look upon every beautiful woman who happened to appear on the horizon as his property acquired in advance.

This time, however, the technique failed, although the offer—twenty thousand pistoles, if Louise would speak highly of Fouquet to the king—was certainly generous. Madame de Montespan reported:

> To his extreme astonishment, this young beauty declined to understand such language. Couched in other terms, he renewed his suit, yet apparently was no whit less obscure than on the first occasion. Such a scandal as this well-nigh put him to the blush, and he was obliged to admit that this modest maiden wither affected to be, or really was, utterly extraordinary.

Finally, according to Louis's biographer, Vincent Cronin, Louise replied, "with scorn in her voice," that "not for a quarter of a million pistoles would she commit such an indiscretion," and she complained to Louis that Fouquet had insulted her.

Fouquet also underestimated the young king. Although Louis XIV had told Fouquet at Mazarin's death that he would be his own chief minister, (*"Il est temps que je les gouverne moi-même"*), Fouquet, knowing Louis's passion for women, hunting, and the ballet—Louis was an enthusiastic and graceful dancer—had not taken him seriously, had not taken the measure of the man with whom he was dealing. Louis, however, understood Fouquet all too well. The king now tricked him into selling the position of *procureur général,* which protected him from investigation, by hinting that he would appoint Fouquet to Mazarin's old post as head of government if only a conflict of interest between his position with the Parliament and his potential position as minister could be resolved. When he learned that Fouquet had decided to sell, Louis informed Colbert, "He is digging his own grave."

The great *fête* at Vaux was the last straw.

Fouquet's building of a grand château at Vaux was not unusual, nor was his invitation to the king. Both Cardinals Richelieu and Mazarin had built sumptuous châteaux while they were ministers to the king. René de Longueil had built Maisons-Laffitte while he was superintendent of finances, and had entertained Louis when the king hunted in the forests of St-Germain-en-Laye. And Colbert, of course, built Sceaux. But this party went beyond the others.

Historians say it was equaled by only one or two celebrations over the entire history of France. Meals were served on solid gold plates; there were ballets, concerts, and a play written by Molière for the occasion. Molière dressed in everyday clothes and greeted the assembled courtiers opposite the cascade, saying he had no actors and no time to prepare the entertainment that was expected, unless some unforeseen help was forthcoming. A shell thereupon opened to reveal a naiad and actors dressed as statues came to life, and *Les Fâcheux* was presented.

Since Athénaïs de Montespan was there, I will let her speak:

On reaching Vaux-le-Vicomte, how great and general was our amazement! It was not the well-appointed residence of a minister, it was not a human habitation that presented itself to our view—it was a veritable fairy palace. All in this brilliant dwelling was stamped with the mark of opulence and of exquisite taste in art. Marbles, balustrades, vast staircases, columns, statues, groups, bas-reliefs, vases, and pictures were scattered here and there in rich profusion, besides cascades and fountains innumerable. The large salon, octagonal in shape, had a high vaulted ceiling, and its flooring of mosaic looked like a rich carpet embellished with birds, butterflies, arabesques, fruits and flowers.

On either side of the main edifice, and somewhat in the rear, the architect had placed smaller buildings, yet all of them ornamented in the same sumptuous fashion; and these served to throw the château itself into relief. In these adjoining pavilions there were baths, a theater, a *paume ground* [tennis court], swings, a chapel, billiard rooms, and other salons.

One noticed magnificent gilt roulette tables and sedan chairs of the very best make. There were elegant stalls at which trinkets were distributed to the guests—notebooks, pocket mirrors, gloves, knives, scissors, purses, fans, sweetmeats, scents, pastilles, and perfumes of all kinds.

But to Louis, aware by this time of Fouquet's financial manipulations, such extravagance was proof of how much his minister had stolen from him. As Athénaïs put it:

It was as if some evil fairy had prompted the imprudent minister to act in this way, who, eager and impatient for his own ruin, had summoned the King to witness his appalling systems of plunder in its entirely, and had invited chastisement.

And finally there was the incident of the forest. The king liked the view from the balcony of his apartment at Vaux—except for one large, rather barren-looking clearing. He mentioned this to his host, who, while the king slept, put hundreds of peasants to work. When Louis awoke the next morning and stepped out on the balcony, the clearing was completely filled with full-grown trees. Recounted Athénaïs:

> Fouquet, with airy presumption, expected thanks and praise. This, however, was what he had to hear: "I am shocked at such expense!"

Louis, infuriated, wanted to arrest Fouquet on the spot, but his mother persuaded him that this would be unseemly behavior for a guest. So he waited for nineteen days, and then, as Fouquet left the royal presence, had him arrested by d'Artagnan, the most trusted of the royal musketeers.

The trial that followed lasted three years. The artists Fouquet had supported now supported him and, as Madame de Sévigné wrote to him, "count chances on their fingers, melt with pity, with apprehension, hoping, hating, admiring; some of us are sad, some of us are overwhelmed. In short, my dear sir, the state in which we live is an extraordinary one, but the resignation and courage of our dear sufferer are almost more than human." It was what she wrote on November 20, after attending his trial, that made me cry:

> As he was returning by the arsenal on foot for exercise, M. Fouquet asked who were those workmen he perceived. He was told that they were people altering the basin of a fountain. He went up to them and gave his advice; and then turning to d'Artagnan [said] "Do you wonder that I should interfere? I was formerly considered clever at these sorts of things."

While most of the judges were in favor of merely exiling Fouquet from France, the king intervened and increased the sentence from exile to life imprisonment. Fouquet, who loved beauty and women, would spend the rest of his life under heavy guard in a cold, damp dungeon in the Pignerol fortress in the Alps.

(Various theories arose to explain the harshness of Fouquet's sentence. One suggested a link to the Man in the Iron Mask, Louis's supposed twin brother and a threat to his throne; this explanation provided Alexandre Dumas with the story line for *Le Vicomte de Bragelonne*. Those preferring a soap opera version saw Fouquet's imprisonment as the result of his attempted seduction of Louise de La Vallière, the king's mistress. Others claimed that Louis, who had been forced to melt his silver to pay for his wars, became furious when served a sumptuous supper on gold plates.)

Louis XIV arrested Fouquet three weeks after seeing Vaux-le-Vicomte, but he entertained no animosity toward the artists who had created it. Instead, the entire team assembled by Fouquet to create Vaux (along with several hundred of Fouquet's orange trees) were brought to Versailles to create the great palace that Louis XIV had envisioned while standing on the escarpment at St-Germain-en-Laye.

Bob and I have been to Vaux-le-Vicomte a number of times. It is not far from Orly, and whenever we rent a car at the airport, we try to stop at Vaux before making our way south.

We have visited Vaux both on days when the fountains are in operation and on days when they are not. I highly advise making

O nly minutes outside Paris I am winging down a country road. There are crisp blue skies and a wisp of wood smoke in the air, but the once-royal forests are still deep emerald and the fields of Ile-de-France still glow golden in the September sun. The historical core of the country, Ile-de-France encircles Paris in a pastoral halo, threaded with rivers and studded with ancient cities, new towns, and an unparalleled wealth of cathedrals, churches, and châteaux—Versailles, Fontainebleau, Vaux-le-Vicomte, St-Denis, St-Germain-en-Laye, Malmaison—magic names all, and all within easy reach.

As I cross the plain south of Paris, blond as the renowned Brie cheese they produce, I am retracing the route of medieval traders as they carried their wares to market in the 12th-century citadel of Provins. Granted safe conduct by the powerful counts of Champagne, they came by the thousands, with dancing bears and musicians, furs and gold, honey and oils, wines and spices, silks and embroideries from Provence, Italy, Spain, Germany, the Baltic, and the Orient.

—Jean Bond Rafferty, "The Magical Secrets of Paris-Ile-de-France," *France Discovery Guide* sure they are on before visiting the gardens. On our last day in France, we decided to visit Louis XIV in Paris. We began at the Louvre, which had been his palace for the first 28 years of his reign, the years he was transforming France into the most powerful and civilized country in Europe. There, in the Louis XIV Galleries, we could see the furniture he used, the Savonnerie carpets he walked on, the Gobelin tapestries and Le Brun paintings that hung on his walls, and the sculptures by Girardon and Coysevox he chose to have near him. We entered the palace grounds as Louis XIV would have wanted—through the pavilion he commissioned. He wanted the pavilion to possess a grand and impressive façade, which would tell the world they were entering the palace of a great king. Voltaire felt he had succeeded, calling this façade "one of the most august monuments of architecture in the world," adding that "no palace in Rome has an entrance comparable." I had seen it before—the whole previous summer I had routinely passed through it on my way somewhere else. I confess, however, I hadn't taken much notice of it. As I stood there looking at it, I realized that it reminded me of something, that its design echoed the style of the Maison Carrée, that perfect Roman temple which had left me totally unimpressed in Nîmes. While I now understood that I could never share Voltaire's ecstatic reaction to the façade—the style is not to my taste—I was nonetheless impressed with the young king who oversaw its construction. The leading architect of the day, the 66-year-old Bernini, who had just completed Saint Peter's Square in Rome, was commissioned to design this façade. Louis XIV, only 27 at the time, demonstrating those aesthetic qualities which set such uncompromising standards for the art of his age, rejected the revered old man's designs. The Baroque pavilion Bernini envisioned would have been inconsistent both with the elegant architecture of Louis's age and with the preexisting pavilions at the Louvre.

Once I was in the Cour Carrée, surrounded by the gleaming white stone and frilly Corinthian columns, the caryatides supporting the dome of the Clock Pavilion, the friezes of cherubs and garlands, it was not difficult to imagine being in the royal courtyard of a palace. I was reminded of the places I had been and kings I had visited on my journey through France when I saw the initials carved in the stone of the four pavilions: the intertwined "H" and "D" of Henry II and his mistress Diane that I had seen at Chenonceau and Anet (initials that Catherine de' Medici, acting as regent after Henry's death, contended were an "H" and a reversed "C"); the solitary "H" of Henry III, Catherine's transvestite son, the last of the Valois line, whom I had visited at Blois; the "H D B" of Henry IV, the first of the Bourbon line, and his initial again, this time joined by the "G" of his favorite mistress, Gabrielle d'Estrées, whose children played at court with the dauphin, the future Louis XIII; and the "LA" for Louis XIII and Anne of Austria, whose union finally produced Louis XIV and the age I had just briefly visited.

Later that day we left the Louvre through the Court of Napoleon and found ourselves facing the Arc de Triomphe du Carrousel, which Napoleon commissioned to commemorate his victories of 1805. It is a triple arch, like the Roman arch at Orange, topped with horses and a chariot, as that Roman arch once had been. Both arches, after their completion, underwent rededication. The four horses Napoleon placed on top were the four gilded bronze horses that his troops had removed from Saint Mark's Cathedral in Venice after he conquered Italy. Those magnificent horses were returned to Venice after Napoleon's defeat at Waterloo. The reins of the horses now there are held by a Goddess symbolizing the restoration—which, after Napoleon's defeat, the arch was then intended to honor. The arch at Orange had originally commemorated the victories of Caesar's Second Legion but was later rededicated to the Emperor Tiberius's victory over a Gallic rebellion led by Sacrovir. Napoleon was dissatisfied with this tiny arch as soon as it was built, and commissioned the Arc de Triomphe to honor the glory of his Imperial Army. In the distance, we could see, as Napoleon never would, that grand and monumental arch atop the Étoile hill, and beyond it, La Défense, the symbol of modern Paris which I wished would go away.

From the Louvre we walked up the great mall to the Hôtel de

Invalides, the last group of buildings in Paris built during the reign
of Louis XIV. Before reading Voltaire, I was unaware that Louis
built this immense hospital and old-age home for his wounded
veterans; I associated the Invalides with Napoleon, since it is the
Emperor's magnificent tomb that dominates its domed church, and
it is the Emperor's accomplishments that are carved in stone in the
crypt encircling the magnificent red porphyry sarcophagus that sits
upon a base of green granite. (Just as I had been unaware that the
Place Vendôme—dominated by a statue of Napoleon atop a tall
column made from 1,200 cannons he captured in one of his victories—had actually been built by Louis, and was once called
"Place Louis Le Grand.")

When we arrived at the Invalides, I remembered at once the
helmeted windows in the Mansard roof, which reminded me of a
battalion of knights, but was surprised to see prominently carved
over the entrance gate a bas-relief equestrian figure of Louis XIV.
There he was, standing between Prudence and Justice, but I had
somehow missed him on previous visits. In my mind, I had associated Louis XIV with Versailles and Napoleon with the Invalides. I
walked through the huge Roman arched entrance into the courtyard with its two tiers of arches marching around its sides, and was
reminded of the Pont du Gard and of the arches marching through
the wilderness of Languedoc that the Romans had built almost
two thousand years before to bring water to the fountains of
Nîmes. To me, those arches in the Invalides brought back the smell
of wild rosemary and the taste of picnics, but to Louis they meant
the glory and power of Rome.

After dinner that night, as we walked back to our apartment, we
passed the Place de la Concorde. There, Paris was a collage of
monuments to kings and emperors, lit against the sky, vying for
posterity's attention. As we came to the Rond-Point, I turned and
saw the freshly gilded and illuminated dome of the Invalides. Louis
had commissioned the huge, soaring, majestic dome above its
church to represent "the glory of my reign." It seemed to float
above Paris, a ghostly golden crown in a velvety blue-black sky,
regal and majestic, a symbol of the Golden Age of France. I felt

Louis was beckoning me to remember the splendor and magnificence of his age, and I was reminded of all the kings before Louis who wore the royal crown.

Ina Caro is a writer and historian who has traveled throughout France since 1978 studying its history. She was the sole researcher on award-winning biographies of Robert Moses and Lyndon Johnson written by her husband, Robert A. Caro, and she is the author of The Road from the Past: Traveling Through History in France, *from which this story was taken.*

❋

Louis XIV had commissioned the Hôtel des Invalides for his old soldiers in 1670. Designed to accommodate 7,000 disabled veterans, it was altogether grander than anything the V.A. has ever come up with. Life within its walls was rigorously, indeed rather monastically, organized and revolved around church observances. What we visit today as two churches, the Eglise des Soldats and the Eglise du Dôme, was conceived as Siamese twins, sharing a common sanctuary and altar. The Eglise des Soldats was intended for the residents of the Hôtel des Invalides; the Eglise du Dôme was reserved for royal use. The first was based on a design by Libéral Bruant, overall architect of the Hôtel; it was elaborated and carried out by Jules Hardouin-Mansart. The second was from the drawing board of Hardouin-Mansart—or, perhaps more precisely, that of his great-uncle, François Mansart, as Hardouin-Mansart seems to have lifted most of the hastily commissioned design from his uncle's plans for an unbuilt Bourbon chapel intended for St-Denis.

Whoever its designer, the Eglise du Dôme is a marvel, the organic perfection of which could only have made inserting a tomb worthy of Napoleon the more daunting. Nor were the problems exclusively aesthetic, as there were those who saw the "usurpation" of this right royal church by the "Emperor" Napoleon as criminal.

An architectural competition yielded a variety of schemes, the best of which was judged to be that of Ludovico Tullius Joachim Visconti, a naturalized Italian. Confronted with altering a beloved monument, Visconti found a solution that was much the same as I. M. Pei's when the latter was faced with an analogous problem at the Louvre more than a century later: dig.

—Catharine Reynolds, "Napoleon's Return to Les Invalides," *Gourmet*

PART THREE

GOING YOUR OWN WAY

✦ ✦ ✦

My Idea of Paris

The city is a tapestry of memory and magic.

"WE KEPT VERY STILL OF COURSE," WROTE ELIZABETH BARRETT Browning, "and were satisfied with the *idea* of Paris."

I sure know what Elizabeth meant. We've been to Paris five times, but the very idea of Paris still seduces—I lust over memories. Yet, at night, when I lie in my husband's arms, it is not recent, sybaritic images I conjure to lure him into that intimate realm only two people who've danced through life together can enter—the realm of memory. No. At night, fancy restaurants, scenic boat rides, châteaux and boutiques evaporate. In their place float up memories, strange and strong. Up floats an *idea* of Paris from my first visit a quarter century ago, when I was 22 and newly wed.

It is a Paris of passion and elemental wonder. It is the Paris I knew when young and poor, and free of all desires except to experience. Of course, even then I had an idea of Paris. That's why when we drove into the city in our VW van, I dressed in what I fancied were "Parisian" clothes. Never mind they were Parisian clothes of some other century. In my long black skirt, black boots, hoop earrings, flea market scarf of pink silk, I felt Paris personified.

The moment I arrived in the City of Light, I was lit. "We must stay at least a month," I told Steve, my husband. "Let's enjoy Paris!"

Paris was expensive and we had little money but I made a fuss so at last he said "All right, we'll stay...but we'll have to camp."

"Camp!" I cried. "In Paris? Nobody camps in Paris!"

We did.

That night we rolled our van, outfitted with no more than a mattress, down the ramp to the Quai de la Tournelle where vehicles are forbidden. We parked at the edge of the river, just past the Pont de la Tournelle. When we looked left, we could see the stone bridge with its little statue of St. Geneviève and beyond, the floodlit Cathedral of Notre Dame. Looking right, we saw our quay merge with the next then vanish in murky shadows. In front of us, across the narrow arm of the river, rose the elegant apartments of the Ile St-Louis.

We climbed in the back of our van, lay on the mattress and looked out the windows.

Magic.

The effect was as if we were both inside the van and out of it too. At once cozy in an enclosed, secret place, and also right out in the city. In its very heart. Above us, apartments loomed into the stars, their lacy iron balconies bathed in light, and at our feet, the Seine flowed discreetly southward.

"Let's enjoy Paris," Steve murmured.

Now a lot of practical things can get in the way of romance, such as the need for a bathroom. But we had the courage of youth and didn't let it. The next afternoon we sat on the riverbank planning just which cafés' restrooms we would discreetly visit at what times of day when a van, big and white as an ambulance, pulled up next to ours. A young man stepped out. He wore no shirt and balanced a hammer vertically on his nose.

"Gidday," he said.

This was Basil Didier, a Mormon New Zealander who'd come to Paris to research his genealogy.

His trick turned the wheel of camaraderie. We had a few laughs together, then, seeing our interest in his Citroen delivery van, he asked, "Would you like a perv?" which is New Zealand for "Would you like to take a look?"

We were awed by the ingenious cabinetry. The seat that evolved into a bed, the stove built into the counter, the table hung on the wall like a picture, and the sink with its clever foot pump, small as a piano pedal.

"I'm a carpenter," Basil said with down-under modesty. But when I opened the narrow door and discovered a flush toilet, I knew he was more than a carpenter. He was our friend.

There must have been something in the air that August of 1971. The next day two more vans arrived. One was inhabited by a young New York couple who'd just returned from North Africa. The other, a rusted black Fiat, contained a bearded artist from Hawaii named Hayden and his black dog, Mahler. Of an evening, the couple would regale us with their adventures in Morocco and Hayden would recount the curious theatrics performed by a tribe of gypsies he'd lived with in Toulouse. For the next month, the six of us shared food, opinions, toilets, and, at sunset, *vin rouge*. Surely there was alchemy at work for though it was totally *défendu* to camp there, directly across, as we learned, from the island home of Prime Minister Pompidou, the *gendarmes* never told us to leave. *Au contraire*! Each night a *gendarme* would stop by our van to check passports and to see that we were all right.

"*Ça va, les jeunes Américains?*"

"*Ça va*," we replied.

Now one warm evening, as Hayden was inside his van painting on its walls by candlelight what he called his "private version of Paris," and the New Yorkers were playing gin rummy, and Mahler was barking at every kerosene barge that chugged up the river, Basil and I sat on the quay, dangling our feet over the water. Steve and I were drinking wine and trying in vain to get Basil to taste the marked-down cheese we'd bought from the Monoprix. But Basil was too busy preaching how French cheeses were decadent. "Food is just matter to fill up space," he said.

Then he went on about sex.

Mormonism forbids sex before marriage and in his opinion that was "too right" for any fool could see sex is merely a fad. A style! A fashion!

"Sex," Basil declared, "is just Gucci Hootchie Kootchie."

𝒟uring our dinner at a bistro somewhere in the Quartier Latin I gave C. a gold necklace studded with tiny jewels and matching our wedding rings, and the wine became even more red and golden and bewitching. Around midnight we were back in the rue Tournon, a little tipsy and a lot happy. I watched C. undress and in spite, or because, of the wine I was able to quote a stanza of Baudelaire's I had memorized twenty years ago: "La très-chère était nue, et, connaissant mon coeur, she had left on her jewels, the bangles and chains whose jingling music gave her the conquering air of a Moorish slave on days her master is pleased..."

—Wulf Diedrich Rehder,
"C., Diderot and I"

Bored with his ideas, we told him one of ours: to drive from France to India. "And what we need," Steve explained, "is a camper, fixed up like yours."

Basil was happy to take the bait for he said he was "right tired of looking up dead Didiers" and would be pleased to help us make our van into a camper. However, our joy turned to dejection when we realized the impossibility of such a project, which required power tools, for we had no electricity nor access to it. "Too bad too," I said, "when there's electricity all around us..."

The maintenance crew at the College de France looked up from their lunches, astonished when we drove into the courtyard.

"Why are you driving your vehicle in here?" demanded a gray-haired man in overalls.

"Where else would we outfit it for the expedition?" Steve retorted.

"What expedition?" the man asked, as the rest of the crew stared.

"What expedition?" I asked myself silently.

Then in the same ringing tone that Métro stations are called out, Steve announced, "*L'Expédition à l'Afrique du Nord!*" The man looked skeptical and the other men laughed. Then Steve began relating the details of our "*expédition scientifique*," how we needed to collect flowers in Morocco and how outfitting the van for this botanical study was part of the project. Steve blended gobbledygook with what the New Yorkers had told us about Morocco.

The man threw his cigarette butt on the ground. "I'm sorry but my men cannot help. Union rules absolutely prevent involvement."

"*Monsieur!*" Steve cried, "We wouldn't dream of troubling you. We only need to use the electricity here…and some power tools."

The man paused, looking hard at Steve and me. And in that pause I dared hope he'd play accomplice to honeymooners. Then in a voice low and sly, like beer trickling out of a jug, the man said, "Well then, it's not impossible, is it?"

For the next three weeks we spent our mornings in construction. Basil drew a blueprint copying the classic VW camper interior. The crew chatted with us every day and cheered us on. They not only supplied power tools, but gave us steel rods and rollers from the lab to make the couch scoot into a bed. They also told us where to find scraps and army surplus items. While Steve and Basil built the cabinetry, I bought the supplies and sewed curtains.

Then, each afternoon, when Basil went off to his French class at the Alliance Francaise, Steve and I fell in love all over again. With each other and with Paris.

We strolled the Left Bank bookstores, plugging head first into musty books, anticipating delight in finding just the right one—for each other. We read Baudelaire at twilight in the spooky ruins of l'Arène de Lutèce, a Roman amphitheater off the rue Monge. We sipped tea in tulip shaped glasses in the garden of the Paris mosque, and every other day crossed the bridge to the Ile St-Louis to bathe at the municipal baths. In our private washroom, as we splashed each other with warm water from the copper pail, we were serenaded by the soulful tunes of the Moslem men who sang in their showers. "Mustafaaaa, Mustafaaaaaaaaa!" they wailed. Rising and dipping, their songs reverberated off the tile walls and washed us in music. Then damp-haired, we'd stroll at dusk along the river bank, our sandals clapping on the cobblestones while above us chestnut leaves fluttered silently like the wings of giant butterflies.

The day our van was finished was also the day Basil ran off to Toulouse with his French teacher, Jacqueline. It was also the day before Pompidou was to return. And the day the *gendarmes* told us to go. "We have to leave all this beauty!" I cried. To cheer me, Steve said we'd have a farewell *tête à tête* in a restaurant. That evening we climbed up the steep market street, rue Mouffetard, but found all the restaurants full. Ambling down an alley we came upon a Chinese restaurant jammed with boisterous diners at tables no bigger than record albums.

"*Entrez! Entrez!*" the diners shouted at us. We were lured inside and before we understood what was happening, tables got squeezed together and we were seated with two men plowing through some inscrutable Chinese dish.

The two were as different as gruyère from gruel. One was tall and elegant with dark wavy hair. An architect, dressed in a chic suit, the other was short, fat and had a ruddy face. He appeared to be some sort of factory worker for he wore the blue working class jacket. In minutes we were drinking wine, enjoying mushy chow mein and listening to the men bemoan how Paris was no fun anymore as nowadays people were obsessed with making a living.

"WHAT A PITY WE'VE FORGOTTEN THE ZANY LITTLE WAYS OF LIFE!" the architect wailed and we all drank a toast to this loss, feeling giddy with joy.

As the evening wore on, I no longer cared that my intimate dinner had turned into a *tête à tête à tête à tête à tête*. We drank a lot of wine and laughed like crazy. In fact, the whole restaurant was a boat of merrymakers on the brink of capsizing.

When the lugubrious waiter asked if we'd like dessert, and I declined, the architect appeared offended.

"Do you mean to say, Madame, that you won't even try *la banane du chef*? It is the specialty of the house!"

"I don't have room for it," I answered.

"Nonsense! No room! You will have the room when you taste it!"

"Very true," the ruddy faced man said. "It tastes like nothing else in the world! Am I not right?" he asked the waiter. The waiter nodded as one might on identifying a body in the morgue.

"Why don't you try it, if it's that good?" Steve urged, knowing my fondness for sweets.

"I'll have *la banane du chef*," I said to the waiter.

As conversation and wine flowed, it occurred to me (through a little haze) that this dessert was taking quite a long time. I was about to question the waiter when the lights in the restaurant went out, plunging us in darkness and causing a collective scream from the patrons. Then the kitchen door was flung open and our waiter walked through the black restaurant holding high a tray with a flaming dessert. Somberly he made his way to our table, guided by the blue-yellow light of the flames. He set the plate in front of me and announced gravely, "Madame, *la banane du chef!*" These words brought a hand-clapping and foot-stomping from the other diners. I looked down.

Banana fritters formed in the shape of a male's private parts.

Every eye in the place was on me, waiting for me to take a bite but I was giggling so much, I couldn't. At last, when I did take that first bite, loud cries of "Ooh La La!" went up and the lights came on. All four of us shared the dessert, which was delicious. After dinner, Steve took my hand and led me up rue Mouffetard. Up and up we wound our way through the medieval street. The night was bright with moonlight which gave the ancient gray houses the look of tarnished silver. We stopped and kissed, our bodies like clasped hands.

"Where are we going?" I whispered.

"You'll see."

We threaded up and around some side streets until suddenly Paris was spread before us. How beautiful it looked then! Exactly like my idea of Paris. Like *everyone's* idea of Paris. Vibrant and askew. The gold-lit Eiffel tower tilted jauntily, and for a beret, wore the moon. The *bâteaux mouches* were now spaceships floating on black iridescent ribbon, while at the Place de la Concorde, the obelisk was a rocket taking off. And far at the city's cusp sailed Sacré-Coeur—a white ship guided by stars. Yes, that night it seemed Paris, in sympathy with us, twinkled and trembled, and leaned too in fervent anticipation. An excited city listing toward love.

So if in the day, I recount some delightful French meal, shopping discovery, historical site or museum exhibit, you'll understand if I say that at night, a more passionate nostalgia beckons. At night, when I lie in my husband's arms, I need only whisper "Gucci Hootchie Kootchie" or "*l'expédition scientifique*" or, if feeling particularly naughty, "*la banane du chef*" to lure us into the realm of memory. Lure us back to that long-ago couple, fearless and fanciful. Back to the quivering nights of a time-distant Paris when the air was dusty with miracles and the stars were hung lower. Closer to our hearts.

Maxine Rose Schur is a travel essayist, marketing consultant, and the author of numerous children's books. She has a passion for discovering a country's art and culture. Her most recent creation is Enchanted Islands: Voices and Visions from the Caribbean, *a gift journal that showcases contemporary art and poetry from the Caribbean islands. An instructor at Mills College, she lives in San Mateo, California and is currently working on an anthology of her essays.*

★

Wet petals sticking to a sky born nude.
The magnitudes, insights, fears and proofs
Were your unconscious gift. They still weigh
With the weight of Paris forever hanging
White throat wearing icy gems,
A parody of stars as yet undiscovered.
Here they tell me I have come to terms.
But supposing I had chosen to march on you
Instead of on such a star—what then?
Instead of this incubus of infinite duration,

I mean to say, whose single glance
Brings loving to its knees?
Yes, wherever the ant-hills empty
Swarm the fecund associations, crossing
And recrossing the sky-pathways of sleep.
We labour only to be relatively
Sincere as ants perhaps are sincere.
Yet always the absolute vision must keep
The healthy lodestar of its stake in love.
You'll see somewhere always the crystal body
Transparent, held high against the light
Blaze like a diamond in the deep.
How can a love of life be ever indiscreet
For even in that far dispersing city today
Ants must turn over in their sleep.

—Lawrence Durrell, *Spirit of Paris: Letters and Essays on Travel*

NANCY LYON

Busking for Supper

Mother and daughter take to the streets.

PEG AND I SAT AT OUR WOBBLY TABLE UNDER THE STARS, HIGH above the molten traffic streams on the rue de Rivoli. I raised my glass of champagne to toast her debut. "Edith Piaf couldn't have done better," I said proudly, and imagined Peg getting so good she'd leave me to my raggedy harp case as little Edith had left her acrobat father to pass his own hat in the smoky alleys of the Latin Quarter.

Peg had always dreamed of Paris, but not like this, hefting a backpack and soliciting money for her daughter in an old goatskin drum. In her younger days she had left Indianapolis, packed off to Mexico for a summer in an old Ford woody with four small daughters and no man and no Spanish. But this was a different kind of adventure, making music in the streets of Europe for crowds of tourists, when all she had ever played was a plastic tonette in a music class for elementary schoolteachers.

"You said you'd show me the Louvre!" Peg laughed. "I expected to see what was *inside*!"

Today all we had seen was the Louvre's Métro station, the museum's endless tunnel façade and those dank, moldy underpasses where flute players vied for good acoustics and foot traffic. After an hour's exploration, we finally made our stage at the top of some stone steps flanked by majestic pillars. I tuned my Irish harp, plugged in my amp, started up a jig, and Peg was on. She would pass around that Irish *bódhran* like a giant offertory plate, charming the tourists into lavishing us with enough francs for dinner and a night on the town.

Members of our audience draped themselves on the Louvre's sunny steps, eating popcorn and hot dogs, feeding the pigeons and smiling blankly, while I attempted to rouse them with stirring battle marches and rollicking hornpipes. Peg smiled at any face and, with quivering lips, held forth the *bódhran*. But when she was expecting roses and *billets-doux* for her lovely daughter, they gave her popcorn and centimes. I played harder, but the spectators took more interest in the tour buses disgorging the belongings of the Muncie, Indiana Bowling Team. There came a moment when Peg might have cringed and gone to eat a hot dog. But instead she narrowed her eyes, tightened her lips, and sidled up to a chic *bon-homme*. *"Aimez-vous la harpe?"* she said in trembling high school French. *"C'est ma petite jeune fille qui joue."*

We didn't make enough for a dinner at La Tour d'Argent, but there was always tomorrow. I wouldn't have invited my mother to Paris if I thought we'd starve. After seven years of "busking," as my profession is called, on stages as diverse as the foyer of a Reno casino, a milk crate in a Dublin alleyway, a flower-pot in a Swiss shopping arcade, and among the vegetable stands at the city market in Indianapolis, I knew how to be resourceful. This adventure was going to revive Peg's spirit of independence, dispel the gloom that had settled over her since the last one of her brood, my younger brother, Robert, had left the nest. And I knew it would be great to have her along as my pal and business partner; mother, 62, daughter, 33, side by side.

Peg took two daisies from our vase of street-corner flowers, put one behind my ear and flamboyantly tossed the other to the traffic below. As it fluttered for eight stories, she exclaimed over the amazing ascent to our room up the dizzying, endlessly spiraling lino-covered staircase echoing with sizzling lamb and Tunisian laughter. From a Poughkeepsie apartment to the Hôtel de Paris. It sounded elegant, and you might say it was. The view from our table was certainly splendid. In one direction, the illumined column of the Place de la Bastille glowed like a lit firecracker, and in the other we could see the floodlit snarling gargoyles of Châtelet. Across Napoleon's grandest boulevard, in the windows of the gracious mansard-roofed apartments, TV sets flickered and burbled with French comedies, and knickers fluttered in the wind. And inside our *petite chambre* was a comedy of backpacks, tent, amplifier, *bódhran* case, lumpy bag of books, the Irish harp I built in a night-school wood-working class in Brooklyn, and Peg's fire-engine red sleeping bag and tin cup, her *bon voyage* presents. Upon that bed was our first day's wages: a tiny heap of francs and centimes, pfennigs, guilders, and miscellaneous lire.

T hen I recalled Jean Cocteau's saying: "Poets don't die, they only pretend to." They live on in their poems, songs, voices, and today it is not just Jacques' songs that "whirl in the streets," but his stories and anecdotes too, which have become part of his legend. One day for example he had came across a blind beggar sitting on the pavement in a town in the South of France, his hat in front of him on the ground to receive coins, and a placard saying: Blind Man Without a Pension.

"How is it going?" asks Prévert.

"Oh, very badly. People just pass by and drop nothing in my hat, the swine!" replied the beggar.

"Listen, let me turn your placard round and I guarantee you a fortune."

A few days later he sees the blind beggar again, and asks how he is faring:

"Fantastic! My hat fills up three times a day."

On the back of his placard Prévert had scribbled: "Spring is coming, but I shan't see it."

—Shusha Guppy, *A Girl in Paris*

Like any business, busking had its good and bad days. It was a gambling game with crazy odds—the public, the cops, the weather, the competition, and your own energy and mood. One day you made lots of money and spent it; the next day the cops shooed you away or it rained or a fleet of street acts took over the town and you lived on baguettes. Sometimes nobody listened and you felt like a fool. But sometimes it was a high-wire circus act with a cheering crowd, a pot of gold, an action-packed street drama—thrilling, joyous, even profound. I knew our act would improve when I taught Peg to play that goatskin drum. She would pound out a leathery beat to my wild tin-whistle reels, and people would fling open their shutters and mob us to see our show.

Peg had ideas of her own. "We need a gimmick," she said intently. "My blue jeans and tennies are just too straight. Wouldn't it be wild if we could find French flics' uniforms. Go busking dressed as *police*!"

"Police! Good God!" Clearly the champagne was having its effect.

No doubt Paris *was* the epicenter of the busking universe: with a traveling circus of Greek panpipers, Romanian acrobats, French mimes, country and western crooners, fiddlers and puppeteers, magicians and jugglers—who could eat fire, juggle plums, pull rabbits from silk hats, and tap dance. To get a good busking pitch was at least as hard as getting a part in a Broadway play. In one Métro tunnel a tiny marionette mimed Stravinsky on a tiny violin while a saffron-robed sitarist sat curled in ragas against the angry tides. In another, a torrent of rock music crashed over us—an eight-piece band in mean leather jackets, while through the din droned a lone accordion. At the peak of rush hour, every time the train doors opened, we heard yet another sound. In the Métro cars commuters were entertained by a strolling Japanese guitarist singing "Ret It Be" over and over, and a fully-staged puppet production of *Le Petit Prince*, red velvet curtain and all.

As we were leaving the last Métro tunnel trudging home toward the Hôtel de Paris, Peg jabbed me and pointed. There stood a thin tube of a woman well into her eighties, dressed in a faded smock that hung loosely above her bobby socks and gumshoes. She stood motionless, like a reed on a bed of brown cloth while people threw money at her feet.

"Look at *that!*" Peg huffed. "Sure I could do *that!*"

June 30, Hôtel de Paris

Bonjour, Robert!

I love this life of wandering troubadour. Last night Nan and I played at Montmartre with the lights of Paris swimming in a mist below us. Nan says I'm getting great on that drum of hers, though the stick keeps flying out of my hand. Yesterday we met a busker who does a trained goat act—the goat climbs a ladder and stands on a tin can. He asked me to play my drum for his goat, and then to join him on the road. Of course I said no. How's P'keepsie? Wish you could see us. Tomorrow we head to the French Riviera, mobs of tourists and broiling sun.

Miss you.

Love,

Mom

July 5, Cassis

Dear Denise,

Peg and I arrived on French Riviera in a hurricane with our bicycles, where it's too mountainous to ride them. And we're a week early for the tourists! Peg nearly mutinied, but last night she met a very nice widower, a fire-eater traveling with his daughter, who took a sympathetic interest in us. I hate these cheap resort towns— bikinis and stiletto heels on motorbikes. No place for an Irish harp.

Love,

Nan

August 31, Paris

Dear Denise,

Here we are at the end of our misadventures and I'm nostalgic already. Peg's notebooks are filled with French noses she sketched in cafés, and detailed descriptions of all the amazing French food she saw in shop windows. She'll never be the same.

Love,
Nan

It was our last Sunday afternoon at the Beaubourg. I was playing sad slipjigs in front of the old cathedral, heartbroken that our summer had come to an end when suddenly the street seemed to explode and everything stopped. The stunned crowd around me stood gaping and a squad of flics appeared, gesturing and shouting, yet I could hear nothing. I had been deafened by a firecracker thrown from a window above. Peg was motioning me to go on with the tune. Was she stunned too? Why was she smiling?

For an endless moment I sat in a macabre silence, devastated that anyone could want to harm a peaceful harp player plucking peaceful tunes. Then suddenly I realized why the flics had ordered me to keep playing: they wanted me for a decoy? I jumped up with my harp and folding seat, grabbed the amplifier, ragged case, and loose coins and stumbled through the crowd with Peg hustling behind me. I had a flash of memories of other buskers' horror stories.

Perhaps it was amazing that nothing had happened to me before this attack. But now I felt like packing up this busking madness forever. Peg was calm. She took me by the sleeve and guided me to a spot some 50 yards from where we had been, and did as she had done when I had fallen face-first into a lake when I was two years old: she put me back into the water so I wouldn't be afraid of it. "*Jouer!*" she ordered.

This time I could hear her, and all the other familiar street sounds I thought I'd never be able to hear again. I started up a frisky polka, and she joined in. When a shiny squad car pulled up and stopped, I nodded and smiled, thinking the cops must be glad to see us unharmed and back in business. But gruffly they ordered us to stop.

"*I-n-s-u-p-p-o-r-t-a-b-l-e!*" cried Peg. "You order us to play and you order us to stop. Go pick on some real criminals!" We took our time packing up, smiling smugly at the four big mustachioed men who glowered at us from their shiny car, and we left the streets of Paris after a bang without a whimper.

The next morning Peg was on her way to Orly Airport, and I was on a train to Cherbourg to catch the ferry back to Ireland, when I heard the news about a French air controllers' strike. Peg had had only her ticket and a 10-*franc* coin to get her back to America. When I got to Cherbourg, I nervously rang Poughkeepsie.

The phone rang and rang, and I imagined her destitute and alone in Paris, when her groggy voice came out of its sleep and cried "I got the very last plane out of France!"

The pilot had said to the passengers, "If we don't make New York before the strike deadline, where would you like to land? Fuel is no problem." And didn't Peg, still tattered and worn from this adventure and with only a 10-franc piece to keep her from vagrancy, start thinking of Vancouver and Peru and Mexico City.

Nancy Lyon is a traditional Irish musician and travel writer/photographer based in Montreal. Her syndicated travel column "Gone" appears in alternative news weeklies and more of her musical journeys are recounted in her collection of travel essays, Scatter the Mud: A Traveller's Medley, *from which this story was excerpted.*

⋆

Let's start out with a positive and friendly word. Everything you've heard about French bureaucracy is true. And the French will admit that their administration is *lourde* (heavy). To complicate matters, the laws are changing as public sentiment shifts and the economy worsens. The overall situation is not getting easier for foreigners who want to live and work in France. Laws concerning the legal status of individuals in mixed (French-non-French) marriages, multi-national kids, political refugees, etc., are in a state of flux. Under normal circumstances, seeking legal status in France can already be taxing. If you are naïve and inexperienced and are planning to stay for a while, you'll be heading for an epiphany. You'll sense the weight of the State as you get sent around feeling like a complete idiot, tracking down a succession of illogical documents for something called your *dossier*, a multi-headed animal that you never quite seem to be able to complete. The French have a love affair with papers, stamps, signatures, and procedures. And procedures are always being changed and modified and modernized, sometimes to your advantage, but often adding only new confusion. The French carry with them at all times their *carte d'identité*, which is proof of their identity. When one French student learned that Americans didn't have national identity cards, he gasped, "How does anyone know who you really are?"

—David Applefield, *Paris Inside Out: The Insider's Guide for Visitors, Residents, Professionals & Students on Living in Paris*

HUGUES DE MONTALEMBERT

✶ ✶ ✶

Mounting Louis XIV

*One chill winter, a man's fancy turns
to the "impossible."*

THE SURGEON STOOD AT THE FOOT OF THE HOSPITAL BED WHERE I was lying with my right leg broken.

"How did you break it?"

"Well, you see Doctor… Don't laugh, but I fell off a horse."

"That is very commendable, in your case."

"Maybe, but it was a bronze horse."

And that was the truth. I could hear the reprobation in his voice: there was the hospital, his position as professor, due respect to the medical profession, and the presence of a nurse which made any kind of joke, at least in his eyes, out of place. I could not blame him and yet that was exactly what had happened.

When life becomes a bore, when everything looks black and you have that sinking feeling, when suicide seems the obvious solution, then the only alternative is to pack your bags or kick something hard enough to shake Heaven and Earth into changing the stars, even if it kills you. Yes, just head for the nearest port, dump your bag on the bridge of the first available freighter and sign on for two years—nothing but sea and contemplation of your inner landscapes.

That morning the sun had risen on one of those days when everything gets on your nerves. Winter, apparently, had come to stay. Below the infinite greyness of the sky Paris was as bleak as Warsaw. Life was mouldy, and going nowhere.

For the last ten years, since I lost my sight, I have been limited to inner landscapes, but that day when I looked within almost everything seemed black, then the phone rang, but it was only the secretary of my dentist making sure I had not forgotten my appointment. I thanked her, assured her I had not and got ready to leave. Of course, I had quite forgotten and dashed out of the house into the hazy street. I should have thought to call for a taxi. I raised an arm in case an empty one was passing by, then felt ridiculous and went into the Mercure Galant, a pretentious restaurant on the ground floor of my building. Thomas, the maître d', hailed a taxi, persuaded the driver to take me and pushed my head down as he opened the door for me to get in, in case I hit my forehead, which always irritates me. However, before I could react the taxi had already sped away from the impatient honking of horns behind us.

"*Quinze, rue du Commerce*, please."

The driver did not reply. So much the better. He was the silent type. My brain mechanically went into automatic pilot and registered the way we were going: left into rue de Richelieu, past the Comédie Française, then rue de Rohan, the entrance to the Louvre, the glass pyramid by I. M. Pei, on the right the Arc de Triomphe du Carousel by Percier and Fontaine. Those two must have made a fortune under Napoleon! They were commissioned all the palaces under the Empire, everything—architecture, decoration, the lot! And I. M. Pei? Under Mitterrand… no, the epoch lacked grandeur.

"What do you think of the pyramid?"

"*Bof.*"

So he was not the silent type after all, but he did not mince his words either. By the time we got to the Chambre des Députés, he asked me whether I wanted to take the tunnel or preferred to stay on the Quai.

"I don't mind," I told him, "Whatever is fastest."

"O.K. Do you smoke?"

"Yes. Why?"

"Because of the pollution. You'd better light up in the tunnel."

We came out on the Boulevard de Garibaldi. There was a presence on the front seat next to the driver.

"You have a lovely white dog, there," I said.

The car swerved, the driver having turned round to look at me.

"How did you know my dog was white?"

He had a point. I had spoken without thinking.

"What colour is your dog?"

"Well, he's white!"

He did not seem at all happy and I felt embarrassed, almost guilty. It was absurd! Thank God we had arrived. I searched in my pockets for some change. Money! In my haste I had quite forgotten to bring any. I didn't have a cent on me. Luckily I found a cheque book in my back pocket. The driver remonstrated, then gave in. I signed the cheque, but he had to fill out the rest himself. I thought, God preserve me from the sum he might fill in.

Half an hour later, with my mouth full of chemical and medicinal tastes, I went into the nearest café and ordered a small black coffee. It was disgusting as it often is in Paris, but piping hot which was marvelous.

"May I pay for your coffee?"

It was a woman's voice, in her 30s. A hit? Women really were getting more and more forward. Maybe she was ugly, but no matter, a man is always flattered to be picked up, even by a plain woman.

"I said that because you don't have any money on you."

Shit! I had completely forgotten. She was right. I had no money.

"But how did you know?"

She laughed.

"I saw you getting out of the taxi, earlier."

She had an indefinable accent. She came from Beirut where her husband was a landscape architect. A landscape architect in Beirut where there was a war going on!

"And does he get any work?"

"Lots!"

I shall never cease to wonder how during a war daily life goes on as usual. I thought of the Vietnamese children I used to see going to school every morning along mined roads, their uniforms perfectly ironed by their mothers the night before.

"Did your husband come to Paris with you?"

"No. He's gone to Sweden to install a central heating system in a cemetery."

"Central heating in a cemetery!"

"They have to heat the graves otherwise the bodies take years to decompose, because of the cold, and it gets overcrowded. Not everybody can afford to buy a permanent plot."

Designing landscapes in Beirut under the shells; heating Swedish corpses! And this morning I thought life was dull! I still had that bitter taste in my mouth.

When I got home I set about several tasks, but accomplished none, so by the time Naïry arrived at the end of the afternoon, I was in a foul mood. Her positively flat voice, devoid of any modulation, exasperated me. It was one of those voices Australia is famous for. I had met Naïry in Jakarta at a dinner. The conversation had revolved around a jewel theft: the victim, an Italian woman, *una caffona*, was smugly detailing each gem. I listened to her thinking that she must be exaggerating the value when I distinctly heard a voice I had not heard before, say: "Shut up, you dead shit!" It had been said calmly, without inflection. An ear as practised as mine immediately discerned alcohol, and the ruthlessness, but also the wound in that voice, in Naïry's voice.

A few weeks later she moved in with me. My house stood among the hills at the foot of Gunung Agung, the sacred volcano of Bali. The evening which always falls prematurely in the tropics, was filled with her low monotonous speech. Sometimes it was difficult to understand her words. Thousands of croaks coming from the layered rice-paddies sloping down the volcano to the sea, pitter-pattered on her flat voice.

She was born in Paramatta, a suburb of Sydney.

"At sixteen, I looked around at my family, and our neighbours, and I swore I'd never stay poor. Not be rich, but free, and have enough money to travel and live surrounded by beauty…and never again find my ass sitting on a flat pile of shit like Paramatta!" she said.

She started working. She was among the first generation of surfers who discovered the beaches of Byron Bay, founded a magazine, planted cannabis…but the big money was not coming in. So Naïry ran a drug traffic between the ANC guerrillas in South Africa and some Zulu movements: arms, money, in exchange for the best quality grass and hash. "The best! When I had enough money I invested it all in Hong Kong and quit. The others wanted to continue. Not me. There were nine of us. Today, the other eight are in jail."

"No husband?"

"No. I can't have children."

She seemed more alone than ever. The croaking of the frogs drowned her silence.

"The customs, the police were on our track. The strain was too much. I started drinking, a lot. One night when I was drunk I killed a child with my car. I realized then that I wasn't responsible enough to have children, so I got myself sterilized."

I listened to her solitary voice in the night vibrating with the insects, frogs and malevolent spirits. What to do with her? I could hear the yearning in her voice: "Take me," it said.…

Wintry Paris rumbled on dully. Listening to both the city and to Naïry I found myself wondering where all the bright days had gone. I live in the heart of Paris, walking distance from French history: the Louvre, the Palais-Royal, rue Chabanais where the most elaborate brothel in Europe had been at the turn of the century. At the top of my street, in the little Place des Victoires, Louis XIV astride a bronze horse was galloping towards the Opera, eternally. In my mind's eye I could see the statue quite distinctly against a black ground. The king was not really galloping. (I am always astonished by the precision of my visual memory. It can conjure up images of an Atlantis permanently plunged in darkness.) No, the king was not galloping, his horse was walking the Spanish pace, the left foreleg raised. The king seemed to be losing his balance while desperately hanging on to the mane of his horse which was too small for him and practically sitting on its flanks. A kind of paralysis emanated from the whole thing. Going around the statue the very first time I saw it I understood why. The artist, who deserves to remain unknown, had used the horse's bronze tail to balance the ensemble by sticking it down into the granite base. As a result the king appeared to be mounted on a horse with five legs....

here were those who swore by the Italian operas of Verdi, and those for whom nothing could bear the Wagnerian epics of Germany, but it was the operatic music of France—emanating from the Paris Opera—that swept the 19th century with its elegant melodies and masterful singing. The French composers of that period were heavily inspired by the great city in which most of their operas were first presented: Paris!

—William Schoell, "The Idols of Opera," *Paris Notes*

"I brought you some photographs of my climb."

Naïry's voice drove King Lulu and his five legged horse into the abyss of my memory. She carefully place the photographs between my fingers and described each one to me.

Where had all the bright days printed on those photographs gone? There was no Port in Paris, no hope of unloading our bags on a ship when the sky was too low, but we could always go to the Café Pouchkine. I put the photographs away and we went out.

We walked around King Lulu in his bronze lace, riding on regardless of the freezing cold. The Café Pouchkine was a tiny place just around the corner from the Place des Victoires: six tables and, at the bar, one customer—always the same customer—reading Russian magazines from the early 1900s, but not drinking. Alexeï, the owner, had been the youngest correspondent of the Tass agency in Peking, that is to say also one of the youngest officers of the KGB. Naturally, he spoke fluent Chinese as well as Swedish,

German, Spanish, Italian, French and English, and was well read in all these languages. That night, Alexeï was in a good mood. He sat down at our table saying drinks were on the house. From a bottle incarcerated in a block of ice, the vodka flowed like syrup.

The hours slipped by and strange people arrived belonging or having belonged—who knows anymore?—to the Soviet intelligencia. They appeared like bubbles rising from a gloomy world. People who came from the aurora borealis, from Arkhangelsk, Murmuansk, the White Sea, but also from Moscow, Novgorod, and other places long forgotten by Western memory. An old ballerina from Petersburg, in black leather, and her girlfriend in lace, a Cossack whip on the table; an impresario without a show, a writer without an oeuvre: Alexeï described them all to me with a mixture of derision and tenderness. Around us, the Russian language, muffled and musical at the same time, warmed my heart along with the vodka flowing into our little glasses. One bottle followed another, and Naïry never said a word. Alexeï, excited by the alcohol, attacked me on the preeminence of Russian literature—its superiority over all literature all over the world, but since I was French and, as he told me, completely ignorant, he limited his field of comparison to France.

"Objectively, take Victor Hugo: *Les Misérables* is as unreadable whereas the novel *Anna Karenina* by Tolstoy, even in French…."

"What about Catherine the Great? She bought Voltaire's library, nothing but French writers, or nearly."

"Catherine II? Pfff…. A German! No, no, the French for that matter don't understand anything about Russian literature. They like Dostoyevsky. That's exotic! They read Dostoyevsky the way they buy postcards. But Pushkin, Gogol, Arhmatova…"

He paused. Three men had just walked into the café.

"Those bastards from Domestic Intelligence," he said, getting up.

There was a confabulation going on by the door.

Suddenly Alexeï's shrill voice rose above the others', "Democracy my ass!"

And the door slammed on a voice which said, "We'll be back!"

Alexeï put a fresh bottle of vodka on the table.

"They keep raiding my place, even though I treat them like dogs."

Nevertheless they must have known that Alexeï had deserted the KGB because as a homosexual he had found himself in a dangerous situation. To escape, he had married a young Swedish diplomat in Peking and ended up in this narrow street in the heart of Paris, incidentally without the Swedish wife. Passionately faithful to Mother Russia, he must have refused to cooperate with the French Secret Service, so they persecuted him a little as a matter of course even though meanwhile the Soviet empire had collapsed.

"The law! The law! It's the only word they can pronounce. To the French, freedom means knowing where the limit lies. To Russians, freedom means knowing there is no limit. We are a mixture of successive influxes of nomadic people on vast plains. Do you understand? It's not Auvergne! Anyway, it soothes my nerves to treat them like dogs."

The night passed in conversation which, thanks to the vodka, seemed more and more brilliant. My dark mood of the morning had been replaced by optimism and certainty—certainty that the good days were not gone. I wondered whether Naïry, who was as silent as ever, was drinking as much as we were. Every now and again I said something to test her and she replied, but her voice was so neutral that I could not tell. She assured me she was not bored.

At intervals a big girl of the Georgian type would come in and sing songs from Okudjava. She would exit without even passing the hat around, leaving you bowled over. Several times I asked Alexeï, "Who is she?"

But each time he replied, "I don't know," which was false.

Life outside was no longer mouldy, the bitter cold hit our faces like a sharp knife and made the alcohol fizz in my veins. It must have been very late because Paris was sound asleep. In the little Place des Victoires, Louis XIV was caracoling on his horse, triumphant.

"I've always dreamed of riding with Louis XIV."

Naïry laughed. "That's impossible, it's much too high."

Impossible was the one word I did not want to hear. That morning everything had been impossible, everything had looked black, but tonight certitude was flowing through me. The bright days were back, everything was possible. Instantly, I let go of Naïry's arm, crossed the street and clambered over the railings around the statue. I do not know how, but I managed to get over the iron spikes and began climbing the granite base. "It's impossible! Hugues, it's IMPOSSIBLE!"

Naïry's cry of alarm in the glacial air echoed from the empty square. Already my hands had reached the top of the base supporting the horse. Now I had to clutch hold of the right foreleg, the one resting on the stone, and from there haul myself up quite easily to King Lulu who would have to make room for me. I chuckled in anticipation. It was as exhilarating as climbing Gunung Agung. To hell with boredom! But where for Christ's sake was the horse's foot? My right hand groped for it in empty space. Clinging to the granite, I moved forward a bit, my left hand firmly gripping the edge of the base. Once again, I searched the air: nothing. Several times I reached out my right hand, waved it around and still met with nothing but freezing air. Down below (and I realized I was already quite high up), Naïry was shouting: "IMPOSSIBLE, it's IMPOSSIBLE."

Suddenly tired, my left hand lost its grip and I plummeted to the ground, between the railings and the base. Feeling my leg and realizing it was broken at the height of the knee, the image of Louis XIV on horseback suddenly surged from within me with unexpected clarity. My God! The king was not galloping, true, but he was not doing the Spanish step either. No, the king was making his horse perform a gait invented in the 17th century by Monsieur de la Guérinière for the stables at Versailles. It is called a curvet, and when the forelegs are flexed, a pesade. In either case the forelegs are raised, therefore it would have been impossible for me to grasp either one of them. My amazing visual memory had failed me!

＊

"You mean a bronze colored horse?" asked the doctor in a conciliatory tone.

"No, made of bronze. Mind you, if it had been doing the Spanish step, I would have succeeded. It was the curvet which…"

The sound of the door closing interrupted my explanation, but I thought I heard someone laugh.

Before being blinded by acid during an assault in New York City, Hugues de Montalembert was a painter, film maker, and writer. In his book, Eclipse, *which was translated from the French into four languages, he writes about his blinding and search for a cure. He still travels widely and writes regularly for French and American publications. He lives in Paris.*

＊

I shall always see Paris as the setting of a novel that will never be written. The times I have returned from long walks through ancient streets with my heart laden with all the inexpressible things I have seen! Is this an illusion? I think not. It happens frequently that, brought up short before, say, a large window draped with mock lace curtains, tucked away in one of the old quarters, I embark on an interminable fancy about the unknown destinies unfolding beyond the dark panes. My eye makes out a little bunch of flowers, which will change or disappear with the seasons, set in the middle of a table covered with a dark cloth; that is all, yet it may be enough. Who lives in that room? Who is dying between those four walls? In the novelist's eyes every life, even the humblest, possesses that itch of mystery, and there is something about the sum total of all the secrets contained in a city that he finds by turns stimulating and oppressive. What a prodigal waste of situations, speeches, dramas, characters, settings! Who would not be moved by such a struggle?

—Julian Green, *Paris*, translated by J. A. Underwood

SHUSHA GUPPY

* *

The Heart Finds a Way

Life goes on in a student's Paris.

To us students in our teens and early twenties Madame
Giroux seemed quite old, although she was around fifty and still
very attractive. She had an apple-blossom complexion enhanced
with a touch of rouge on high cheekbones, and harmonious features. Her hair, dyed to its original chestnut brown, framed her oval
face and was held back by small combs and *barrettes* which never
varied. Her figure was "matronly"—middle-aged spread checked
by corsets and sober clothes, arms and legs still shapely and slim.
With the students she was dignified, even politely cold, but when
a man other than a dishevelled student appeared on the horizon,
such as Mr. Raheem, she melted into a pool of feminine charm: a
girlish smile displaying a set of even white teeth, green-grey eyes
wistfully narrowed into a soulful expression: "*Monsieur*? You wish?"

Madame Giroux was not often in the office/reception, preferring to do her work in her apartment, on the ground floor behind
the stairs. We did not dare knock on her front door, however urgent the matter, but instead left a request for an interview with the
receptionist and in due course were summoned. As she had the
power to expel us at a moment's notice, we were afraid of her and
on the whole never broke the rules.

Madame Giroux was a widow. She had been "blissfully happy" with her husband, an army officer who had died just after the war. She had never worked while he was alive, but after his death she had taken this job, not from necessity but to placate loneliness, as she had no children. She liked "the girls" whom she found bright and usually "serious." She did not seem to have many friends either, for she seldom went out in the evenings and hardly ever received anyone in her apartment. But she had one friend who called on her regularly, twice a week. Often they sat at the back of the office and chatted over a cup of coffee or a glass of white wine. If you entered the reception to pick up your key while the Major was there, you could see her laughing while he talked, leaning forward to impart a secret. At such moments she ceased to be the stern Madame Directrice, and you saw the pretty teenage girl who had turned the head of a young officer 30 years before.

The Major had lost a leg at the start of the war—"You should've seen those German Panzers! *O la la*!"—and his wife at the end of it; his two sons had married and left home, and now he lived alone, not far from the Foyer, and came to visit his old regimental friend's widow.

All this I learnt from Madame Monique, the daily cleaner. She believed that there was "an understanding" between the two of them, and that they did more than indulge in remembrance of her late husband. We did not believe her, as the Major was bulky, flabby, bald, and a cripple to boot—how could she fancy him? "For some women any man is better than none," Madame Monique would answer with a contemptuous snort. I remained incredulous, for it was impossible for the Major to enter Madame Giroux's apartment or emerge from it without being seen, and the picture of a crippled bear with an artificial leg climbing through a narrow window was too awkward to be contemplated. But Madame Monique maintained that they found a way: "People always do."

The Major had replaced his missing limb with an artificial contraption that ended in a round metal disk. As he entered the Foyer you could hear the contrapuntal thuds of his walking stick and artificial leg on the stone entrance, followed by his stentorian saluta-

tions: "*Bonjour, Madame!* How are you today!" he would boom at
the receptionist, who would rush to alert Madame Giroux.

One night I went to bed with a cold and woke up with a temperature. A weak bulb was left on each floor after blackout in case
we needed to use the lavatories at the end of the corridor. I heard
the familiar rhythmic sound that announced the Major's presence
coming from the floor below. At first I thought it was happening
in my feverish head, but as I listened it became unmistakable.
Thud, thud, thud…receding in the courtyard behind the building
and disappearing into the night…

"The heart finds a way to the heart," goes the Persian saying.

Madame Monique was in charge of keeping the stairs and corridors, the office and waiting room clean, while the girls were
responsible for their own rooms. She arrived at eight o'clock,
started downstairs and worked her way to the top, which she
reached some time in the afternoon, and she left around four. She
used old-fashioned tools—a bucket, cloths, brushes, and dusters,
crouching on all fours. Around noon she stopped, sat on the stairs
and consumed her sandwich and coffee which she brought with
her. One or two girls asked her to help them for an hour a week
to keep their rooms tidy and clean, which she did, more to oblige
than for the extra cash it provided. Indeed she showed utter contempt for money and always took it with an expression of haughty
disgust, as though it soiled her hand. I too asked her to help me
once a week, and she accepted. On Thursdays she knocked on my
door at three, or let herself in with my key if I was out, whirled
round with her duster and broom, and left. But if I was in she
talked non-stop while working, and sometimes sat down for a
while afterwards to rest and chat. When one day by chance I told
her that I had joined the Communist Youth at the *lycée* in Persia,
my stock rose, she relaxed her diffidence and began to talk about
her life.

Madame Monique came from the Eastern Pyrénées and her
voice had the resonance and cadences of her lofty mountains—
loud and heavily accented. She rolled her Rs like cartwheels over
gravel, with dramatic variations. During the Spanish Civil War she

had helped Republican refugees across the frontier hills and learnt some Catalan. Many of her friends were Spanish exiles, and she cursed Franco and "all the Fascists in France who supported him" for their none-too-easy plight.

She had married young and moved up to Paris with her husband in search of work. He had found a job in a factory where he stayed for the rest of his life, while she did cleaning. They had remained devoted until his death, at the end of the war, of a heart attack. They had joined the Communist Party in their youth and were unwavering in their faith. During the war they were among the first Communists to join the Resistance, early on in 1942, and several times had nearly been caught by the Gestapo.

Madame Monique was still a card-carrying member and harboured a soft spot for the Party Leader, Maurice Thorez: "A miner, son of a miner, grandson of a miner, no bourgeois he!" She spat out the epithet with all the disgust and hatred she could muster. She had toed the Party line through all its twists and turns—the Hitler-Stalin pact, the show trials, the purges, etc.... Any threat to her staunch belief was brushed aside as "lies, lies, lies!" American and bourgeois machinations. When the Khrushchev report to the 20th Congress of the Soviet Party leaked in 1956, she treated it as yet another diabolical fabrication: "Comrade Khrushchev is one of the architects of the Soviet miracle, how could he say things like that? Why didn't he say anything while Stalin was alive?" There was no point telling her he would have been shot, like the others—she would not have believed you. When Soviet tanks crushed the Hungarian uprising in 1956 and killed thousands of workers, she believed it was a "*coup monté*" by counter-revolutionaries on the payroll of America. All her own and her husband's emotional and religious capital was invested in the Party, so how could she give it up? That would render their lives meaningless. Madame Monique sustained her faith by reading *L'Humanité,* the organ of the Party, every day, from cover to cover, swallowing its content hook, line and sinker, like a devout Muslim saying his daily prayers or a Christian going to Mass every Sunday. In her I understood the meaning of "blind

faith," and would encounter it in the years to come in many ide-
ologically committed people.

The only time Madame Monique showed any weakness was
when she recounted her husband's death. Then the hard, angry
mask that had become part of her melted away, her eyes filled with
tears and a wan smile glided over her lips like the shadow of a
cloud over the plain. He had died suddenly at daybreak as he got
up to leave for work, leaving her forever with the night. She had
spent all she had and bought a ten-year lease on a grave for him at
the Père Lachaise Cemetery. Since then every Sunday without fail
she went "to visit him," taking a bunch of flowers. I imagined her
clearing up dead leaves, silently communicating with him, willing
him into some sort of life.

"Why, Madame Monique, do you go to his grave? He won't
know, and since you are an atheist and don't believe in the survival
of the soul, nor in an afterlife, there is no one to communicate
with, except in memory, which you can do in your own room?"

"I do it for me. I talk to him, I feel better for it."

"What will happen when the lease runs out?"

"If I'm still around I'll renew it for another ten years, otherwise
that's that!"

Perhaps another widow will buy it then, I thought, bury her
husband and go to his grave on Sundays, taking a bunch of daf-
fodils or violets... "The heart has its reasons which Reason does
not know."

Madame Giroux's part-time assistants who sat in the office during the day were innocuous enough, but the night receptionist,
Mademoiselle Mori, was "a case"—"*Ah! C'est un cas!*" Madame
Giroux used to say, rolling her eyes to heaven. She had lived in the
Foyer for as long as anyone remembered, on the top floor where
the rooms were divided by thin partitions into what they called
"boxes," using the English word. No one had ever succeeded in
befriending her—she responded to smiles and greetings with a
blank expression, as though someone else had been addressed. As
she worked all day in an office and became our receptionist in the

evenings and on Sundays, she only went to her room to sleep. Sometimes strange noises emanated from her box in the middle of the night, which her neighbours attributed to nightmares, and often she snored loudly, which kept them awake. As the partitions went up from the floor to a foot below the ceiling, a couple of inquisitive girls had once climbed on chairs and tables and each other's shoulders like circus acrobats to have a peep inside her room. They found it packed with years of accumulation: cardboard boxes, tatty clothes, disparate objects—a cross between a bric-á-brac flea market stand and a tramp's hovel. And there she lived out her existence as if in expiation for a terrible sin.

Mademoiselle Mori was of medium height, thin and shapeless, without any female protuberances on her body. Her hair, short, grey and wiry, stuck out on her scalp and gave her the allure of a hedgehog, an impression increased by her diffidence. Her eyes were bird-tiny and expressionless, her complexion the colour of whey. As the night receptionist she was in charge of switching off the lights and locking up at midnight sharp. At five minutes to twelve she lit a candle, stuck it in a cracked saucer, and as soon as the clock of the nearby military hospital of Val-de-Grâce struck midnight she switched off the electricity at the main and locked the front door. By the time the twelfth stroke resounded in the slumbering district she was half way up the stairs. Sometimes she waited behind the door, inserted the key into the lock, and turned it decisively upon sensing the clock's will to chime, so that her gesture coincided with the first stroke. That single, long iron key, similar to those castle keys illustrated in fairy tales, gave her enormous power over us, for if we were so much as ten seconds late, we found ourselves locked out for the night.

Once I put forward the idea of purloining the key, taking an impression of it and having a copy made. But it proved impossible to penetrate her room and find it, and anyway my friends decided that I had seen too many gangster movies! A midnight curfew may not seem too unreasonable, except when you consider that nearly all shows—theatres, operas, concerts, even political meetings—ended around midnight. As the underground ran until one o'clock in the morning there was no difficulty in getting home, but even leaving at 11:30 and running all the way from the station to the Foyer was risky. Countless last acts, encores, finales, were thus missed by us for fear of being stranded in the street.

Having failed to meet the curfew, you could sit in cafés till two or three, which was usually their closing time, then walk till five or six when others opened, but it was dangerous for girls on their own to roam the streets. There were some all-night cafés, usually near mainline stations, but they were not respectable haunts in the small hours, and a single girl (or even two or three) was bound to be harassed. We were constantly warned against the "recruiting agents" of the White Slave Trade, their methods of persuasion and coercion, their uncanny stratagems, the police's connivance with them. Harrowing stories circulated about girls who disappeared suddenly, having been put to sleep by an anaesthetic needle in a cinema or an empty bus, and then abducted. By the time they re-gained consciousness they were on their way to some brothel in Africa for legionnaires! None of it was of course true, but it scared the daylights out of us and we avoided risky circumstances and sinister men who invariably approached us with offers of "model-ling" and "film contracts." It was better to miss the show than take the risk.

As my room was above the entrance, I often heard girls bang-ing on the door and pleading with Mademoiselle Mori to please open it and let them in, since she was still there, and they could hear her. Ruthlessly she would click the key, turn round and slowly walk up the stairs, candle in hand, like a ghost carrying out a pre-ordained task. One night hearing a girl bang the door and calling out supplications, I came out to the landing and confronted Mademoiselle Mori, begging her to let me go down and open the door to her. She looked at me impassively, and kept climbing like a somnambulist. I perceived the shadow of a malignant rictus on her then dry lips, and I wanted to hit her and pry the key from her,

> "*To drive people to fury is my greatest joy.*"
> —Tartuffe to Orgon, *Tartuffe*
> by Moliere (1664)

but I was glued to the ground. I went back into my room, leaned out of the window and discussed ways of hoisting the girl up to my room, but it was impossible without a long ladder. Eventually we decided that the only solution was for her to take the last Métro back to her friends' house, where she had spent the evening, embarrassing as it was to wake them up.

Several times Madame Giroux was approached with petitions to extend the curfew by one hour, but she was adamant: the Foyer was not a hotel, she wished us to know, but a respectable home for "*jeunes filles de bonne famille.*" In fact she did not wish to pay for the extra time, nor was Mademoiselle Mori willing to accept the new arrangement.

Since the war sexual mores had changed a great deal in France, to the chagrin of the older generation, who did their best to stem the approaching tide of what is now referred to as "the permissive Sixties." At first limited to artists and intellectuals in *la vie de bohème*, where it had always existed, the relaxation was now spreading, as a sort of undertow. Yet the majority of people lived by the old customs and restrictions based on religious precepts, and most young people still refrained from pre-marital sex. Even the Communists who denounced "bourgeois marriage" as "legal prostitution" frowned upon "looseness" and advocated monogamous commitment. The supreme exemplars were the General Secretary of the Party, Maurice Thorez and his "companion" as she was officially called, who had lived together for years and had several children, without having gone through legal and "bourgeois ceremonies"—social defiance combined with puritanism. The fact that some notable communist intellectuals and fellow travellers led such promiscuous lives as to make Casanova and Mata Hari seem positively chaste was not known by the rank and file, who only saw their outwardly monogamously happy marriages.

For Madame Giroux, as for most people, girls were still either "serious" or "light"—*légère*, and she did not approve of the latter. But the strict rules designed to protect the girls' virtues produced the opposite effect and contributed to their "downfall." Many a Foyer student lost her virginity by being a few seconds late. Her boyfriend offered her hospitality for the night at his place, which was often no more than a tiny room with a single bed, and the inevitable happened. Sometimes the circumstances were engineered by the young couple themselves: running back at midnight and reaching the door a few minutes before midnight they lingered over the parting kiss within a few yards of the door. You saw them flattened against the wall and in doorways as you hurried past, and you were reminded of Prévert's song:

> Children in love
> kissing on their feet
> Against the gates of the night…

They would hear the key turn in the lock, unwind themselves, and rush…. Quick! Quick! Too late—Mademoiselle Mori's steps thudded away in the entrance like the ticking of fate's clock. *Et voilà!*

Shusha Guppy also contributed "St-Germain-des-Prés" in Part I.

★

Rilke wrote that the spirit of Paris "is the desire to live in haste, in pursuit; it is the impatience to possess all of life right away, right here. Paris is full of this desire; that is why it is so close to death."

—JO'R, LH, and SO'R

Hair Pierre

Put on your high-heeled sneakers
and your wig-hat on your head.

I LAND IN FRANCE AT THE AGE OF NINETEEN WITH A STUDENT loan and the belief that an address in Paris is the precursor to a literary, artistic, or at least interesting life. I have come to attend the Sorbonne's French Language and Civilization program. One month in Paris and I too will be sitting in the cafés, draped in black, suffering through excessive bouts of second-hand smoke, looking bored—always bored—complaining how my life is so underfunded. My lips will be fantastically pouty. I will meet only fascinating people—the soon-to-be-famous—and have an immediate rapport with them. I will be welcomed into their tight weave of friendship, partially due to the above-mentioned pouty lips, and partially due to my ability to say outrageously witty and insightful things at the appropriate time.

None of these traits have ever formed any part of my existence prior to moving to Paris. Why I will suddenly transform into this stylish, clever person is an inconsistency I easily dismiss. Who needs logic when they have Paris?

The first month passes with the usual excitement and frustration of a new routine. And I find the shopping areas. I remind myself that I am here to learn the language. And maybe have a deeply intriguing adventure. If I acquire a spectacular wardrobe and a sense of chic along the way, I won't complain.

I regularly deposit myself and my journal in a café to watch the world, and more importantly, the Parisians, pass. I am initially taken by the style and *je ne sais quoi* of the men. However, they are taken by the style and *je ne sais quoi* of the French women. So I too become a student of the women's ways.

After much study, I note in my journal, Things to Do to Become a Parisienne:

Always wear tight jeans. Anywhere and anyhow. A must. Even at funerals.

And heels. Podiatrists must retire early in France.

Have your hair managed. Stuck in place, really, so that it looks the same at 11:00 p.m. as it did at noon. In fact, it probably hasn't moved.

Make sure your earrings match something on your person. Or have a serious reason for wearing them.

Carry an overstuffed shoulder bag. Watch for signs of curvature of the spine.

Ensure your lips are always a deep red.

Never have an appetite.

And always wear a scarf. Preferably silk.

I believe that I am eight items away from being mistaken for a Françoise, or Michelle or Marie. I march off to the markets. Most of these prerequisites are for sale. I search out an oversized shoulder bag and a new collection of bright or bold earrings. I have never frolicked in the costume jewelry section before with so much determination. I have a mission.

Being cursed with curly hair, however, the Parisian women's ability to manage their tendrils is beyond comprehension. I drag myself to a hair salon, clutching a photo of Princess Stephanie of Monaco. She is my age and is always considered *à la mode*. Maybe I am only a haircut away. Instead, after a long conversation with

Pierre where I stress the need to be *bien coiffée*, he trims and poofs. I don't believe Stephanie ever poofs. She may slick and groom and pat, but never poof. I leave Chez Pierre with an extra three inches in height and a potential to be a hazard in the Métro. I cannot afford enough gel to tame my cut, and to give it that royal style. Maybe my hair will sense the Parisian-ness of the rest of me and fall into place. The rest of me will be easier to manage.

In between classes I wander the Latin Quarter—with my big Pierre hair, shoulder bag, and earrings—to observe the locals: what they wear, what they order at the cafés, how they carry themselves. This is the greatest classroom for me. At the Sorbonne I diligently conjugate my verbs, polish my pronunciation, and learn the social implications of the May '68 uprising. But my passion is for the lessons of the street, and the chicness that somehow comes with a French birth certificate.

Three months in Paris and I still look as if I belong at a right-wing political fund-raiser, rather than on the Left Bank. I realize that this transformation is not just going to happen. I must take action.

After class I traipse down to a shopping area, or the department stores. This is the pulsing, intoxicating, and free version of the fashion magazines. The most overwhelming of these shops is Galeries Lafayette. Eight stories of exclusiveness built around an atrium. I'm not sure it gets any better than that.

One afternoon I collect some nerve—or maybe the second installment of my student loan has come through—and I enter Galeries Lafayette with a purpose. A full makeover. To allow the most Gaullic of women to spread as many concoctions on my face as the surface area will allow. They seem to see me as a challenge, a mound of fresh clay to mold and manipulate. Foundations and creams and shadows and liners all find their way onto my face. And lipstick. The ubiquitous Parisian red. My face is cracking but my lips are pulsating with color as I ride the escalator to the section "20 *ans*" where I plan to buy the remaining articles of a *de rigueur* wardrobe. It is time for the jeans and heels. I try. And try and try. But when you dwarf the men around you, the jeans don't have the same effect. I totter in shoes that make me even taller, and pour into jeans that are meant to celebrate my natural lack of appetite. Instead they only cheer reinforced stitching. I decide to wear my new outfit out of the store. Onto the streets of the city I saunter, bottles of potions clanking in my massive, recently acquired, over-stuffed shoulder bag. I walk past cafés trying to notice if anyone is noticing me. From behind this canvas of cosmetics I feel more European, more sure that I am on the way to being "one of them," and then maybe attracting an Etienne or a Tristan or a Jean-Paul. I'll even settle for a Claude.

After a strutting tour of every public gathering spot I can manage, and with not even one proposition, I return home, limping but mostly undamaged, to survey the success these women have wielded on me. I poke and prod my pores, hoping to discover the secret and realizing that as I paid little attention to what they were doing, my hopes of replicating the result are fairly small. I struggle to remove my overpriced jeans. I got them on. The laws of physics comfort me: they must be removable. My feet are throbbing as I step out of my new shoes and back on solid ground. My arches have had too much of a workout.

The next morning I greet my face. It looks as if it has just landed in the emergency room. Colors blend in to black and red and blue that seem to be everywhere but where they were yesterday. I scrub and cleanse and exfoliate and start again. When I am done, however, half the bottles remain unopened, and I don't look much different than I always have. But for those new, red pouty lips. Actually they aren't pouty at all. They are red though, and I figure that counts for something.

Six months have passed and I still don't possess that natural style. Maybe I just need the scarf.

Between struggling with the subjunctive tense, the French political structure and excerpts of Proust, I return to Galeries Lafayette to watch other women, and see how they do it. Just to hear the sound of their accents: "*Les écharpes*," they say as they describe the scarves. The sound flows like the Seine, the last syllable rolling forward in the mouth. I've solicited other shops for their scarving expertise, but none are as good as Mlle. Vincent (as it says on her name tag) at Galeries Lafayette. Every week I canvas the area. She smiles at me, like a regular in a local pub greeting a familiar but unnamed face. This beautifully draped woman demonstrates how, with two flicks of the wrist, I could turn any piece of silk or cotton or polyester into a "fashion accessory." As hard as I try, my scarves only ever look like a bib from Big Bob's House of Ribs.

And each Sunday I devour another of the weekly *Elle* magazines, or *Dépêche Mode*, or anything glossy that proclaims French style. And still, after planning and plotting my texture options the night before, every morning is a chore, as I try to create some well structured outfit. And no matter how hard I try, I still look like I just stepped off the campus of Bowling Green.

Nine months have passed. I've mastered the tenses, an overview of French history and their beloved literature. I have acquired a nice social circle, but none of my friends are literary figures. In fact most of them have jobs. And none of them smoke. I am feeling a failure. Then I get a letter. A note, really.

A friend is coming to visit. An ex-boyfriend, passing through town on a "Europe in six weeks" pre-packaged expedition. Looking as Parisian as possible is mandatory for our meeting. This is my test. My watershed.

The morning of our meeting arrives. I try to tame my hair, slip into the volume-challenged jeans, apply a bright color to my lips, insert the appropriate earrings and elevate myself two

France, native land of Jean Nicot, the 16th-century French ambassador who introduced tobacco to France and gave his name to the poison it contains, was the first European country to impose a ban on smoking in all enclosed public places—including offices and factories—except in specially designated smoking areas equipped with suitable ventilation.

—The Economist

inches in the shoes. I casually toss a scarf (as I now own several) around my neck. Actually I place it carefully, hoping for it to look casually tossed. I grab my massive shoulder bag, and I descend into the Métro to meet The Ex. He is on a tight schedule, which allows me the comfort of knowing this encounter will last only a few hours.

I ascend gracefully from the Métro stop. There he is, looking like the sorest thumb in *tout-Paris*. Shorts and a baseball cap and Converse running shoes. He screams North America. He is startled to see me approach. He doesn't quite recognize me at first. I greet him and offer him my cheek. He doesn't know what to do with it. He tries to hug me. An awkward exchange follows, half cheek kisses, half insubstantial hugs. He trails me as we enter and seat ourselves at the bistro. I translate the menu for him and highlight the most interesting items. I order for both of us, and complain when an item doesn't arrive. I introduce him to a friend of mine and his girlfriend who pass in the street. I recommend places to visit and towns to explore. Dazed, he comments; "You look...different." I laugh at his naïveté. I toss my hair, but it catches on my earrings. I smile, but he tells me that I have lipstick on my teeth. I play with my precious scarf, but its ends persist in falling into my café au lait. I search for my wallet, but it is lost in the pounds of necessities that I have managed to stuff into my oversized shoulder bag. I realize I have attained a high-maintenance look. Which, given the circulation-inhibiting nature of my clothing, is not a particularly comfortable one.

I feel, however, as if I've made it. I have soaked up French culture and it is soaking into my pores. I lean forward and try to flirt, as I've seen the Parisian women do every day in the cafés, but he only pulls back, as if I've invaded his personal space.

My chicness has been on display now for two hours. He must be in awe of my new-found grace, and stunned by my transformation. He looks at his watch and proclaims that this encounter must end. He picks up his baseball cap and puts it back on his head. I flinch. He fumbles at his velcroed money belt for cash. I cringe. He pulls out some francs and tries to understand the exchange rate. I cower. As he leaves he puts his arm around me. I smile. It's true. I must be irresistible, like all those French women. He lowers his voice: "You know I'm impressed. You've learned a lot this past year. You speak French really well. But do you really think you look good like that?"

Cailín Boyle's days consist of working as a freelance writer in San Francisco, and plotting trips to places with really bad plumbing. She was last seen looking for a good latte in the Khyber Pass.

✳

Before Louis XVI mounted the throne in 1774, women's hair styles had already reached a volume of such enormity that the weight on their necks was oftentimes insupportable. There were cases where the mouth of a lady in *grande toilette* would be at a point equidistant between the top of her coiffure and her feet. "The head was transformed alternatively into mountain, forest, or garden," wrote Éze and Marcel, summing up the extravagances of the period of Mme. du Barry. "It was an orgy of butterflies, birds, tree branches, cardboard cupids. The hair was teased, crimped, loaded with feathers, gauze, ribbons, garlands, pearls, and diamonds. One went so far as to ornament one's coiffure with vegetables."

One went further than that and carried a whole tableau on one's head. According to a contemporary witness, Louis Petit de Bachaumont, the Duchesse de Chartres wore an eye-catching scene, the central figure of which was a seated female wet-nursing an infant who was said by the Duchesse to represent M. le Duc de Valois. "To the right was a *perroquet* on its stand, pecking at a cherry, the bird being precious to the Duchesse, and at the left, a blackamoor," Bachaumont noted in his *Mémoires Secrets*.

By 1778, the monster hairdos were taking a nautical turn and heads bearing frigates in full sail were the going fashion; one style, "à la Belle-Poule," was named after a French ship that was victorious in a skirmish with part of the British fleet off the coast of Brittany. In 1783, the Montgolfier brothers and their lighter-than-air ballooning inspired new soaring coiffures. Benjamin Franklin's discovery of atmospheric electricity did not give birth to a new French hairdress, but he was honored with a hat, "*le chapeau paratonnerre*," with a little metal chain to attract lightning extending from the back of the hatband down to the wearer's heels.

—Phyllis and Fred Feldkamp, *The Good Life…or What's Left of It*

A Night in Gay Paree

The author puts his best foot forward.

Soon after the end of World War II, when it was again possible to visit the continent of Europe, and when I lived in England, I went with two friends for a week to Paris. It was a dream come true. We were in our early twenties, quite innocent, and on a very tight budget.

We took the day train from London and arrived in the evening at the Gare St-Lazare, which conveniently and dramatically brings the traveler right into the center and bustle of Paris. As we stood in the square outside the station and breathed the heady air and ambiance of Paris, we felt that it was a major achievement merely to have arrived there. We walked with our luggage to the rue du Colisée where, we had heard, there were small hotels which offered cheap rooms for *men who liked the color green* or who were *musical*, or *so*—the word *gay*, in those days, was used only to mean lively, merry, light-hearted, given to pleasures.

At the Hôtel du Colisée, they showed us a three-bedded room; but each of us hoped, although we had never discussed this, to meet a rich beau who, in return for certain favors granted, would pay for our dinners and theater tickets and other amusements—so we took three single rooms. There was a rudimentary bathroom along the corridor.

My friends were as graceful as a pair of swans, and within 24 hours of our arrival had established amiable relationships. John's friend was a tall, black American, the leading dancer in the revue at the Lido night club; Neville's *amour* was an Egyptian playboy whose mother was such a well-connected *grande dame*, that he could take the three of us to a showing of the highly publicized New Look collection at Christian Dior for which it was impossible to obtain tickets. He had enormous hands. "We all know what *that* implies," Neville gloated.

I was the ugly duckling of this trio; and after the days' dutiful cultural sightseeing, when darkness fell and the lights lit up and Paris became truly *la ville lumière* and as romantic as we had expected, my friends would go off to dinner with their protectors, and I was left to my own devices. I had barely enough money for food; the cost of theater and even cinema tickets was prohibitive. The cheapest way to spend the evening was to go to the *Bain Vapeur* in the nearby rue de Penthièvre, a bathhouse in a working-class district chiefly patronized by men who lived in that area and had no bathrooms in their homes. But there was an army barracks close by, and some of the young soldiers had no more money for entertainment than I had, so they went there to while away many hours. There was some furtive sexual activity in dark corners and where the steam was most dense.

But toward the end of our week's stay, I felt that I had to see more of Paris by night than the

One of France's most celebrated and esteemed authors, Colette, immortalized the lesbian society of Paris in her The Pure and the Impure, *which she considered to be her best book. The shocked and offended readers of a Paris weekly,* Gringoire, *in which it was serialized in 1930, disagreed: after its fourth installment the editor, bowing to his readership, discontinued the serialization so abruptly that, according to Janet Flanner, "the word* FIN, *The End, appears in the middle of a sentence that is never completed."*

—Andrea Weiss, *Paris Was a Woman: Portraits from the Left Bank* interior of that sordid, unclean bathhouse; I would splurge just once and go to the famous *Boeuf sur le Toit* bar, the meeting place of all the richest, most famous, talented, and beautiful homosexuals; it was said that Jean Cocteau and his gorgeous lover Jean Marais were there almost every night. Young men—painters, playwrights, poets, actors, musicians—had been discovered there; careers had been born. It was a must for an impecunious, ambitious young man.

I rested in bed all afternoon and early evening in order to look my best; I brushed my best suit, made sure I had kept a clean shirt for the occasion, selected my most handsome tie. A drop of cologne went behind each ear, more was sprinkled onto the pristine, hand-hemmed Irish linen handkerchief which was arranged to peep just a little more flamboyantly than usual from the jacket's breast pocket. With hair brushed vigorously *en brosse* and with considerable trepidation, I entered the door of this elegant, dimly lit bar.

Drinks were exorbitant, I had been warned, but less so at the bar than at tables. I went to the bar, where not many places were taken, and sat down three stools away from a little woman in a rather mannish grey skirt and jacket with matching hat. I ordered a gin fizz because a tall drink can be made to last a long, long time.

The mirror behind the bar reflected the whole room, and in it I began to notice that the men seated at the tables behind me were glancing at me—no, openly looking at me. I was very surprised, but there was no doubt of it: they were watching me, studying me; I was tremendously flattered and elated by this attention. Was it because I was a new face there? Was it my crew cut—not yet fashionable at that time in Paris? Whatever it was, I glowed in all those admiring looks; I preened, pretending not to have noticed them; I gave the room the benefit of first one profile, then the other; I toyed with my glass, and dipped a finger into the gin and made it fizz and pulled my finger back out again and licked it ever so sensuously. I was a vamp of the silent screen; I looked dreamily into the far distance, and then swiveled slowly, seductively around on my stool, leaned back on one elbow against the bar, posed with my legs thrust apart, and looked directly at the men who were looking at me.

But they were *not* looking at me, nor had they been at all. Not one of them had paid any attention to all my ridiculous posing and preening. Their eyes were all directed to my right, on the drab little woman three stools away—and no wonder, for now that I had become used to the dim lighting, I saw that this woman was Marlene Dietrich.

Oh, the shock of it! The realization stunned me so much and I was so mortified that I gulped down the remainder of my drink and knew that I couldn't afford to order another one when the highly efficient bartender immediately appeared to serve me. The entire pretentious bar, all the men and that famous actress in it— the whole of Paris had become hateful. I wanted to run away, but I sat still, as if I were glued to the seat of my humiliation, pretending to the barman that I was waiting for someone, a rich admirer, a handsome lover, the editor of the *Spectator* who had asked me to allow him to publish my story about meeting the King of Swaziland; a theatrical producer who had begged me to design the decor and costumes for his next opera at La Scala, at Covent Garden, at Bayreuth. But, as in the best remembered line of my favorite book, *it was all play…a striving and a striving, and an ending in nothing*. I was a miserable failure.

And then, as in a dream or a film with a happy ending, a tall and well-dressed man rose from one of the tables and on his way out of the bar made a little detour and came right up to me. Without stopping, he said "Do you plan to waste more time here, or will you go home with me now?"

I was rescued. I followed him out of that dark bar and to a taxi which drove us around the Place de l'Etoile into the tree-lined Avenue d'Iéna to a late 19th-century mansion which had been converted into apartments, and, in an incredible *fin de siècle* elevator that was all glass and bronze, we went up to his flat.

He switched on a table lamp and I found myself in a small, very neat studio room, sparsely furnished in what seemed to be a military style, with framed ancient photographs of quaint groups of soldiers all over the walls. "This is not my home, you know; I live mostly in England. It's just my little Paris *pied-à-terre*, a foot on the ground, you know. I have others in Cairo and Lahore."

Of course, when the British complained about French self-indulgence and immorality, they were referring not to haute cuisine and not even to the urban ratio of dogs to human beings but to other matters, such as naughtiness in sex; and here, it must be admitted, the French have little of what they like to call Anglo-Saxon puritanism, no laws against any sort of consensual, adult sexual behavior. (It was not by accident that Oscar Wilde, persecuted in Britain, went to Paris after his imprisonment in the Lord Douglas case, dying there in 1900.)

—Richard Bernstein, *Fragile Glory: A Portrait of France and the French*

I was impressed. My rescuer was clearly a rich and cultivated man. As Oscar Wilde had pointed out, the possession of several addresses inspires confidence—and not only in tradesmen. His charmingly old-world upper-class English accent was more reassuring, too. I knew he was a real gentleman and that I would come to no harm with him.

While I looked at the photographs he had taken the fur rug off the narrow bed and folded it neatly. "Go to bed," he told me. "I'll join you." And he went to the bathroom, from which he reappeared after I was between the sheets. I caught a glimpse of him, naked and very thin and tall, a silhouette against the doorway before he turned out the light behind him and came to bed. He smelt clean and good, and we were both tired, and I went to sleep in his arms.

When I awoke the next morning, pale daylight was coming into the room through the window blinds. My host appeared from the bathroom in a magnificent floor-length Eastern robe and went into the kitchen. "I'll make us a pot of hot chocolate before you leave," he called out. It was a strong hint that he did not want me to linger, and I was disappointed.

I dressed and walked around the room to look more closely at the framed sepia photographs that filled the walls, all of which depicted groups of late 19th-century soldiers of the British Army—*officers and gentlemen*—sitting with spiked and plumed Shikar helmets held on their laps, their ceremonial swords or sabres beside them, wearing highly polished, spurred boots almost to their knees, very tight trousers, and uniform jackets criss-crossed over and over with masses of heavy braid and tassels, fancy facings on the sleeves and on the high-necked collars, and ornamented shoulder epaulettes. Their legs were always thrust far apart in manly poses; most of them sported fierce moustaches. Behind them, or demurely posed at the sides of the pictures, were their native servants in turbans and white robes with wide sashes across their chests, some holding regimental mascots—mostly dogs, but an occasional goat. In the background there were tents, trestle tables laid for elaborate meals featuring many bottles of wine, bungalows set among palm trees, or the veranda of a gymkhana club.

Some of the pictures were not of large groups but showed only four, five, or six officers, bachelors all, at their ease in front of the stuccoed white chummery in which they lived, one reposing gracefully on the ground and the others sitting on camp stools behind him, with their household servants, their grooms, their polo ponies, and their pets arranged artistically around them.

All these military group portraits were handsomely framed behind glass, and on their cardboard mats they bore in black or in embossed gold letters the names of the regiment, the date, and location, and, in small type, the names of each man pictured. It was a delightful, unusual collection of photographs, and when my host returned with the hot chocolate I complimented him on them. "They're so amusing, so quaint, such fun," I said. "Wherever did you find them all?"

"*Find* them? What *can* you mean?" he said, quite sternly. "They're mine, of course. They're my regiment; I'm in every one of them."

It was impossible to extricate myself from my faux pas. "But they're all so old," I said, feebly.

"Of course they're old. So am I. I fought at Majuba Hill, you know."

This was inconceivable. I had gone to school in Johannesburg and knew South African history. "Majuba Hill!" I cried. "But the battle of Majuba Hill was in 1881!"

"So it was, and a bloody mess it was, too. I was a nineteen-year-old subaltern."

He walked to the two windows and snapped down the little acorns at the bottom of the blinds so that they rolled up and let in the sunlight. It shone upon him like a spotlight. He was not Frankenstein's Monster—not quite—but the gentleman with whom I had shared a bed was all too obviously 86 years old.

It was a shock, and I felt extremely foolish, but the lighting in the bar, in the street outside it, in the taxi, in the lobby and elevator of the apartment building had all been very dim. The flat had been lit only by the small table lamp. I had never clearly seen his face the previous evening; all that had mattered to me, was that a kindly and well-spoken gentleman had rescued me from that hateful bar and taken me to his cozy bed.

"But who are you? Are you a general?" I asked this ancient warrior who had played an active part in the rise of the British Empire and then witnessed its fall.

"What does that matter?" he said. "No questions, no pack drill."

We drank the hot chocolate, which was delicious.

He had been up the Nile with Wolseley in 1885, and in the Afghan Frontier Campaign of 1897, and then back in Egypt and the Sudan in 1898, and at the battle of Omdurman.

"*Omdurman!*" The cavalry charge—Winston Churchill was in that," I said in awe. I was an ardent admirer of Britain's great wartime Prime Minister.

"Yes, and what a nuisance he was, too."

After that he had returned to South Africa and fought in the Boer War. "And in the First World War?" I asked.

He wanted me to leave. I finished my hot chocolate; we shook hands; he took me to the glass-and-bronze elevator, and watched me descend in it.

I did not know whether to feel ashamed or proud of my exploit as I walked down the Avenue des Champs-Elysées to the rue du Colisée to have breakfast with John and Neville and exchange accounts of our night's adventures. Unlike wines and violins, bed companions are not prized for their age. I felt that I had made myself ridiculous—but, on the other hand, I had inadvertently made an interesting link with the past.

Hanns Ebensten runs a travel agency in Key West, Florida. He wrote this story for Christopher Street.

✦

In 1958 we went to the Folies-Bergère like good Americans, lured by Jo Baker as mistress of ceremonies. She shimmied and shimmered. She wore a clinging black gown and danced a variation of a tango with a slinky but sturdy partner who lifted her and draped her around himself in the best ballroom dancing tradition—elegant and detached. She changed into some ruffles by Balmain—a simple country girl who warned you not to touch her tomatoes but threw favors out to her guests from time to time. We were all her guests—that was what was most striking. She gathered up us thousand souls and hugged us to her as closely as those volumes of *mousseline* would permit. She was glamorous and folksy. The stage was her living room and she wanted you to be as comfortable as she was. She went to great lengths to teach us the words and melody of the refrain, allowed us to sing it once and then shifted on to another song like *tout de suite*.

But her apotheosis quite literally was her appearance at the Folies three years later—another Farewell Appearance as Mary, Queen of Scots, crowned, wearing an enveloping white, six-foot-wide crinoline gown and a fifteen-foot train, held and maneuvered by uniformed attendants as she came down that Folies staircase, majestically unhurried.... It was all absurd and sublime. It was Liberace and Radio City Music Hall's East Pageant rolled into one. She announced this as her final stage appearance and when she came forward to sing her adieu, the burden of the song was an account of her responsibility to her village, her castle, her dozen adopted children, and her threatening bankruptcy. She wept on cue at every performance and held out her hands to her beloved public. Men and women—all those bourgeois and concierges streamed down the aisles, weeping loudly and screaming "Josephine, don't leave us! Don't leave us!" Mountains of flowers were thrown on the stage. She hugged and kissed everyone in reach—tears mingled, love crossed the footlights, hovered, and settled. The curtain didn't come down for an hour.

—Julian Heath, *Deep Are the Roots: Memoirs of a Black Expatriate*

BOB BRADFIELD

Air Château

*The author fulfills a dream and gets a
bird's-eye view of the Loire Valley.*

IT WAS A BRIGHT BEAUTIFUL MORNING IN PARIS, AND FOQUET'S
sidewalk café on the Champs Elysées was definitely the place to be
because a German crew was filming a scene for a World War II
film at this historic landmark. I had just arrived on the Red Eye
from California, and could have used a few winks. But my friend
Bernard was in his element. Like most airline press officers, he
always had a good story idea, which invariably involved his company. I always thoroughly enjoyed listening to his yarns, and pretended to believe most of them. But this time he had gone too far.
He had arranged to play an extra in a German film about occupied Paris because it appealed to his sense of the ridiculous—he
had been a French Air Force pilot during the war, but he had also
organized a small part for me in the café scene, and shooting
started in five minutes. After the 15th take I quit, maybe I was
fired; it's a little hazy, but taking 3 hours to complete 30 seconds of
film was too much of a drain on life's juices for me.

"Bobby," he said, "our film careers are in a shambles, but life
must go on. Tomorrow is Sunday. If you could do anything you
wanted to do anywhere in France tomorrow, what would you like
to do?"

I mulled it over a few moments and replied, "I would like to do something very few people have done. I would like to get a small high-wing plane or glider and go along the Loire River at low altitude photographing the most interesting castles and châteaux from the level birds see them. I want to know from the land why they are located where they are. I want to look down on the complicated royal gardens surrounding the châteaux to get a better idea of what the designers had in mind, from a perspective even they did not have. I want to see how they used flowing water as a design element, whether natural or created."

His face lit up, and he almost shouted "*C'est magnifique!*" His eyes sparkled. "I've never done it either, and don't know of anyone who has. If I set the whole thing up tomorrow, could I go up with you?"

"*Mais oui, compadre,*" I agreed. He was transfixed with my newer knowledge of French.

Yet he looked worried. "But, Bobby, there are more than 400 châteaux and castles along the Loire, you will have to choose just a few."

I replied, "Not to worry, Bernard. I have always wanted to visit just three; Chenonceau, Chambord, and Azay-le-Rideau. Chenonceau because it is unique and looks like I imagine a royal residence should look. The River Cher runs right through it, and it has elegant gardens best seen from the air. It reeks of both British and French royal history. Chambord is enormous, structurally very different, solid-look-

"Château" has two quite distinct connotations— fortified castle and grand country house. In many places the second meaning gradually evolved from the first, as the strongholds of local barons (built to safeguard their families and retainers, their villagers and as many cows and sheep as could be crammed within the walls) were enlarged and altered in more peaceful times, rebuilt with a view to luxury rather than protection or domination, surrounded by parks and formal gardens, embellished with ornament. The high walls which surround these mansions now had social rather than military significance: they guarded the grand bourgeois from unwelcome intrusion by the peasants at his gate.

—Simon Loftus,
Puligny-Montrachet: Journal of a Village in Burgundy

ing, and it is located in an enormous park. Azay-le-Rideau just *is*, a jewel of a château designed just right for an ideal location. If I were president of this country I would make it the presidential residence. And all three of these properties are within 25-50 miles of each other."

He smiled. "I'll organize it right now."

He was back in an hour. "We have a single-engine, high-wing plane at Chartres laid on for 9:00 a.m. It's an old trainer, but we'll manage. I'll pick you up at your hovel"—he knew I preferred inexpensive lodgings on the Left Bank—"at 5:30 a.m. because I want you to see the stained glass at the Chartres cathedral by early light, and it opens at 7:30 a.m. Take a very wide angle lens, the cathedral is narrow, but more than 400 feet high." He rubbed his hands together with glee. "Today we lost our opportunity to be matinee idols, but tomorrow will be a better day."

Bernard swung by bright and early the next morning in an old black Citröen, the doors-the-wrong-way model so familiar to movie fans from Jean Gabin's classic gangster films, and we headed towards Chartres, about 60 miles south and west. The horrible clog of Paris traffic was a breeze on the weekend, and we were out of town in twenty minutes. There is an awe-inspiring view of the cathedral from the junction of two highways just outside Chartres. The architectural details are best seen when the sun is low. The commanding presence of the cathedral over the town can best be appreciated from here. Rodin described the cathedral as "the French Acropolis," and it is a particularly appropriate description. Both the Acropolis and the cathedral are impressive structures perched high on rocky promontories in the middle of town.

I found it interesting to explore the town of Chartres on foot, particularly the narrow cobblestoned lanes near the River Eure. Locally-made stained glass windows can be seen around town, and glass workshops can be visited without much fuss. Near the cathedral, the International Stained Glass Center is well worth a visit. The cathedral has nearly 150 stained glass windows containing 27,000 square feet of stained glass beauty, depicting mainly religious subjects. Many are 700 years old and extraordinarily complex. They are best seen in the early morning or late afternoon when the light enters at an angle.

But we came down to fly, and we headed off to the airport. The airport manager was singularly unimpressed that Bernard had flown a Flying Fortress many years ago, and assigned a pilot who didn't appear to be more than fifteen. I wasn't sure if he had begun to shave, but he told us he knew the plane, and not to worry, flying over the châteaux would be a piece of *gâteau*. He told us to keep in mind that all of these structures had been created more than 400 years ago. When the manager wasn't looking, I removed the passenger-side window to have an unobstructed view.

The three of us piled in and headed down the runway, anxious to witness history from this unusual viewpoint. It seemed like miles before we were able to get up enough speed to take off, but finally the old crate lifted and we were on our way. Flying near the cathedral was off limits because the city fathers feared small planes would buzz around the cathedral like gnats all day, so we banked away from the city and headed for the Loire. I found the chugada-chugada–chugada of the prop motor reassuring, but it made it difficult to talk, so we shouted and used hand signals. Bernard translated above the din.

Low-level fluffy cumulus clouds gave the landscape a dappled look as we went from sun to shade and back to sun again. When we climbed we found that the clouds were all at the same level, as if they had been pasted to an invisible net at 500 meters, so we continued climbing to 1000 meters for a smoother flight. When the Loire River first came into view Bernard shouted in my ear, "Bobby, if you know the history of that river down there you will understand much of the history of France." There was no doubt Bernard was having a marvelous time. Even if I didn't get a single picture the trip was already a huge success for him. He was trying to talk to the pilot over the noise of the motor, gesticulating and laughing as memories of flying flooded back.

The pilot pointed down with the pride of Lindberg approaching LeBourget, and Bernard shouted "There it is, Chenonceau."

But the cloud cover had thickened and we had to go down through it if we were going to get any pictures. Because of limited cabin space available and anticipated plane movement I was using my trusty old Leica M2 range finder camera with just a wide angle and short telephoto. As we came into the clouds the old cloth plane groaned, creaked, twisted, and pitched. Suddenly it dropped several hundred feet, as if the bottom had fallen out. Then it hit an invisible bottom, and it felt like the plane had stopped dropping, but the passengers hadn't. I thought I might lose my croissant, and remembered news stories of old crop-dusters breaking up in low-level turbulence. The creaking noises made me worry the wings would fall off. But suddenly we broke through and the château exploded into view, set in formal gardens which can only be fully appreciated from the air.

The centerpiece is a 75-yard two-storied gallery that spans the slow-moving River Cher by means of five massive arches. I signaled the pilot with a stiff hand that I wanted to bank on the side of the open window so I could look down without wing or strut obstructions, and then moved my hand in a circle to suggest doing a tight circle. The pilot nodded and set about it, but I hadn't realized that a tight circle meant practically standing me on my head with gravity pull, nor that going through each pretty cloud meant I would be bouncing and hanging on to the bracings of the plane for dear life, rather than taking pictures. The next time around we made a larger circle, avoided the clouds, and I was able to squeeze off some shots emphasizing different aspects of the castle and grounds. We went around again for good measure so I could just look at this magnificent sight.

Bernard shouted that more than one million people visited every year and enjoyed paintings by Rubens and 16th-century tapestries in the sixteen rooms open to the public. Henry II gave the castle to his mistress, Diane de Poitiers. But when the king died his wife, Catherine de Medici, gave the mistress the boot and moved in, making many changes, particularly the gallery and the formal gardens. The castle became a royal social center and over time François II, Charles IX, and Henri III and their courts resided here.

Chambord was just a few minutes away, but it is very different from Chenonceau in concept and execution. We went jouncing through the clouds again and circled the property at different altitudes, this time with less turbulence. My eyes were directed to the large, boxy, three-story structure by a very long, royal-looking, tree-lined road leading straight to it like an arrow, through patches of woods within the 13,000-acre hunting park. The gardens were neat but smaller, less complex, and less impressive than Chenonceau. A most curious collection of spires, domes, cupolas, gables, and turrets on the château roof looked like a small village from the air.

Some say Chambord lacks the woman's touch seen in Chenonceau, but others say it was constructed as a basic hunting lodge by François II, not as a château, and its three-story rectangular structure was appropriate for its 440 rooms and 365 chiseled turrets and chimneys. Several days later I visited the château and the guide described the roof scene as a "busy terrace." The royal château is known for the extraordinary superimposed circular stairway, and is well decorated with furniture, paintings, and tapestries of the time. François chose the salamander as his royal emblem, and the guide told us there were more than 700 representations of salamanders within the structure. I took his word for it. Although it took many years to construct François lived there only about a month. During World War II the art treasures of the Louvre were hidden there.

Leaving Chambord, we followed the Loire River towards the ocean to Blois with its fine castle on a rock spur overlooking the river. Now we were free of clouds. The castle is located on a hill overlooking the town with a commanding view of the river in both directions and the bridge across it. A large wall surrounds the castle, emphasizing its importance. The pilot said there was enough space to house the townsfolk inside the walls in an emergency. More than the other locations we had viewed this morning, Blois gave the impression that this castle was built with the idea it would have to be defended.

Azay-le-Rideau was just a few more miles down river. I was prepared to like Azay-le-Rideau from pictures I had seen, but they did not prepare me for the jewel-like setting in a tiny tributary of the Loire, the Indre. Unlike the larger stand-alone counterparts we had seen earlier which dominated their surroundings, Azay-le-Rideau is small, just the right size for the setting, and blends into the willow-lined banks of the Indre. It belongs there. It exudes peace, class, and style; it is the Jackie Kennedy of châteaux. I re-membered Balzac had described Azay as "a multi-faceted diamond in the setting of the Indre," and we saw the diamond aspect when the sun glinted off the river. We circled around several times at dif-ferent altitudes trying to get a balance of the château, the river, and the trees to capture the harmony it reflects; to put on film the im-pression I had in my mind.

The pilot waved cheerfully as we climbed to our cruising alti-tude. He was very proud of his châteaux, and he had been right, the trip had been a piece of cake, but it was a gift of unforgettable memories as well, hopefully now on film. The view of the châteaux from the air had given us a perspective as to why they were placed where they were, in a way that walking around on the ground could not. We had seen the design of the royal gardens as the makers intended. It also helped me to understand the histori-cal perspective—what had gone on in these buildings. Bernard cupped his hand and shouted, "The portion of the river we are fol-lowing was the path Joan of Arc took when she led the army in Chinon to victory over the British in Orleans several months later—about 100 years before these châteaux were constructed."

We landed in Chartres without incident and repaired to the bar to have an opportunity to chat with our young pilot without shouting over the noise of the motor. He told us he was a univer-sity student and found it thrilling to study what had happened in these châteaux during the week and then on the weekend be able to view them from the perspective of a bird, something even the royal families had not been able to do. We headed back to Paris in the squat old Citröen. It had been a marvelous day, and we decided we much preferred the spontaneous reality of high adventure to the disciplined creation of fantasy in films.

Dr. Bradfield directed Harvard's program on the Amazon River, carried out research at Cambridge as a Guggenheim Fellow, and was a clinical professor at the university of California at Berkeley and a civil rights attorney. He has lived in many parts of the world and has now returned to his first love— travel writing.

★

If the rest of us go to Paris for romance, where do the Parisians go? Some go to one of the most beautiful country houses in the world: a 443-year-old château with lovers' initials intertwined over the door.

Château d'Esclimont is only 37 miles southwest of Paris, next to a village you've probably never heard of—St-Symphorien-le-Château—off the main road to Chartres. But those directions are misleading. Esclimont is not on the way to or from anyplace. For two people who have a great deal to say to each other, it is a hidden place far from anywhere.

—Richard Reeves, "Château d'Esclimont," *Travel & Leisure*

IRENE-MARIE SPENCER

Sacred Hill of the North

An artist becomes part of an eternal tapestry.

THE TOLLING OF THE BELLS OF SACRÉ-COEUR SERVED AS A DAILY reminder of the sacred aspects of Montmartre. Their heady, metal pandemonium blotted out all other sound, emptying everything from my head for the minutes of the tolling. The bells were both a mantra and a white-out. I was living at the foot of Sacré-Coeur, the sugar-coated triple-domed spectre of white, which rules one of the seven hills of Paris, where the spirits of generations of mystics and artists have all played a role in the creation of this place.

The *quartier* is diverse, ethnic, Arabic, decaying. It does not possess the modern aura of Montparnasse. On some streets just below Sacré-Coeur, it takes a good hard look to realize you are not walking the marketplaces of Tunisia or Egypt. Shop vendors stand outside, heckling you as you pass, *Monsieur, Mademoiselle, beautiful, please come in, want to buy a suitcase, a watch*? You name it. None of the trendy shops of Boulevard St-Germain or St-Michel here.

To go home, I got off at Métro stop Château Rouge. One long block up, past the mostly Tunisian open market which was there on Wednesdays and Saturdays, a block left, and two blocks up. My studio apartment was located on a long narrow passageway, Passage Cottin, at the foot of an interminable flight of decrepit cement

steps frequented by stray cats. The building had a decidedly industrial appearance, very basic. And my one-room studio on the
third floor had only one window, which looked out to a blind
court, a square of walls and rooftops, windows which glowed
strangely orange in the lavender-indigo twilight. I could, on occasion, see the moon and a few stars by craning my neck and looking straight up into the black square. There was a large vent fan on
the wall perpendicular to mine, which turned ceaselessly around
and around, throwing shadows across the court at a certain time of
day. I had no kitchen, just a hotplate. And a bathroom with a very
deep but short bathtub, in which I spent many hours soaking in
an embryonic trance induced by sandalwood bath oil, in the af-
termath of a freezing afternoon visiting art galleries with my port-
folio. The primordial landscape of my tiny apartment at the foot
of Sacré-Coeur was not drawn with visual elements, however. It
was the tolling of the bell, La Savoyarde, the largest in France, I'm
told, the bell of Sacré-Coeur. This bell was the landscape which
flooded my body, my eyes, my soul. I began to live according to
the tolling of this amazing bell, as a monk's day is delineated with
ethereal chiming reminders signifying a transition, such as the call
to vespers. Inside, I felt this way about the sound of this bell. It had
become a call to prayer.

One night walking in Montmartre, I felt a longing—I wanted
to see the ghosts of Picasso and Apollinaire come strolling arm-in-
arm around the corner from a no-longer existing Bateau
Lavoir, or Toulouse-Lautrec and Aristide Bruant, smoking and
chatting outside the Chat Noir. The sky was a deep violet, and
the windows were all yellow and orange lit salons, as if by gas
lanterns, with people in them living out different Paris dreams.

> *"You are born French, but become Parisian."* I never learnt who said this, but it is true. All foreign students soon become Parisians and navigate the turbulent waves of the great city to their advantage.
>
> —Shusha Guppy, *A Girl in Paris*

I felt myself go inside those lives. I smelled the smoke of a wood
fire. I walked past Erik Satie's house. I thought about a "way" of

living in Paris, a style which flows with the character of the city, and blends in continuously. G.I. Gurdjieff frequented the cafés of Montmartre. He could not have been blind to its charm, to the subtle sounds and sublime vision through the fog of a deserted Sacré-Coeur towering above the butte. Vestiges of the ancient pagan tradition were everywhere, if you looked through Paris eyes. I had met so many people here who directed me to new paths, and that's what living in Montmartre seemed to be about. But just what was it about Montmartre? The history I began to look at revealed some new twists.

The rue des Abbesses is named after L'Abbaye aux Dames, an infamous cloister of Benedictine nuns founded in the early Middle Ages who ruled the *butte sacrée* with a zest for pleasures of the flesh. Henri IV's wild escapades in the convent while making Montmartre his headquarters are notorious. As far back as the 18th century, Montmartre had already gained a reputation for sex and abandonment, even before a parade of artists and bohemian fun-lovers had made it popular. Mothers sold their daughters to wealthy officials in the likes of such frolicsome taverns as A la Fontaine d'Amour and Au Veau Qui Tète. The 19th-century art scene provided the current guidebook reputation of Montmartre as an enclave for hedonistic artists: Toulouse-Lautrec, Van Gogh, Pissarro, Degas, Cézanne, Gauguin, Utrillo, Corot, Bonnard, Modigliani, Dufy, Ernst, Picasso, to name a few. Cabarets, underground theatre, dance-halls, and drinking establishments like the Chat Noir and the Lapin Agile proliferated in the twisted and cobbled passageways of the *quartier*. Today the vapid portraits and serene cityscapes displayed by the current "artists" of the Place du Tertre are a far cry from the energy and creativity of earlier times.

Leisurely afternoons spent browsing out-of-the-way, minuscule bookstores provided me with an unexpected surprise: a little rag-edged book in French, *Les Racines Sacrées de Paris* by Pierre Gordon, or *The Sacred Roots of Paris*. A chapter on Montmartre traced the history of the *colline sainte du nord*, or sacred hill of the north, back to pre-Christian times. Now here was some interesting material. Montmartre, according to Gordon's little book, did not derive its name from *mons martyrum* or "martyr hill," as the prosaically-minded would have us believe, but instead had received

the designation Mont Mercure, after the God Mercury, back in times of the Roman conquest. In the year 742 A.D., under the Carolingians, Montmartre was still called Mont Mercure. Mercury, or Hermes, was primarily the god of initiations. It was Caesar who designated Mercury the representative god of the Gauls. You can see the winged symbol for the god on a very *quotidien* blue square package of Gauloises, the prototypical filterless French cigarettes. And in the pervasive French cartoon, "Astérix."

From 700 to 500 B.C., hordes of Celts from Bavaria, Bohemia, and central Europe descended on fertile France and swallowed (or were swallowed by) the existing Cro-Magnon mixture. The Romans, observing that these Celts kept fighting roosters (in Latin, "rooster" is gallus), called them Gauls.

The French adore their Gallic ancestors. In the delightful comic strip Asterix, the little Gallic hero always outwits the block-headed Romans. The Gauls must have looked like today's French from the Midi—of medium height, brown haired, brown eyed—contrary to the idealized French belief that the Gauls were tall, blond, and blue eyed. This belief persists: recently, the nativist politician Le Pen found it necessary to deny publicly that he used a peroxide bleach to produce his blond hair.

—Henry S. Reuss and Margaret M. Reuss, *The Unknown South of France*

The Christian version of the Montmartre legend primarily describes the decapitation of St. Denis at the summit of the sacred hill, hence the appellation of Mount of the Martyrs which most standard guidebooks subscribe to. Gordon, however, maintains that initiation cults of pagan times frequently depict a "rite of the severed head," thus ascertaining that a symbology existed prior to Christian interpretations of site-specific events. The severing of the head represents a psychological and spiritual death and rebirth, particularly in the case of an initiation rite. There is evidence that Dionysian initiation cults took place here as well.

Initiation was my prevailing mood at the time. There was my

own cultural initiation of being a stranger in a strange land, learning the language and customs of a new country. I felt like a baby, groping for ways to express myself accurately. The French pay particular attention to the details of their language, especially pronunciation. I was also experiencing a deep personal initiation, of getting in touch with my self, turning 30. I had finally found my own apartment in Montmartre, after months of unsuccessful living experiments and sleazy hotels, house-sitting and transitional living with various acquaintances of old friends. And now, everyone I had met and knew was leaving Paris. I would stay on alone. The Paris I was getting acquainted with had the perpetually revolving face of Janus. Looking up as I wandered, I would see green and gold ancient gallic links of ivy, one crescent moon linking to the next, the spaces of sky reflecting between the trees and the medieval stone sides of buildings. After an inspired, formless day spent drinking Grog au Rhum in the afternoon café, I would find myself wandering aimlessly through the dark, misty streets, completely and utterly lost and alone.

One foggy February day I had decided to take the Métro rather than a bus. After the automatic doors banged shut, I had an intuition that I had made a grave mistake. Claustrophobia pierced my outer calm, and my worst fears were confirmed as fumes filled the car and then the lights went out. The train pitched us forward as brakes squealed. Dead calm and darkness. There was a black-out between Château Rouge and Barbès-Rochechouart. Smoke filled the train, which moved along like a slug through the dark tunnels, stopping every five seconds. I felt the invasion of fear, my palms sweating. There I was, a messenger with letters which had to be mailed. But no one was allowed to get on or off the train. At each stop, a voice from nowhere announced, "No one may descend at this stop. Please stay on the train."

The following day, Paris showed me a different face. I walked through the winding streets, watched the old men playing *pétanque*. The sky was bright blue, and the sun was out. A large plant being unloaded from the back of a car resonated green against the ancient stone walls and I felt full of a Paris I loved, a place of intense magic. I went to the Musée de Cluny. One room was huge and white, full of headless white statues on a stage. I could imagine living in that room. The whiteness and mystery of that scene pitted against the roughness of 11th- and 12th-century artifacts fascinated me, and I lingered over the rich detail of the medieval tapestries, jewelry and relics. Paris, a sphinx of a city, could change like that in a day. And Paris was changing me.

One day I noticed a small, peculiar sign on the door of the neighbor who lived directly across from me, a man I rarely caught a glimpse of. He was apparently African, and wore a traditional long and colorful robe. I stopped to read the sign. He was a shaman, a medicine man! His sign read "The Grand African Medium." Fascinated, I began to look for him every time I came in or out. Eventually, I found a reason to knock on his door. He was there, and kindly invited me in. His apartment was very plain, no decoration, just a few colorful African cloths thrown over a chair or two. He chatted with me very sociably, unpretentiously. I gradually got to know him better as time went on. He told me of his village in Mali where his grandfather was medicine man. He even invited me to stay with them if I ever got down to Mali. I felt very lucky to have been his neighbor, although I never did make it to Africa.

I wandered the winding streets of Montmartre on foggy nights, visited Masses in Latin at Sacré-Coeur (which seemed like pieces of performance art to me), heard Gregorian chants sung live in a medieval chapel, bickered with the Tunisian vendors at the Wednesday market, and suffered daily pilgrimages to the top of the Sacred Hill. I climbed the belltower of Sacré-Coeur, a tightly-wound spiral of endless stairs straight up a narrow stone cylinder, but well worth the bird's-eye view. And I spent many hours inside my apartment making art: magical, mystical paintings overwrought with shamanistic symbolism. I made the acquaintance of a French man, an enigmatic person and artist himself, who became my constant companion as we strolled the maze of streets, drank, and played chess in the cafés of Montmartre. Living there, in that place, turned out to be a turning point in my travels and in my life. From there, I traveled on to Turkey, where I later spent long periods of time and gathered experiences that changed my life completely.

One last vivid memory of Montmartre remains in my mind. After I had moved out of my apartment, and was leaving with my belongings—my cat and a large suitcase mostly filled with books which I dragged to the bus stop—I passed a man I did not know or recognize who said something to me. I will never forget what he said: "You haven't changed." I was shocked, and stopped to find out what he meant, who he was, but he seemed to disappear. I was left with only the image of his face looking directly at me, the eyes burning, and his mouth moving with those words. To this day, I take that experience as a visionary one. What he said was full of truth, but I did not realize it at the time. The enigmas of that man and his unexpected words had sealed off my time in Paris with a fitting postlude. I had to recognize in that moment, as I was getting on the bus, with the tolling of La Savoyarde in the background, that this hill had infused me with its very old magical spell. Montmartre would change my life, only much later.

Irene-Marie Spencer writes fiction and poetry, and has just completed her first novel Tales of the Moon and Water, *based on her experiences living in a fishing village in Turkey. She is also a fine art photographer. Spencer lives near Stoughton, Wisconsin with her husband and four daughters.*

✻

We stood in awe watching the red sunset behind Sacré-Coeur at the summit of Montmartre and its pink and orange reflection in the pools before the Palais de Chaillot. Silently we congratulated ourselves on providing the memory of a lifetime for the mature, cultured young gentleman that Kevin had become on his "Grand Tour." With the magnificence of Paris laid out at our feet, I turned to my son and asked gently, "Kevin, what are you thinking of right now?" Expecting a nugget of inspired brilliance, I was dismayed to hear him say, "I wonder how my Little League team is doing tonight."

I was crushed! Despite our best efforts, our son's mind was still back in the all-American pastime.

To most, thoughts of Paris bring back memories of lost passion, lingering kisses along the quays, whispered conversations in sidewalk cafés. But my heart fills with love when I recall this light-hearted memory of my son's childhood.

To this day, eighteen years later, whenever someone expects us to hold forth with some brilliant reply, our stock answer, followed by knowing smiles all around, is "I wonder how my Little League team is doing tonight."

—Sharon Huck, "*Bon Anniversaire*"

LAWRENCE OSBORNE

⋆ ⋆ ⋆

Turkish Baths

Our peasant explores the world
of Parisian hammams.

IT IS ALMOST CERTAIN THAT THE ARABS LEARNED THE SECRETS OF
the art of public bathing, with its meditative and homoerotic
dimensions, from the 400 bath houses of the Alexandria they conquered. In the modern equivalent of Alexandria the Islamicized art
of corporeal purification has come home to roost in the city where
the largest Roman ruin is a municipal bath and in which the desire for solitude is so intense that its ultimate gratification may rest
only with the *hammam aturki,* the *bain turc.* Our peasant, now that
some months have passed and he is firmly established as a naturalized citizen of the City, has become so addicted to this far from
gratuitous pastime that he spends almost all his money on the joys
of steam rooms, refrigerated pools and the manic manual skills of
the little Maghrebian masseurs who can be picked up almost as
easily as street girls and for a fraction of the cost. A light and
intensely individual eroticism holds court in the depths of the *hammam* in almost alarming harmony with a communal serenity en-
forced by the habit of the masseurs in the smaller establishments of
interrupting all operations at five o'clock precisely, unwrapping
their wicker mats between the massage tables in the direction of
Mecca and offering up their devotions in quiet but heartfelt un-

dertones. The object of the *hammam* is to escape the City and the world around it. Not only does the Moslem, as in the mosque, escape the City of War, but the sensual atheist, too, escapes from the asphyxia of the present and exiting by a series of illusionist doors in the form of underground chambers and ante-chambers, of mystic waters and fountains, leaves his existence behind, flirts more openly than ever before with his own body and suffers a sudden and vertiginous loss of toxicity—a brutal advent of cleanliness that leaves him in a state of memoryless disorientation for hours and even days afterwards.

The Turkish bath, with its mystique derived from the tendency of the European to indulge in infantile fantasies of the opulent, promiscuous, sorbet-eating East, the East of exemplary consumerist living which was never actually observed from close to, retains—in the high-class tourist establishments at least—the aura of the opium-smoking 1920s. The guides who cater to well-heeled international itinerants or local businessmen, the Gault-Millau for example, do not hesitate to include sections on the Turkish baths and the baths which they recommend are all devoid of true alien content, with the notable exception of the glorious *hammam* of the Mosquée de Paris. They are approximations to the original which compromise with Scandinavian modes of ablution. The systems of massage used, for example, with their—to our mind—tame and unimaginative hand-chopping and shoulder-kneading (as opposed to the more athletic and strenuous tendon-wrenching of the masseurs of the Middle East), seem to us to be entirely heretical in the context of the true *hammam*, as are their inclusion of such contraptions as saunas, exercise bicycles, vegetarian restaurants and bars. Let us be as explicit as possible: the true *hammam* is not a health club or a glorified gym. It is a place of non-activity, of withdrawal. The slightest athletic movement spoils the peculiar spiritual density of the small rooms, where every occupant is aware of every other down to his fingernails and the trails of sweat moving down his spine. Slowness of movement and reaction, a dropsical detachment, enable the bather to feel intimate with his fellow sufferers and to feel a primitive sympathy for his greatest defects, even for the rolls of diseased fat, the distended and craven bellies, the shrivelled-up penises that tempt bravura—or, for that matter for his greatest points of superiority, for the baths sometimes throw up disciplined and poetic male bodies that move with the ease of hammerhead sharks and which restore the dim memory of Roman court favourites, Neronic love-boys and professional Adonises expert in the nibbling of imperial testicles.

An example of the *hammam* that has missed its destiny is the Hammam St-Paul on the rue des Rosiers in the Marais. It might have been difficult, of course, to maintain a scrupulous Moslem profile in this Jewish neighbourhood, with kosher

ot only did the Hammam St-Paul miss its destiny, it's become part of history. It is now a hip clothing store.

—David Applefield, "Paris Review"

butchers and cinnamon-scented bakeries filled with seven-armed candelabra only a few doors down, and the façade itself betrays other points of origin: the gold mosaic lettering set into a chocolate wall and sculpted lions' heads on either side of a window with a blue push-out blind are clearly affected with 1930s mannerisms. A cramped lobby downstairs in a quaintly rectilinear style provides you with a staircase leading up to the first-floor restaurant and reception area housing a bar, a large and sunny space with rows of empty tables, rubber plants and semi-recumbent male forms draped in white bath towels. Subtending to this area are the mauve cubicles reminiscent of an obsolete swimming pool and from here, after undressing in distressing and anemic solitude, you descend the stairs to the baths. A crude thermal titillation awaits you. You sweat even before you push open the door that leads into the nondescript showers and by the time you have penetrated one set of doors further into the hexagonal steam lounge—the purgatory between the hell of the full steam room and the paradise of the ice-cold pool in the central atrium—your armpits are thrashing about in a swelter of racing moisture, you are reeking, your heartbeat has tripled, your eyeballs are popping like fragile ceramic objects accidentally thrown into a roaring oven. In this gasping, vapid little

room long spruce deckchairs are ranged around a circular table of
the same wood bearing a variety of French newspapers. You are intended to seat yourself, prevent yourself from passing out by
checking the dairy odours emanating from your boiling skin, and
leaf through one of these soggy and glutinous journals with nim-
ble fingernails.

*Purity is the ability
to contemplate defile-
ment.*

—Simone Weil, "Oppression and
Liberty" (1958)

It is not intended that you
should be able to stand much of
this sly thermic sadism and so it
is that before long you desire to
change direction and mood
and—why not?—temperature.

On either side of the door from the showers are the sauna and the
steam bath. We would sincerely recommend you not to waste time
in the sauna, which is naturally indistinguishable from all other
saunas, and whose dry heat we find unbearable: direct yourself to
the left-hand door and plunge into the inferno of the herbal steam
room, where the moans of the dying are Dantean and where you
can sit on any one of the ascending steps that recede back into in-
visibility: behind the wall of vapour, each one getting hotter as it
gets nearer the ceiling. The heat here is abusive, the burning com-
bustion that can be imagined on the surface of a wretched moon
of Jupiter, except that here the steam is scented with eucalyptus
and a piercing and tonic freshness quickly fills the lungs. The only
criticism that can be levelled against this exemplary steam room,
which is properly sealed at the correct temperature, is that far from
our much-awaited ideal of repose and abstraction we find here fat
businessmen discussing their sad little scandals in voices only half
hushed and farting at regular intervals.

Needless to say, such vulgar interruptions are highly distressing
to our refined and aristocratic peasant and you too may well find
yourselves leaving prematurely and searching out the cold bath in
order to attain your Sufic ecstasies. But you would be well advised
to wait until you are on the verge of unconsciousness before making a move, and then you should move quickly, stride with closed
eyes through the reading area, push through the aluminum doors

into the atrium (which is cool and distinguished) and, ignoring the notices in 1930s demotic advising you not to hurl yourself about, hurl yourself into the small pool, at the bottom of which a multitude of tiny blue and white checked tiles dazzles the eye. You should be aware, of course, that this brusque but exquisite gesture, given the size of the pool and the room, will drench every occupant of every chair around you, but unlike the true *hammam* a certain egoism is permissible here. In any case, the atrium (for want of a better word) will now allow you to dry off in relative anonymity, being equipped with foam mats ranged along a raised dais on either side of the pool and here you can contemplate the hexagonal cupola cut into the ceiling in clear reference to its Andalusian model, the Roman clock presiding over the pool, the unfortunate and completely inappropriate photo-murals of Hawaiian beaches and the plethora of yellowing notices on the walls arguing for silence, respect and cleanliness. Here, the same businessmen who irritated you in the steam bath come out gasping for air, brutally naked and half-boiled, and lower themselves quietly swearing into the icy water. You can see that they have difficulty breathing. They have the appearance of flabby consuls of the late empire, addled with erysipelas, or St. Anthony's Fire. So they wheeze and disport themselves like wounded dolphins in the blue and white shimmer of the pool and the clock ticks slowly while you sleep in the shadow of the arcade on your foam bed and hours pass by in the continual migration from steam to water, from heat to cold, from moaning to gasping, from sickness to health. After a while you notice that you have begun to smell differently, a smell of foul yogurt that comes with the exposure of your inner filth. It is time for that modern necessity, soap, and you can only regret that the masseurs available here, and who cost an additional 40 francs to the 90 you have already paid, are not authentic despite the fact that they soap you down as they should. You will have to go into the shower and do it yourself.

The truth is, we are not convinced that for 90 francs we are experiencing the *hammam* at its most disconcerting and gratifying. In fact, our peasant rarely consents to part with 90 francs at the St-

Paul unless he feels the need for the cold swimming pool—admittedly a luxury at most *hammams*. Depending on the area he finds himself in, there are numerous alternatives that remind him more of the *hammams* he has crawled through in the cities of North Africa, and more particularly of the exquisite massages he has enjoyed in the cheap unmarked bathhouses of Meknes and Fez, where the hot flagstones touched in the dark, the powerful hands of masseurs, the overpowering heat of underground vaults, produced in his mind the most powerful memories of all his various travels across the globe. His passion for these places was born in these distant cities and has mostly been prosecuted ever since on the margins of deserts, where the poignance of the public bath— the most potent and rich symbol of urban civility and utility—is at its greatest faced with the puritanism of the nomad. It was here that he discovered his distrust for the nomad, the scorner of bathhouses and therefore of libraries.

As in Alexandria, the *hammam* is the pivotal point of urbanity. It is the place where accumulated surplus time is spent and where the equivalent excess of eroticism is displayed and dissipated without action or violence. How significant that it is at the heart of the Islamic world that the *hammam* has imposed itself, as much at the centre as the much-vaunted mosque: that heart which is contested by, on the one hand, the classical urban tradition of intellect, leisure, tolerance and development and, on the other, the nomad pastoral tradition of disruption, perpetual violence, ascetic scorn, military rigour and social fluidity…the whole gamut of desert puritan values so glorified by Ibn Khaldun for the sake of its austerity and moral purity, but which can only destroy the precious fabric of the *hammam*, refusing to recognize as it does anything but the sterility of the moving man. In this way, invisibly seduced by our own desert jeremiads, our whining nomadism in the form of a thirst for the purity of the primitive, we see the Turkish bath as a locus for unparalleled sybaritic corruption, for discreet copulations and the begetting of illegitimate children. The fate of the bath in the life of the European city reflects this prejudice. Contrary to our myths of the Middle Ages, public bathing was popular in the European cities of the 14th century. The Church's edicts against "washing," so beloved of those desiring to prove in the most irrefutable way the pitiful backwardness and barbarism of this otherwise irritatingly arrogant continent, turn out on closer historical inspection to be tirades against the bi-sexual public baths of which the German city of Augsburg contained dozens, eventually closed down on orders from the bishop and in which—men

and women being entitled to rent private cubicles—a vast number of bastards were reported to have been sired. The Church did not care whether people were clean or not, it cared about their legitimacy. And yet the Church also, beyond its sense of spiritual responsibility, perpetuated the sneer of the original nomads, the greatest of whom is Moses. The urban mind of the Mediterranean, with its own fascination for the

I love prostitution in and for itself.… In the very notion of prostitution there is such a complex convergence of lust and bitterness, such a frenzy of muscle and sound of gold, such a void in human relations, that the very sight of it makes one dizzy! And how much is learned there! And one is so sad! And one dreams so well of love!

—Gustave Flaubert, writing to his mistress, Louise Colet (1853)

human body, only relinquished its bathroom habits under intense pressure from the outside, from the spiritual guerrillas of the desert. It seems to us, lying in the arcaded courtyards of the world's *hammams*, subdued by the bubbling of fountains and drowsily aware of the naked bodies propped against classical pillars and scraping oil from their arms, willingly immersed in the only form of collective masculinity devoid of aggression, in a calm enjoyment of architectural details, self-enclosing fraternity, absence of loud throats and locker-room wit, borne along by the immemorial forms of a relaxation that is eminently horizontal and silent, that we have returned to our Greco-Roman roots, however uproariously funny this may seem to fellow hyperboreans. Even the smallest Parisian *hammam* gives us this nostalgia—the "pain of returning."

There is, for example, the small place on the corner of the rue de Tombouctou and the Boulevard de la Chapelle in the Goutte d'Or, called El-Baraka but ominously missing from the telephone books. Situated between the railway lines fanning out behind the Gare du Nord which sprawl under the boulevard and a gaping hole at the angle with the rue de Chartres formed by the destruction of a block of tenements and which is now like a chalk quarry covered with gargantuan figures of street art, cubic skeletons and running gangsters depicted falling into the hole, the El-Baraka is announced by its delicate blue tiles and Moorish lancets rising unexpectedly out of the hurly-burly of the boulevard. A small neon sign is all that tells you there is not the usual Moroccan restaurant with whining lutes underneath. Instead, the vestibule is cramped, dark and hot and above all it is grave as all true *hammams* are. There is no joking and elbow-nudging here. The bath is a serious enterprise. For 50 francs you have a straightforward sweat and for a further 20 you can hire one of the two or three white-haired masseurs at the top of the stairs and take him down with you into the depths. The baths themselves are simple in the extreme: a shower and spotless defecation area, a long hot-room in dark blue tiles with basins set at regular intervals into the wall with a continuous bench running between them and, at the far end, properly screened by heavy plastic ribbons, the steam bath itself, a small triangular room in the same blue tiles. Despite the absence of extra luxuries the El-Baraka is a place of asylum. It is used only by the local Moslems, sandalled loan sharks, grocers scarred with smallpox, oily clerics, students, train drivers, small-time landlords. It is an advantage of the familiarity that reigns in the El-Baraka that the attendants personally tie the knot in your bathrobe and in general speak to you with a certain outlandish deference. The drying and rest room, where the wet clients stretch out on their mattresses, has high mirhab-shaped windows giving on to the rue de Tombouctou and the boulevard—where the Métro trains crash along the overhead track—and lying between the walls of tiles in the heat of a burning afternoon while the myriad voices babbling in Arabic and Turkish on the suffocating boulevard seep into the silence of the baths, you know that you are no longer in the Paris of the glass towers and Napoleonic relics, you are in the Nilotic Paris, the Paris of Mesopotamia, the Flower of the Desert. And all this, at the Baraka, for 50 francs!

But whatever the advantages offered by the small baths of the Goutte d'Or and however much our peasant resorts to them because they are in his neighbourhood, it cannot be denied that no *hammam* in Paris, or in the West, can equal in vertiginous decor and graceful eroticism the baths of the Paris Mosque situated on the Place du Puits de l'Ermite. Although we have made a resolution not to stray into descriptions of the tourist dimensions of the New Disneyland, we cannot help descending into the much-frequented and familiar Hamman of the Mosque, which is in addition charmingly attached to the tearoom where blow-dried nymphets and pouting schoolgirls with their quaint little Maghrebian pastries, tiny one-mouthful "gazelle horns" and *keblahs*, oblivious to the fantastic world on the other side of the wall, where loin-clothed male bodies slump in an oleic dungeon of heat, where time moves slowly backward. As always, we have no idea what the female side of the baths is like, but here at least the ethos of the Ottomans ferments like yeast in the warmth. You wonder, in a moment of crass vulgarity, why there is not a mad Sultan spitting

I paid the entrance fee and proceeded tentatively past the door, through a double layer of curtains made of heavy woolen weavings. A few more doors followed, and then suddenly I was at the opening of an enormous room, with naked bodies reclining languorously all about.

I was taken aback. The scene was of a harem, painted by Ingres or Matisse, now come alive with the soft burbling of the women talking in different languages. The ceiling was decorated in intricate designs of red and dark green. In the center of the marble-floored room was a tall fountain, the cool water continuously gurgling out and over, splashing into a mosaic bowl. On all sides of the room were canopied platforms covered with carpets, on which small mattresses were placed, side by side. In every space there were lounging odalisques.

This must be Tunisia, but no, it was the center of Paris, and no, these were not harem slaves, but Parisians.

—Zona Sage,
"Hunting the *Hammam*"

foam in one of its nooks and crannies or why at least there are no
eunuchs in evidence—the calmness and luxury of the rest area
with its veined marble columns and quietly murmuring fountain
should be the ideal terrain for a multitude of obedient and heavily armed eunuchs....

Of all the secluded retreats which the City offers this is by far
our favourite: the proliferation of geometric figures, assorted poly-
gons, lozenges and stars in the painted wooden panels, the octagonal cupola opening up above the fountain, the dark red that pre-
dominates in the woodwork, the filtered light and the columns of
the raised dais that surrounds the fountain on three sides are offset
in the realm of sound by the steady murmur of the water sliding
over the upper lip of the fountain and into the basin below, where
bottles of water lie cooling. The dais is heated from below so that
the tiles are always warm and mint tea is served with oranges to
the reclining clients. Beyond the narrow doors that lead to the
baths the decor is more Spartan and cavernous: white vaults brim-
ming with condensation, raised alcoves framed with classical pillars
with basins and taps where the stone flags are hot to the touch, the
massage room with its single slippery bench and, in the middle
room, an elegant central platform surrounded by columns with
simply carved capitals bathed in a single shaft of light. The rooms
become hotter progressively until at the far end you enter the final
steam bath, a small chamber with, on the left, a raised platform and,
on the right, a large circular cistern filled with sediments of grey
clay. On the far side of the uncertain crater are two ventilators
belching forth an agonizing heat. It is a point of masculine bravura
to walk slowly around the cistern passing within inches of the searing ventilators, with no gesture of disbelief except a casual wipe of
the brow and it is an athletic achievement to do this even once
without passing out and tumbling ignominiously into the cistern,
from where you would be fished out covered in horrible and outlandish burns. Here the fat men do best, leaning on their ther-
mostable guts and, for once, eyeing their thin rivals with contempt.
They do not blush or quiver as the slim carcasses do; they absorb

patiently like heat-seeking reptiles and the sweat that rolls off them is measured and wise. For those less endowed by nature with subcutaneous armour it will be necessary to retire quickly to the lesser steam room, where the basins are thoughtfully equipped with hoses attached to the cold-water taps.

The massages, by the axolotyl-like Hamid, are worth the 50 francs—but since you have only paid 55 francs to enter this stupendous *hammam* in the first place you will assume you have profited from a bargain. The massage is exactly as it would be anywhere in the Moslem world, since the movements are laid down according to physiologically tested ritual and are always executed with a methodical and patient exactitude. Contorting their bodies into bows, they stretch out the client from underneath by clasping his ankles and wrists, inflect his spine, pull the arms across the chest and move their hands along them as if squeezing a tube of toothpaste, displace each finger a millimetre from its joints, twist, thump, arch, distend, wrench, hiss, and cluck. The service involves maximal effort on their part, using every part of their own body. Those so-called masseurs who content themselves with slapping a supine pair of shoulder blades with the sides of their hands seem worse than absurd by comparison. At the end of this gruelling set of figures the client feels broken apart, unstuck and magically reassembled. No ligament, tendon, muscle or nerve seems to have escaped the treatment. The spine, in particular, suffers a realignment suggestive of blissful fracture. At the same time the masseur oils and soaps the entire surface of the body with scrupulous attention to detail—although unlike the masseurs of the Maghreb they do not hurl buckets of scalding then cold water over it, much to our regret. The washing of the extremities of the fingers, carried through with such thoroughness, expresses an inadvertent tenderness which is communicated through the square, flattened nature of Hamid's toes and the similar bluntness of his fingers: through long hours of immersion in the tropical heat of the *hammam* they have become vegetal. They have the fibrous strength of tendrils of liana. You might well spend days of ecstasy in the Hammam of the

Mosque, never quite able to tear yourself away from it through whole afternoons, as our peasant does (not only because he is indolent by nature but also because he can think of no better way to change identity). We might well suggest other *hammams* to you, the one next to the Chope des Artistes on the rue du Faubourg St-Martin, for example, ensconced at the bottom of its grimy little passageway next to the Buzy Body clothes store, or the incredibly simple and secretive baths at 126 Avenue d'Italie announced by an old fashioned black and gold sign—Bains et Hydrothérapie—and similarly hidden at the end of a run-down passage and courtyard which is truly in the middle of nowhere. But for the minimum price of around 50 francs it is impossible to improve upon the Mosque and nowhere else outside of the Goutte d'Or will the imperialism of the City be more easily disrupted. When will the day come when *hammams* are built on every street corner complete with muscly masseurs and carved *moucharabiehs*, polylobal arches

I continued my explorations and discovered the "gommage" room, where white-clothed attendants were vigorously scrubbing down women on two concrete tables. I asked some of the women waiting in line along the wall what this process was about. They said "gommage." Even though I had no idea what that meant ("erasure?"), I was game for the total experience at this point, so I joined the others and waited in line. Several women in the large open showers on the side were smearing themselves with green mud.

My turn came up for gommage and I lay on the concrete table. It turned out that this was not for the tame or tender. It was more intense than any spa treatment I had ever received anywhere, and felt like very stiff bristles scraping all over my body. By the time I had been completely gommaged I was down to a layer of skin that hadn't seen the light of day in a generation.

—Zona Sage,
"Hunting the Hammam"

and ceramic *zelliges?* When will the public bath drive out the fatuous private bathroom and regain the gigantism of Caracalla and Diocletian? When will the scent of scorched eucalyptus replace the obnoxious odours of shower gels and talcum powder? No doubt we are guilty once again of rash nostalgia of the past, but on this occasion we can claim the excuse that the *hammam* is not yet dead, that it thrives furtively under the City's skin and that one day it might just possibly erupt back into the national habits. When that happens the Age of Plenty will have returned to earth, the Golden Age, the Innocent Age, the Oh How Much Better It Was Age…the Age of the Turkish Bath.

But the *hammams*, as you slowly begin to realize, are only oases of peace in the livid organism of the City and like all oases they frame large tracts of desert between them. And one of these hostile Gobis of the Mind exists in all its terrifying largeness and imponderability inside the head of an ex-abattoir manager who lives on the third floor above the peasant's apartment at no. 37 rue André Antoine, who—as it happens—is right at this very minute having a ferocious dream about Genghis Kahn and the Golden Horde. For M. Soufflet has something of an obsession with the Golden Horde. You see, they're going to come back one day, that old bastard Genghis Khan will come back too and destroy our beloved Paris…for everything is at risk, the barbarians are coming—indeed, they're already among us!—and it is only a matter of time before they start eviscerating children on the boulevards from the saddles of their stinking little ponies. It'll be like the Boches, only worse. The Mongols aren't even Aryans! And as history shows, the only thing they know how to do is wipe out cities, whole metropolises. Remember Baghdad, remember Delhi, remember Kiev! Curious to say, the pugnacious little ex-meat man has a moving and thoroughly noble attachment to the values of urban civilization and we can only listen with the utmost gravity to the dire warnings of his dreams…it is only to be regretted that M. Soufflet, in his hatred for everything alien, throws the baby out with the bathwater by associating the Mongols with Turkish baths. In this way we see that curious nightmares inspired by the City leave no room for fine definitions. And M. Soufflet, fearing the contaminating breath of those ear-chopping goblins from the steppes, will never ever put a foot inside a *hammam*. There is nothing for him to do but suffer and dream.

Lawrence Osborne is the author of The Angelic Game, Ania Malina, *and* Paris Dreambook: An Unconventional Guide to the Splendor and Squalor of the City *from which this story was excerpted. He lives in Paris.*

★

My thighs ached and I strained to breathe as I ground slowly up the hill, leaving the Seine River below. The cool Foret de Meudon was only a short distance away, if I could only keep running. With close to twelve thousand other runners, I was following the course from the Eiffel Tower to Versailles. Approximately eleven miles long, the run is one of the most popular races in Paris. Each year in September, thousands of Parisians and foreigners gather at the base of the Eiffel Tower. Groups of runners are started minute by minute, each contestant's number individually electronically scanned. By the time those of us near the end of the line begin running, the winners of the race have already been announced over the loudspeaker. But we are not running as competitors, rather for the pleasure of running from the Eiffel Tower along the banks of the Seine as far as Chaville, where the route leaves the river and takes us up the hill, through the Foret de Meudon and down the other side, to the grand boulevard leading to Louis the XIV's palace at Versailles. Local bands enthusiastically play popular songs, classical music, or rock at strategic points along the route. In September the weather is still warm—downright hot two of the three times I ran it—and the shade of the forest provides a welcome relief. Descending the hill towards Versailles, runners relax in the fern-filled woods, feeling as though they have left Paris and city streets a vast distance behind. Entering the town of Versailles, runners make their way up the tree-lined boulevard, approaching one of the most extravagant palaces ever built. We succumb to the illusion of grandeur, even tired and sweating as we are.

—Barbara J. Euser, "Running in Paris"

GEORGE VINCENT WRIGHT

✦ ✦ ✦

Wounded and Healed

Father and son enjoy a final trip together.

IT WAS LATE NOVEMBER AND I WAS IN PARIS WITH MY FATHER who was 93 years old. We had been in France for almost three weeks. It had been a delightful, elegiac and harrowing trip. Delightful in that people were charmed by this sturdy old man with frailty at the edges and a crinkly sense of humor. Elegiac in that there was more truth between us than ever before in our lives, and although his health was good, I think we both knew, somewhere, that this was the last trip, and everything came roaring out of the woodwork: high intelligence, perception, poetry, insight, and that which made it harrowing: deep green bile anger and underhandedness on both our parts, and envy and out-of-normal mental states: at times he thought I had brought him to France to kill him, that the hotel we were staying at was a mental hospital (he was right, some of them did look like mental hospitals) and that I was the doctor keeping him locked up. Other times he would see what he called "zombies": groups of six figures dressed in black, with black veils over their faces; they would disappear when he got closer to them than twenty or thirty feet. He was to die seven weeks later, peacefully without illness, in his sleep.

It was a cold, damp, gray, grainy day. We had just had breakfast at our hotel in the Left Bank and we were in a taxi going to the Louvre. We got out in front of the Louvre and there was an unusually high granite curb, about ten inches from the cobblestone street to the sidewalk. As my father mounted the curb, he faltered and his left shin struck the hard granite.

He cried out in pain and I helped him sit down. I lifted up his pant leg and through the white support stocking I could see blood pouring into his shoe.

I was scared and light-headed with fear. I felt slow and sleepy, and it seemed as though I could not react and make things happen fast enough. There was a security guard 100 feet away, so I signaled him and he came over and called for help on his walkie-talkie. Very quickly two more security guards came over and gave my father a coat to put over his legs to keep him warm. He sat on the sidewalk shivering with the cold. I was holding a handkerchief over his wound; my father was drawn into his physical self, concentrating on enduring. I was making conversation with the security guards and help arrived with the typical French siren "aah-uuh, aah-uuh"—high sound on the "aah" and low sound on the "uuh."

They were the Pompiers/Sapeurs—the combination of firemen and ambulance medics. They were take-charge, fast, efficient. And cute. I just don't know where to begin in describing these beings....They were shortish, mid-twenties, dark hair, beard-grain on the face and a jauntiness only the French have. Lithe and slender, they had the clean-limbed and intimate physicality that comes from a well-practiced team performing tasks together. And their uniforms! Navy blue with a clerical-type collar without the white, all of the same material, perfectly proportioned. The restraint and elegance in this envelope of clothing gave such contained power to the occupants, who had the bearing of those who are constrained from bursting into backflips. They had that Parisian fine bubble and spritz in everything they did, and although individuals, they had the simplicity of we-are-men-working-together, the gruff sweetness of toy soldiers. I could see them breaking into song

and dance but with more Schoenberg in it than music hall to mirror their boyish gravity. After weeks of sleeping in hot rooms with
my father (his age required great warmth) and washing his dirty
underwear, this energy before me was…I couldn't believe my
eyes.… How did I wake up here?… I wanted to take it all in and
pour it all over me but I couldn't find the method to do so.

They took us to the emergency room of the Hôtel Dieu, a hospital built in the 1600s and recently renovated. My father was put
on a wheeled gurney and we waited while more pressing cases
were taken care of. Looking down the corridor I saw a tall young
man, beatitudes coming out of him. I said to myself, "I want that
guy to work on my Dad." As fate would have it, he's the guy we
got.

He was good-looking and had élan gentled by intelligence with
loft, just like his height. He had big friendly ears, an inquisitive
smile and a sympathetic connection which was clear in the way he
used his hands in examining my father. Through all this my father
was quiet and content and making an occasional comment. X-rays
were taken, everything was fine. The doctor directed the young
aide to stitch the wound, which he accomplished with a synco-
pated grace. He was quick and deft in his motions but then he
would have brief, hesitant stops in midstream where he would
check upstairs, mentally speaking, and then continue.

It was all so subtle, my neurons were a-tingle. I could sense that
the connection between this young aide and my father was strong.
No anesthetic was given to my father, yet he was tranquil and alert.
The aide would revert to accented English and ask my father: "It's
all right? It's all right? Good?" My father would nod and say yes
and the aide would stick his thumb up and nod in approval. He
checked in with my father this way every twenty or thirty seconds
and gave the same thumbs-up. This energetic tenderness continued throughout the sewing-up process during which time he told
me how my father reminded him of his grandfather whom he
loved very much and who was also 93 years old. Sewn up, doctor
approved, bill paid (only $50!) we left the Hôtel Dieu. What a flip-

flop day. From worry and fear to the most sublime experience of human beings. This was the most amazing day of our trip, and it led us to experience a whole different side of Paris.

Two hours later we took a taxi back to the Louvre, mounted the high curb correctly, smiled at the same security guard, who was obviously surprised at our re-entry and obtained a wheelchair for Dad. Just as he was getting into the wheelchair, my father bumped his other shin into some protrusion of the device. Momentary heartskip for me and string of curses from Dad, but just a blood blister and we wheeled away into fields of art.

Seen close up, the Sun King was less radiant than one would think. He had two teeth when he was born, but when he was a little over twenty he had to have all his teeth extracted by the court surgeon, because of an illness. There are various accounts of this matter: some say all, some say many, some one. (His father, Louis XIII, on the other hand, had forty-eight teeth instead of the usual thirty-two.) In any case, the operation was not a success; the King lost a piece of this palate, and during meals bits of food often came out of his nose, which etiquette did not permit his fellow diners to notice. The King, for his part, would have liked to eat alone, but not even he could escape the etiquette that prescribed his presence at the table.

—Aldo Buzzi, *Journey to the Land of the Flies and Other Travels*, translated from the Italian by Ann Goldstein

That evening we were near St-Germain-des-Prés sniffing around for a good restaurant. We finally chose one on a little street, a cozy restaurant in Art Nouveaux style.

We went inside and were greeted by a charming and pretty woman who was passing into early middle age ripeness and maternal warmth but still with the air of the world about her; she had a knowing look, lasciviousness with grace, the special character of which seems to be the domain of lower middle-class French women. I don't mean this to be a supercilious put-down, but to identify it as a quality.

She was charmed by my 93-year-old father and escorted him down the stairs to our table. He, of course, relished this lovely female attention.

When we were seated at the table, the charm of the place sank into me. There were all these nooks and crannies and built-in cabinets with specially made handles and curving lines. There was an upper level by the street which had little tables that had the coziness of an old railroad dining carriage. The area where we sat was the larger dining area, about three feet lower than the other level. But it wasn't like looking up or down at people. It seemed more that you were looking at people from a different angle. This subtlety, and sense of floating in space was promulgated by the lilt of the design. The only straight lines were the four exterior walls. Everything else was curved and tendrilled—like some enchanted little beings from Walt Disney's *Fantasia* had put on ice skates to mark out the design.

The curves were not smooth and continuous but were partial and interrupted as if the curve maker was always getting a better idea and so would stop the curve he was making in favor of another. Everything was curved: the platform, the stairs, the recess in the ceiling, the railings, the windows. The place abounded with little places where something delightful and surprising could be hidden, popping out at any moment. And, oh the lamps, ten to twelve inches high, also of a tendrilled design, with amber parchment shades with long vermicelli fringe hanging down from the edge, one lamp on each table. With people huddled over the tables deep in conversation, lamps glowing in the middle, it looked like a scene of forest beings gathered around their many individual fires. Urban fauns and leprechauns could call this home.

I ordered a Sauterne, actually it was a Cadillac, which was a town across the river from the Sauterne region. It was some Cadillac, *very* golden in color and with spritz in it! I had never had a Cadillac with spritz in it. And it was great—the little spritz cut the oily sweetness of the Cadillac. Then came the pâté—it was thick and rich with essence of fowl taste. Like the essence of Thanksgiving turkey gravy velveted into the silk of divine fat. What was a big surprise was how good the oily Cadillac tasted with pâté of fat goose. I enjoyed a supernal OPEC dinner.

I don't remember the rest of the dinner very well except that
there was some kind of soup, some kind of meat and potatoes,
some kind of dessert. But just as we were finishing the pâté, two
women came in and sat down at a small, round table across the aisle
from us. An older one and a younger one. In her 40s and in her
30s. They were aloof and engaged. Striking, but not bizarre.
Angular, but not hard. There was a special spaciousness and intimacy to their relationship. Were they lovers or good friends? It was
hard to tell.

The older one was much more intriguing. She was long and
drawn out, but the maker knew just where to stop before distor-
tion. She had some of that Princess Di quality of a sumptuous
thoroughbred, the equine quality shining through human form
most clearly as when exiting from the rear seat of a limousine, legs
together as in a canter, the high heels going down elegant, hoof-
like. I turned my head and looked at her; she slowly turned her
head and looked at me. A gaze of several moments—and then back
to our eating. The whole dinner was like that, back and forth. It
was as if we were both busy typing, and when we went to the left
to draw the carriage back to the right of the typewriter, we would
pause and look at each other for a few seconds.

I kept coming back because I was fascinated with her and I had
never quite had an experience like this before. I had recently read
a story on flirting in Paris so I was prepped that it was common,
light-hearted, and playful—and that it could happen. But here it
was. And actually, although there was flirting going on, there was
so much more going on at the same time. It felt as if we were two
computers downloading data into one another with the organiza-
tion and meaning yet to be done. Her skin was pale and healthy,
her eyes were hazel. Her physical envelope had a dullness like the
plumage of female birds. But the dullness was not unhealthy or un-
interesting. It concealed a gleaming which I could sense behind
the cells. The orbits around her eyes were large; the eyebrows spa-
ciously arched. A wide mouth, slender lips with just a bit of puff
in them. A long neck. Hipped but not full. She had the intrigue of
a woman on the edge of the homely.

There was a sense of a smile-in-formation with us but we never smiled the whole evening. While there were sophisticated levels as well, we were looking at each other the way small children look—with unvalued and undetermined curiosity. Something delphic and wise in her, like an oracle. I could feel her cruelty, her judgment, her long nose, her disdain, her contempt, her hardness, her snobbism, her cold good taste, her putting someone to the sword, her enjoyment of blood, the witch in her. What was so deeply satisfying in this encounter was that I had all of those same qualities in me, showing as were hers, but under wraps in a way that kept curiosity and a squeak of tenderness going between us. I felt that I had met an equal and that I could let out all of my DNA without arranging it into acceptable forms.

But their dinner was over and they took their long legs out into the night. And I continued to read selections of poetry to my father from the *Oxford Book of English Verse*.

George Vincent Wright grew up in Bayside, Queens (New York) and graduated from the Yale School of Architecture. In addition to designing, renovating, and building houses for more than twenty years in Maine, San Francisco, and the Bay Area, he's traveled the world, ever curious about water culture bathing, history, music, and cuisine sauvage. *He has also harbored a long interest in being president. He returned to Bayside in 1994 to spend time with his father and now lives in the family home where he writes and gardens.*

✱

In the time of the Sun King, the *souper à sonnette* was invented—the "bell dinner," during which the ladies sat at the table dressed only in powder, perfume, and jewels. On the backs of their chairs hung loose robes, to put on whenever the servants, summoned by the bell, entered to perform their duties. No servant of the time has left a memoir that might enable us to understand what thoughts passed through his mind while he was serving. Perhaps the most aphrodisiac effect was reserved precisely for the servants; and perhaps in the silvery sound of the bell one can discern the first signs of the future revolution.

—Aldo Buzzi, *Journey to the Land of the Flies and Other Travels*, translated from the Italian by Ann Goldstein

DAVID APPLEFIELD

Montreuil-sous-Bois

An updated version of Paris thrives in the city's suburbs.

IN AN INTERVIEW FOR HIS COLUMN "POSTCARD FROM PARIS" IN the *Washington Post* the American journalist Mort Rosenblum once quoted me as labeling Montreuil "the Montparnasse of the *fin-de-siècle.*" To anyone familiar with both bohemian Montparnasse of the twenties and thirties and this large working-class town of 100,000 at the eastern edge of Paris, jammed with Malian and Moroccan immigrants and teeming with all sorts of creative and marginal types, the comparison at first rings with irony. But on second thought, the somewhat stretched metaphor begins to leak some truth. The Paris of vibrant intellectual exchange, of lively debate in the cafes, of blissful artistic decadence in the artistic circles—at pittance prices—today belongs to tired folklore. Present-day Paris, frankly, is way too expensive for all but a few expatriate artists and writers to endure open-endedly. Legal immigration restrictions have grown far too stringent to encourage the once-privileged American literati to come in flocks and stay. Even the word "expatriate" has lost its original sense of protest: AT&T, for one, uses the term to label its permanent resident accounts, most of which belong to rather patriotic people who work for IBM, Citibank, Disney, or one of the other large corporate citizens with international outreach, and enjoy the ubiquitous presence of such iconic Goliaths as Haagen Daz, Nike, and Pizza Hut.

To understand Paris today, one has to be willing to suspend many of the cliches that nonetheless continue to drive the city's international reputation, and venture out beyond the sacrosanct 4th, 5th, 6th, and 7th *arrondissements*. This is hard for visitors, tourists, and much of Paris's mass of migratory addicts who aren't so willing to update their fix or readjust their sights. Psychic resistence is powerful. Francophiles and general tourists alike need a certain gilded Paris as their symbolic capital of love, art, and style. They need this "let them eat cake" place in the world where things are beautiful, women are slim, and poodles are welcomed in chi-chi restaurants. Touching these icons is a bit taboo because writers and readers alike need a celestial French capital—a real and imaginary place outside of the confining ropes of anglo-saxon puritanism, American mall culture, historically-void notions of the past and contemporary functional aesthetics. As one aging American literary publisher who had spent lots of glorious weeks in Paris in the fifties and sixties crudely whispered to me at a book fair recently, "It's always been easier getting laid in Paris." Others would put it differently: "In Paris you feel more alive."

For those of us who continue to live in Paris, it's at times painful to observe how the city continues journalistically to be painted more in memories and dreams than in truth. The story of the expat American writer in the Paris garret is one of the great cliches of the century. And one that just won't go away. It's hard to forget that afternoon in the late 80s when I got my 90-second on-camera chance at stardom: for a 4-minute segment on American Writers in Paris, CNN completely rearranged my apartment to fit the decor of a pre-determined thesis statement. And in the great young tradition of sound-bite editing, I went on record as affirming exactly what I'd been trying to dispel: the cliches no longer applied.

The fact is that most people who write about this city don't live here and write for others who also don't live here, many of whose only travel need is to imagine Paris. One guidebook editor once explained to me that 25 percent of the Paris guides sold in the United States are purchased by people who'll never make the trip. Nonetheless, some five million do actually arrive each year, and the terms in which they visit Paris and return periodically are the ones I'd like to help freshen-up. First, we have to get beyond the Marais and St. Germain-de-Prés and wander out into the outer districts and *banlieu proche* in search of what remains of a *Paris populaire*, the Paris that Jacques Chirac as former mayor sacrificed to the delight of private developers. Moving to Montreuil at first was painful in that somehow an American in Paris who is not within eyeshot of the Seine tends to wonder what he or she is doing here. But the move from the bourgeois rue Monge in the 5th *arrondissement* to the *banlieu rouge* was a pertinent step into being part of Parisian life as opposed to remaining just an admiring spectator.

Bringing you to Montreuil helps reveal much about the Paris that travelers and visitors don't see and rarely come to know. And telling its story becomes a vehicle for slashing back much of this sappy, albeit pleasurable, fairy tale and enhancing perhaps a new urban serendipity.

Montreuil, industrial and delivery-truck studded, is not particularly pretty, it has no outstanding monuments, and brags of nothing exactly quaint. Once upon a time it was France's leading manufacturer of *bonbons* and porcelain-headed dolls. Today, the town makes knock-off *prêt-a-porter*, and is loaded with noisy print shops and binderies. The sharp steel sculpture in honor of the Resistance movement which towers over the Place Duclos at the Croix-de-Chavaux, although admirable for its message, is reminiscent of the hideous eastern bloc aesthetics of the fifties and sixties. No, it's not beauty that drives Montreuil. In fact, in the late winter when the municipal Christmas lights are belatedly swinging in the breeze over the shabby rue de Paris beyond the Porte de Montreuil, I think more of East Orange, New Jersey than Paris, France.

But don't be mistaken; Montreuil is not East Orange.

Montreuil-sous-Bois today, when mentioned in the guidebooks, is noted for its bustling *Marché aux puces*, where great piles of used dress shirts and slacks, neckties and lacey blouses at ten francs an item await being picked over. This can be seen as a metaphor. Montreuil is also known for its colorful patchwork of multicultural residents, a fact the town advertises as an asset with its plastered slogan *Vive la différence*! More Malians, for example, live in Montreuil than anywhere else in the world, except, of course, Mali. Sixty-three languages are spoken by the kids in the town's public schools—languages that most anglo-saxons haven't even heard of, like Bambara or Pull or Mori or Kabile. Along the rue de Paris, one finds felafels, pilpil, nems, gyros, crepes, roasted sheep heads, spicy olives... Around the Robespierre Métro station, stunning, coal-black women in brightly patterned batiks walk past with multiple babies bundled on their backs. My ten-year-old son's best friend, Mamadou, lives a few hundred meters away from us in a family cluster that includes his polygamous father and a dozen siblings and half siblings. Mamadou calls my son his "*frère*" and me "*papa*." On the Moslim *fête de la mouton*, Mamadou's father slaughters a healthy sheep with a sharp knife in front of the house and divvies up the meat for friends and neighbors. On the tiny rue Bara over 1000 African workers live in a packed residence filled with laborers, students, tailors, barbers, and merchants of bananas, wild yams, grilled corn, and imported cassettes from Abidjan, Dakar, and Douala. Meters away a cello maker carves wood for his instruments, labor unionists distribute flyers announcing a strike in protest to factory closings, the National Conservatory of Music and Dance is conducting ballet classes, platters of couscous are being served for lunch, an exhibition on Albatros, the Russian school of cinema in Montreuil in the twenties is opening, and the Portuguese owner of the Italian restaurant Jardin de Florence is prepping his *bacalhau*. This is Montreuil on any day.

Montreuil also has one of the highest per capita rates of artists per square meter anywhere in France. The availability of affordable work space, the community of like-minded people, and the progressive cultural politics of the town, make Montreuil a logical choice to make art. What's remarkable about Montreuil is the cultural life that lies within the dailiness of its residents and the political biases of its traditionally communist city government.

Montreuil is a mainstay in the cluster of towns circling Paris to the north, east, and south popularly called the *Banlieus Rouges*, the Red Suburbs, a score of municipalities that have continually voted-in communist city governments—towns like Bagnolet, St. Denis, Malakoff, Montrouge, Creteil, and La Courneuve, which sponsors the exciting Fête de la Humanite each September with the communist daily newspaper, *l'Humanité*. The word alone, communist, even years after the fall of the eastern bloc, shocks most Americans. And in the eighties some of us joked with the absurdity that Montreuil would hang on longer than extremist Albania. Who would have guessed that that presupposed absurdity would become a prophesy?

For those who read French, there are seven major daily newspapers in Paris to choose from. On the left there is L'Humanité, *the Communist dinosaur; on the far right,* Le Quotidien de Paris; *moving towards the middle, one can enjoy* Le Monde, *which tends to be intellectual; the lighter afternoon paper* France Soir; Info Matin, *whose articles might prove easier to read for the French-impaired visitor;* Libération, *which has good coverage for art lovers; and* Le Figaro, *which dates back to 1866 and often rails against the government from a conservative viewpoint.*

—JO'R, LH, and SO'R

By communism in France, we only mean a more egalitarian distribution of local taxes and services. Culture, for one, is seen as a necessity for enriching the daily life of a community and its citizens—not a luxury or a privilege that comes last on the priority list. Culture is the core of a civilized and intelligent society. In Montreuil, the Office of Cultural Affairs employs 22 full-time people and spends over five million francs each year on the performing and plastic arts, cinema, literature, and music. Several years ago I had the bright idea of inviting the Culture Director for the town, Jean-Michel Morel, and the Cultural Attache of the U.S. Embassy in Paris for a local lunch to brainstorm on some potential projects. I nearly choked on my *steak frites* when the American diplomat asked Morel in complete seriousness if "he had a budget." Morel squinted at me with cynicism and disbelief. He answered, "Why? Don't you?" The reply was "no." And the lunch meeting died on the spot. The fact is the town of Montreuil spends more on culture than most large American cities and nearly as much as the entire National Endowment for the Arts budget for literature! Montreuil and other French towns don't believe in being reliant on large corporate gifts from Mobil or Philip Morris to get a dance company to perform or a painter's works on the walls of a gallery. Culture isn't a PR stunt.

The town subsidizes and administers an *art et essai* cinema which takes its name from one of the founding fathers of the French film industry, Georges Melies, France's equivalent of Thomas Edison, the "Magician of Montreuil," who set up his ground-breaking studios in town over a hundred years ago. Ticket prices are kept low for all those who live and work here, and all the public schools integrate the modern moviehouse into their curricula. In fact, Montreuil-sous-Bois is credited as the birthplace of Western cinema, having housed the studios of the Freres Lumiere, Leon Gaumont, and the Pathe brothers. Over 1200 silent films were made in the Croix-de-Chavaux area between 1896 and 1929! The town's commitment to this tradition is clear, and Morel, who writes for the cinema himself and edits an imprint at the prestigious literary publishing house Le Seuil, has done much to help young *cineastes*. Not only are numerous contemporary films shot in Montreuil, production and animation houses, including those affiliated with Disney, are known for their Montreuil design and illustration studios. In the last few years, some of France's most important high tech software and entertainment publishers, like UbiSoft, have helped affirm Montreuil's future, and the town's emerging Institute of High Technology inaugurated in the fall of 1996 the opening of one of France's most robust fiber optic Internet cable networks.

As you enter the town from Paris's McDonald's-studded Porte de Montreuil, a large mural commemorating the centennial of cinema greets you on a massive wall that is part of the architecturally-impressive national headquarters for the CGT, the largest and most provocative of the French trade unions. Initially attached to the

Communist Party, the CGT no longer wears this ticket, but is still wholly known for its left-wing orientation.

Just a few hundred meters down the rue de Paris, on a small side street to the right there is a progressive jazz club called L'instant Chaviré, the only club of its kind in the Département Seine Saint Denis, known as the 93rd which corresponds to its postal code and is embossed on all the license plates in the state. Here on any given night you can hear anyone from the American transplant jazz innovator Steve Lacy to a battery of *Camerounais* percussionists or a hot Cuban or *antillais* salsa combo. On the walls of this converted garage are the paintings and photographs of local artists, and around the small tables the young and not-so-young Montreuillois culture-set talk loudly about art and life while downing quantities of reasonably-priced red wine. Although a private initiative, l'Instant Chaviré has been substantially supported by the town since its opening, mostly because the "Assistant Mayor for Culture," Catherine Puig, recognizes that such public places contribute to the overall quality of daily social and cultural life of its citizens. A refreshing outlook for government.

Theater people have come to Montreuil too. A well-known clown called Hoppman left Paris three years ago for a space near the Croix-de-Chavaux. The popular singer Enzo Enzo calls Montreuil home. As does the film star Marie Rivière and the Olympic track stars Michel Jazy and Serge Hélan. The French-American painter Daniel Kohn lives and works in Montreuil, and the megastar African jazzman Manu Dibango not only lives in town but donates gigs to Montreuil all the time. The American drummer, Kenny (Klook) Clarke, one of the founders of Bee-bop who played with Dizzie Gillespie and Charlie Parker, lived in Montreuil in the sixties. And the poetic and tragic singer, sailor and actor Jacques Brel lived in Montreuil for much of the sixties and seventies.

Behind their renovated rue de Paris townhouse, stuck in between an Algerian bakery and a Cambodian vegetable shop in which incense is always burning as an offering to Buddha, Colorado-born painter Ralph Petty and his wife Lisa Davidson, who translates French articles for travel and art publishers, settled into Montreuil around ten years ago and built a stunning studio out back. As Lisa, who left Seattle nearly two decades ago, brags, "We're cultural refugees." Now their kids, like ours, are native Montreuillois, polyglot, deeply exposed to people from around the world, and are a wholly new kind of American in the world. A typical roll call in the local primary school Jules Ferry includes first names like Bandiougou, Karim, Haïtem, Souphien, Kianouch, Thibaud, Hamed, Mhemet, Nasrine, Djadje.... Back in New Jersey in the sixties we all were Jeff, Mike, Steve, David, Jennifer, Lisa, Mary, Judy, Lori, Barb.

On the eastern edge of the mythic French capital, just beyond the famous and forever congested *périphérique,* another reality thrives: Montreuil-sous-Bois. There isn't much forest anymore, or peaches for that matter—the town was once famous for its indigenous fruit trees. "The Montparnasse of the *fin-de-siècle"* might still seem a bit over the top, but then again, so are prices of drinks at La Coupole in Paris's irreplaceable Montparnasse.

David Applefield, an American writer and publisher from Boston, has lived in Paris and Montreuil since the early 1980s. Author of the guide Paris Inside Out *and the novel* Once Removed, *he edits the international literary journal* Frank *and* Paris–Anglophone, *a directory of English-speaking Paris, along with a popular Paris web site (http://www.paris-anglo.com).*

＊

Ce qu'il y a de plus étranger en France, pour les Français, c'est la France.
What is most foreign in France, for the French, is France.
—Honoré de Balzac

$*$ $*$ $*$

The Frog and the Periscope

A case of time travel.

THE FROG SIGN CREAKED AS IT SWUNG ABOVE OUR HEADS. WE opened the door directly under it and crossed the courtyard. Although it wasn't necessary, my husband knocked on the door of Roger's just as he did the night he discovered it. After a few seconds, the door squeaked as it was opened by a woman looking very formidable in a severe black dress. I smiled. No wonder he thought she was the madame of a brothel all those years ago.

"*Oui?*" Although she had aged, her voice still had the sultry Simon Signoret quality to it.

"*Bon soir, madame. Est-ce que possible,*" Dave hesitated, searching for the French words hiding in the back of his memory, "*pour moi et ma femme manger ce soir?*"

"*Oui, monsieur,*" and she stepped aside so we could enter her restaurant.

Tables and diners lined each side of the long, narrow room. The din of conversation and a variety of mouth-watering aromas surrounded us. Madame led us half way down the aisle and seated us at our table.

So this was the famous Roger's I'd heard so much about. We were on our honeymoon and we'd come to Paris not only to see the celebrated historic sights of that beautiful city but to go in search of a piece of Dave's past, hoping it too still existed. I desperately wanted this restaurant he'd frequented to be the same for him. So far so good, but knowing how things change, I vowed to eat my *cuisses de grenouille* with crossed fingers.

It wasn't long before a robust, middle-aged man, with a cigarette dangling precariously from his mouth, approached us. I recognized Madame's husband and the proprietor, Roger, immediately from Dave's description of him. His soiled white t-shirt overhung a long, white apron. He tossed a hunk of bread onto the bare wood table and extracted a couple of bottles of wine from under his arm. After upturning our glasses, he first poured some red and then some white into each one: Roger's celebrated "*rosé*" *apéritif*. And true to form, he took the ashtray, dumped the contents on the floor and wiped it out with the bottom of his t-shirt.

Dave ventured some more rusty French. "*Bon soir, monsieur. J'ai mange ici beaucoup ans passé. Est-ce que possible le même t-shirt?*" he laughed and pointed at Roger's shirt.

"*Mais oui! Un très vieux t-shirt*," and he made a face while holding his nose. "*Vous êtes américain ou anglais?*"

"*Américain. J'ai travaille à Paris pour l'Armée des États-Unis en cinquante et un. Mes amis et moi mange ici tout les Mercredi soirs. J'ai apporte ma chérie*," he pointed to me, "*ici manger vôtre grenouille—le meilleur à tout Paris!*" My chéri's French was now rolling off his tongue and my heart swelled with pride.

Roger cooed at the compli-

*O*ne evening I found myself making a speech about Australia to a group of French journalists. I apologised for my appalling French, stumbled through my short speech, felt relieved when they laughed at the joke at the end, wiped the sweat from my brow, and sat down, relieved it was over. At which point a charming French woman came over, said she'd enjoyed it and was pleased I had not done what so many English language speakers do in similar situations, apologise that their French is lousy and, therefore, make their speeches in English. "Oh no," she said, "you went on to prove it!"

—Tony Wheeler, "Life in Paris"

ment. "*Merci beaucoup monsieur. Merci.*" And with a devilish grin, he whispered conspiratorially, "*Le périscope pour vous?*"

"*Certainement! Et* binoculars *aussi s'il vous plaît!*"

Fantastic! Roger was going to perform his periscope trick. I glanced around at the other diners to see who might be the likely victim.

He returned and handed the binoculars to me so I could see the chalk board menu on the wall at the end of the room. But I had eyes only for the periscope. It was handed to Dave upside down so the sight was focused *under* the table. While he looked through it, Roger walked up to a woman sitting facing us at an adjacent table and lifted her skirt. She obviously knew him because in mock anger, she slapped his hand and for our benefit, pronounced him "a naughty old man" in heavily accented English. The three of them howled with laughter. I beamed. Our time travel trip back to the old Roger's was so far totally successful. Now it was up to the waitress to perform the grand finale. But it was ridiculous for me to even consider the possibility that she could be the same one. Then I quickly chastised myself for such negative thinking.

I scrutinized her out of the corner of my eye when she brought our wine and *grenouille* and concluded that she was, after all, about the right age.

"Don't you remember her?" I asked.

"No," he answered very definitely, cruelly dashing my hopes.

As we sipped wine and dug into succulent, tender little frogs legs dripping with garlic butter, Dave told me the story again.

In 1951, Lt. David Brown, U.S. Army, was stationed in Paris during the Korean War. (He's always been grateful for that roll of the dice.) Since he lived on the French economy instead of on an army base, the Hotel Bon St. Jour was home. (The rate was a dollar a day which included laundry service.) He usually ate his meals at the same neighborhood bistro but every Wednesday, the monotony was broken by dining out at various restaurants with his friends and superior officers, Major Frank Bayard and Captain Tony Biando. That is until one particular Wednesday when they took a friend up on his recommendation of an unpretentious and fun Left Bank place called Roger La Grenouille. It was fated to become The Wednesday Night Restaurant.

According to directions, they took the Métro to St. Michel, walked along Quai des Grands Augustins and turned left onto the rue des Grands Augustins. On that particular moonless night, the street lights weren't operating. And not a ray of light escaped from the tightly shuttered windows. The street could-

The Left Bank called me and even now it does not cease to call me and to keep me. I cannot imagine that I could ever leave it, any more than an organ can leave the place that is assigned to it in the body.

—Adrienne Monnier

n't have been darker. Or quieter. The three officers huddled together. As they approached number 28 the silence was broken only by the creaking of a frog sign swinging in the breeze above them. Since the entrance wasn't on the street, they assumed it was off the courtyard on the other side of the door. The officer of lowest rank was sent to reconnoiter the territory. Lt. Brown bravely opened the door and tiptoed across the courtyard toward the only door which had a strip of light escaping from the bottom. He knocked softly and waited while listening to his thumping heart.

The door squeaked and creaked as it was slowly opened by a very mysterious woman dressed in black. Dave tried to ignore the chill running down his back.

"*Oui*?" She strung out the "oui" in a sexy, throaty voice.

His jaw came unhinged when it finally registered that he was facing the madame of a brothel for the first time in his life. (Or so he told me.) Funny trick the friend had played sending them to a brothel! But then again he thought, what did it matter? Brothel or restaurant, they couldn't lose.

"*Un moment s'il vous plaît madame*," and he turned to give his superiors, who were hiding in the shadows, the all-clear, come-ahead sign. As the three entered, Dave barely stifled a laugh. Were they ever going to get a shock! But the aroma of garlic butter told him the friend hadn't tricked them after all.

Roger, the "frog," compensated for any disappointment Dave may have felt. He performed his bit with the trio from his "*rosé*" to his periscope. But the finale was performed by the waitress.

After spending a leisurely three hours over a very enjoyable dinner, Frank and Tony rose from the table, leaving Dave to compute the tip. (Those were the days before *service compris*.) When he reached the door, the waitress blocked his way.

After pressing something into his hand, she whispered, "*Un baiser. Donnez un baiser à moi*," and she pointed to her puckered red lips.

Dave's eyes bulged. There was no mistaking *this* French! She wanted him to kiss her! Not the other guys who had been politely shoved out the door but him! He eagerly leaned forward and just as he was about to kiss her lips, she quickly turned her cheek to him.

"*À bientôt, monsieur. À bientôt*," and she ushered him out.

Well, she was just being coy, Dave thought. Since she was going to see him soon, she had obviously slipped him her phone number along with something that felt cold and hard in his palm. A key to her apartment?

Outside, he joined the others who were busy looking, with the aid of a cigarette lighter, at little lead frogs they'd been given as souvenirs. With anticipated dismay, Dave opened his hand. Yep. Another frog.

"I suppose she kissed you guys too?"

"Kissed?" Frank questioned. "I didn't get a kiss. What about you Tony? Any kisses?"

"Not a one. I guess she liked you best Dave."

And so the evening was salvaged for my husband by two good friends.

We'd arrived at Roger's at eight. Now it was almost midnight. We had devoured *cuisses de grenouilles, cassoulet, coq au vin, salade de tomate*, a generous portion of the huge cheese tray (passed from table to table by the diners themselves as it had always been) and finally strawberries with *crème fraîche* and coffee. I didn't want to leave. I wanted to postpone the disappointment I was sure would accompany our departure. But it was time to face reality: *she wasn't going to be the same waitress.* I consoled myself with the fact that it had been a wonderful evening, full of surprises from the past and certainly no reason to feel disappointed.

It was time to go. We stood and walked up the aisle. But as we approached the door, she was waiting…and making unmistakable eyes at Dave! I took a deep breath. Her lips puckered. His eyes bulged.

"*Un baiser!*" she demanded and pointed repeatedly at her mouth.

While I gaped ecstatically, Dave happily complied. Or tried to. At the last second, her head swiveled ninety degrees and he got a mouthful of cheek again.

Then she pressed a little lead frog into his palm. "*J'étais aussi ici en mille neuf cent cinquante et un et je me rappelle très bien de vous,*" she smiled coquettishly.

I simply couldn't believe it. Had any time elapsed at all since 1951?

"Ohhhhh *mademoiselle,*" Dave gushed. He kissed her hand and told her in his best French how very much he also remembered her.

Like Frank and Tony before me, I stepped outside to wait for my friend and to blissfully savor the fact that not a single second had passed in 27 years.

We have returned to Roger's twice since then. During our last visit in 1992, we sadly discovered that he had passed away. However, "Madame Roger" was holding down the fort nicely. No longer were they handing out lead frogs, but mademoiselle was still doling out kisses.

Tish Carnes Brown resides with Dave in Media, Pennsylvania. They take the time machine to Paris every chance they get. Her articles have appeared in France Today.

✦

It is said that the world's first café opened in Istanbul (the Turks were great popularizers of coffee) in 1550. Paris got its first one in 1686, when a Sicilian named Francesco Procopio dei Coltelli opened an establishment called Le Procope on the Left Bank, on what is now the Rue de l'Ancienne Comédie. It is still in existence on the same site, having closed and opened several times—reviving most recently in 1952 as a restaurant now mainly patronized by tourists, who may or may not be impressed by the fact that Voltaire, Diderot, and Rousseau drank on the premises.

In the 19th century, the focus of Parisian café life shifted from the Left to the Right Bank, to the gilded and chandelier-hung establishments of the Grands Boulevards—that once-elegant series of broad thoroughfares that leads from the Opéra to the Place de la République. At the same time, painters, writers, and all-purpose bohemians began to haunt the steamy cabarets of Montmartre.

The everyday corner café, or *café du coin*, now so emblematic of Paris, began to flourish in the city around the turn of the century, when hardy rural types from the Auvergne in central France began to set up shop in the capital to sell coal and charcoal for heating and cooking. They offered wine and strong drink to their customers along with other kinds of fuel, thus providing meeting places for ordinary Parisians who weren't interested in gilt or bohemian pursuits. The descendants of these establishments are everywhere in Paris today—scruffy generic places that supply such basic components of Parisian life as jolts of thick black *café serré*, darkly aromatic French cigarettes, stamps and lottery tickets, telephones and lavatories of dubious sanitation.

—Angela Mason, "Café Society," *Los Angeles Times Magazine*

Au Revoir Paris

Take heart, Paris will be here when you return.

THE TAXI PULLED UP IN FRONT OF MY HOTEL LIKE AN EXECU-tioner, masked by dawn and anxious to be the means of taking me from this world to the next.

This was how I felt as I relinquished my two small bags to the driver, a man in his 60s, still straight and tall in his starched white shirt and black pants.

"Gare du Nord," I said as I settled into the rear seat, resigned to my fate. I was leaving Paris and didn't know when I would return. Paris and I have an ongoing love affair, and I become sullen and unbearable when I am away too long.

As we started down the rue de Cherche Midi, we passed the small tea room owned by my friends. I had dined with them until two o'clock in the morning, until they drove me back to the hotel to pack. I thought of our parting, their strong hugs, and the kisses. There are always at least three kisses, sometimes four, on alternating cheeks. A sign of true affection. "*Au revoir,*" they whispered. "*A bientôt.*"

"*A bientôt, mes amis,*" I replied, although I knew that despite what I had said, my return would not be soon, but in a year, or more.

How different the words for departure are in French and English. Perhaps, in some subtle and subconscious way our attitudes about a place, and of leaving people behind become entangled in the turns of phrases.

In English we say, "Good-bye," a contraction of "God be with you." Or, "farewell," wishing the departing person a safe journey. We focus upon the act of leaving and the trip itself.

But in French it is always, "*au revoir*"—"until we see each other again." Or "*à bientôt*," meaning "see you soon."

Every departure carries with it the promise of a return and reunion. Even "*bon voyage*," seems never to be used except to address those taking brief holidays, and in context, always carries with it the implied promise of a glass of wine together in the near future.

And so I take heart. Perhaps by saying my good-byes in French I have predetermined my own quick return to Paris.

In the midst of this linguistic reverie, the driver turned his head towards me and asked, "What time does your train depart?"

"Don't worry," I told him. "We have plenty of time. My train doesn't leave until 8:10."

It was not yet 6:45.

"In fact," I asked him, "would you drive slowly and take the longest route to the Gare du Nord?"

He seemed delighted to oblige.

Turning right onto the Boulevard Montparnasse, we headed toward the gold dome of the Hôtel des Invalides where Napoleon sleeps for eternity, sealed in an elaborate sarcophagus of red granite.

I remembered that above the crypt is an inscription written by the emperor during his final exile from France. Loosely translated, it says, "Bury me on the banks of the Seine River, among the people of Paris whom I love." Even Napoleon, banished twice from France, got his wish to return to Paris.

Then the driver turned right again, and we traveled on streets parallel to the Seine, past the Musée d'Orsay and the Louvre. We approached Notre Dame near the corner of the Boulevard St-Michel. The day before, a terrorist bomb had exploded in a crowded commuter train in the St-Michel station just below us, killing seven and injuring over one hundred people. In the long pale rays of early morning sunlight, there were still some shards of glass scattered about. Police were mining the area for clues. My driver shook his head and made an attempt at small talk, commenting on the hot weather.

As I looked out the taxi's window, I thought of Paris as a dowager actress for whom the show must go on, no matter what. The café owners and shopkeepers were washing and sweeping the streets in front of their stores.

They watered the boxes of primulas, impatiens and violets that sit like jewel chests at every doorway and window. Bakeries were stacking warm loaves of bread, crusty *baguettes* and *pains au chocolat* in their windows. The whole city had a warm, comforting, yeasty smell.

Along the river, the *bouquinistes*, the merchants who run tiny stalls that sell books and prints, were unlocking their bins and arranging their wares by stringing them up with clothes pins on tentatively hung lines. A thin mist rose from the river like a veil lifting.

> *I* first met Napoleon some 40 years ago in a Chinese school textbook, which told me that Na-p'o-lun *was a great man of France who won many battles, made a code of laws, and did other famous deeds. The names of the battles were transcribed in Chinese characters and sounded very odd. I had not the slightest idea where the battlefields were; indeed, I did not even know where France was. At the age of ten it never occurred to me that I should ever want to see Napoleon's tomb or the Empire he ruled over somewhat beyond the horizon. Hero-worship formed no part of my education, and I did not pay attention to the importance which the textbook seemed to attach to Napoleon. But now as I walked about Paris I felt the presence of the Emperor in every corner of the city, as though his unseen, powerful hands had moulded it. In this he is unique. Rome, for example, is not stamped with Augustus, nor Peking with Genghis Khan.*
>
> —Chiang Yee,
> *The Silent Traveller in Paris*

Across the street, tables and chairs were being taken outside and set up in front of cafés. Awnings were unfurled and adjusted for the morning light.

Paris was preparing herself for another day, even though the constant flash of the blue *gendarme* lights and the periodic sound of sirens were reminders of how tenuous all this could be.

The cab driver was shocked by the bombing. He shook his head again while surveying the hordes of police, and said, "This is worse than when the Germans occupied Paris, and that was awful. At least they never bombed Paris."

His remark recalled to mind the German general who defied direct orders from Hitler and refused to blow up Paris in the face of the advancing Allied troops. The general did not wish to be remembered by history as the man who destroyed Paris. Terrorists, on the other hand, seem to have no fear of history.

"Were you in Paris during the occupation?" I asked the driver.

"Oh yes," he said, "I was just a boy, but I remember it well. It was awful. I still feel nauseous when I think about it. It was four years of nausea."

"But what was it like?" I persisted.

"For days they came. The Germans. The soldiers entering Paris, sitting in cafés, ordering beer. You could hear gunfire, explosions in the distance. At night, sometimes, the sky would light up like fireworks, but you knew that it wasn't that. Leaflets were being passed out urging Parisians to cooperate and that nothing would change. Heh!"

He paused, overcome by memories.

"But the march down the Champs-Elysées, it was the most terrifying thing I have ever known," he continued. "I expected the German tanks to be scary, but it was the rows and rows of soldiers that were most frightening. I will never forget

We return to the palatial Meurice Hotel on the rue de Rivoli, itself almost 200 years old ("I'd like a room overlooking the executions"). In the lobby, I meet a senior French diplomat and ask: "Wasn't this hotel where the high Nazi generals stayed during the war?" Diplomat, stiffly: "So it is said." "And," I went on, "wasn't Coco Chanel shacked up here with a German general?" "I have no knowledge of that," said the diplomat. "I must go now." To this day, the French dislike talking about the German occupation and the incidents of collaboration.

—Herb Caen, "The Walking Caen," *San Francisco Chronicle*

the way tens of thousands of feet made the streets tremble. And the sound of their feet marching all together was to me, like the sound of Hell cracking open. A terrible sound…"

He became lost in thought as we turned left and crossed the river at the Ponts de Sully, past the Colonne de Juillet, where the infamous Bastille prison once stood, and down the Boulevard Beaumarchais. We rode in silence for a few minutes.

"So," he finally said, "are you going away on vacation?"

This question struck me as odd. "I am on vacation," I responded. "I'm taking the train to London to see some friends, and then I fly back home to the United States, to California."

"Oh, you are an American. I thought I detected a bit of an accent," he responded. "But you speak French very well."

To be told that you have not mangled the French language is the highest compliment a Frenchman can pay a foreigner.

"Americans don't come to Paris like they used to," he continued. "And they don't take taxis."

"It's too expensive," I reminded him. "The dollar is not so strong. Paris is very expensive for Americans."

"Yes," he said. "Now it is all Germans and Japanese. It is ironic, isn't it?"

But before I could commiserate with him, we pulled into the taxi stop at the Gare du Nord. He got out, removed my bags from the trunk, placed them on the sidewalk and then let me out of the taxi. I handed him a 100 franc note for the fare, and a 10 franc piece as a tip.

He handed back the ten francs, and said, "No, you will need this to rent a luggage trolley."

I was touched. We had become friends and now he worried about me. I showed him that one of my bags had wheels and a pull-up-handle; the other bag would ride on top.

"Thank you," I replied, "but I don't need a trolley. Here, please take this." I held the 10 franc piece out to him again.

He refused it, and instead, cupped his hands around mine. Looking me in the eyes, his voice a little shaky, he said, "Remember, Americans are always welcome in Paris."

I was almost in tears. All that I could get out was, "*Merci. Merci, monsieur.*"

He released my hands, and as I took my bags and turned to walk towards the door he shouted loudly at me, "*Au revoir, madame.* Take care. *Au revoir.*"

I stopped, and waved back at him with my free hand. "*À bientôt. Au revoir.*"

Claudia J. Martin fell on her head as an infant, which her mother believes explains everything about her. She has worked as a worm-picker, go-go dancer, trial attorney, law instructor, editor, cocktail waitress and pastry chef. Her travel essays regularly appear in The San Francisco Examiner.

★

"They say…that when good Americans die they go to Paris."

—Oscar Wilde, *A Woman of No Importance*

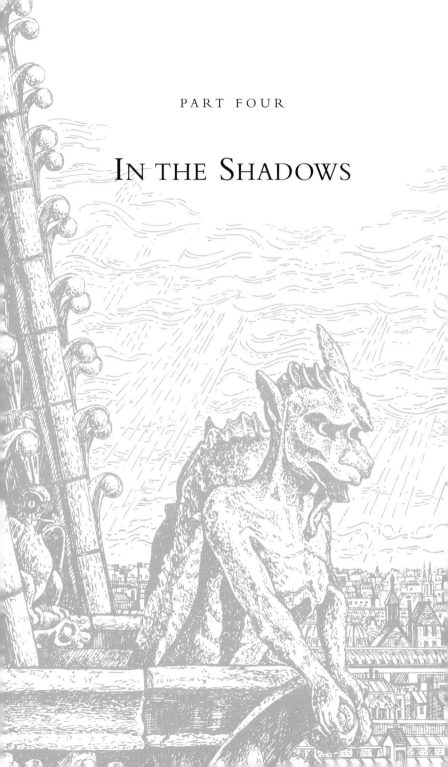

PART FOUR

IN THE SHADOWS

MARCEL F. LAVENTURIER

Destination Paris

A young man meets his destiny.

BEFORE REACHING PARIS, I ESCAPED FROM ST-QUENTIN.
The town of St-Quentin, the capital of Picardie in northern France.

The year was 1940. The German army had invaded Holland, Belgium, Luxembourg, and France. The only remaining obstacle to Hitler's total domination of Western Europe was Great Britain, a few tantalizing miles across the Channel. In the fall, the German High Command implemented the first phase of Operation Sea Lion: saturation bombing of the British seaports and the London Blitz. South of the Belgian border, north of Paris, the invasion force was readying an attack for the spring of 1941.

At the time, I was nineteen, an American student living with an uncle in Belgium. The German authorities in our small town had paid scant attention to me until September 10 when it was announced that President Roosevelt had transferred 50 American destroyers to the Royal Navy. The local commandant considered this an overt act of war for which he held me personally responsible. I was ordered to report to the Kreiskommandatur in Brussels to justify my status as a non-combatant neutral alien. There was a

313

complication—I carried a valid American passport and was U.S. born, but the fact that both my mother and father had been born in France made me a French citizen according to French and German laws. My other problem was that I had failed to report for conscription in the French army when I reached eighteen; this made me a deserter as well. Rather than report to the Germans to face jail or deportation, I joined the Belgian Underground.

as the last word been spoken? Must hope die now? Is our defeat decisive? No," the voice thundered, "nothing is lost for France!"

This was the "immortal message of June 18," the radio appeal to Frenchmen to take heart, to resist the Germans, delivered by General Charles de Gaulle. It was the message that lived on in history in the oft-cited phrase, "France has lost a battle, not the war."

De Gaulle never pronounced that phrase in exactly those words. What he said was, "This war has not ended with the battle of France. This war is a world war," but the shorter, more dramatic version that lived on was close enough to what de Gaulle actually had said to be valid.

—David Schoenbrun,
As France Goes

My best friend was the leader of a small group of resisters who helped escaped allied prisoners evade the Gestapo. He controlled black market and smuggling rings which he used to finance his clandestine operations. He signed me on as a courier. For a couple of months I lived in safe houses and smuggled uncut diamonds from Antwerp across the border into France; occasionally, I served as an English interpreter. That November, the Germans changed the currency laws for the occupied countries, and our group was able to steal one million newly printed Occupation Reichmarks. The money had to be spread around to our operatives in a way that it could not be traced. As my final job for the Underground, I was given the opportunity to earn my passage back to the U.S. by smuggling part of the loot to our safe house in Paris. Up to that time the border was fairly porous, our couriers carrying false papers moved people and money back and forth regularly. What we didn't realize was that this red zone, as it came to be known, had been placed on high alert by the Germans to prevent spying on the troop movements. Special passes from the Kreiskommandatur in Brussels were required for civilian travel. All I had was my American passport. To hide my share of the swag, 150,000 Reichmarks, I divided the bills into two bundles which I wrapped in brown paper then baked in two large loaves of peasant bread. Bread was rationed and I would not attract attention by carrying some in my luggage. When I boarded the Brussels–Paris express, I carefully selected a seat in a second class compartment closest to an exit.

The train had been chugging along for some time through the wintry countryside when it slowed down and finally stopped. I stepped out of the compartment and saw two German military policemen wearing the insignia of the "Feldengendarmerie" enter at the opposite end of the carriage. As the train started slowly, I reached for the handle on the exit door, ready to jump, but there were sentries posted every few feet along the track. The door to the rest room was at my back, I opened it and locked myself in, trapped like an animal. In a cold sweat with my pulse racing, I prayed that the police would overlook my hiding place. Soon, I heard a rap on the door. I didn't respond at first but when it persisted, louder and louder, I opened the door and two of the largest German soldiers that I had ever seen walked in; one stood in front and one in back of me.

"*Papiers?*"

I showed them my passport, they compared me to my photo then the largest one said, "*Zu schen sein passierschein?*"

"*Nicht Verstehen,*" I answered.

He smiled, "*Mitkommen.*"

They frisked me for weapons and took me back to my seat where one of them guarded me until we reached the next stop— St-Quentin. A six-man squad of soldiers waited on the platform. The policeman handed my passport to a corporal; three other prisoners joined us, then we were marched double file across the tracks, over a bridge, then right in the center of the street going uptown. Curious civilians stopped to stare at us, traffic went around us. Soon, we stopped at a building over which flew a huge swastika flag. The troopers herded us into a room filled with frightened men and women; some were crying. They didn't make room for me so I sat on my fancy yellow leather suitcase. The corporal of the guard handed our papers to two Gestapo men who sat at the opposite end of the room. One of them came to me, motioned me off my suitcase and took it away. The smell of my terror was added to that of the other prisoners. A Gestapo seated at the table piled high with papers pointed and shouted questions at us in German. An interpreter translated his questions. I understood most of what the Gestapo was saying, but when my turn came, he pointed at me and shouted, "*Sprechen Sie Deutsch?*"

I looked blankly at him and kept silent.

The translator said, "Do you understand German?"

"Unfortunately, no. Only English and French."

My answer sent the Gestapo into a rage, he got red in the face, started shouting louder and banging his fist on the table. He threw some papers in a folder but kept on raving and making menacing gestures.

The translator said, "He is turning you over to the judge for immediate sentencing. He says that you are a Frenchman with a fake American passport sent here to spy for the British. If it was up to him, he'd call out the firing squad and shoot you without a trial, this minute."

The other prisoners moved away from me as if I were a leper. I began to perspire, my hands shook and my mouth and throat went dry. One of the Gestapo soldiers pushed me into the next room, past the raving maniac who was still screaming.

It served as a court room. On an elevated dais a small bald-headed, sour-faced man dressed in a black uniform sat at a large desk. He picked through my papers, looked at me with disgust and speaking in French said, "This court is tired of adjudicating cases that are not in our jurisdiction. You will be tried in a military court in Brussels. You are remanded back to Belgium."

In German, he ordered the Gestapo to take me away and to ship me back on the next train.

I was taken to a small room where three French *gendarmes* sat at a small table playing cards. The guard propelled me towards them and in an accented French told them to push me across the red line as soon as possible. They interrupted their card game and looked at me with professional interest, trying to place me in some criminal category. What was this well-dressed young man up to?

One of them, not unkindly said, "Sit down and relax. It will take some time for the Germans to fill out all their forms. They love paper work. There isn't a train north until tomorrow anyway. You will sleep in our jail tonight."

Ever since my arrest I had lived in a state of disorganized terror as if I'd been thrown overboard in a vast ocean full of man-eaters. I was desperately paddling to stay afloat while dozens of other prisoners were clinging to the sides of a boat. They were torn away, one by one, by the attacking sharks. Sitting in the boat, which flew the swastika, drunken soldiers amused themselves, pushing men, women and children over the side. I was living a nightmare.

The benign attitude of the French *gendarmes* reassured me. It changed my outlook from terror to simple fear. It is astonishing what a kind word can accomplish in a desperate situation. The *gendarmes* ignored me and returned to their noisy game. In about an hour, a German brought my suitcase and handed the policemen a manila envelope. I asked the sergeant if I could get some cigarettes out of my bag. He nodded yes. I opened it. I could tell that it had been searched, but both loaves of bread appeared intact. My spirits

At dawn on July 16, 1942, police across Paris arrested more than 16,000 Jews and bused them to the Vélodrome d'Hiver, an indoor cycling stadium.

It was the first major roundup of Jews in Nazi-occupied France. The families were held inside without food or water for three days. Those who survived were transferred to concentration camps in France and, ultimately, to Auschwitz.

—George Rodrigue, "France Reopens its WWII Wounds," *The Dallas Morning News*

soared from despair to hope. Everything was not lost. My luck was changing; with courage, imagination, and determination, I might escape the sharks. When the card game ended, the *gendarmes* added their score, exchanged money and then turned towards me. I offered them cigarettes and asked them if it was possible for us to stop and buy some food on our way to the jail.

"If you have money to pay for it, we'll gladly take you to a restaurant."

"If it's OK, I would gladly buy drinks and dinner all around."

They looked at each other, but they didn't answer. One of them escorted me out, through a back door, down an alley to a closed restaurant. We entered through the kitchen. It was empty except for the owners. We were finishing our first drink when the other two *gendarmes* showed up. I called for more drinks. We enjoyed a five course dinner with bottles of expensive wine with each course; then cognac and more wine. I told them that I was an American student trying to reach Paris prior to returning home. My arrest was a total mistake. I am sure that they didn't believe me. We played cards and drank until midnight. Naturally, I lost heavily. Since it was past curfew, the jail was closed and I was such a grand fellow and model prisoner, they decided that I should take a room upstairs; drunk as I was they said that they were certain that I wouldn't try to escape. Afterwards, hugged by the comfort and warmth of a feather bed, I decided that the odds were so poor that I could run away in the middle of the night, without papers, in a strange town crawling with Germans, that I planned to wait until daybreak before making my move. I fell asleep and dreamt of Paris.

Next morning, shaved and dressed in my tweeds, I was ready to step out onto the wet pavement when one of the *gendarmes* showed up. He seemed surprised that I was still around. They must have really thought that I was a spy. Mustering all my courage, I asked him if he carried a gun. No, the Germans didn't trust him, he was armed with a night stick and a whistle. If a prisoner tried to run away, his orders were to try to restrain him and to blow his whistle to alert the German and French police to come to his aid. Outside, the rain had stopped but had been replaced by a cold gray fog, the kind that chills you right through to the bone marrow. I took an envelope filled with currency and put it in his hand.

"I'd appreciate it if you could give me my passport and wait a couple of hours before blowing your whistle."

He put the envelope in his tunic pocket, handed me my passport out of the manila folder, opened the door, pointed down the hill towards the railroad station.

"That is the way south. Keep off the paved roads, try the fields. If you get caught tell them that you knocked me down and overpowered me. Good luck."

The streets were deserted, I walked across the Marne canal without seeing anyone. When I reached the railroad tracks, I entered the plowed fields slippery with brown clay. The fog was thicker around the waterways and the going so tough that I doubted that any patrols would venture into the countryside that morning. I stumbled along keeping the barely visible railroad lines to my right. From time to time, I stopped to rest and to listen to the sounds around me. I heard voices, dog barks, train, car and wagon noises. I was floating in a sea of fog with everything near but out of sight. Once, I was stopped by a canal. I didn't panic, I backtracked alongside it and crossed the water at a railroad bridge which was left unguarded. Around noon, the fog eased a little. I had reached the outskirts of a small city. It was the town of Tergniers, a rail center with squat houses huddled around the station. Since leaving St-Quentin I hadn't been challenged by anyone, my luck was holding. Before entering the town, I sat down and changed to a clean pair of shoes from my suitcase. I left my muddy ones in a culvert and, nonchalantly carrying my suitcase, I walked into the station. The platform was full of German soldiers. When a train with a Paris destination ground to a noisy stop, everyone including me jumped on board.

Struggling with my suitcase, I walked through the first class section until I located a compartment with an empty seat. All other seats were occupied by young officers. They helped me heave my coat and my bag onto the rack. They spoke to me, I answered

"*Guten tag. Jawohl....*" and smiled a lot. I intimated that I was Flemish, "*Flemmisch Sprechen. Deutsch Verstehen.*"

Looking around, I noticed that all the signs in the car were in German. God. In my haste, I had jumped on a troop train which had originated in the Fatherland. My traveling companions mistook me for one of their civilian surrogates—a collaborator. They couldn't have treated me nicer; having exhausted most of my vocabulary and before I could arouse any suspicion, I had to find a way out—not the toilet this time. A steward playing a glockenspiel stuck his head in the compartment and announced the second seating for lunch. I followed him to an ornate dining car. He thrust a reservation book at me to sign in. I wrote something illegible followed by the street address of a hotel in Antwerp. He waved me to a small table for two; except for some ladies, I noticed that I was the only civilian there. I tried to make myself as inconspicuous as possible by looking out the window. The sun had finally broken through the mist. At a large table opposite mine, four German officers in full dress, their tunics covered with iron crosses, ribbons and medals were lingering over their desserts and plotting the train's itinerary

In a sense, the wartime French government—headquartered in the resort town of Vichy and led by Marshal Philippe Petain—began to be rehabilitated under postwar President Charles de Gaulle. A vengeful bloodletting had followed the war, with perhaps 10,000 suspected collaborationists executed without trial. But then, for the sake of French pride and unity, the leader of the Free French helped build the myth of French resistance. Since then, French and foreign researchers have been systematically unraveling that tale, often against the wishes of the French government.

The groundbreaking research into Vichy was performed by an American historian, Robert Paxton. His 1973 book, Vichy France: Old Guard and New Order 1940–44, *drew upon German records to prove that Marshal Petain's government not only collaborated voluntarily, but in some cases went beyond German demands.*

—George Rodrigue, "France Reopens its W W II Wounds," *The Dallas Morning News* on a map. They observed the countryside with binoculars and talked about having traveled through there before. I overheard them say respectfully "General." When the train reached Compiègne, the place where the armistices in 1918 and 1940 had been signed, they laughed and called for champagne. The General stood and proposed a toast. Everyone in the dining salon stood, including me. He noticed that I was raising my water glass so he directed the steward to bring me some champagne. On command, we toasted Germany's victorious armies. As the only person not in uniform, I realized that I stood out like a sore thumb and expected the worst. Should the General try to talk to me, I was finished. When he stood up to leave, he directed the waiter to bring me two half-filled bottles of white wine and some cake from his table. I stood up, bowed and said, "*Danke Schön, Herr General.*"

He gave me the Nazi salute, "Heil Hitler."

I responded in kind. When I sat down, I was pleased with my performance. My Heil Hitler to the General certainly impressed the rest of the diners who cast furtive glances in my direction. I really must be important for the General to take notice of me. The waiter brought the menu and I ordered sausage and red cabbage in my most guttural Flemish. The dining room was full and there were some officers waiting to be seated but because of my short acquaintance with my host I was allowed to savor their best Rhine wines and eat their gourmet food at my leisure like a privileged member of the Master Race. Had I been dressed in shabby clothes, worn muddy shoes and sporting a two day's growth of beard, I would be traveling on a train going in the opposite direction to a certain death. Clothes make the man; this morning I was haggling with a French policeman for my freedom and now I was dining in the German senior officers' salon. My long walk and the dangers I had faced sharpened my appetite; I did justice to the meal and the chocolate cake, the first chocolate that I had tasted in months. The waiter brought a box of cigars and a brandy snifter. He opened the box and I selected one as he poured me a half glass of Courvoisier from the General's bottle. When I reached for a lighter, he gave me a light and I lit the cigar like an expert. I gave him a couple of

hundred francs for his trouble. For my taste I find Courvoisier a little sweet—not enough oak. I prefer a more robust Cognac, but this
being wartime and given the circumstances I must learn to make
do…. The cigar was Dutch Sumatra perfect, it built a wonderful
cone of ashes. The train rattled through the last miles of our journey. I smiled with contentment and a young lady two tables away
smiled back. I hadn't meant to smile at her, it was a reaction to my
change of fortune; happiness like misery is easily transmitted. I was
jettisoning my anguish every mile that I traveled away from St-
Quentin and towards Paris. Here I was in the midst of my enemies,
enjoying their hospitality while in my bag I carried 150,000 stolen
marks. I went from the depth of despair to the heights of elation.
Paris was not only my destination, it was my destiny. When we
reached the drab industrial approaches to the city, the train slowed
and I decided that it was safe for me to return to my seat. The rail
lines around the Gare du Nord were guarded by anti-aircraft bat-
teries. When the train stopped, all the military personnel were allowed on the platform. When I tried to exit, my passage was
blocked by military policemen. I looked out the window and saw
the reason why. The huge glass and steel building was festooned
with swastikas. An honor guard stood at attention facing the train.
A band played "*Deutschland Über Alles*." The General and his staff
reviewed the troops, saluted them, then the honor guard changed
formation, and the band attacked a lively march tune as they
goose-stepped out of the station. The General and all the troops
followed, then me, whistling and marching in step, carrying my
precious yellow leather suitcase towards freedom and the Paris
boulevards.

  I soon learned that the General who unwittingly helped me
achieve the first stage of my escape was the new military governor
of Paris.

*Marcel Laventurier was born in the United States but spent his youth in
Belgium and France. After escaping from the Nazis he served in the US
Navy throughout World War II, married in 1945, and became a pharmacist*

*in California. This story is one of a series that he has written about his war-
time experiences.*

✷

During the long war years, when I was living far from Paris, I often used
to wonder how so large a city found room inside a tiny compartment of
the human brain. Paris, for me, had become a kind of inner world through
which I roamed on those difficult dawn hours when despair lies in wait
for the waking sleeper. I needed time, though, to take a conscious step
over the threshold of this secret city that I was carrying around inside me;
first there were the black weeks during which the mere mention of the
name Paris broke the hearts of all who heard it. So I barred the gates of
my city against myself; I banished its avenues as far away as possible. At
night, however, flouting my own orders, I would slink along its streets like
a spy or a thief, restlessly going from house to house. Suddenly I would
appear in a room where friends were hiding. "What—*you* here? It *is* you!"
And one of those interminable conversations would start up and not stop
until daybreak. Things we could not tell one another with the width of
the Atlantic between us we communicated from heart to heart in those
imaginary conversations. Gone was all the water that separated us; I had
abolished space; I was there. I wanted to know everything. As I left I used
to touch the stones of the houses and the trunks of the trees with my
hands, and I would wake with a curious feeling of having been both ful-
filled and frustrated.

Thinking about the capital all the time, I rebuilt it inside myself. I replaced its physical presence with something else, something almost super-
natural; I don't know what to call it. A map of Paris pinned to the wall
would hold my gaze for long periods, teaching me things almost sublim-
inally. I made the discovery that Paris was shaped like a human brain.

—Julian Green, *Paris*, translated by J. A. Underwood

Bearing Witness

Every city has its sorrows.

I RECENTLY SAW AN ARCHITECTURAL ARTICLE ON MITTERRAND'S final grand project, the new national library, *Bibliothèque Nationale*, and the memories returned in a flood.

I had been living in Paris for many years, but every excursion still held the promise of discovery and the unexpected; being innocently mistaken for a camera-wielding Japanese tourist who could speak French would turn into a front-seat ride with a Métro driver on an interesting aerial stretch of the #2 line.

It was a sunny day of July, 1991, the first good day for my black and white film. I took the Métro out towards the encampment of 30 or so homeless West Africans at the Quai de la Gare. The encampment was on the edge of the site of the much-heralded national library, for whose design prominent architects had competed. At that time the site was an immense vacant lot criss-crossed by narrow, ghostly streets. An entire neighborhood had been razed, as in a war except the process was surgically precise, dislocating thousands. These people came to symbolize the City of Light's disenfranchised.

Although most held jobs and could pay some rent, they could not find decent lodging in this increasingly gentrified city, whose very charm and identity had originated in the many villages which had come to constitute greater Paris's quartiers.

I was there with the urge to "bear witness."

At the entrance a large white banner proclaimed, *"Un toit, un droit."* (A roof, a right.) It was hot and dusty from the nearby construction and the traffic rushing by. Inside the sheet metal fence, a table, makeshift like the tents, for petitions and information. Had I a right to intrude on these people who tried to live with dignity? How much support and visibility of this sort did they really need? Certainly little from me, who am neither journalist nor politician nor Abbé Pierre, their champion, France's conscience.

Barely arrived, and already in doubt, I told myself to stick to inert matter, such as the beautifully textured old walls of the Marais, updated with poetry and protests, or the peeling layers of old maps and advertisements on the Métro walls; in the meantime, two well-equipped photographers before me were refused the right to photograph the site; so much for my plans and nascent activism.

Disappointed yet relieved, I was about to walk away when one of them approached me with a curious invitation—he would be taking photographs of children he'd been visiting in Belleville later in the afternoon, would I be interested in accompanying him?

This seemed intriguing enough, in spite of oft-repeated warnings about French males, and I love children, so I accepted. Belleville, at the confluence of the 10th, 11th, 19th, and 20th *arrondissements*, is known for its lively cultural mix of North and West Africans, Vietnamese and Chinese or both, holdouts of the French Communist Party (whose headquarters were in the area) and their obligatory leftist intellectual sympathizers, and elderly working-class French, in the best tradition of French solidarity. Blue-collar Belleville is far from the mind and eyes of tourists. Small, unpretentious corner cafés and bistros still teem with the locals. It is one of my favorite haunts to rediscover the Paris of my childhood, and its diversity makes it always interesting and friendly.

But first, I went on to the rue Watt, one or two large blocks away, whose images did not pose moral dilemmas. It had been ren-

dered famous by Robert Doisneau, the photographer of quintes-
sential Parisian life, when couples still danced the Java and kissed
on the street.

This short, wide underpass of a road ran below the Austerlitz
train line heading southeast from Paris. In the right light, the metal
grating shielding it from the trains creates an intricate interplay of
light and dark upon the dotted lane divider, a flickering pattern
which moves with the sun's path in the sky, and undulates upon
humans and speeding vehicles alike. Elaborate, traditional iron ban-
isters and streetlight globes separate pedestrians from the street on
a raised sidewalk, turning it into a promenade. The warmth and
lightness of the metal cast a new nostalgic glow on New York's
elevated train tracks and fire es-
capes, the urban eye-sores of my
adolescence in Queens.

You might wonder why so
much love was put into the design of an essentially unseen, unknown street in a forgotten part
of town—probably this was not
always so. Paris's elegant and romantic façade belies centuries of
transformation, often brutally
sweeping, as under Baron
Haussmann or in today's unre-
lenting, accelerating pursuit of
modernity; all along rue Watt are
sterile forms of concrete and
glass not unlike the cold polished
geometric stone slabs, unworn
by time, now covering the renovated Champs-Elysées and Les
Halles. The Library would be
just one more brick in the master plan. If the rue Watt was the
final expression of an entire

*As an administrator
Haussmann was over
bearing, irresistible, indefatigable,
and efficient. He spoke habitually
of his staff as his "militant personnel," an army whose task was "to
go forth to the conquest of Old
Paris." This army "would permit
me to undertake ripping the quarters of the center of the city from
the tangle of streets virtually im-
penetrable to traffic," gutting "the
sordid, filthy, crowded houses which
were, for the most part, but entryways to misery and disease, and
subjects of shame for a great country like France...." It is one of the
hallmarks of a great administrator
that all the business of his bureaucracy be considered important.
From paper clips to patronage to
boulevards, Haussmann oversaw
everything.*

—David P. Jordan,
*Transforming Paris: The Life and
Labors of Baron Haussmann*

quartier's bygone way of living, it would not survive much longer, but I did not know this. After one roll of film, I went on to meet my new acquaintance.

It was four o'clock on this Sunday afternoon in Belleville, and streets were busy with conversation or the game of *boule*. The photographer paused to chat with an elderly stranger, in an easy yet detached manner.

The older man, like most people, but particularly those with memories of desolation of wars and celebrations of peace, gushed with so many stories to tell, and so few to tell them to. But the young man listened with a distracted ear.

Discretion and respect for privacy always got the better of my yearning to ask, and perhaps it should not have. Unexpressed empathy remains invisible, after all. Earlier that year, in the little town of Terrasson, in the valley of Dordogne, which still openly bears war's ravages, a woman cried as she told of the courageous lives lost during the Resistance, and of the terrible division between French and French. And not just the old, as it turned out, but many young lives as well who need to share theirs.

Down a narrow alley, about a dozen African children aged perhaps from two to ten passed away their time in a small, treeless inner courtyard surrounded by four stories of windows, presumably behind which some elder would keep a watchful eye. They greeted us gently, without wariness; the boys resumed playing soccer, and I kicked the ball a couple of times with them. The man started shooting away with his Nikon, and the girls rushed to me with curiosity and warmth.

In this society where each is still defined by his role, it didn't take long to realize that mine was to keep the children occupied. A role not only assigned by the photographer, but unintentionally as well by the children's parents, whom I never met. In no time I became their big sister, as we hugged and chatted, huddled on the ground, against a wall. Two of them eagerly rushed back to their ground floor homes and gave me their prized possessions, colorful paintings they had done in school.

Rarely in my travels to the ends of the world have I encountered such sensitive, spontaneously trusting, but affection-starved, tender young souls. The girls said their mothers were busy working, sharing the same husband who seemed to return often to Africa. They were thus pretty much left to their own devices. They were so many, yet so lonely.

As I debated whether to photograph them, the same doubts nagged at me, compounded by the additional sense of betraying a child's trust, in spite of their apparent obliviousness to the photographer. And there was also the question of the act of photography, by which I was backing away, consciously or not, instead of surrendering my heart to them as they had to me. Perhaps I unconsciously knew what would eventually transpire.

Photography by its very nature creates a distance, establishing the relationship of subject and object through the intermediary of the lens, a safe but disengaged sort of distance. Perhaps both through this detached yet faithful capturing and reflection of object, and subjective sentiment, true photography is nostalgic in essence.

But I refused the role of caretaker and companion which was assigned to me, all the more readily, it seemed, because of the Oriental stereotypes which preceded me. I saw shapes, texture; I sensed reflections of mood, theirs and mine.

There is a photograph of hands, theirs, one atop another. I reflect with a certain sadness that my hand could not have been one of them. There is another of the eldest beaming proudly with her painting, which almost overwhelms her.

In yet another, in the blinding sun, against dirty white-washed walls, a little boy who did not take to soccer to fill his void, sits with sad, expressive eyes, looking at nothing in particular. This vision transported me to a certain Africa where perhaps his dreams are not strangers.

In Paris, this apparent dislocation is not more or less unusual than that of the regal West African woman coifed with her brilliant headdress riding the Métro with the black-on-black Parisian sophisticate; or, on that same Métro, the long-robed Senegalese Muslim (much like the one who sold me an exquisite sculpture from Mali), next to the dignified, humble gentleman wearing the same formal tweed jacket he has owned for the last 30 years, in a careful life without waste.

I hoped to redress the imbalance between subject and object by letting the children take a turn at the camera. But the sweetest, youngest, and the most sensitive girl finally asked me to put it away. So I did.

I did not fully grasp the meaning of this encounter until it was time to leave, after two hours. The same little one would simply not let go of me. Between her tearful pleadings and my attempts at reassurances, the only way I could leave without traumatizing her on the spot was to promise to return. It was then that the eldest explained that the man brought different female companions each time, and this was difficult for the younger children who would get attached—this time, they wished I would stay.

On the way home, I was very pensive and heartsick—not only about the means to obtain photographs of people, but also of

My flight had been dictated by my hope that I could find myself in a place where I would be treated more personal, and my fate less austerely sealed. And Paris had done this for me by leaving me completely alone. I lived in Paris for a long time without making a single French friend, and even longer before I saw the inside of a French home. This did not really upset me, either, for Henry James had been there before me and had had the generosity to clue me in. Furthermore, for a black boy who had grown up on welfare and the chicken-shit goodwill of American liberals, this total indifference came as a total relief and even as a mark of respect. If I could make it, I could make it—so much the better. And if I couldn't, I couldn't— so much the worse. I didn't want any help, and the French certainly didn't give me any. They let me do it myself and for that reason, even knowing what I know, and unromantic as I am, there will always be a kind of love story between myself and that odd, unpredictable collection of bourgeois chauvinists who call themselves la France.

—James Baldwin,
No Name in the Street

the casual human contacts which may not be so "casual" to some. Usually particularly careful with children, I had not foreseen this. Or had I?

On one hand, isn't it better to give a little than not at all? On the other, how much can one give if it is without long-term commitment? What could really be a substitute for a parent's love? The boys, who did not cry, emitted a certain sadness and perhaps repressed bitterness at being lightly befriended as objects of photographs the man will sell.

I was torn between the desire to return for the children, and the inevitably daunting task of filling the maternal, or paternal, void in their emotional lives. With time, it became increasingly difficult to go back, and I'd hope they would forget so as to soothe my guilt, even though experience had already taught me children never forget promises.

Was this not best after all than to re-open an ever-growing wound? I was only a transient myself, far from entrenched and stabilized in life. I couldn't assume responsibility over fragile lives for which I could do little but offer unattainable dreams.

I still don't know. As I write, I wish to see them again, and offer a painting or photograph in return, a piece of my soul they could keep when I'm gone.

But I won't be able to look up rue Watt anymore. Even Robert Doisneau could not save his beloved street as it was literally obliterated from the map, another sacrifice to the Bibliothèque and its underground parking. In ancient places like Paris, one routinely treads upon the past. History and the unseen always catch up in surprisingly mundane ways, such as the time commuter train renovation work encountered possibly live bombs from the two World Wars, immobilizing circulation for a few days. On a brighter note, Louvre excavations yielded a nearly structurally complete medieval version under the one we now know.

I did not want to know whether the street was just buried for future archeology, or bulldozed through. The lives it touched threw a boisterous farewell street party, complete with live bands, street art and street artists, to this inert object whose soul and brief existence remains enshrined by the camera, as the light was slowly banished.

As for the photographer, his ulterior motives became transparent when he called me the following weekend for a houseboat party on the Seine. I gently turned down his offer, while expressing willingness to see the children again, but he hung up.

Much later, a friend related to me his experience as a naïve amateur photographer venturing onto a houseboat party with his model. It had been advertised as a photographic opportunity, and turned out to be a shocking promotion of sexual voyeurism. Apparently this is quite common, and in banal coexistence with the great French camera tradition, many newsstand "photography" magazines sell erotic female nudes and other less provocative photographs of "charm." This was not necessarily the kind of party I had been invited to, but it was a reminder of a certain type of exploitation for strictly personal interest, in the name of art.

Inside a crate, in the hull of a ship which left Le Havre several months ago on its way to the New World, lie a drawing and a dozen photographs of the girls to whom I can no longer attach names, whose melancholy and thirst for love and life still haunt me.

Thérèse Lung is a software engineer who travels as often as she can. She has lived in Taiwan, Geneva, New York, and Boston and currently calls San Francisco home.

*

Nothing is more relaxing than to live among people who let you be yourself—not as a favor to you, but because they want the same freedom for themselves. The French have the virtue of their vice: an individuality so fierce it has produced a dozen political parties and made France almost impossible to govern, yet, at the same time, has produced Paris, the most civilized of cities, and made France the second home of all civilized men. If you personally assume the mission of straightening out your neighbor's morals, behavior, and non-conformist politics, you might as well forget your peace of mind.

—Joseph Barry, "La Relaxe and French Skepticism"

ROBERT DALEY

* * *

Monsieur de Paris

Who will execute the executioner?

BEHIND THIS WALL AT 35, RUE DE PICPUS THERE COME TOGETHER a number of strands of French history, and some of American history as well. It is a plain address on a plain street in the working-class 12th *arrondissement*. It is not mentioned in guidebooks. There are no tourist buses pulled up outside. The first time I came here I wasn't sure it was the place, because from the sidewalk nothing shows. I had been round and round the block searching. I kept coming upon two great wooden doors in the wall with a smaller wooden door inset into one of them, and finally I opened the small door and peered inside. I saw a large gravel courtyard surrounded by buildings, including a church. The concierge's *loge* was off to the right, together with a sign: "Visits permitted only from two o'clock to four."

A woman of about 60 answered my knock. This was the right place, she said, but it was now five past four and closed.

I gave her a smile. I was late by only five minutes, I said, and actually I had been here on time, but I couldn't find it—

"Je regrette, monsieur."

I don't know why I persisted, for I knew Parisian concierges. But I had come all the way from America, I told her. I was going home tomorrow. I was only five minutes late. This was my last chance to see something important to me.

"Je regrette, monsieur."

It occurred to me to slip her 50 francs. But to succeed at bribing people takes a certain grace. "Perhaps if I give you something you could make an exception," I said. Instead of just doing it I had had to announce it first. Beautiful.

Her manner became haughty. She said *"Je regrette"* again and closed the door on me.

There was an iron door in the wall beside the church. It was locked. I knew what was behind it. I wanted to go through it, and couldn't.

I went into the church. The usual gloomy church, lit principally by candles. About a dozen nuns wearing the elaborate white habits of my youth knelt in pews in prayer, keeping a permanent vigil there. They worked around the clock in relays. That's what they did for a living. They belonged to the Order of the Sacred Heart and were semicloistered. I watched one or two new ones come in and others go out. I had forgotten there were nuns who still dressed in such habits, that prayer vigils still existed.

In the lateral chapels, immense white marble plaques bordered in black were fixed to the walls. On them were inscribed the names, ages, professions, and dates of each of the victims out in the garden. I walked over and peered up at the names, first in one chapel, then in the other. Some were familiar to me. The nuns on their knees paid no notice. There were about 1,500 names in all. For a moment 1,500 living people marched through my head. The impression it made was overpowering, and I resolved to make one more try at the garden.

A side door up by the altar rail might lead out into the garden. I went through it. The worst that could happen was that I would run into some nun; if so, I would bluff my way past her. I had gone through grade school with nuns like this. I was not afraid of nuns.

But I had come out into a corridor, not the garden, and I met not one nun but three. The first two gave me a startled look. The third said sharply. *"Monsieur, vous désirez quelque chose?"* And she pointed, exactly in the manner of my grade-school teachers, back in the direction I had come.

Thoroughly humiliated, I went back into the church, out the front door, and back to my hotel.

Today I knock again on the concierge's *loge*. Some months have passed. This time she is all smiles. I am acquainted with few important people in France, but one is the Count de Chambrun, a descendant of Lafayette, who has called her on my behalf. Normally, she tells me with a smile, visitors are not permitted at this hour. However, she's always happy to make an exception for a guest from America like me. I smile right back. Clearly she does not remember me. I remember her well enough. She hands me a heavy bunch of keys and points to the gate to the garden. I tip her 50 francs. It would seem churlish not to. The money disappears into her apron and she thanks me profusely.

The keys are as big as the keys to a jail, and I open the iron door and go through.

The garden is much bigger than I had thought: about 300 yards long, about 60 wide. It is bigger than some parks, an enclave of greenery entirely surrounded by buildings. There are long alleys of trees, mostly horse chestnuts and lindens, and flat sweeps of lawn. The cemetery is in the far right corner. Its gate is locked too—the French lock up everything. But one of my keys opens it, and I go in.

Lafayette's grave is easy enough to find, for over it flies an American flag. I don't know when the flag was first put up, but it has never come down. It flew all during the German occupation, which surprises me less than it evidently does some people. Probably, like most modern tourists, the Germans didn't know it was there, nor the tomb, not even the garden. Lafayette's wife Adrienne lies beside him, I note, and George Washington de Lafayette behind them both. Just beyond these tombs under the trees, stones mark the place where are buried almost 1,500 headless corpses.

At the start of the Revolution this was a convent, as it is now, but the nuns were forced out, their sacred vessels, paintings, and stained glass confiscated, their chapel demolished and its stones sold to builders. A man named Riedain rented the property from the State, lived in one of the buildings, and in partnership with another man ran what was called a *maison de santé et de détention*—a euphemism for a kind of prison hospital. Actually what they ran was a profitable extor-

> *The more I see of the representatives of the people, the more I admire my dogs.*
>
> —Alphonse de Lamartine,
> *Count d'Orsay*

tion. "Enemies of the nation" (a great many euphemisms were in vogue at this time) could claim to be sick, get themselves sent here, and, for as long as their money or their relatives' money held out, avoid the guillotine. Usually they did not stay long. As more and more goods and property got confiscated, as relatives got arrested too, they were dumped back into the mainstream, en route towards what the men in charge called the Sword-Blade of the Law—the populace, being less pious, called it the National Razor.

By the summer of 1794 the guillotine and the nauseating odor that went with it had been moved several times. Death by decapitation was incredibly messy. The blood pooled on the paving stones underneath. The executioner had a hose and at the end of each day's work would hose off the scaffold, the blade, washing more blood down among the stones. In the summer heat it decomposed rapidly, attracted flies, and gave off a stench. Whole neighborhoods first stank, then protested.

In June of 1794 the instrument was moved again, just in time for the start of the Revolution's busiest summer. Over 1,300 men, women, and children were executed in a month and a half at the new site, the Place du Trône, today's Place de la Nation, which is four or five blocks from where I stand. Thirty-eight heads were lopped off on the first day, including 26 belonging to members of the Toulouse parliament, 42 heads two days later, and 61 the day after that. The record seems to have been 68 on July 7, including the 80-year-old Abbé de Salignac Fénélon (some accounts say he was 69), who had founded a home for the small orphan boys who were the chimney sweeps of Paris. A detachment of weeping boys followed the tumbrel to the scaffold, where the priest asked that his hands be unbound so he could give them a final blessing. The entire mob went to its knees as he traced the cross in the air. Ten days later, singing hymns, a convent of Carmelite nuns, about whom Poulenc later wrote an opera, genuflected to their Mother Superior, climbed the steps one by one, and were decapitated. There were sixteen of them in all. One was a novice. Two were 78 years old.

Next the heads of Lafayette's mother-in-law, her mother, and one of her daughters rolled into the basket, all for the crime of being aristocrats; and the head of André Chenier, 31, poet, about whom Giordano would write an opera 100 years later. Chenier's crime was that he had written articles in the *Journal de Paris* protesting the excesses of the Revolution.

Day by day the guillotine worked. It killed the rich and poor, the known and unknown, 1,109 of them men, including at least one seventeen-year-old boy; 197 of them women, including 51 nobles and 23 nuns, the rest being for the most part maids, hairdressers, and seamstresses from noble households.

The problem became what to do with the corpses, and one morning Riedain woke up and found that a hole had been broken through the wall at the bottom of his garden. Hordes of men were chopping down his fruit trees, digging vast ditches in his lawn, building a heavy door into the breach in his wall. Riedain rushed up and protested. The nation has need of your place, he was told. The ditches got deeper and deeper. He shouted, pleaded, got nowhere. He ran off to plead before the proper ministry. What about his prison hospital? He was doing important work for the Revolution. Again he got nowhere. The first ditch was twenty-five feet long, fifteen wide, twenty deep. The second was even bigger, thirty by twenty by twenty-four.

Night fell, and here came the cartloads of corpses into the garden. Men worked by the light of torches. The headless male, female, and adolescent bodies were first stripped, then dumped naked into the hole. The heads were shaken out of sacks.

Sometimes one or another escaped and was booted in like a soccer ball. The bloody clothing, meanwhile, was being inventoried
by scribes to be sold.

It rained a lot that summer and the garden turned to mud. The
carts were heavy and some nights the men could barely push them
up to the edge. Night after night the carts came through, and the
corpses fell one upon the other in the ditches, where they were
sometimes covered by a light dusting of lime. The ditches remained open, and through the neighborhood on every night
breeze moved clouds of stench. After almost two months, neighborhood outrage reached such a pitch that the guillotine was
moved back to what is now the Place de la Concorde in front of
what is now the Hotel Crillon. But at night fresh corpses continued to arrive here. Finally the order was given: the immense
ditches, containing now about half of all the victims of the Terror,
were to be filled in. The depths were measured. In the first ditch
the headless corpses lay eight feet thick, in the second only five.

Altogether more than 3,000 people were executed in Paris
alone, among them many of the best men France had. More than
110,000 others, including all the rest of France's best, had fled
abroad, where they stayed. Napoleon, 30 years old, walked into an
empty capital and took over.

By 1802 some of the *émigrés* had trickled back to Paris, many
wanting to visit the graves of guillotined loved ones. In most cases
they were unable to find out where they were, for although the
executions had taken place in public, the burial details had worked
at night and in secret lest grief or rage provoke demonstrations.
Officially, the mass graves at 35, Rue de Picpus did not exist. But
the surviving Noailles sisters, Adrienne de Lafayette and Pauline de
Montagu, learned of a lacemaker who had followed the cart containing the corpses of her father and brother.

The girl led them here.

The two women decided to buy the property. But they had no
money anymore and so were obliged to sell subscriptions to other
bereaved relatives, the ones they knew, the ones with blood as blue

as their own. In time they invited the present order of nuns to establish a new convent here and to build a new church over the ruins of the old.

They also set aside a corner of the garden as a private cemetery for themselves—this cemetery in which I stand—with the result that I walk now past tomb after tomb of counts and marquesses and princes and dukes and their female equivalents. There can't be such a conglomeration of nobility anywhere else in the world. Hardly a commoner's tomb anywhere. It is very strange. The commoners are all back there under the trees, headless, buried twenty feet deep, indistinguishable from the aristocrats who died with them.

I am quite alone in this enormous garden, and I walk over to look at the wall where the breach was made for the carts. The carts were painted red so the blood would not show, or at least not show so much. The breach is still visible. After the Revolution it was filled in with stones that are not quite the same color. Also the lintel is still there—the great thick beam that the workmen embedded in the wall so that the doorway would not collapse on the horses and carts.

There are plaques by the breach and more plaques on the wall that surrounds the mass graves—to the sixteen Carmelites, to André Chenier, and to others. If you enjoy reading such things, this is the place for you. You will be busy a long time. Nor is there any similar place elsewhere. There were mass graves in other parts of Paris at the time, but as the city expanded the others were built on; this is the only one extant.

The 1,500 people piled together under my feet, plus that many again who lie today under buildings, were all beheaded by one man, Charles-Henri Sanson. Sanson, who was 50 years old in 1789, came from a family of executioners. The Sansons were themselves the executioners, or were related to the executioners, of eighteen cities in all, and Charles-Henri was the fourth generation in an unbroken line from father to son to serve as executioner of Paris. After him the post would go to his son, and then his grandson, six generations in all before the line petered out.

At the beginning executioners were not allowed to marry out-side the profession. By law their houses were painted red. If they had daughters they were sometimes obliged to nail a sign to the front door to warn suitors away. The baker baked their bread apart, and in church their pew was set apart. Commissions brought to them were not handed over but tossed at their feet.

Their job was even messier at first than it later became. In addition to merely killing people, the early Sansons and their relatives and colleagues in other places also had to cut off hands, cut off ears—the left one first because it was thought to control sexual activity—and stretch people out on the wheel so as more easily to break their legs with iron bars. If the court's sentence called for it they had to peel a criminal like an orange with red-hot pincers or stretch him on the rack until all his limbs were dislocated. Sometimes the executioner used the retentum immediately, or almost immediately. The retentum was a cord so fine the mob couldn't see it. The executioner strangled the victim, then performed the heavy stuff on the corpse. Whatever happened, eventual death was certain. Vagrants and petty thieves were hanged. Homosexuals were burned. Bad women or bigamists were scourged. Serious felons were decapitated: swords for the nobility, axes for commoners. Executions were popular entertainment. To get the best places, spectators began to gather the night before; they lit fires, bought food from vendors, who abounded.

The first four Paris Sansons were all named Charles, the last two Henri. The sire of the dynasty was an army lieutenant stationed in Rouen who had the misfortune to fall in love with the Rouen executioner's daughter. He was, in more ways than one, invited into the family. At his first execution, when ordered to start clubbing the condemned man, he is said to have fainted. This was the origin of the legend that the Sansons were at heart kind, sensitive, gentle. There would be more publicity of this nature during the Revolution. Once inside the profession this first Charles found he could not get out. The top job in Rouen being already taken, he moved to Paris, where he made a name for himself.

His son, the second Charles, performed his first execution at eighteen. The prisoner was a woman who had tried to poison her husband. The windows all around were selling, it was said, for 50 *louis d'or* apiece. The boy's father ordered him to sword off her head. Butchery. He was trembling so much it took him five or six swings.

The third Charles inherited the post at seven, his father having willed it to him on his deathbed. His mother, née Marthe Dubut, had to hurry him over to the public prosecutor's office, where she pleaded for the appointment to be approved, and it was. From then on the child had to witness every execution to make it legal. He did not himself perform one until he was eighteen. At thirty-five and in bad health he resigned—one almost wants to say abdicated—in favor of his oldest son, the Charles-Henri of the Revolution, who was then only fifteen—too young. Back to the public prosecutor went Marthe Dubut, dragging her grandson by the hand. The boy had been assisting his father on the scaffold from the age of eleven, she testified. He was certainly experienced. Grandma claimed the job as the family's right, and again got her way.

This newest Sanson was supposedly the most soft-hearted of the lot, and the execution of a man who had murdered his mistress's husband is offered as proof. Charles-Henri, by then sixteen, could not watch. A mulatto assistant began bludgeoning the man while Charles-Henri looked away. The mistress, meanwhile, was being made to watch; she was later hanged.

Soon afterwards a man named Damiens stabbed Louis XV. Although the King was only nicked, Damiens was sentenced to horrendous torture. Knowing himself too tenderhearted to carry out the sentence, the boy executioner (so the story goes) went to his grandmother for help. Marthe Dubut must have been one tough lady. She summoned one of her other sons, who was executioner at Reims, and they bought strong horses. On the appointed day the boy and his uncle went to the *conciergerie*, where the prisoner had his arms dislocated by *estrapade* and his feet twisted in the boot. Onwards to the scaffold, where the uncle held the would-be renegade's hand in the brazier and an assistant began peeling off his skin with red-hot pincers. Other assistants poured boiling oil and boiling lead onto the wounds. The limbs were then attached to the four horses, which tried three times to pull the man apart. Finally his limbs had to be severed with axes. Every rooftop around was crowded with people.

This was the climate in October 1789 when Joseph Guillotin, 51, a medical doctor and delegate, made a speech in the Estates Général. A quick and humane method of capital punishment had to be found, he argued. All persons regardless of rank should be similarly executed. Torture must be abolished once and for all. There should be no confiscation of the condemned man's property—justice did not permit the nation to ruin his family as well. After execution his family should be allowed to claim his body if it wished.

Guillotin was from Saintes. He had once studied for the priesthood in Bordeaux. He had left to study medicine in Paris and was by now an extremely high-priced doctor—consultations cost 36 livres, about double what others dared charge.

Guillotin began to research capital punishment. He found engravings by Dürer, by Cranach, that showed primitive guillotines. He found descriptions of such machines elsewhere, and he brought this information to Charles-Henri Sanson.

The executioner, we are told, had grown tall and strong. His features were classic, his manner pleasant. He took himself seri-

In Sentimental Education, *set in the 1840s, Flaubert wrote: "'But do you imagine the press is free? Do you imagine we are free?' said Deslauriers passionately. 'When I think that you have to fill in anything up to 28 forms just to keep a boat on the river, I feel like going off to live among the cannibals.'"*

—Mort Rosenblum, *The Secret Life of the Seine*

ously, and he was a snob. He had tried to call himself the Chevalier de Longval, but this did not catch on. He had tried to dress himself in blue, the color reserved for the nobility, had gotten officially reprimanded, and so took to wearing green coats stylishly cut. His title was *Bourreau*—axman—which he found undignified, and he had petitioned the King to be called instead the Executor of Criminal Judgments. The King, now Louis XVI, had so decreed it. The people went on calling him Bourreau anyway—or else, cynically, *Monsieur de Paris.* He played the violin and the cello, how well we do not know, and was friends with Tobias Schmidt, a maker of harpsichords.

It was to Schmidt that he brought Dr. Guillotin's ideas. It was Schmidt, whose name has barely come down to us, who designed the guillotine, but it was the humane Dr. Guillotin whose name got attached to it. He came to be seen as one of the villains of the Revolution, and even of history. During his lifetime—he lived until 1814—he often seemed an object of horror, or else an object of fun. People who passed him in the street would shake their head or give themselves karate chops to the back of the neck. He died a disillusioned man.

In March of 1792 Sanson and Schmidt submitted their designs to a government official at the Tuileries. The King came in and looked them over. He was an enthusiastic amateur locksmith, and it is said that he made suggestions for improving the design of the machine that would ten months later lop off his own head.

The first guillotine was built, and on April 15 Sanson tried it out on some live sheep. Two days later he decapitated three corpses—two men and one woman—in the courtyard of the hospital at Bicêtre, while a crowd of officials, including Dr. Guillotin, looked on. Eight days after that it was used on a thief named Jacques Pelletier. It worked so perfectly that Tobias Schmidt, the harpsichord maker, got orders for 34 more. Someone is supposed to have said: I hope this doesn't make killing people too easy.

The Terror began the next year, and a guillotine mentality, guillotine fads, swept over the city, together with insane rumors. Did severed heads feel pain, was the guillotine humane or not? Learned men, and some not so learned, disputed this point. Experiments were conducted on heads. When pricked with a knife point, tongues were said to retract into the mouth; when turned to the sun, pupils were said to dilate. Charlotte Corday's cheeks were said to have blushed when one of Sanson's assistants slapped her face as he showed her head to the crowd. The general belief seemed to be that severed heads continued to feel pain until they had cooled.

Meanwhile, there were charms for bracelets in the form of guillotines, and toy guillotines for children. Small guillotines were sold to farmers for beheading chickens. At dinner parties similar guillotines beheaded tiny dolls; out flowed a red liqueur into which men dipped their fingers, women their handkerchiefs. Songs were written. Cartoons appeared, in one of which Sanson himself lay bound under the blade; according to the caption he had guillotined everyone else, so there was no one left to guillotine but himself.

Sanson had four assistants, then seven; two tumbrels, then nine. Some days he worked from dawn to dark. He complained of overwork, of burgeoning expenses. He kept asking the Committee of Public Safety for more money; eventually he got it, a bonus of 20,000 *livres*. Between March 1793 and July 1794, a period of 502 days, he, his brothers, his sons, and whatever other assistants were on the scaffold with him killed 2,362 people. Sensitive? Softhearted? Some were people Sanson knew and had had official contact with; others he came to know, for the ride to the place of execution was frequently long, sometimes two hours or more, and he would converse with them. In addition there were rain delays— Paris is a rainy place—and a rainy, bloody scaffold with that great snaggletooth hanging overhead was too dangerous to work on. While the rain lasted, executioner and condemned prisoners alike would huddle under the scaffold, and again Sanson would converse with them. Sometimes he would apologize for making them wait.

He executed everyone sent to him, no questions asked, nine men over 80, sixteen artists, twenty-five writers, the King, the Queen, the actress Marie Grandmaison and her 18-year-old-serving girl, and eventually, Danton, Robespierre, Public Prosecutor Fouquier-Tinville, and most of the others, the signers of the death warrants, the very men he had been taking his orders from.

Under the Revolution he became, in his own eyes at least, a figure of importance. As he saw it he was respected everywhere he went. He was certainly good at his job. The mass graves in this garden attest to that. He once killed 21 men in 38 minutes. He made them get out of the carts and stand in rows facing away from the scaffold. One by one he ordered them to mount the steps. On top their legs were bound together with ropes. Their arms were already bound. They were strapped to the bascule. Their heads were tipped into the lunette. The two halves came together and locked. Down came the blade. Unstrap him. Undo the ropes. Into the basket with him. Next.

Such speed was possible because virtually none of the victims made a fuss. They were all too proud. The rich were especially haughty. They looked out over the cheering mob, their lips came together in what was close to absolute contempt, and they went to their deaths without so much as a grimace. Madame du Barry, once the mistress of Louis XV but now a raddled, middle-aged woman, did kick and scream. It took three men to hold her while her hair was cut and her arms bound. But she was the exception. It was the opinion of a number of witnesses that if everyone had behaved just like her the public would have sickened of the spectacle much more quickly than it did; the Terror would never have lasted so long.

As far as Sanson was concerned the Revolution produced only one tragedy. One day his son Gabriel, who had been assisting him on the scaffold from the age of eleven, but who was by then a grown man, was parading around the perimeter showing someone's head to the mob. He fell off the edge and was killed instantly. There were railings around every scaffold after that, but Sanson, it was said, was never the same.

The guillotine devoured nearly everyone who came near it, with one glaring exception—Sanson himself—which seems, on the face of it, incredible. He was arrested twice. A Royalist press was found in a room in his house that he had rented out. He argued his way of that one. Later on he and his two brothers were arrested and charged with being Royalist sympathizers—they had hanged, clubbed, and broken the King's enemies for years, had they not? What else could they be? A charge like this was sufficient to send scores of men to the scaffold, but the Sanson case posed a special problem: who do you get to execute the executioners? In the 1790s you could not just phone up some other town and fly in a substitute. Meanwhile, death warrants were piling up on somebody's desk. People were waiting to be executed, and there was no one to do it.

So again they let the Sansons go. Soon afterwards Charles-Henri became so busy and also so essential that he was never bothered again.

There were not even recriminations once the Terror finally ended. Outraged or grief-stricken relatives might have come forward. None did. There might have been cries for revenge, but if there were no one heard them. By the standards of the Nuremberg trials Sanson would certainly have been arrested and prosecuted as a war criminal. But this was not 1945. He was a government functionary. He had obeyed orders. He had done his job. He died in bed in 1806.

By then he had been succeeded by his son. Later came his grandson, sixth and last in the line, who got himself fired. He lost his job, and his descendants lost their jobs at the same time. Between 1840 and 1847 this last Sanson guillotined only eighteen people. He was supposed to be a tenderhearted executioner too, and this is offered as the reason he gave himself to gambling and fast women. He felt an intense revulsion for who he was and what he did that could be assuaged in no other way. But the result was unfortunate: he went heavily into debt and faced debtor's prison.

He pawned the guillotine for the sum he needed, 3,800 francs. He was hoping to be able to redeem it in time.

But someone took a shot at the King (for France had kings again now). The would-be assassin was caught, and the authorities went looking for the executioner. Then they went looking for the guillotine. At first they couldn't find either. Finally Sanson came back. He was 48 years old. The authorities redeemed the guillotine for him, the execution took place, and then they sacked him, and the family dynasty, after just under 200 years, was over.

A new one promptly started. Louis Deibler became *Monsieur de Paris*. In 1870 the number of executioners was reduced to one, whose jurisdiction encompassed the entire country. There was only one guillotine too, plus a spare, of course; he and it moved about the roads as needed. *Monsieur de Paris* had become *Monsieur de France*. Louis Deibler was succeeded by his nephew Anatole Deibler, who was succeeded by his nephew Henri Desfourneaux, and then by André Obrecht, another nephew of Anatole, who performed the last public execution in 1939 and who later was credited with having "perfected" the guillotine—he put ball bearings instead of grease in the grooves. The great blade still weighed seventy pounds—now it dropped more quickly. When it spoke, people listened. With it Obrecht executed 387 criminals to 1977. He was something of a natty dresser. That is, he became famous for wearing his hat while he worked. There was perhaps something subliminal there—his clients had nothing to wear hats on. He kept going until he was 78 years old, then retired in favor of his nephew by marriage, Marcel Chevalier, the present incumbent and perhaps the last in history, for France abolished the death penalty in 1981.

Every country has its "traditional" method of execution. The Spaniards garrote, the English hang, the Americans electrocute, and the French guillotine; and although the result is the same in all cases, it is the last-named that has so fascinated the world. The very thought of it, it is said, is enough to make a man feel a chill on the back of his neck. No method is "nice," nor are they always instantaneous. Men in electric chairs jerk and sometimes fry. Men hanged sometimes squirm, strangling, for some time. However, the sensibilities of onlookers are not assaulted. The mess is self-contained. Hanging, garroting, electrocution—these can seem almost euphemisms for killing. The guillotine, by contrast, is graphic, noisy, bloody—the real thing.

And so to a good many people, though not to the French, who remained married to it for so long, it has seemed by far the most horrible method of judicial death. The condemned man, philosophically speaking, is more than executed. His arteries fountain after he is dead, and he goes into his coffin mutilated, his head under his arm, retribution having been carried out seemingly even on his corpse. He will remain both killed and mutilated until the

end of time. This is a heavy notion, and everyone who ever pon-
dered the guillotine as a method of execution (condemned men in
their cells have tended to ponder it a lot) has had to come to grips
with it.

Robert Daley is the author of 24 books, including Prince of the City. *He
lives with his wife in Connecticut and Nice.*

★

The Musée du Pain is not an homage to the Marquis de Sade; *pain* means
"bread" in French. This astonishing little museum, tucked away in an
unassuming courtyard next to a working mill, celebrates the eternal connection between humanity and the loaf—for as is written in the museum's little brochure-cum-manifesto, "The life of bread is the life of
Man." Where is this relationship more evident than in France, a country
where bread became a rallying point for revolution?

Nonetheless, we visit a museum like this anticipating the worst kind
of kitsch. Come on—bread? But founder Jacques Lorch, who opened the
museum's doors in 1972, has done an amazingly tasteful job. Lorch, a true
connoisseur of all things doughy, has invested a fortune in amassing a collection of historic memorabilia that must be unique.

Here you will find the world's oldest surviving communion wafers
(from the 17th century) and seven rather stale, discus-shaped loaves exca-
vated from a 4,400-year-old Egyptian crypt. There are grains of wheat
from Masada, antique waffle irons, and "breads of the world" interspersed
with statues of millers and bakers from the four points of the compass.

Those with a hunger for history will find plenty to sink their teeth
into. There is a letter from Marie Antoinette to a new master baker, explaining his rights and responsibilities; correspondence from the Emperor
Napoleon to his chief baker; and an edict issued by Joseph Fouche, minister of police during the Revolution, in which he forbids the baking of
inferior loaves for sale to the poor.

—Jeff Greenwald, "Discovering the Hidden Museums of Paris,"
San Francisco Examiner

La Photo

Your life can change in a flash.

OFF TO A ROMANTIC DINNER AT LE PRE CATELAN, A SWANKY restaurant nestled in Paris's Bois de Boulogne, we settled into the roomy back seat of a luxurious Mercedes taxi. Trees in the dense woods took on shadowy forms as darkness descended early on this cool October evening. As traffic slowed down, we began to notice striking figures strategically positioned under certain trees, posing for passing motorists. We gazed in amazement as gorgeous women with long flowing hair sensuously opened skimpy kimonos to reveal curvaceous bodies clad only in minuscule G-strings.

"They must be freezing!" I said, while my husband gazed raptly at this cornucopia of delights, here a redhead, there a brunette, opening and closing their short kimonos with tantalizing slowness. With a photographer's zeal, he grabbed his trusty Nikon to record the scene. The brief flash lit up the crisp night air. Once past the site, we wondered if we had seen a mirage, but our thoughts quickly turned to the three-star dinner that awaited us.

Moments later we heard a horrendous clattering on the sidewalk, rapidly approaching. In fact, it was the sound of six pairs of high heels in hot pursuit of our taxi. Traffic was only inching along, so we were almost stopped when the back door was yanked open by the fastest runner, who screamed in our faces, "*La photo! Nous demandons la photo!*" Our shock at the forceful demand was overshadowed by the realization that this was no Folies showgirl! Instead, we were confronted with a heavily made-up male face— bright red lipstick, eye-shadow and rouge thickly applied to jowly rough skin. This apparition screamed French obscenities in a deep, angry voice, while banging on the taxi with a huge, hairy fist. The sheer kimono barely covered the male transsexual's voluptuous breasts so recently bared.

Momentarily stunned, I shrank into the deep recesses of the seat while my husband argued valiantly in broken French. By this time they had all arrived. Any attempt at feminine allure was cast aside. No more preening for the voyeurs. Now they were guys and they were mad, swaggering, yelling, and threatening. The makeup and peek-a-boo outfits notwithstanding, we knew they were serious.

Somehow my husband managed to wrest the car door away and slam it hard, imploring the taxi driver to "Go quickly!" All he got in reply was a blank stare until he repeated in French, "*Allez, vite, vite!*" A quick getaway was impossible, given the situation, but the car pulled away and had picked up a little speed when we heard outraged squealing and loud protestations that someone's hand was caught in the door. I had visions of our taxi "dragging a drag queen" through the Bois de Boulogne. Would our insurance cover the lawsuit?

> *The French law is very clear and strict about impromptu street encounters. Regardless of fault, in the case of a dispute, the person who touches the other first is wrong.*
>
> —William Wharton,
> *Houseboat on the Seine*

We had no choice but to stop, realizing too late that they were faking the hand-caught-in-the-door routine. Now they were *really* mad. Brawny fists pounded on the taxi while the driver held his head, lamenting "*mon taxi, mon taxi,*" and the car came dangerously close to rolling over with us in it.

Why didn't we simply hand over the film? It was one of the last shots on a roll of 36 which we had taken over the course of a week. My husband had won a free trip to Paris for six people, and we shared his prize with my sister and her family. It was a rare opportunity for us to spend a week in Paris together, and that film had captured many magical moments.

However, strongly outnumbered, we had few options left. With great reluctance, my husband opened the camera and surrendered the film to the menacing horde, who snatched it up and scrutinized it under the street lamp, muttering to themselves. As the taxi carried us slowly away, we trembled with residual fear and the beginnings of relief. During dinner, fortified with good French wine, we heatedly discussed what we should have done, could have done, and would do next time.

Parisian friends to whom we related this incident nodded knowingly to hear of the parading transsexuals but threw their hands up in horror when we mentioned taking "la photo." How gauche! After all, as one Parisian reminded me with a shrug, "this is Paris."

Cori Kenicer is a travel and golf writer who lives near San Francisco. She has teed it up in the King of Morocco's golf tournament, wielded her putter in Aruba, and shared the greens with the wild elk in Banff. This is her first published work that has nothing whatsoever to do with golf.

★

I found Henri Beyle, for one, he who was known, among some three hundred other names, as Stendhal. Protean Henri introduced the word "tourist" into the French language. This was fitting, as he lived his early 18th century life at a distance, as a sort of tourist, an original romantic, a prototypical modern man. In him, as in his English contemporary William Blake, the period's insistence upon rationality—upon thinking making the man—took its fuller dimension: a preference for the self-created universe, for the world within. "How many precautions," wrote miserable Henri, whom I knew as I knew myself, "how many precautions are necessary to keep oneself from lying."

—Jim Paul, *What's Called Love: A Real Romance*

KATHERINE GIBBS

Paris Light and Dark

*For these visitors, the Fête de la Musique is
different the second time around.*

M Y HUSBAND AND I HAVE DONE PRETTY MUCH EVERYTHING HAV-
ing to do with our romance backwards. This is how it happened
that our first trip together to Paris was an oddly timed honeymoon
during which I was six months pregnant with our first child. It was
early summer and we had arrived for five days together, alone (except for the constant kicking in my lower abdomen) in the City of
Light. Life was good.

We had secured a perfect room in a little hotel on Rue Jacob
on the Left Bank. We were three blocks from the Deux Magots
and six from Notre Dame. Our hotel was lovely, clean, and tiny and
served the best kind of French breakfast—dark, rich coffee; hot,
steamed milk; croissants; very fresh baguette; jam and butter.
Heaven.

During our five days, we were dedicated tourists. Both of us are
serious walkers, and we toured everything possible on foot. We
would start out our day with a plan to consume a particular area
of Paris. Our first task was to get to the middle of the area on the
Métro. Once there, map in hand, our walk started. We didn't stop
until exhausted when we would find the nearest Métro stop and
head back to our hotel.

This was the type of day we spent on June 21, 1983. We had toured on foot all day, then tired and happy, we had returned to our room to rest before dinner. We trudged up the stairs and collapsed on the bed, feet up. The huge old window and its shutters were open to the warm, late afternoon. A tiny breeze blew by, catching the sounds of the city and pulling them to us. We dozed.

Evening crept through the city. Since it happened to be summer solstice, this evening was more like a typical late afternoon. The sky was bright, the sun well up from the horizon, and the clock read 7:00 p.m. The sounds of the street still swirled through our room, but now, we heard music. Notes came from guitars, drums, a flute somewhere far away, bells ringing, a violin just down the block. We shook off our nap, changed into only slightly wrinkled clothes, and wound back down the stairs. What was this sound of music all through the streets?

As we walked out of the hotel, we could see that an on-street transformation was taking place. The usual bustle of city people, hurrying to work, to school, to meetings, had changed into a strolling group of festival goers. Couples walked leisurely, arm-in-arm. Groups of students laughed and talked. Parents and children stood and listened. On every street corner, in every nook and cranny of our temporary neighborhood was music. The violinist on the corner was a girl of twelve or thirteen, solemnly playing hard-learned classical movements. In the next block, a single saxophonist played mournful jazz. Still further, in a small square, a flatbed truck was parked with an immense organ balanced on its back. Puffs of air and music bleated from the huge machine, sounding, appropriately, like background music for some great horror film such as The Hunchback of…well, you get the idea.

Music was everywhere. String quartets, jazz quartets, the French version of the barber shop quartet combined somehow with electric-acid-punk-rock and opera. Listening to the music and strolling through the ever-present sun of midsummer were happy groups of Parisians and tourists alike. The scene was magic. We strolled and listened and laughed until our feet (and my back) could carry us no more. After complete darkness settled in at about

11:00, we walked ourselves home and silently crept up our hotel stairs. As we climbed into bed, windows still open to the summer night, we could hear that we were clearly some of the first to bed. The streets buzzed with music, laughter, and talk as we drifted off.

Let's move ahead now in time. It is exactly eight years later, June 21, 1991. We are back in Paris to renew the bliss. Now, of course, we have a few more people in our party, including the almost eight-year-old, Sam, and his five-year-old sister, Rachel, as well as my sixty-eight-year-old mother-in-law. We also have, fortunately as it turns out, met up with our friend, Helene, who is a native Parisian. We all decide to relive the wonder of our first summer solstice at the Paris Music Festival. After dinner at Helene's, the kids, Gramma, Helene, my husband and I head hopefully for the inner workings of Paris. Our first stop is the Place des Vosges, a secluded square between the Marais and the Bastille. Surrounded by attached houses, most of which were built in the 1600s, including Victor Hugo's house in the corner, the Place des Vosges holds centuries of peace, seclusion, and silence. The stone is the color of dark, warm sand, and the architecture is cloister-like, the entire interior consisting of an almost uninterrupted string of archways. This night, music dots the square, just as we had hoped.

We decide not to linger here, though, and head back across the river into the heart of the Left Bank. We arrive at about 9:30, and we are definitely not alone. It appears that the summer solstice festival is now shared with the population of most of the surrounding areas of France, half the foreign tourists in Europe, and all available drunks in a 30-kilometer radius. The Paris Music Festival has changed in a big way. It is now big. Not just big, huge.

The tiny streets of the Left Bank are pressed solid with people. The music is still there, struggling to rise above the people and into the night air, but the crowds block it, closing its sounds to earthbound beings. We are in the most intense crowd I have ever seen, and we can't seem to get out. My husband is carrying the five-year-old now so that she won't suffocate with all the tall bodies around her. I am clutching the hand of my mother-in-law as I pull her behind me, all the while keeping a lock on my son's shoulder as I maneuver him ahead of me. Where are we and where are we going? Again, thank God for Helene.

> *We decided to carry on to Trocadero and see what was going on there. It was really cool, there were two trucks with people on them dancing away. OK it was techno music and techno may severely suck but it was such fun to watch people dancing. The Germans were going sick because they love techno and they dance so cool; it was sooo cool to just watch, but it's really bad to hang around there if you are young, female, and blonde because some of the guys there were blahhhh.*
>
> —Tashi Wheeler, 15

Helene leads us slowly through the press. We all agree that we need to get out of there, but the kids are tired of walking, and our hotel, this time, is far from where we are. We need the Métro. Helene knows where a stop is. We snake and wind through the crowds. This takes us a long time. We creep past a mass of people trying to see a jazz group; we stumble right next to a lone electric guitar; drums rattle us as we try to work through a crowd in an intersection.

It takes us almost an hour and a half to make it the few blocks to the Métro stop. We slowly move down the steps, still mired in a crowd. The station is packed. Everyone wants out of there. We wait; a train comes; we move with the crowd closer to the tracks. We cannot get on this train; it is much too crowded. We wait some more; a train comes; we move ahead again. Again we cannot get on. The third train arrives; it is now almost midnight. We get on and move to the other side of the car. The car fills, and fills, and fills with people. I have grabbed onto two poles in order to form a barrier to keep my son and my mother-in-law protected from the crush. My husband holds our daughter high to keep her up where she can breathe. Somehow, though, the flow of the crowd has moved him away from me. He is half way down the car. Helene is even farther down.

The conductor tries to shut the doors. They will not shut. There are so many people on the train that many of them must stand with their arms straight up in the air. There is no room for arms here. I am guarding my kin while a short, fat, drunk old man leans heavily into my back. Is he feeling me up or is he unwillingly compromised? At this point, who knows?

The train does not move, and a sulky French voice crackles over the loud speakers, "The train is too full. Too full. Get off the train. We will not leave until people get off."

Nothing happens. No one moves. Silence reigns. The train stands still. "The train is not leaving," the now petulant voice crackles again.

In our car, three lithe young men next to the door leap out onto the platform. They stand, we all stand, in stifling silence. The buzzer warning that the doors are about to close goes off. The young men leap in. The doors close. We leave the station. As it turns out, this is the last train of the night.

The drunk behind me says something. He doesn't like something I am doing but my French is not great, and I can hardly hear him over the train. Suddenly the train lurches, stops and all the lights flicker off. We are in total darkness. Silence again overtakes us. It is incredibly hot in the cars, and no one knows why we have stopped. I can see faint lights out the window. It is the station just down the track. I plan what to do in a fire. I stand silent, wanting to scream, grab the children, and run like crazy. There is nowhere to go, and the fat drunk is into my side and back again. Finally, the announcement, still sulky, "Someone has pulled the emergency brake and it will take time to reset."

The lights go on, and we lurch ahead. The fat man is right in my ear now, and I can hear him and understand him. He is angry at me because I have broken a Métro rule. He hates it when people break rules. He wants to know why I think I can allow my son and mother-in-law to sit on the special pull-down seats which are not supposed to be used when the car is full. I blast him back.

"For God's sake, this is a child and his grandmother. What difference does it make?"

"No," he says. "The rules are for everyone. They should not sit."

This is absurd, I think. We are all just trying to survive here.

The train stops at the station. No one gets off. It lurches again. As it jerks out of the station, I feel searing pain shooting up from the floor. The fat, old drunk has ground his solid, heavy heel into my toes. All his weight and the force of the overloaded train car are crushing my toes into the dark of the floor. But, I am a stoic. I have maintained emotional stability so far tonight, and I will never give him the satisfaction of breaking me. However, if we ever get out of this car, this guy is dead.

The train lurches through two more stops before a few people actually start to get off. The fat, old drunk is swaying now with the train, and I have managed to move my foot under my son's seat. The next stop is ours. We peel ourselves out, gratefully spewed onto the dark platform. But, the drunk thinks he is not finished with me. He follows me out, weaving and cursing. I am free now, and I am sober, and I am young and strong. I turn on him, ready to give my kids a lesson in the down side of city life. I look him squarely in the eyes with the same piercing glare reserved for bad dogs and bad drivers. He stumbles and falls halfway to the ground. His breath bursts from him, and his friend, who has followed him out of the car, catches him. They lean and stagger on each other. I leave, vindicated.

It's late and the evening is warm as we struggle out of the Métro. The kids are exhausted. My husband is still carrying the five-year-old while I push and cajole the almost eight-year-old up the long, silent stairs. Helene and Grandma take up the rear. We stand now on a quiet street, under leafy plane trees, in the half-light of the city. We made it. And under that dim street light we are still alive, still together, still friends, and still, after all, in Paris.

Katherine Gibbs is a freelance travel writer who relives her family's travel adventures through her stories. Her articles have appeared in The Washington Post *and* Travelers' Tales France. *When she's not traveling or writing, she teaches in the Psychology and Education departments at the University of California, Riverside. She lives with her two children, husband, and dog in an old house in the downtown section of Riverside.*

✳

Descending the stairwells to the Métro's cavernous tunnels, we wondered vaguely why no one was there to take our fare.

We were enroute to the Champs-Elysées and the Arc de Triomphe and in the beginning our spirits were high. Trains thundered by, vibrating our seats on the empty platform. I looked around. Under a neon green/yellow haze we were quite alone save for one other—a young fair-haired fellow sitting nearby. He returned my now-strained smile. Together we watched as, intermittently, jammed trains swollen with people actually hanging out the sides, shot through at great speeds.

"Are you Parisian?" I asked.

"Yes," he said with a gentle smile.

"Uh, we're waiting for the train to the Arc de Triomphe. Where *is* everybody?" Whereupon he explained that a Métro strike was just beginning and only a few trains remained in service. Perhaps ours would come, he added, hopefully. He smiled again.

We chatted a while about the beauties of Paris and he nodded, but added words about how we should take care and not go to the *bois*— Paris' nearby woods—as well as other dangerous areas.

About this time, a gang of ruffians descended the stairs—an unruly looking bunch as can be seen in all major cities. They eyed us and came alongside, some sitting to our right and others to our left. We suddenly realized we were surrounded and our exit was cut off.

The young fellow smiled up at them while beckoning us to follow him. He walked right through as they gave way for us to pass and soon we were safely up the stairs into the soft Parisian sunlight once again.

"I'll try to get you a taxi," he offered.

We smiled our appreciation, not daring to expect *that* possibility during a Métro strike, but as he raised his hand, an empty taxi pulled to the curb. Our friend leaned in, gave directions, and we were once again on our way.

I often think about him—our Parisian angel. Was he real, or one of the Louvre angels come to life? I think the latter.

—Jeanne Conte, "An Angel in Paris"

INA CARO

Fleeing the Splendor

A visitor finds fault with the abode of the Sun King.

BOB AND I VISITED VERSAILLES ON OUR FIRST TRIP TO FRANCE. I suppose everyone does. We visited it again eleven years later, in 1985. Both visits had exhausted my supply of superlatives. We had taken the guided tour, which I thought wonderful. We had seen the king's antechamber, where, we were informed, Louis XIV dined alone while 24 violins played. We were taken to his bed-chamber, where 100 courtiers were given the honor of attending the morning ritual of *lever* and another 100 the evening ritual of *coucher*. When these descendants of fighting knights donned *their* armor, they were probably heading off not to battle but to one of the innumerable costume parties that set the immense palace glittering in the evenings.

In the Hall of Mirrors, the Galerie des Glaces, we saw busts of Roman emperors in porphyry and marble, antique statues of Greek gods—and, under a vaulted ceiling painted by Le Brun, crystal-and-silver chandeliers, and gilt-and-crystal candelabra reflected in seventeen arched mirrors. Now, in 1991, fondly remembering the hall—and Versailles as a whole—as I planned this journey through France's history, I felt it would be the perfect prism through which to see the Age of Louis XIV. The silver furniture that once sparkled in the light of four thousand candles may have been melted down to pay for Louis's wars—and Louis's vases of gold, inlaid with diamonds, agate, emeralds, turquoise, jade, and pearls, may have been transferred to the Louvre—but, remembering my earlier visits, I felt that the splendor and magnificence of this hall encapsulate for the tourist France's Golden Age. The arcade of seventeen arched mirrors reflects more than the seventeen arched windows, more than the chandeliers and candelabra or the splendor of the Grand Siècle; it illuminates also the socioeconomic foundation that lay beneath the gilt. For example, the mirrors at Versailles were manufactured in France. Previously, fine mirrors had been imported from Italy, because no one in France knew how to make them properly. Louis XIV and his minister Colbert were determined that France be economically self sufficient, but they could not simply begin to manufacture mirrors. Venice made the finest glass in the world, so Venetian artisans were enticed to France by extravagant salaries and perquisites to teach the art; then Venetian foremen were recruited to set up a factory in Paris. Economic competition in the seventeenth century was not taken lightly, and when Italian authorities learned that two of the best mirror artisans had been lured to France, the authorities had them poisoned before they were able to teach their secrets to French apprentices. As soon as the industry was in place, the tariff on imported mirrors was doubled, thereby discouraging imports. By the end of Louis's reign the finest mirrors in the world were made in France, and Voltaire could write, "The fine mirrors made in our own factories, which now decorate our houses, cost far less than did the little ones that used to be imported from Venice." Louis and Colbert did the same for other industries, encouraging high quality by awarding prizes to the French master craftsmen who produced the finest quality products (or "master pieces"). "We have beautiful and ornamental materials that are both cheaper and better than those brought from abroad," Voltaire wrote.

Other incentives were used. "In order to establish the manufacture of tar in France," Colbert later recalled, "the king brought from Sweden a certain Elias Hal. This man, after three or four years' work, informed me of his desire to settle in France. His Majesty ordered me to take the trouble of arranging marriage for him—he gave him 2,000 *écus* for use at his marriage and disposed 2,000 livres of appointments for him annually, which has always been regularly paid. I found a girl at Bordeaux who brought him a very honorable marriage."

Colbert desired not merely to limit imports but to increase exports, so Versailles was designed in part as a showcase, displaying to ambassadors and foreign visitors French products of such excellent quality and taste that they returned home wanting to buy the products themselves and singing their praises throughout the world. Foreign dignitaries attending state functions held at night in the Hall of Mirrors could hardly help being impressed by the reflected glow of 4,000 candles—and by the silver furniture, the Savonnerie carpets, the Gobelin tapestries, and by the vases, the laces, the marble from Languedoc used throughout the palace.

Has God forgotten all I have done for him?"
—Louis XIV, upon hearing the news of the French defeat at Malaquet

Look up at the ceiling painted by Le Brun for the Hall of Mirrors. It glorifies Louis's victories in a war with Holland, the country most competitive with France. If normal means of commercial competition proved inadequate, Louis and Colbert went to war. Descartes, the French philosopher, who lived in Holland, wrote that "everybody but myself is in business and so engrossed with his profits that I could live here all my life without being noticed by anyone.... All their toil helps to adorn the place of my abode, and supplies all my wants...the vessels arrive which bring an abundance of all the produce of the Indies and all that is rare in Europe." Louis said the Dutch "absorb nearly all profits of trade in all parts of the world and leave only a very small portion to the other nations." The last straw was an embargo that the Dutch placed on French wine and brandy. Louis declared war on them in 1672.

In planning this journey through French history, I had expected, when we reached the Age of Louis XIV, to recommend

Versailles as a magical place to visit the pinnacle of monarchy. I had felt, moreover, that the 20th-century visitor, viewing the Sun King's bedroom, visualizing there the crowd of dukes and counts—men who once were independent masters of fiefdoms like Carcassonne, Beynac, and Castelnaud, but who now filled their hours with useless court functions, waiting around to watch the king get into or out of bed, helping him put on his clothes—would see how under Louis the king's favor had become the sole source of power in France.

And a visit to Versailles, I had felt, would reveal the tyranny of Louis XIV not only over his courtiers but over the arts as well. The function of art, to Louis, was simple: his glorification. He was being quite candid when he told the members of the French Academy, "I entrust to you the most precious thing on earth—my fame." (The artists proved faithful trustees—not that they had much choice. Molière may have mocked the rest of society, but he never mocked Louis XIV. One gentleman who ventured to criticize the length of a prologue praising Louis XIV promptly found himself in jail.) For twenty years Louis XIV was the primary patron of the arts, and for twenty years, Le Brun, director of the French Academy, saw to it that the arts were devoted to enhancing the splendor of Louis XIV's palace and glorifying his image. It was Le Brun's identification of Louis XIV with Apollo—an identification evident throughout Versailles—that created for posterity the image of the Sun King that Louis desired.

In August of 1991, Bob and I were concluding a test tour of the places I wanted to include in the book I was writing, to check whether those I had fallen in love with over a period of twenty years were still as I remembered them. Arriving at Versailles on a beautiful summer day, we found the parking lot in front of the palace filled with a herd of large tour buses, and the line to purchase tickets to visit the palace far longer than either of us had the patience to endure. Not wanting to spoil our memory of Versailles, we went back to Paris without visiting the palace. Without Versailles, however, I was afraid the plan of my book would be incomplete. I told myself that August, the month the

French go on vacation, was no the time to visit Versailles or, indeed, any place in France. We would, I decided, go to Versailles before Easter, not only before the French vacation but before the colleges and schools let out for the summer. We returned on a rainy day in early April 1992.

The first thing I saw on emerging from the train station at Versailles was a sign for a McDonald's. Horrors! And yet the vast palace did not disappoint, nor was it even crowded that day, in the depth of winter and a chill rain: we supped on the glories and follies of the dead to our heart's content. Outside, in the gardens, we briefly lost two of our children, only to find them weeping, squatting before a puddle of rain, the Sun King's vast edifice rippling on its surface as they poked it with sticks.

—James O'Reilly,
On and Off the Autoroute

We took the Métro to the Invalides station, where there is a connection with the RER to Versailles/Rive Gauche. (The train to Versailles-Chantier does not go to the palace.) The ride was only 38 minutes. Versailles is easy to get to—perhaps too easy.

It was a Tuesday morning, cold, overcast, and intermittently rainy. But again the lot was filled with buses, huge single-deckers and even larger double-deckers. I counted over thirty-five of them—and then stopped counting. When we arrived at the gilt-and-black wrought iron gate leading to the courtyard, the serpentine line of tourists waiting to visit the palace extended past the gate curving around Bernini's equestrian statue of Louis and across the entire length of the enormous courtyard. In 1985 I had been overwhelmed by the crowds. Oh, well, I thought bitterly, even in the Age of Louis XIV, Versailles had been commercial.

Giving up on seeing the inside of the palace, we retreated to the gardens. The long line of visitors queued up to take a little train to the Trianons was so long that the train would have had to make four or five trips to transport the people already in line. And even as we watched, the line was getting longer.

One of the greatest things about the gardens at Versailles is the fountains. An aqueduct and the Marly Machine were built to bring water four miles to fill 1,400 fountains. (One reason contemporaries were so opposed to Louis's construction project at Versailles was the lack of an adequate water supply nearby.) The fountains, however, were silent during our visit. I later found out they are so expensive to operate that they are rarely turned on.

Descending into the gardens, we sat down on the edge of Le Brun's Fountain of Apollo. Bob, having noticed that I hadn't spoken for quite some time, tried to whip up some enthusiasm by pointing out the geometric beauty of the terrace, the arch of dark green hedges in a great horseshoe behind it, and the arcs of Grecian urns and Grecian statues framed by the hedges circling the Fountain of the Sun God—and, behind it, the palace of the Sun King. Someone, I thought, had been a 17th-century public relations genius. At the time Louis was king, over a hundred years had passed since Copernicus had shaken the foundations of the medieval world by proving that the earth revolved around the sun. To the subconscious mind of some 17th-century visitors, the garden of Louis's palace must have suggested that the planets revolved not around the sun but around the Sun King.

I turned to my book on gardens and read once again that Le Nôtre had designed the gardens here to be an earthly paradise—the Elysian Fields that the Greeks had imagined. But I had to confront the fact that Versailles was no paradise to me. Originally built to destroy the independence of the nobility, in the 20th century it may work just as well to destroy tourist's desire ever to tour again. It creates a curious dilemma: Versailles is so sumptuous and magnificent that you ask yourself, "How can I not visit it?" But after I had visited it, I began to consider buying a summer house, my desire to tour having totally dissipated. My advice is to buy *Versailles: Complete Guide of the Tour of the Château and Gardens* in Paris and read it in the gardens at Vaux-le-Vicomte, Rambouillet, Dampierre, or Sceaux. I recommend that you skip Versailles.

In 1992 it was no longer possible to sit in, or even enter, the wonderful Colonnade, the circle of 32 arches supported by columns of blue and pink marble from Languedoc, which, after my earlier trips, I would have suggested as a particularly lovely place to sit while reading a book. The whole Colonnade was now fenced off. When I saw a VIP being given a private tour, I became truly annoyed. I was angry at Bob, too. I could have arranged for a special tour of Versailles and many of the other places I was visiting, but Bob had asked me when I started doing the research for this book, "How can you write honestly about places where you are given special treatment and the average traveler isn't?" So I had come to Versailles as an ordinary tourist and the experience had become truly unpleasant. When I glared at Bob, he had no idea why. Exercising my divine right to leave, I headed for Les Trois Marches, a charming, romantic restaurant in the town, where in 1985 we had enjoyed a meal whose asparagus wrapped in pastry I still remembered melting in my mouth—but the restaurant had moved, probably to larger quarters to accommodate more tourists.

When, hungry and tired, I settled back in my comfortable seat on the train for the ride back to Paris, I heard sighs of other people settling into theirs. Don't get me wrong: these were not sighs of contentment but of relief—of escape from a truly enervating and depressing experience. The train was packed with tourists, and the gloomy atmosphere of disappointment reminded me of a subway ride I had taken many years before from Giants Stadium in New York after the loss of a championship football game.

Since I always like to travel with someone from the century I am visiting, I had stuck Voltaire's *The Age of Louis XIV* in my oversized purse along with my camera. On our trip back to Paris I sat silently reading it for a second time. I was amused to see how, within a few hours, my reading of this paean to Louis XIV had changed. On the trip to Versailles, hoping to experience the brilliance and splendor of the Sun King's court by visiting the setting of endless rounds of feasts, ballets, masked balls, and hunts that all of Europe wanted to emulate, I had approvingly underlined: "*It seems clear that one of Louis XIV's main preoccupations was to inspire, in every field, that spirit of emulation without which all enterprise languishes.*" On the way back, being in a nasty mood, I found a bit of malicious pleasure in recalling that Voltaire's book had not been well received. It was published twenty years after the Sun King's death, and the king at the time, Louis XV, considered Voltaire's praise of Louis XIV's reign to be a criticism of his own. In addition, a line I had read right over on the way to Versailles now stuck in my mind: "*If he had spent…a fifth of what it cost to force nature at Versailles on embellishing his capital, Paris today would be, throughout its whole extent, as beautiful as is the area around the Tuileries and the Pont-Royal, and would have become the most magnificent city in the Universe.*"

As we emerged from the Métro station, the good thing, I thought, about our trip to Versailles was that it was still early in the afternoon and we had plenty of time that day to spend in Paris.

Ina Caro also contributed "The Fairy Palace" in Part II.

✳

The palace allowed Louis XIV freely to indulge his passion for hunting and other courtly pleasures, such as entertaining mistresses and staging concerts and ballet. The palace was also an exercise in power architecture, whereby Louis emphasized his social and political superiority. Basic amenities counted for less than conspicuous display: accommodation for courtiers was often cramped, and toilet facilities were few. Versailles became the center of power and court patronage, where sycophantic nobles vied with one another for the king's favors. The court also became a fashion center, imposing its own lavish styles on an aristocracy that was dependent on royal largesse.

—John Ardagh, *Cultural Atlas of France*

PART FIVE

THE LAST WORD

JULIAN GREEN

St-Julian the Poor

Enter the city of infinite doorways.

A SCORCHING HOT SUMMER'S DAY IS THE RIGHT TIME TO PUSH open the slightly rickety door that shuts off a treasure trove of coolness. I enter and stand motionless. In here the great shout of Paris is reduced to a murmur, overpowered by the greater silence of this little church. The stocky pillars glow pink in the afternoon light that falls from narrow windows of clear glass set between panes of blue. The pillars support the Romanesque barrel vault, beneath which thought takes wing like a bird beneath a woodland canopy. They are so strong, so still, as if waiting for the Last Judgement, lost in a kind of contemplation that cuts them off from our century. Like kings engrossed in dreams of greatness, they scorn the sad modern anxiety of which I have my share and make me, unawares, a gift of some of the peace they hold within them. Crowns of foliage are set on their heads, and they bear them towards the altar like baskets of offerings in a procession that has been going on for 800 years; a winged siren here, a Christian knight there are like symbols of the solemn thoughts they harbour beneath the rounded sky of the vaults.

This could be the spot where Dante knelt, between these green-stained walls that look as if an ocean has draped them with its algae; this was where the visionary hailed the invisible, and he later recalled the narrow Paris street where his meditation had enjoyed a moment's respite on its journey towards the abysses of the inner world.

It is hard to imagine the sumptuous past of St-Julian the Poor today. The church appears to have waited for our sad modern age in order fully to deserve its name. We catch only a feeble glimpse of the way it was when a priory adjoined it and 50 monks filled its vaults with the sound of their chanting, and it is difficult for us to appreciate that one of the loveliest ceremonies of the Middle Ages was held in a place that our spiritual poverty has brought so low. Yet this is where the *rector magnificus* of the Sorbonne handed over the ermine cloak and the velvet bag containing the seal of the university to the person who was to succeed him. It was here, too, that on June 11 each year the teaching staff gathered with great pomp before proceeding to the annual fair in St. Denis Fields to purchase their parchment requirement. The rue Galande, the rue du Fouarre, the rue Saint-Séverin, and the rue Saint-Jacques would be roused at dawn by the drums and trumpets of the students, many of whom brandished spears, swords, or sticks for no other reason than that they were young and loved a rumpus. Of all that full, strong, joyous life that belonged to an age we cannot match, what is left in this quarter, apart from one name? It is that of the rue du Fouarre, which reminds me of when Pope Urban V enjoined students to sit not on benches but actually at the feet of their masters. The ground being hard to sit on, the lads would go running to the street vendors who sold straw for stuffing in the shadow of St-Julian. There is nothing to stop us picturing Dante doing as everyone else did and coming here for his bundle of straw before attending the lessons of his excellent master Brunetto Latini, whom he subsequently pitched into hell, though he did in a way make up for it by slipping the name of the little rue du Fouarre into a tercet of the *Paradiso*.

The 17th century shook its ignorant wig at the venerable church and pronounced it barbaric. No doubt it was not thought significant enough for wholesale modernization; probably, too, St-

Julian, situated on the very edge of the Romanesque, though already subject to the first stretchings of the new style, did not strike Mansart's contemporaries as possessing the Gothic character that so got their goat and that they did their best to obliterate in the choir of St. Séverin, St-Julian's less fortunate neighbour. But it was the prior of St-Julian himself who shortened the nave and replaced the Romanesque portico with a façade that that tonsured ass believed to be Doric. Latterly, in a final metamorphosis, a wide iconostasis put in by Eastern Orthodox priests bisects what is left of one of the loveliest and most ancient churches in Paris.

Even so, St-Julian the Poor has kept its sturdy grace and mysterious youthfulness. You can imagine it surrounded by fields, for it has the charm of a country church. Its solid, artless countenance is so different from the fevered flights of St. Séverin, which withdraws into itself behind great tatters of shadow. St-Julian embraces the day and holds the light in its walls until dusk; it is as foursquare, firm, and placid as a Scholastic argument. Neither doubt nor distressing visions will ever disturb its pensive, serene solitude. It is a simple-hearted divine, sitting in his white robe on the bank of the Gallic river.

You used to be able to push open the little side door inside the church and find yourself in a delightful piece of waste ground, covered with vegetation, where your feet might stumble against some of the oldest stones in Paris. Hard by the chevet of St-Julian one of the last vestiges of "Philippe Auguste's Wall" stuck up abruptly out of the long grass like a rock emerging from the sea, and a twisted tree, slowly dying beneath the weight of several centuries, still sprouted leaves that quivered overhead. Who remembers that place, so attuned to daydreaming? In the distance the towers of Notre Dame, white in stormy weather, looked black against the July sky, and the occasional tugboat on the Seine would utter a long-drawn-out, melancholy cry, the misty note lingering and fading into the blue beyond. Yet the hubbub of Paris seemed to die at the edges of that small solitude where I loved to come and think. The silence around me was like a dwelling in which the past had sought refuge; that inner peace seemed to me to hold a real feeling of Romanesque France, of which St-Julian's ancient stones offered a tangible image. That was what so attracted me in my sixteenth year or thereabouts. Having come across the little church by accident on one of my walks, I went back there again and again.

Sometimes we do things, without thinking, that make no sense to us until much later and yet appear to have been prompted by the most alert part of our being. In the spring of 1940, which ended so tragically for civilised Europe, I instinctively visited those places in Paris where I had most memories, and certain churches detained me at length, though I did not then imagine I should be deprived of them so soon. St-Julian was the one I found hardest to leave: having crossed the threshold on my way out, I re-crossed it a moment later, touched by a misgiving too vague to find expression in words, and took one last look at those columns, which the setting sun had invested with a melancholy glow.

Born in 1900 of American parents living in Paris, Julian Green spent most of his literary career there, writing in French for a wide and enthusiastic European readership. He has published over sixty-five books in France: novels, essays, plays, and so far fourteen volumes of his Journal. Initially writing in English, he published five celebrated books in the United States before writing exclusively in French.

★

Recommended Reading

We hope *Travelers' Tales Paris* has inspired you to read on. A good place to start is the books from which we've made selections, and we have listed them below. Many general guidebooks are also worth reading and the best ones have annotated bibliographies or sections on recommended books and maps.

Applefield, David. *Paris Inside-Out: The Insider's Guide for Visitors, Residents, Professionals & Students on Living in Paris*. New York: Houghton Mifflin Company, Inc., 1995.

Ardagh, John. *Cultural Atlas of France*. Oxfordshire, England: Andromeda, 1991.

Baldwin, James. *No Name in the Street*. New York: Dell Publishing, a division of Bantam Doubleday Dell Publishing Group, Inc., 1986.

Barry, Joseph. *The People of Paris*. New York: Doubleday, a division of Bantam Doubleday Dell Publishing Group, Inc., 1966.

Beauvoir, Simone de. *Witness to my Life: Letters of Jean-Paul Sartre to Simone de Beauvoir, 1926-1939*. Translated by Lee Fahnestock and Norman McAfee. New York: Charles Scribner's Sons, 1992.

Bernstein, Richard. *Fragile Glory: A Portrait of France and the French*. New York: Alfred A. Knopf, Inc., 1990.

Buzzi, Aldo. *Journey to the Land of the Flies & Other Travels*. Translated from the Italian by Ann Goldstein. New York: Random House, 1996.

Campbell, James. *Exiled in Paris: Richard Wright, James Baldwin, Samuel Beckett, and Others on the Left Bank*. New York: Scribner, 1995.

Camus, Albert. *Notebooks 1942-1951*. New York: Alfred A. Knopf, Inc., 1965.

Caro, Ina. *The Road from the Past: Traveling Through History in France.* New York: Doubleday, a division of Bantam Doubleday Dell Publishing Group, Inc., 1994.

Carroll, Raymonde. *Cultural Misunderstandings: The French-American Experience.* Chicago: The University of Chicago Press, 1988.

Daley, Robert. *Portraits of France.* London: Hutchinson, Random House, 1991.

Durrell, Lawrence. *Spirit of Place: Letters and Essays on Travel.* New Haven, Connecticut: Leete's Island Books, Inc., 1969.

Feldkamp, Phyllis and Fred. *The Good Life...or What's Left of It.* New York: Harper & Row Publishers, Inc., 1972.

Flaubert, Gustave. *Early Writings.* Translated by Robert Berry Griffin. Lincoln, Nebraska: University of Nebraska Press, 1991.

Gentleman, David. *David Gentleman's Paris.* London: Hodder and Stoughton, 1991.

Gold, Herbert. *Bohemia: Where Art, Angst, Love and Strong Coffee Meet.* New York: Simon & Schuster, Inc., 1993.

Green, Julian. *Paris.* Translated by J. A. Underwood. New York: Marion Boyers, 1991.

Guppy, Shusha. *A Girl in Paris.* London: William Heinemann Ltd., 1991.

Heath, Gordon. *Deep Are the Roots: Memoirs of a Black Expatriate.* Amherst, Massachusetts: The University of Massachusetts Press, 1992.

Jordan, David P. *Transforming Paris: The Life and Labors of Baron Haussmann.* Chicago: The University of Chicago Press, 1995.

Landes, Alison and Sonia. *Pariswalks.* New York: Henry Holt and Company, Inc., 1991.

Loftus, Simon. *Puligny-Montrachet: Journal of a Village in Burgundy.* London: Ebury Press, New York: Alfred A. Knopf, Inc., 1993.

Maspero, François. *Roissy Express: A Journey Through the Paris Suburbs.* London: Verso, 1994.

Miller, Stuart. *Understanding Europeans.* Santa Fe, New Mexico: John Muir Publications, 1990.

Morris, Jan. *Locations.* Oxford, England: Oxford University Press, 1992.

Osborne, Lawrence. *Paris Dreambook: An Unconventional Guide to the Splendor and Squalor of the City.* London: Bloomsbury Publishing Ltd., 1990.

Paris Notes. The newsletter for people who love Paris. Published by
Mark Eversman. To subscribe send check or money order
($39.00 for 1 year, 10 issues) to *Paris Notes,* P. O. Box 3668,
Manhattan Beach, California 90266 or call 310/545-2735.

Paul, Jim. *What's Called Love: A Real Romance.* New York: Villard
Books, a division of Random House, Inc., 1993.

Reuss, Henry S. and Margaret M. *The Unknown South of France: A
History Buff's Guide.* Boston: The Harvard Common Press,
1991.

Rosenblum, Mort. *Secret Life of the Seine.* Reading, Massachusetts:
Addison-Wesley, 1994.

Weiss. Andrea. *Paris Was a Woman: Portraits from the Left Bank.* San
Francisco: Harper San Francisco, an imprint of HarperCollins
Publishers, London, 1995.

Wells, Patricia. *The Food Lover's Guide to Paris.* New York: Workman
Publishing, 1987.

White, Edmund. *Our Paris: Sketches from Memory.* New York: Alfred
A. Knopf, Inc., 1995.

Yee, Chiang. *The Silent Traveller in Paris.* New York: W. W. Norton &
Company, Inc., 1956.

Glossary

à pied	on foot
à bientôt	see you soon
accouchement	childbirth; labor and delivery
aérateurs	ventilators
allée	path, avenue, drive
allez	go
alors	then, at that time, in that case
amis	friends
arrondissement	a district or section of Paris
atelier	workshop, studio
au revoir	good-bye
auberge	inn, small hotel
aubergine	eggplant
auteur	author
autoroute	freeway
bain	bath, swim
baiser	a kiss
bal musette	dance with accordion accompaniment
bateau mouche	tour boat of the Seine in Paris
belle	beautiful
beur	French-born Arab
beurre noir	brown sauce
billets-doux	love letters

bis	The street number "9 *bis*" means 9a
bof	expression meaning "I don't know" or "I don't care"
bonbon	candy, sweet
bonhomme	fellow
boule	ball
bouquinistes	booksellers
brasserie	informal eating establishment
bricolage	do-it-yourself; patched-up job
bricoleur	handyman; do-it-yourselfer
brocanteur	dealer who sells used goods
butte	knoll, hillock
Ça va?	How are you?
cache-sexe	G-string
calme	calm
carrefours	crossroads
carte d'identité	identification card
chanteurs de charme	crooners
chanteuse	female singer
chaos	pile of boulders
chose	thing
choucroute	sauerkraut
cinémathèque	relating to the cinema
citron pressé	fresh lemonade
clochard	hobo, tramp
coifeuse	hairdresser
Comment?	What did you say?; How?
commerçant	shopkeeper, trader
conseiller	to advise, to recommend

coucher	to go to bed, put to bed
coulisse	behind the scenes
coup monté	put-up job
coups d'œil	glances
croustillant	crisp, crusty
cuisse	thigh
danseuses	female dancers
de riguer	compulsory; the rule
de trop	too many
désolé	desolate; sorry
déviation	detour; diversion
difficile	difficult
dossier	file
eau	water
eau-de-vie	brandy
écharpes	scarves
écorché	someone who is flayed alive
élan	style, flair, enthusiasm
entrepôt	warehouse
essai	try; attempt
extrêmement	extremely
faire les vitrines	to window shop
femmes fatales	women of seductive charm
fête	feast; festival, party
fin	done, finished, end
fin de siècle	end of the century
fine	brandy
fiston	son, lad
flâneur	stroller; street wanderer

fontaine	fountain, spring
frère	brother
fruits de mer	seafood
gendarmes	police officers
grand magasin	department store
gratteurs de guitare	guitar-scrapers
grenouille	frog
habitués	regular visitors
hammam	Turkish bath; spa
haute couture	high fashion
immédiatement	immediately
impairs	odd numbers
indigènes	natives, indigenous people
je déteste le rouge	I detest red
je regarde	I am just looking
joie de vivre	joy of living
jouer	to play
légère	light, slight, weak
littéraires	literary people
loge	dressing room; concierge's apartment; spectator's box
louche	dubious, shady, fishy
lourde	heavy
luxe	luxury
maison	home
malade	sick
merde	shit
midinette	silly young townie
mon	my
mort	death

nacelle	basket
n'est-ce pas	isn't it?, won't you?
naturellement	naturally
noir	black
non	no
oui	yes
pairs	even numbers
Parisienne	female Parisian
péniche	barge
péridurale	epidural
périphérique	outlying, peripheral; expressway surrounding a city
pétanque	lawn bowling
petit peu	a little bit
peu	a little
pied-à-terre	secondary or temporary lodging
politesse	politeness, courtesy
pommes	apples
privée	private
procureaur général	attorney general
promenades	walks, promenades
quartier	district, quarter
quelque	some; a few
quincaillerie	hardware
quotidien	daily; ordinary; everyday
raie	skate; ray
relations	contacts, relations
rouge	red
sage-femme	midwife
salon de thé	tea room

sentier	path
sentinelle	(vulgar) turd; sentinel
societé	company, society
sous-sol	basement
spectacles	shows
sportive	athletic
steak frites	steak with French fried potatoes
terrain vague	empty lot
tout	all
tout de suite	immediately, right away
vendeuse	sales lady
vespasiennes	urinals
ville lumière	city of light
vite	quickly, fast
volupté	sensual delight, pleasure
votre	your
Voulez-vous quelque chose	Do you want something?

Index

Index of Contributors

Acknowledgements

Heartfelt thanks to Wenda Brewster O'Reilly, Andrea, Noelle, and Mariele O'Reilly, Paula Mc Cabe, Brenda O'Reilly, Clement, Seumas, Liam, and Tobias O'Reilly, Timothy O'Reilly, Cindy Collins, Raj Khadka, Susan Brady, Judy Anderson. Special thanks also to David Applefield, Mark Eversman, Brigitte Chemouni, Hélène de la Salle, Don George, Mary Lou Miller, Keith Granger, Cynthia Lamb, Deborah Greco, Trisha Schwartz, and Jennifer Leo.

Publishing. Published by Bloomsbury Publishing in 1990, £14.99.

"Wounded and Healed" by George Vincent Wright reprinted by permission of the author. Copyright © 1997 by George Vincent Wright.

"Montreuil–sous–Bois" by David Applefield reprinted by permission of the author. Copyright © 1997 by David Applefield.

"The Frog and the Periscope" by Tish Carnes Brown reprinted by permission of the author. Copyright © 1997 by Tish Carnes Brown.

"*Au Revoir Paris*" by Claudia J. Martin reprinted by permission of the author. Copyright © 1997 by Claudia J. Martin.

"Destination Paris" by Marcel Laventurier reprinted by permission of the author. Copyright © 1997 by Marcel Laventurier.

"Bearing Witness" by Thérèse Lung reprinted by permission of the author. Copyright © 1997 by Thérèse Lung.

"*Monsieur de Paris*" by Robert Daley excerpted from *Portraits of France* by Robert Daley. Copyright © 1991 by Riviera Productions Ltd. By permission of Little, Brown & Company.

"La Photo" by Cori Kenicer reprinted by permission of the author. Copyright © 1997 by Cori Kenicer.

"Paris Light and Dark" by Katherine Gibbs reprinted by permission of the author. Copyright © 1997 by Katherine Gibbs.

"St-Julian the Poor" by Julian Green excerpted from *Paris* by Julian Green, translated by J. A. Underwood. Reprinted by permission of Marion Boyars Publishers, Inc. Copyright © 1991 by Marion Boyars Publishers, Inc.

Additional Credits (arranged alphabetically by title)

Selection from "An Angel in Paris" by Jeanne Conte reprinted by permission of the author. Copyright © 1996 by Jeanne Conte.

Selection from "Architecture View" by Alastair Gordon reprinted from the December 22, 1991 issue of *The New York Times*. Copyright © 1991 by the New York Times Company. Reprinted by permission.

Selection from *As France Goes* by David Schoenbrun published by Harper & Brothers. Copyright © 1957 by David Schoenbrun.

About the Editors

James O'Reilly and Larry Habegger first worked together as late night disc jockeys at Dartmouth College in New Hampshire. They wrote mystery serials for the *San Francisco Examiner* in the early 1980s before turning to travel writing. Since 1983, their travel features and self-syndicated column, "World Travel Watch," have appeared in magazines and newspapers in the United States and other countries. James was born in Oxford, England, raised in San Francisco, and lives with his family in Leavenworth, Washington and France. Larry was born in Minnesota and lives on Telegraph Hill in San Francisco.

Sean O'Reilly is a former seminarian, stockbroker, and bank slave who lives in Arizona with his wife Brenda and their four small boys. Widely traveled in Europe, he most recently spent time roaming East Africa and the Indian Ocean. He is also at work on a book called *Politics and the Soul: The River of Gold,* which he describes as a "re-examination of classic Greek, Roman, and Christian philosophies as tools for moral excellence in modern society."

TRAVELERS' TALES

LOOK FOR THESE TITLES IN THE SERIES

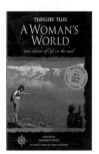
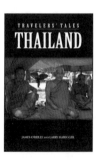

"Only the lowest wattage dimbulb would visit Brazil
without reading this book."

—Tim Cahill, author of *Jaguars Ripped My Flesh*
and *Pecked to Death by Ducks*

TRAVELERS' TALES BRAZIL

Edited by Annette Haddad & Scott Doggett
1st Edition January 1997, ISBN 1-885211-11-2

"Sterling's themes are nothing less than human
universality, passion and necessity, all told in stories
straight from the gut."

—Maxine Hong Kingston, author of *Woman Warrior*
and *China Men*

TRAVELERS' TALES FOOD

Edited by Richard Sterling
1st Edition November 1996, ISBN 1-885211-09-0

"As glimpsed here through the eyes of beatniks, hippies,
surfers, 'lavender cowboys' and talented writers from
all walks, San Francisco comes to vivid, complex life."

—*Publishers Weekly*

TRAVELERS' TALES SAN FRANCISCO

Edited by James O'Reilly, Larry Habegger & Sean O'Reilly
1st Edition June 1996, ISBN 1-885211-08-2

The first smaller format, "tips" book in the Travelers' Tales
series, Gutsy Women is an indispensable pocket guide with
travel tips for women on the road. It offers a wealth of
fresh ideas on how to travel safely, comfortably, within
your budget, alone, with your mother or children.
It's packed with instructive and inspiring travel vignettes—
a must-have for novice as well as experienced travelers.

TRAVELERS' TALES: GUTSY WOMEN
TRAVEL TIPS AND WISDOM FOR THE ROAD

By Marybeth Bond
1st Edition October 1996, ISBN 1-885211-15-5

"A superb, eclectic collection that reeks wonderfully of gazpacho and paella, and resonates with sounds of heel-clicking and flamenco singing—and makes you feel that you are actually in that amazing state of mind called Iberia."

—Barnaby Conrad, author of *Matador* and *Name Dropping*

TRAVELERS' TALES SPAIN
Edited by Lucy McCauley
1st Edition November 1995, ISBN 1-885211-07-4

"All you always wanted to know about the French but were afraid to ask! Explore the country and its people in a unique and personal way even before getting there. Travelers' Tales: your best passport to France and the French!"

—Anne Sengés, *Journal Français d'Amérique*

TRAVELERS' TALES FRANCE
Edited by James O'Reilly, Larry Habegger & Sean O'Reilly
1st Edition June 1995, ISBN 1-885211-02-3

"The essays are lyrical, magical and evocative: some of the images make you want to rinse your mouth out to clear the dust."

—Karen Troianello, *Yakima Herald-Republic*

TRAVELERS' TALES INDIA
Edited by James O'Reilly & Larry Habegger
1st Edition January 1995, ISBN 1-885211-01-5

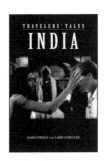

"*Travelers' Tales Mexico* opens a window on the beauties and mysteries of Mexico and the Mexicans. It's entertaining, intriguing, baffling, instructive, insightful, inspiring and hilarious—just like Mexico."

—Tom Brosnahan, co-author of Lonely Planet's *Mexico–a travel survival kit*

TRAVELERS' TALES MEXICO
Edited by James O'Reilly & Larry Habegger
1st Edition September 1994, ISBN 1-885211-00-7

VISIT TRAVELERS' TALES
ON THE INTERNET

READ A STORY. ENTER A CONTEST. PLAN A TRIP.

Way back in 1993, we were the first travel book publisher on the World Wide Web, and our site has been growing ever since. Point your Web browser to **http://www.ora.com/ttales** and you'll discover which books we're working on, how to submit your own story, the latest writing contests you can enter, and the location of the next author event. We offer sample chapters from all of our books, as well as the occasional trip report and photo essay from our hard-working editors. Be sure to take one of our Webtours, an exhaustive list of Internet resources for each of our titles, and begin planning your own journey.

SUBMIT YOUR OWN TRAVEL TALE

Do you have a tale of your own that you would like to submit to Travelers' Tales? We highly recommend that you first read one or more of our books to get a feel for the kind of story we're looking for. For submission guidelines and a list of titles in the works, send a SASE to:

Travelers' Tales Submission Guidelines
101 Morris Street, Sebastopol, CA 95472

or send email to *ttguidelines@online.ora.com*
or check out our website at **www.ora.com/ttales**

You can send your story to the address above or via email to *ttsubmit@ora.com*. On the outside of the envelope, please indicate what country/topic your story is about. If your story is selected for one of our titles, we will contact you about rights and payment.

We hope to hear from you. In the meantime, enjoy the stories!